# Experimental Economics

# Schools of Thought in Economics

*Series Editor:* Mark Blaug

Emeritus Professor of the Economics of Education, University of London and Consultant Professor of Economics, University of Buckingham

For greater convenience, a cumulative index to all titles in this series will be published in a separate volume number 12.

# Experimental Economics

*Edited by*

# Vernon L. Smith

*Regent's Professor of Economics*
*University of Arizona*

EDWARD ELGAR

Published by
Edward Elgar Publishing Limited
Gower House
Croft Road
Aldershot
Hants GU11 3HR
England

Gower Publishing Company
Old Post Road
Brookfield
Vermont 05036
USA

**British Library Cataloguing in Publication Data**

Experimental economics. — (Schools of thought in
  economics; v. 7)
  1. Experimental economics
  I. Smith, Vernon L. (Vernon Lomax)  II. Series
  330′.0724

**Library of Congress Cataloging-in-Publication Data**

    p. cm.  − − (Schools of thought in economics : 7)
    Includes bibliographical references.
    ISBN 1-85278-061-4
    1. Negotiation in business. 2. Decision-making.
  3. Microeconomics. 4. Markets. 5. Oligopolies. I. Smith, Vernon
  L. II. Series.
  HD58.6.E95 1989
  658.4 − −dc20                                                                89-23490
                                                                                   CIP

ISBN 1 85278 061 4

Printed in Great Britain by Galliard (Printers) Ltd, Great Yarmouth

# Contents

# Acknowledgements

The editor and publishers wish to thank the following who have kindly given permission for the use of copyright material.

Academic Press Inc. (London) Ltd for essay: Vernon L. Smith (1980), 'Relevance of Laboratory Experiments to Testing Resource Allocation Theory' from *Evaluation of Econometric Models*, edited by J. Kmenta and J.B. Ramsey, pp.345−77.

American Economic Association for articles: R. Mark Isaac and Charles R. Plott (1981), 'Price Controls and the Behavior of Auction Markets : An Experimental Evaluation', *American Economic Review*, 71, June, pp.448−59; Don L. Coursey and Vernon L. Smith (1983), 'Price Controls in a Posted Offer Market', *American Economic Review*, 73, March, pp.218−21.

The Econometric Society for article: Robert Forsythe, Thomas R. Palfrey and Charles R. Plott (1982), 'Asset Valuation in an Experimental Market', *Econometrica*, 50, May, pp.537−67.

McGraw-Hill Book Company for chapters 2, 3, 4 and 5 from *Bargaining Behavior* by Lawrence E. Fouraker and Sidney Siegel (1963), pp.11−59.

North Holland Publishing Co. for article: R. Mark Isaac, Valerie Ramey and Arlington W. Williams (1984), 'The Effects of Market Organization on Conspiracies in Restraint of Trade', *Journal of Economic Behavior and Organization*, 5, pp.191−222.

The RAND Corporation for article: Don Coursey, R. Mark Isaac, Margaret Luke and Vernon L. Smith (1984), 'Market Contestability in the Presence of Sunk (Entry) Costs', *The Rand Journal of Economics*, 15, Spring, pp.69−84.

Society for Economic Analysis for articles: James W. Friedman (1969), 'On Experimental Research in Oligopoly', *Review of Economic Studies*, 36, October, pp.399−415; Charles R. Plott and Vernon L. Smith (1978), 'An Experimental Examination of Two Exchange Institutions', *Review of Economic Studies*, 45, February, pp.133−53.

Southern Economic Journal for article: John Carlson (1967), 'The Stability of an Experimental Market with a Supply-Response Lag', *Southern Economic Journal*, 33, January, pp.305−321.

The University of Chicago Press for articles: Vernon L. Smith (1962), 'An Experimental Study of Competitive Market Behavior', *Journal of Political Economy*, 70, April, pp.111−37, and Errata in 70, June 1962, pp.322−3; Raymond C. Battalio, John H. Kagel and Morgan O. Reynolds (1977), 'Income Distributions in Two Experimental Economies', *Journal of Political Economy*, 85, pp.1259−71; Elizabeth Hoffman and Matthew L. Spitzer (1985), 'Entitlements, Rights and Fairness : An Experimental Examination of Subjects' Concepts of Distributive Justice', *Journal of Legal Studies*, 14, June, pp.259−97; Arlington W. Williams and Vernon L. Smith (1984), 'Cyclical Double Auction Markets with and without Speculators', *Journal of Business*, 57, pp.1−33.

Western Economic Association for article: David M. Grether and Charles R. Plott (1984), 'The Effects of Market Practices in Oligopolistic Markets : An Experimental Examination of the Ethyl Case', *Economic Inquiry*, 22, pp.479−507.

In addition the publishers wish to thank the Library of the London School of Economics and Political Science for its assistance in obtaining these articles.

# Introduction

Experimental economics includes the study of individual decision making in which an isolated individual chooses among alternatives that have a monetary (or commodity) value defined quantitatively by the experimenter. For example a subject might be asked to choose between two uncertain outcome prospects, with specified monetary returns, that will then be 'played out' in extensive form and the stated monetary prize which is the outcome is then paid to the subjects. My research interests have concentrated on the study of markets in which there are two or more subject agents who engage in exchanges in a sequence of market trading periods. Microeconomics is prominently concerned with the study of the price and efficiency properties of markets. The economist's interest in decision theory stems from the study of markets. Thus Adam Smith's work on the nature and function of markets preceded by a century the articulation of a utilitarian theory of demand, and the cost-productivity theory of supply. The Swedish economist Gustave Cassel is known for his championship of the notion that supply and demand (market response) functions were the appropriate primitives of market theory because he doubted that one could meaningfully derive market response functions from assumptions about individual preference and choice. Experimental methods over the last quarter century provide modest support for this dichotomy in the sense that choice tests of individual decision theory based on preference theory has faced more serious, and controversial, challenges than tests of market theory. I do not mean to suggest that market predictions are always supported in the laboratory, but by and large they have fared well and have encouraged the proposition that elementary economic theory is on the right track empirically. Similarly, in the context of experimental *markets* individual decision and preference theory performs much better than it does when we confront isolated individuals with choice questions. In Smith (1988) I suggest that the latter experiments show that people do not think about economic choices the way we economists do. But this does not mean that their actions in markets are inconsistent with the predictions of theory.

My immediate intellectual forbear was Chamberlin (1948) who, to the best of my knowledge, was the first scholar to conduct a market experiment − in this case it was in the form of a classroom exercise designed to demonstrate the poor predictive power of competitive price theory. It is worth emphasizing that Chamberlin's experiments were two-sided markets with real subject sellers *and* buyers. In the early oligopoly experiments (1959 − 1963) the demand side of the market was always stimulated.

It is a curious fact that during the years 1956 − 1960 when I was conducting the experiments that would be published in 1962, several others were independently starting to make use of the techniques that would ultimately become known as the methodology of experimental economics. These included Hoggatt (1959), Sauermann and Selten (1959, 1960), the unpublished Pennsylvania State Working Paper by Fouraker, Shubik and Siegal (1961), Siegal and Fouraker (1960, 1963), Suppes and Carlsmith (1962) and Friedman (1963). Here, indeed, seems to be an example in which the time was ripe for an idea, and more than one person responded. It is my hypothesis that there were a number of us at this time, about whom it can be said that we were (1) dissatisfied with the state of our empirical knowledge of the credibility of economic theory and (2) harboured considerable curiosity about how economic processes actually worked. I was a doubter who perceived experiment as a means of testing these doubts. At the same time I was curious about the trading rules (the double oral auction) used in organized markets. Economic theory had nothing to say about this institution. Again, Martin Shubik has long been known for his passion for understanding the details of how markets work, and how they might be related to game theory. His interest in the extensive form game-theoretic interpretation of trading institutions goes back a quarter century. Similarly, from my brief personal knowledge of Sidney Siegel I can attest to the depth of his interest in developing rigorous empirical tests of all aspects of microeconomic theory.

Laboratory experimental methods have a number of advantages over traditional methods of empirical investigation in economics. However, in no sense are laboratory methods a substitute for studies based on field data, and the strengths of each help fortify the other. All field empirical tests of the predictive implications of a microeconomic theory are necessarily *composite tests*. For example, suppose one desires to test the proposition that in one market with N buyers the extent of demand revelation is greater than in another separated (say because of commodity perishability or high transportation cost) market with $M < N$ buyers. The test is motivated by a theorem stating that demand revelation is greater, the larger the number of buyers. Such a test is necessarily a joint test, not only of the theorem, but also the following (not necessarily complete) list of maintained or auxiliary hypotheses: (1) buyers act to maximize their surplus subject to the institutional rules that govern their trading, (2) the incentive for demand revelation in the two situations is not affected by differences in the trading institutions used, (3) the unobservable maximum-willingness-to-pay demand in the two markets is comparable, and (4) supply conditions in the two markets are not different. In the laboratory, where we use cash reimbursements to induce well-defined demand schedules, we have a clear benchmark for measuring demand underrevelation. Similarly we can control 'supply conditions'. Finally, by controlling the institution, or rules of contract, we can prevent this effect from confounding our interpretation of the effect of the number of agents on demand revelation. Consequently, the first important advantage of laboratory methods is to enable us to formulate sharper tests of the *component elements* of a theory.

Laboratory experiments also permit us to articulate more rigorously the empirical properties of exchange institutions. This can be a valuable preformal exercise for motivating theory development by providing a clearer picture of the observable regularities of trading under a particular market institution as a function of changes in the cost-valuation environment. This is much different than *ex post hoc* theoretical 'explanation' in that once a general theory is articulated that accounts for the historical experimental results, the theory can be used to design entirely new experiments to test the excess empirical content of the general theory (Lakatos, 1978). An example is the extensive experimental study of oral double auctions which is starting to motivate theoretical efforts to model this challenging, but remarkably efficient form of exchange institution.

This volume offers a collection of fifteen papers in experimental economics that span the years from 1962 to 1985. These years cover the formative period up to about 1976 and the decade from 1976 to 1985 in which experimental methods have enjoyed a vast expansion in the quality, depth and diversity of economic questions to which laboratory experiments have been applied. The formative period was characterized by a growing recognition that markets are most meaningfully studied and understood within the context of institutions. This collection attempts to include influential, as well as representative, examples of this quarter century of development and growth.

The first chapter in this volume, 'An Experimental Study of Competitive Market Behaviour', was my first experimental paper. I conducted the first experiment reported in this paper in January 1956; the last would have been conducted in early 1960. The results of this paper contrasted sharply with those of Chamberlin (1948) who used bilateral bargaining with the pairs self-chosen by the participants in a random encounter process, whereas I used a multilateral double oral auction similar to that used in the commodity and stock exchanges. Hence the institution (I called it market organization in 1962) is seen clearly as a treatment condition in price formation that cannot be ignored. Similarly, variations on the oral double auction, such as the one-sided offer auction shown in Chart 8, have an evident impact upon price behaviour. These results made it clear that the concept of an 'institution free' theory of economic behaviour was in question.

It should be noted that *none* of the experiments reported in this paper used monetary payoffs. The latter are discussed and the results of replicating the experiment in Chart 4 using monetary payoffs is reported in footnote 9. In all my later work monetary payoffs were used. But it is clear that except for certain boundary cases, they are not necessary to establishing the convergence properties of the oral double auction where one has 'captive' subjects as in the classroom. It is standard practice to use such rewards, and any work omitting them is suspect. I think rewards should always be used to guard against the possibility that they will make a difference in any particular study, but we should not be too surprised to find that there may be circumstances in which they appear not to be important. Many people seem to be programmed to do their best, and appear to perform for short periods of time as if maximizing even if it is a 'game' in the popular sense. Any result obtained without pay-offs should be replicated with pay-offs to determine its robustness. But don't try to recruit subjects to come to an experimental session without making it clear that they will earn money because nonpayment is feasible only with captive groups. In the context of choice among uncertain prospects, Binswanger (1980) found that where substantial rewards were used behaviour was so different from the hypothetical responses elicited in the manner used by Kahneman and Tversky that the latter were not useable in assessing risk attitude.

In their seminal 1963 study Fouraker and Siegel (FS) tested noncooperative equilibrium models of (1) posted price leadership bilateral bargaining, (2) simultaneous move quantity adjustment, or Cournot, duopoly and triopoly, and (3) simultaneous move posted price, or Bertrand, duopoly and triopoly. Each of these institutions and environments is studied under incomplete and complete information conditions. In FS 'incomplete' information meant that each agent knew only his (throughout S. Siegel's experimental research career only male subjects were used) own cash pay-offs. This corresponds to what we call private pay-off information today. 'Complete' information referred to each agent knowing both his pay-offs and that of all other participants in the market. Today we know this as common knowledge of pay-offs if each agent knows that all others know all pay-offs. The recognition by FS of the importance of the distinction between private and complete information is merely one of the many reasons why this is a classical work.

This collection includes only the FS study of bilateral bargaining. In place of the FS treatment of oligopoly we include James Friedman's more comprehensive subsequent survey piece. But we should note here the fundamental findings across all the FS experiments, whether in bargaining, quantity adjustment or price adjustment oligopoly: the noncooperative equilibrium concept receives its greatest experimental support under private pay-off information and its least support when there is complete information on pay-offs. This is just the opposite of the conventional wisdom among game theorists whose criticism of noncooperative equilibrium theory is its strong information requirements, namely that all agents *must* know the preferences of all other agents. An exception is Shubik (1959) who asserts the opposite. 'The more information there is in a market, the more likely it is that combinations will result' (p. 171).

John Carlson's examination of markets with a supply response lag yielded the significant finding that theoretically unstable supply and demand environments are not behaviourally unstable. According to the cobweb theorem, price and the lagged production response to price, will diverge from the fixed market clearing point if the slope of the demand function is sufficiently steep (or inelastic) relative to supply. Behaviourally, such 'unstable' cases turn out to be just as stable as those for which the cobweb theorem predicts convergence. The key assumption of the theory is that agents expect next period's price to be the same as the current period's price. But it is the unstable case in which this assumption is most quickly revealed to be erroneous. Agent behaviour is much more flexible and adaptable than is implied by this model with the result that all the markets studied tend to converge to a relatively small region in the neighbourhood of the fixed market clearing point. This phenomenon has also been observed in the context of the Groves–Ledyard mechanism applied to the provision of public goods. The Cournot divergent and convergent theoretical cases are both convergent behaviourally (Smith, 1979, p. 90).

Friedman's survey of experimental research on oligopoly covers his own work, and that of Austin Hoggatt and Fouraker and Siegel. The first papers by Friedman and Hoggatt and the book by Fouraker and Siegel span the pioneering years from 1959–1962 when experimental methods were successfully being applied to a wide range of the basic topics in microeconomics. Other contributions in this period not covered by Friedman's survey include that of Sauermann and Selten (1959, 1960), which unfortunately did not become known generally to experimental economists for a decade or two after its publication, and the work of Shubik. Although Martin Shubik was not a co-author of the Fouraker–Siegel book, he had been so listed in a working paper partially reported in their book, and his contribution is acknowledged in the preface to their book.

This collection includes the only study (of which I am aware) of the distribution of income among experimental subjects that has been attempted. In this original work by Battalio, Kagel and Reynolds, two findings are particularly prominent: (1) the similarity between various measures of the distribution of income in the experimental economies and those of national economies; (2) the similarity between male – female differences in earnings in the experimental economies and these differences in national economies. In spite of this pioneering study, no one has examined the income distribution implications of the immense data base that exists from a wide variety of different market experiments.

Charles Plott and I had spent many hours in the late 1960s and 1970s discussing experimental economics by sunlight, firelight and moonlight on fishing trips in the canyons of Utah's Lake Powell. Our paper examining and comparing oral auctions and posted price institutions was our initial collaborative effort. This collaboration had been made possible by my two-year (1973 – 1975) tenure at Cal Tech; first as a Fairchild Scholar, then as a visiting professor at Cal Tech and USC. Charles Plott had been instrumental in making this visit possible. It was in this research that, I think, we both first began to appreciate the power and importance of the institutional rules of contract in determining price and allocation outcomes. It was this collaboration that opened our thinking to the institutional interpretation of the results obtained in the earlier study of posted pricing by Fred Williams (1973). As we saw it his study was about institutions and not about 'the multiunit case'. Also, in our paper, we gained important insight into the institutional and behavioural similarities between sealed bid auctions and posted bid pricing. All this seems elementary from the perspective of a decade later. The intervening years have brought a vast deepening of our understanding of the central role of institutions in affecting individual behaviour and, *ipso facto*, market outcomes.

In 1957 and 1958 I started giving seminars on the experimental research that I had in process. People didn't know what I was up to or why. This was reflected in the questions put to me by seminar participants, and later by journal referees. This forced me to think about methodology. Why do we do what we do in the ways that we do it? None of my research outside of experimental economics required me to come to terms with this question. When you do mainstream research everyone takes for granted your right to do it. In confronting these issues I was led to write about them. One such effort was in Smith (1976). The next effort is the 'Relevance ...' paper appearing in this volume. More recently two additional methodological pieces have been published or are in process (Smith, 1982, 1988). The most comprehensive is in Smith (1982), but most of the basic ideas were generated in the paper appearing in this volume. This sort of writing seems inevitable if you want to convey some appreciation for the role of experiments in increasing economic understanding. It is not enough to just do experiments, and to report them, because they are not part of the culture of your audience. Their questions and doubts require a response. Of course all that is now changing – experimental research is now a part of the culture, but still only a small part. Hence the need continues for coherent explanations of why, how and to what ends we experiment in economics.

Isaac and Plott's innovative study of price controls in the context of double oral auction markets continues to stimulate interest in the many replicable properties of this trading institution. However, to Don Coursey's and my surprise the qualitative effects of price controls and their subsequent removal that are documented by Isaac and Plott are also observed (although attenuated) in the much more sedate posted offer market institution. Hence these phenomena are robust across at least two institutional treatments, although the quantitative response is different in the two cases.

The Coase theorem states that where agents can harm each other by their decisions, and it is possible for them to negotiate with each other, they will bargain to an efficient outcome whichever one of them might have the legal right to harm the other(s). Previous work by Hoffman and Spitzer yields results which, without exception, are consistent with this prediction. However, all of the subjects also divide equally the joint maximum profit from this efficient bargain. This directly conflicts with the prediction of game theory, which states that each party should hold out for a share of the total which is at least equal to what he/she could get without bargaining at all. Hoffman and Spitzer address this issue in their paper included in this volume. They hypothesize that the use of a coin flip to randomly assign one of two subjects to the 'controller' (prior property right) condition is not benign; *i.e.* it is actually a treatment. Their hypothesis is that if you acquire a property right by a chance procedure then you have not 'earned' it and it is not 'just' to exploit it for personal gain. They proceed to replicate their earlier experiments, but with important differences that allow the subject to perceive and feel (even say) that the property right, or position of controller, was 'earned'. This changes the results dramatically. This is a very important finding, not only in the specific context of the Coase theorem, but in general. It tells us something of permeating importance about when we might, and when we might not, find individually rational behaviour dominating egalitarian behaviour. It also reminds us that anything we do to 'set the stage' for an experiment is potentially an important treatment variable. Mere procedure, and of course randomization is the bedrock of all experimental methods, may not be neutral in its effect on human decision behaviour.

Grether and Plott report the results of an experimental investigation of certain contract specifications commonly employed in the sale of lead-based anti-knock compounds in the gasoline industry. These specifications include: (1) advance notice and public announcements of all price increases, and (2) 'most favoured nation clauses' that guarantee to each customer that no other customer will obtain the product at a lower price; *i.e.* the seller agrees not to practice price discrimination. The hypothesis is that these contracts limit competition by facilitating collusive price competition. Any cut in price to a customer is costly to the seller because it must be extended to all customers. This study was motivated by an FTC complaint against the industry charging anti-competitive practices. The claim that failing to price discriminate is anti-competitive is particularly interesting in that under the Clayton Act price discrimination is prohibited because it is thought to be anti-competitive. One might conjecture that the Clayton Act helped to induce most favoured nation clauses since they provide a solid legal basis for defending against the charge of having violated the Clayton Act. In any case it is clear that the implications of price discrimination cannot be understood except in an institutional context. For example the continuous double oral auction generates much price discrimination in disequilibrium and it has been the most competitive institution we have studied.

Isaac, Ramey and Williams examine the effect of the opportunity to conspire on the prices and profits of sellers under the posted price and continuous double auction trading institutions. These results are compared with the actual behaviour of posted price monopolists, and of posted price markets in which sellers are not given an opportunity to conspire. The 'opportunity to conspire' means that the sellers were given an opportunity to discuss all aspects of the market for a short period of time before the beginning of each new market pricing period. Generally, these conspiracies did not result in prices at or near the theoretical monopoly prediction under either posted price or double auction trading, although the posted price conspiracies tended to be more successful in raising prices than the double auction conspiracies.

The final paper in this volume studies the effect of sunk entry costs on market competition where scale economies allow only one firm to satisfy the entire demand. This paper was motivated by the considerable recent literature on contestable markets. The basic idea is an old one: the power of a monopoly firm is limited by the potential as well as the actual entry of a competitor. Included in this idea is J.B. Clark's (1901, p. 13) concept of potential competition in which 'the new mills that will spring into existence will break down prices; and the fear of these new mills, without their actual coming, is often enough to keep prices from rising to an extortionate height'. The concept of 'limit pricing' in industrial organization reflects this idea; *i.e.* if an incumbent firm prices low to 'limit' entry this is just an alternative way of describing the effect of potential entry.

Vernon L. Smith
1989

## References

Binswanger, Hans P. (1980), 'Attitudes Toward Risk : Experimental Measurement in Rural India', *American Journal of Agricultural Economics*, 62, August.

Chamberlin, Edward (1948), 'An Experimental Imperfect Market', *Journal of Political Economy*, 56, April.

Clark, J.B. (1901), *The Control of Trusts*, The Macmillan Co., New York.

Fouraker, Lawrence, Martin Shubik and Sidney Siegel (1961), 'Oligopoly Bargaining : The Quantity Adjuster Models', Pennsylvania State University, University Park, Pa.

Fouraker, Lawrence and Sidney Siegel (1963), *Bargaining Behavior*, McGraw-Hill, New York.

Friedman, James (1963), 'Individual Behavior in Oligopolistic Markets : An Experimental Study', *Yale Economic Essays*, 3.

Hoggatt, Austin (1959), 'An Experimental Business Game', *Behavioral Science*, July.

Lakatos, Imre (1978), in *The Methodology of Scientific Research Programmes*, vol. 1, J. Worrall and G. Currie (eds), Cambridge University Press, Cambridge.

Sauermann, Heinz and Richard Selten (1960), 'An Experiment in Oligopoly', *General Systems Yearbook of the Society for General Systems Research*, vol. 5, Ludwig von Bertalanffy and Anatol Rappoport (eds), Society for General Systems Research Ann Arbor. Translation of 'Ein Oligopolexperiment', *Zeitschrift für die Gesamete Staatswissenschaft*, No. 115, 1959.

Shubik, Martin (1959), *Strategy and Market Structure*, John Wiley and Sons, Inc., New York.

Siegel, Sidney and Lawrence Fouraker (1960), *Bargaining and Group Decision Making*, Macmillan, New York.

Smith, Vernon L. (1976), 'Bidding and Auctioning Institutions : Experimental Results', in *Bidding and Auctioning for Procurement and Allocation*, Yakov Amihud (ed.), New York University Press, New York.

Smith, Vernon L. (1979), 'Incentive Compatible Experimental Processes for the Provision of Public Goods', in *Research in Experimental Economics*, vol. 1, V.L. Smith (ed.), JAI Press, Greenwich, Conn.

Smith, Vernon L. (1982), 'Microeconomic Systems as an Experimental Science', *American Economic Review*, 72, December.

Smith, Vernon L. (1988), 'Theory, Experiment and Economics', *Journal of Economic Perspectives*, 3, Winter.

Suppes, P. and J.M. Carlsmith (1962), 'Experimental Analysis of a Duopoly Situation', *International Economic Review*, 3, January.

Williams, Fred E. (1973), 'The Effect of Market Organization on Competitive Equilibrium : The Multiunit Case', *Review of Economic Studies*, 40, January.

# [1]

# THE JOURNAL OF
# POLITICAL ECONOMY

| Volume LXX | APRIL 1962 | Number 2 |

## AN EXPERIMENTAL STUDY OF COMPETITIVE
## MARKET BEHAVIOR[1]

VERNON L. SMITH

Purdue University

### I. INTRODUCTION

RECENT years have witnessed a growing interest in experimental games such as management decision-making games and games designed to simulate oligopolistic market phenomena. This article reports on a series of experimental games designed to study some of the hypotheses of neoclassical competitive market theory. Since the organized stock, bond, and commodity exchanges would seem to have the best chance of fulfilling the conditions of an operational theory of supply and demand, most of these experiments have been designed to simulate, on a modest scale, the multilateral auction-trading process characteristic of these organized markets. I would emphasize, however, that they are intended as simulations of certain key features of the organized markets and of competitive markets generally, rather than as direct, exhaustive simulations of any particular organized exchange. The experimental conditions of supply and demand in force in these markets are modeled closely upon the supply and demand curves generated by the limit price orders in the hands of stock and commodity market brokers at the opening of a trading day in any one stock or commodity, though I would consider them to be good general models of received short-run supply and demand theory. A similar experimental supply and demand model was first used by E. H. Chamberlin in an interesting set of experiments that pre-date contemporary interest in experimental games.[2]

[1] The experiments on which this report is based have been performed over a six-year period beginning in 1955. They are part of a continuing study, in which the next phase is to include experimentation with monetary payoffs and more complicated experimental designs to which passing references are made here and there in the present report. I wish to thank Mrs. Marilyn Schweizer for assistance in typing and in the preparation of charts in this paper, R. K. Davidson for performing one of the experiments for me, and G. Horwich, J. Hughes, H. Johnson, and J. Wolfe for reading an earlier version of the paper and enriching me with their comments and encouragement. This work was supported by the Institute for Quantitative Research at Purdue, the Purdue Research Foundation, and in part by National Science Foundation, Grant No. 16114, at Stanford University.

[2] "An Experimental Imperfect Market," *Journal of Political Economy*, LVI (April, 1948), 95–108. For an experimental study of bilateral monopoly, see S. Siegel and L. Fouraker, *Bargaining and Group Decision Making* (New York: McGraw-Hill Book Co., 1 60).

Chamberlin's paper was highly suggestive in demonstrating the potentialities
of experimental techniques in the study
of applied market theory.

Parts II and III of this paper are
devoted to a descriptive discussion of the
experiments and some of their detailed
results. Parts IV and V present an empirical analysis of various equilibrating
hypotheses and a rationalization of the
hypothesis found to be most successful
in these experiments.

Part VI provides a brief summary
which the reader may wish to consult
before reading the main body of the paper.

## II. EXPERIMENTAL PROCEDURE

The experiments discussed in Parts
III and IV have followed the same general design pattern. The group of subjects
is divided at random into two subgroups,
a group of buyers and a group of sellers.
Each buyer receives a card containing
a number, known only to that buyer,
which represents the maximum price he
is willing to pay for one unit of the
fictitious commodity. It is explained that
the buyers are not to buy a unit of the
commodity at a price exceeding that
appearing on their buyer's card; they
would be quite happy to purchase a
unit at any price below this number—the
lower the better; but, they would be
entirely willing to pay just this price
for the commodity rather than have their
wants go unsatisfied. It is further explained that each buyer should think
of himself as making a pure profit equal
to the difference between his actual contract price and the maximum reservation price on his card. These reservation
prices generate a demand curve such
as DD in the diagram on the left in
Chart 1. At each price the corresponding quantity represents the maximum
amount that could be purchased at that

price. Thus, in Chart 1, the highest price
buyer is willing to pay as much as $3.25
for one unit. At a price above $3.25
the demand quantity is zero, and at
$3.25 it cannot exceed one unit. The
next highest price buyer is willing to
pay $3.00. Thus, at $3.00 the demand
quantity cannot exceed two units. The
phrase "cannot exceed" rather than "is"
will be seen to be of no small importance. How much is actually taken at
any price depends upon such important
things as how the market is organized,
and various mechanical and bargaining
considerations associated with the offer-
acceptance process. The demand curve,
therefore, defines the set (all points on
or to the left of DD) of possible demand
quantities at each, strictly hypothetical,
ruling price.

Each seller receives a card containing
a number, known only to that seller,
which represents the minimum price at
which he is willing to relinquish one unit
of the commodity. It is explained that
the sellers should be willing to sell at
their minimum supply price rather than
fail to make a sale, but they make a
pure profit determined by the excess
of their contract price over their minimum reservation price. Under no condition should they sell below this minimum. These minimum seller prices generate a supply curve such as SS in Chart
1. At each hypothetical price the corresponding quantity represents the maximum amount that could be sold at that
price. The supply curve, therefore, defines the set of possible supply quantities
at each hypothetical ruling price.

In experiments 1–8 each buyer and
seller is allowed to make a contract for
the exchange of only a single unit of
the commodity during any one trading
or market period. This rule was for the
sake of simplicity and was relaxed in

subsequent experiments.

Each experiment was conducted over a sequence of trading periods five to ten minutes long depending upon the number of participants in the test group. Since the experiments were conducted within a class period, the number of trading periods was not uniform among

has been closed, and the buyer and seller making the deal drop out of the market in the sense of no longer being permitted to make bids, offers, or contracts for the remainder of that market period.[3] As soon as a bid or offer is accepted, the contract price is recorded together with the minimum supply price of the seller

CHART 1

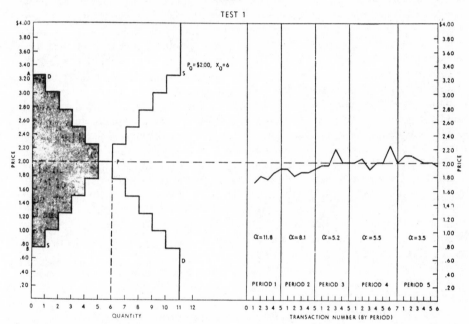

the various experiments. In the typical experiment, the market opens for trading period 1. This means that any buyer (or seller) is free at any time to raise his hand and make a verbal offer to buy (or sell) at any price which does not violate his maximum (or minimum) reservation price. Thus, in Chart 1, the buyer holding the $2.50 card might raise his hand and shout, "Buy at $1.00." The seller with the $1.50 card might then shout, "Sell at $3.60." Any seller (or buyer) is free to accept a bid (or offer), in which case a binding contract

and the maximum demand price of the buyer involved in the transaction. These observations represent the recorded data of the experiment.[4] Within the time limit

[3] All purchases are for final consumption. There are no speculative purchases for resale in the same or later periods. There is nothing, however, to prevent one from designing an experiment in which purchases for resale are permitted if the objective is to study the role of speculation in the equilibrating process. One could, for example, permit the carry-over of stocks from one period to the next.

[4] Owing to limitations of manpower and equipment in experiments 1–8, bids and offers which did not lead to transactions could not be recorded. In subsequent experiments a tape recorder was used for this purpose.

of a trading period, this procedure is continued until bids and offers are no longer leading to contracts. One or two calls are made for final bids or offers and the market is officially closed. This ends period 1. The market is then immediately reopened for the second "day" of trading. All buyers, including those who did and those who did not make contracts in the preceding trading period, now (as explained previously to the subjects) have a renewed urge to buy one unit of the commodity. For each buyer, the same maximum buying price holds in the second period as prevailed in the first period. In this way the experimental demand curve represents a demand per unit time or per trading period. Similarly, each seller, we may imagine, has "overnight" acquired a fresh unit of the commodity which he desires to sell in period 2 under the same minimum price conditions as prevailed in period 1. The experimental supply curve thereby represents a willingness to supply per unit time. Trading period 2 is allowed to run its course, and then period 3, and so on. By this means we construct a prototype market in which there is a flow of a commodity onto and off the market. The stage is thereby set to study price behavior under given conditions of normal supply and demand.[5] Some buyers and sellers, it should be noted, may be unable to make contracts in any trading period, or perhaps only in certain periods. Insofar as these traders are submarginal buyers or sellers, this is to be expected. Indeed, the ability of these experimental markets to ration out submarginal buyers and sellers will be one measure of the effectiveness or competitive performance of the market.

The above design considerations define a rejection set of offers (and bids) for each buyer (and seller), which in turn

defines a demand and a supply schedule for the market in question. These schedules do nothing beyond setting extreme limits to the observable price-quantity behavior in that market. All we can say is that the area above the supply curve is a region in which sales are feasible, while the area below the demand curve is a region in which purchases are feasible. Competitive price theory asserts that there will be a tendency for price-quantity equilibrium to occur at the extreme quantity point of the intersection of these two areas. For example, in Chart 1 the shaded triangular area $APB$ represents the intersection of these feasible sales and purchase sets, with $P$ the extreme point of this set. We have no guarantee that the equilibrium defined by the intersection of these sets will prevail, even approximately, in the experimental market (or any real counterpart of it). The mere fact that, by any definition, supply and demand schedules exist in the background of a market does not guarantee that any meaningful relationship exists

[5] The design of my experiments differs from that of Chamberlin (*op. cit.*) in several ways. In Chamberlin's experiment the buyers and sellers simply circulate and engage in bilateral higgling and bargaining until they make a contract or the trading period ends. As contracts are made the transaction price is recorded on the blackboard. Consequently, there is very little, if any, multilateral bidding. Each trader's attention is directed to the one person with whom he is bargaining, whereas in my experiments each trader's quotation is addressed to the entire trading group one quotation at a time. Also Chamberlin's experiment constitutes a pure exchange market operated for a single trading period. There is, therefore, less opportunity for traders to gain experience and to modify their subsequent behavior in the light of such experience. It is only through some learning mechanism of this kind that I can imagine the possibility of equilibrium being approached in any real market. Finally, in the present experiments I have varied the design from one experiment to another in a conscious attempt to study the effect of different conditions of supply and demand, changes in supply or demand, and changes in the rules of market organization on market-price behavior.

EXPERIMENTAL STUDY OF COMPETITIVE MARKET BEHAVIOR    115

between those schedules and what is observed in the market they are presumed to represent. All the supply and demand schedules can do is set broad limits on the behavior of the market.[6] Thus, in the symmetrical supply and demand diagram of Chart 1, it is conceivable that every buyer and seller could make a contract. The $3.25 buyer could buy from the $3.25 seller, the $3.00 buyer could buy from the $3.00 seller, and so forth, without violating any restrictions on the behavior of buyers and sellers. Indeed, if we separately paired buyers and sellers in this special way, each pair could be expected to make a bilateral contract at the seller's minimum price which would be equal to the buyer's maximum price.

It should be noted that these experiments conform in several important ways to what we know must be true of many kinds of real markets. In a real competitive market such as a commodity or stock exchange, each marketer is likely to be ignorant of the reservation prices at which other buyers and sellers are willing to trade. Furthermore, the only way that a real marketer can obtain knowledge of market conditions is to

[6] In fact, these schedules are modified as trading takes place. Whenever a buyer and a seller make a contract and "drop out" of the market, the demand and supply schedules are shifted to the left in a manner depending upon the buyer's and seller's position on the schedules. Hence, the supply and demand functions continually alter as the trading process occurs. It is difficult to imagine a real market process which does not exhibit this characteristic. This means that the intra-trading-period schedules are not independent of the transactions taking place. However, the *initial* schedules prevailing at the opening of each trading period are independent of the transactions, and it is these schedules that I identify with the "theoretical conditions of supply and demand," which the theorist defines independently of actual market prices and quantities. One of the important objectives in these experiments is to determine whether or not these initial schedules have any power to predict the observed behavior of the market.

observe the offers and bids that are tendered, and whether or not they are accepted. These are the public data of the market. A marketer can only know his own attitude, and, from observation, learn something about the objective behavior of others. This is a major feature of these experimental markets. We deliberately avoid placing at the disposal of our subjects any information which would not be practically attainable in a real market. Each experimental market is forced to provide all of its own "history." These markets are also a replica of real markets in that they are composed of a practical number of marketers, say twenty, thirty, or forty. We do not require an indefinitely large number of marketers, which is usually supposed necessary for the existence of "pure" competition.

One important condition operating in our experimental markets is not likely to prevail in real markets. The experimental conditions of supply and demand are held constant over several successive trading periods in order to give any equilibrating mechanisms an opportunity to establish an equilibrium over time. Real markets are likely to be continually subjected to changing conditions of supply and demand. Marshall was well aware of such problems and defined equilibrium as a condition toward which the market would move *if* the forces of supply and demand were to remain stationary for a sufficiently long time. It is this concept of equilibrium that this particular series of experiments is designed, in part, to test. There is nothing to prevent one from passing out new buyer and/or seller cards, representing changed demand and/or supply conditions, at the end of each trading period if the objective is to study the effect of such constantly changing conditions on market behavior.

In three of the nine experiments, once-for-all changes in demand and/or supply were made for purposes of studying the transient dynamics of a market's response to such stimuli.

### III. DESCRIPTION AND DISCUSSION OF EXPERIMENTAL RESULTS

The supply and demand schedule for each experiment is shown in the diagram on the left of Charts 1–10. The price and quantity at which these schedules intersect will be referred to as the predicted or theoretical "equilibrium" price and quantity for the corresponding experimental market, though such an equilibrium will not necessarily be attained or approached in the market. The performance of each experimental market is summarized in the diagram on the right of Charts 1–10, and in Table 1. Each chart shows the sequence of contract or exchange prices in the order in which they occurred in each trading period. Thus, in Chart 1, the first transaction was effected at $1.70, the second at $1.80, and so on, with a total of five transactions occurring in trading period 1. These charts show contract price as a function of transaction number rather than calendar time, the latter of course being quite irrelevant to market dynamics.

The most striking general characteristic of tests 1–3, 5–7, 9, and 10 is the remarkably strong tendency for exchange prices to approach the predicted equilibrium for each of these markets. As the exchange process is repeated through successive trading periods with the same conditions of supply and demand prevailing initially in each period, the variation in exchange prices tends to decline, and to cluster more closely around the equilibrium. In Chart 1, for example, the variation in contract prices over the five

trading periods is from $1.70 to $2.25. The maximum possible variation is from $0.75 to $3.25 as seen in the supply and demand schedules. As a means of measuring the convergence of exchange prices in each market, a "coefficient of convergence," $\alpha$, has been computed for each trading period in each market. The $\alpha$ for each trading period is the ratio of the standard deviation of exchange prices, $\sigma_0$, to the predicted equilibrium price, $P_0$, the ratio being expressed as a percentage. That is, $\alpha = 100 \, \sigma_0/P_0$ where $\sigma_0$ is the standard deviation of exchange prices around the equilibrium price rather than the mean exchange price. Hence, $\alpha$ provides a measure of exchange price variation relative to the predicted equilibrium exchange price. As is seen in Table 1 and the charts for all tests except test 8, $\alpha$ tends to decline from one trading period to the next, with tests 2, 4$A$, 5, 6$A$, 7, 9$A$, and 10 showing monotone convergence.

Turning now to the individual experimental results, it will be observed that the equilibrium price and quantity are approximately the same for the supply and demand curves of tests 2 and 3. The significant difference in the design of these two tests is that the supply and demand schedules for test 2 are relatively flat, while the corresponding schedules for test 3 are much more steeply inclined.

Under the Walrasian hypothesis (the rate of increase in exchange price is an increasing function of the excess demand at that price), one would expect the market in test 2 to converge more rapidly than that in test 3. As is evident from comparing the results in Charts 2 and 3, test 2 shows a more rapid and less erratic tendency toward equilibrium. These results are, of course, consistent with many other hypotheses, including the

## TABLE 1

| Test | Trading Period | Predicted Exchange Quantity ($x_0$) | Actual Exchange Quantity ($x$) | Predicted Exchange Price ($P_0$) | Average Actual Exchange Price ($\bar{P}$) | Coefficient of Convergence [$\alpha = (100\sigma_0)/(P_0)$] | No. of Submarginal Buyers Who Could Make Contracts | No. of Submarginal Buyers Who Made Contracts | No. of Submarginal Sellers Who Could Make Contracts | No. of Submarginal Sellers Who Made Contracts |
|---|---|---|---|---|---|---|---|---|---|---|
| 1...... | 1 | 6 | 5 | 2.00 | 1.80 | 11.8 | 5 | 0 | 5 | 0 |
|  | 2 | 6 | 5 | 2.00 | 1.86 | 8.1 | 5 | 0 | 5 | 0 |
|  | 3 | 6 | 5 | 2.00 | 2.02 | 5.2 | 5 | 0 | 5 | 0 |
|  | 4 | 6 | 7 | 2.00 | 2.03 | 5.5 | 5 | 1 | 5 | 1 |
|  | 5 | 6 | 6 | 2.00 | 2.03 | 3.5 | 5 | 0 | 5 | 0 |
| 2...... | 1 | 15 | 16 | 3.425 | 3.47 | 9.9 | 4 | 2 | 3 | 1 |
|  | 2 | 15 | 15 | 3.425 | 3.43 | 5.4 | 4 | 2 | 3 | 1 |
|  | 3 | 15 | 16 | 3.425 | 3.42 | 2.2 | 4 | 2 | 3 | 0 |
| 3...... | 1 | 16 | 17 | 3.50 | 3.49 | 16.5 | 5 | 1 | 6 | 2 |
|  | 2 | 16 | 15 | 3.50 | 3.47 | 6.6 | 5 | 0 | 6 | 1 |
|  | 3 | 16 | 15 | 3.50 | 3.56 | 3.7 | 5 | 0 | 6 | 0 |
|  | 4 | 16 | 15 | 3.50 | 3.55 | 5.7 | 5 | 0 | 6 | 0 |
| 4A...... | 1 | 10 | 9 | 3.10 | 3.53 | 19.1 | None | None | None | None |
|  | 2 | 10 | 9 | 3.10 | 3.37 | 10.4 | None | None | None | None |
|  | 3 | 10 | 9 | 3.10 | 3.32 | 7.8 | None | None | None | None |
|  | 4 | 10 | 9 | 3.10 | 3.32 | 7.6 | None | None | None | None |
| 4B...... | 1 | 8 | 8 | 3.10 | 3.25 | 6.9 | None | None | None | None |
|  | 2 | 8 | 7 | 3.10 | 3.30 | 7.1 | None | None | None | None |
|  | 3 | 8 | 6 | 3.10 | 3.29 | 6.5 | None | None | None | None |
| 5A...... | 1 | 10 | 11 | 3.125 | 3.12 | 2.0 | 7 | 0 | 7 | 0 |
|  | 2 | 10 | 9 | 3.125 | 3.13 | 0.7 | 7 | 1 | 7 | 0 |
|  | 3 | 10 | 10 | 3.125 | 3.11 | 0.7 | 7 | 1 | 7 | 0 |
|  | 4 | 10 | 9 | 3.125 | 3.12 | 0.6 | 7 | 0 | 7 | 0 |
| 5B...... | 1 | 12 | 12 | 3.45 | 3.68 | 9.4 | 4 | 0 | 3 | 2 |
|  | 2 | 12 | 12 | 3.45 | 3.52 | 4.3 | 4 | 0 | 3 | 0 |
| 6A...... | 1 | 12 | 12 | 10.75 | 5.29 | 53.8 | 5 | 3 | None | None |
|  | 2 | 12 | 12 | 10.75 | 7.17 | 38.7 | 5 | 3 | None | None |
|  | 3 | 12 | 12 | 10.75 | 9.06 | 21.1 | 5 | 2 | None | None |
|  | 4 | 12 | 12 | 10.75 | 10.90 | 9.4 | 5 | 0 | None | None |
| 6B...... | 1 | 12 | 11 | 8.75 | 9.14 | 11.0 | 4 | 1 | None | None |
|  | 2 | 12 | 6 | 8.75 | ......... | ......... | 4 | 1 | None | None |
| 7...... | 1 | 9 | 8 | 3.40 | 2.12 | 49.1 | 3 | 1 | None | None |
|  | 2 | 9 | 9 | 3.40 | 2.91 | 22.2 | 3 | 0 | None | None |
|  | 3 | 9 | 9 | 3.40 | 3.23 | 7.1 | 3 | 1 | None | None |
|  | 4 | 9 | 8 | 3.40 | 3.32 | 5.4 | 3 | 0 | None | None |
|  | 5 | 9 | 9 | 3.40 | 3.33 | 3.0 | 3 | 0 | None | None |
|  | 6 | 9 | 9 | 3.40 | 3.34 | 2.7 | 3 | 0 | None | None |
| 8A...... | 1 | 7 | 8 | 2.25 | 2.50 | 19.0 | 5 | 0 | 4 | 0 |
|  | 2 | 7 | 5 | 2.25 | 2.20 | 2.9 | 5 | 0 | 4 | 0 |
|  | 3 | 7 | 6 | 2.25 | 2.12 | 7.4 | 5 | 0 | 4 | 0 |
|  | 4 | 7 | 5 | 2.25 | 2.12 | 7.0 | 5 | 0 | 4 | 0 |
| 8B...... | 1 | 7 | 6 | 2.25 | 2.23 | 7.8 | 5 | 0 | 4 | 0 |
|  | 2 | 7 | 6 | 2.25 | 2.29 | 6.1 | 5 | 0 | 4 | 0 |
| 9A...... | 1 | 18 | 18 | 3.40 | 2.81 | 21.8 | 6 | 3 | None | None |
|  | 2 | 18 | 18 | 3.40 | 2.97 | 15.4 | 6 | 2 | None | None |
|  | 3 | 18 | 18 | 3.40 | 3.07 | 13.2 | 6 | 2 | None | None |
| 9B...... | 1 | 20 | 20 | 3.80 | 3.52 | 10.3 | 4 | 3 | 2 | 0 |
| 10...... | 1 | 18 | 18 | 3.40 | 3.17 | 11.0 | 4 | 2 | None | None |
|  | 2 | 18 | 17 | 3.40 | 3.36 | 3.2 | 4 | 1 | None | None |
|  | 3 | 18 | 17 | 3.40 | 3.38 | 2.2 | 4 | 0 | None | None |

# CHART 2

## TEST 2

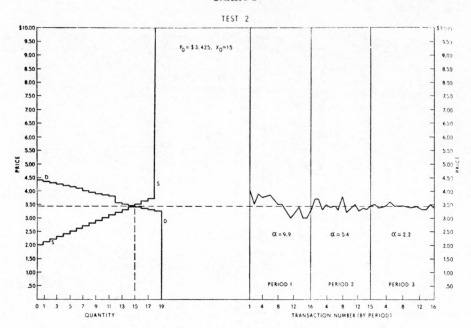

$P_0 = \$3.425, \ x_0 = 15$

# CHART 3

## TEST 3

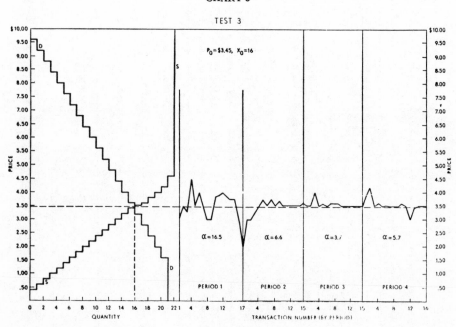

$P_0 = \$3.45, \ x_0 = 16$

EXPERIMENTAL STUDY OF COMPETITIVE MARKET BEHAVIOR 119

excess-rent hypothesis, to be discussed later.[7]

The tests in Chart 4 are of special interest from the point of view of the Walrasian hypothesis. In this case the supply curve is perfectly elastic—all sellers have cards containing the price $3.10. Each seller has the same lower bound on his reservation price acceptance set.

equilibrium since there is a considerable excess supply at prices just barely above the equilibrium price. From the results we see that the market is not particularly slow in converging, but it converges to a fairly stable price about $0.20 above the predicted equilibrium. Furthermore, in test $4B$, which was an extension of $4A$, the interjection of a decrease in

CHART 4

TEST 4A AND TEST 4B

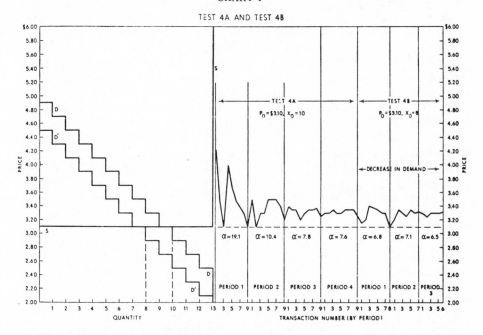

In this sense, there is no divergence of attitude among the sellers, though there might be marked variation in their bargaining propensities. According to the Walrasian hypothesis this market should exhibit rapid convergence toward the

demand from $DD$ to $D'D'$ was ineffective as a means of shocking the market down to its supply and demand equilibrium. This decrease in demand was achieved by passing out new buyer cards corresponding to $D'D'$ at the close of period 4 in test $4A$. As expected, the market approaches equilibrium from above, since contracts at prices below equilibrium are impossible.

The sellers in this market presented a solid front against price being lowered to "equilibrium." In the previous mar-

[7] The results are inconsistent with the so-called Marshallian hypothesis (the rate of increase in quantity exchanged is an increasing function of the excess of demand price over supply price), but this hypothesis would seem to be worth considering only in market processes in which some quantity-adjusting decision is made by the marketers. The results of a pilot experiment in "short-run" and "long-run" equilibrium are displayed in the Appendix.

kets there was a divergence of seller attitude, so that only a very few marginal and near-marginal sellers might offer serious resistance to price being forced to equilibrium. And this resistance tended to break down when any of the stronger intramarginal sellers accepted contracts below equilibrium.

From these results it is clear that the static competitive market equilibrium may depend not only on the intersection of the supply and demand schedules, but also upon the shapes of the schedules. Specifically, I was led from test 4 to the tentative hypothesis that there may be an upward bias in the equilibrium price of a market, which will be greater the more elastic is the supply schedule relative to demand.[8] For example, let $A$ be the area under the demand schedule and above the theoretical equilibrium. This is Marshall's consumer surplus, but to avoid any welfare connotations of this term, I shall refer to the area as "buyers' rent." Let $B$ be the area above the supply schedule and below the theoretical equilibrium (Marshall's producer surplus) which I shall call "sellers' rent." Now, the tentative hypothesis was that the actual market equilibrium will be above the theoretical equilibrium by an amount which depends upon how large $A$ is relative to $B$. Similarly, there will be a downward bias if $A$ is small relative to $B$.

Test 4 is of course an extreme case, since $B = 0$. In test 3, $A$ is larger than $B$, and the trading periods 3 and 4 exhibit a slight upward bias in the average actual exchange price (see Table 1). This provides some slight evidence in favor of the hypothesis.

As a consequence of these considerations, test 7 was designed specifically to obtain additional information to support or contradict the indicated hypothesis. In this case, as is seen in Chart 7 (see below), buyers' rent is substantially smaller than sellers' rent. From the resulting course of contract prices over six trading periods in this experiment, it is evident that the convergence to equilibrium is very slow. From Table 1, the average exchange prices in the last three trading periods are, respectively, $3.32, $3.33, and $3.34. Average contract prices are still exhibiting a gradual approach to equilibrium. Hence, it is entirely possible that the static equilibrium would eventually have been attained. A still smaller buyers' rent may be required to provide any clear downward bias in the static equilibrium. One thing, however, seems quite unmistakable from Chart 7, the relative magnitude of buyers' and sellers' rent affects the speed with which the actual market equilibrium is approached. One would expect sellers to present a somewhat weaker bargaining front, especially at first, if their rent potential is large relative to that of buyers. Thus, in Chart 7, it is seen that several low reservation price sellers in trading periods 1 and 2 made contracts at low exchange prices, which, no doubt, seemed quite profitable to these sellers. However, in both these trading periods the later exchange prices were much higher, revealing to the low-price sellers that, however profitable their initial sales had been, still greater profits were possible under stiffer bargaining.

A stronger test of the hypotheses that buyer and seller rents affect the speed of adjustment and that they affect the final equilibrium in the market would be obtainable by introducing actual mon-

---

[8] Note that the Walrasian hypothesis might lead one to expect a downward bias since excess supply is very large at prices above equilibrium if supply is very elastic relative to demand.

etary payoffs in the experiment. Thus, one might offer to pay each seller the difference between his contract price and his reservation price and each buyer the difference between his reservation price and his contract price. In addition, one might pay each trader a small lump sum (say $0.05) just for making a contract in any period. This sum would represent

any such reluctance that is attributable to artificial elements in the present experiments.[9]

The experiment summarized in Chart 5 was designed to study the effect on market behavior of changes in the conditions of demand and supply. As it happened, this experiment was performed on a considerably more mature group

CHART 5

TEST 5A AND TEST 5B

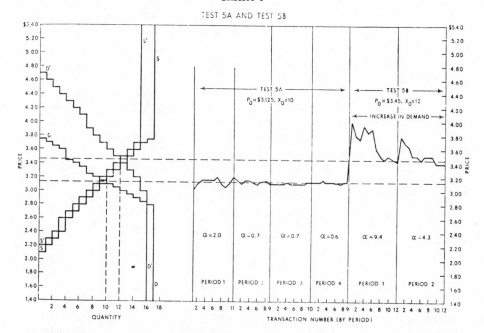

"normal profits," that is, a small return even if the good is sold at its minimum supply price or purchased at its maximum demand price. The present experiments have not seemed to provide any motivation problems. The subjects have shown high motivation to do their best even without monetary payoffs. But our experimental marginal buyers and sellers may be more reluctant to approach their reservation prices than their counterparts in real markets. The use of monetary payoffs, as suggested, should remove

of subjects than any of the other experiments. Most of the experiments were performed on sophomore and junior engineering, economics, and business majors, while test 5 was performed on a

[9] Since this was written, an experiment has been tried using monetary payoffs and the same supply and demand design shown in Chart 4. The result, as conjectured in the text, was to remove the reluctance of sellers to sell at their reservation prices. By the second trading period the market was firmly in equilibrium. In the third period all trades were at $3.10! Apparently $0.05 per period was considered satisfactory normal profit.

graduate class in economic theory. In view of this difference, it is most interesting to find the phenomenally low values for a exhibited by test 5A. The coefficient of convergence is smaller for the opening and later periods of this market than for any period of any of the other tests. Furthermore, trading periods 2–4 show a's of less than 1 per cent, indicating an inordinately strong and rapid tendency toward equilibrium. In this case, no offers or bids were accepted until the bidding had converged to prices which were very near indeed to the equilibrium. Contract prices ranged from $3.00 to $3.20 as compared with a possible range from $2.10 to $3.75.

At the close of test 5A new cards were distributed corresponding to an increase in demand, from $DD$ to $D'D'$, as shown in Chart 5.[10] The subjects, of course, could guess from the fact that new buyer cards were being distributed that a change in demand was in the wind. But they knew nothing of the direction of change in demand except what might be guessed by the buyers from the alteration of their individual reservation prices. When trading began (period 1, test 5B), the immediate response was a very considerable upward sweep in exchange prices with several contracts being closed in the first trading period well above the new higher equilibrium price. Indeed, the eagerness to buy was so strong that two sellers who were submarginal both before and after the increase in demand (their reservation prices were

$3.50 and $3.70) were able to make contracts in this transient phase of the market. Consequently, the trading group showing the strongest equilibrating tendencies exhibited very erratic behavior in the transient phase following the increase in demand. Contract prices greatly overshot the new equilibrium and rationing by the market was less efficient in this transient phase. In the second trading period of test 5B no submarginal sellers or buyers made contracts and the market exhibited a narrowed movement toward the new equilibrium.

Test 6A was designed to determine whether market equilibrium was affected by a marked imbalance between the number of intramarginal sellers and the number of intramarginal buyers near the predicted equilibrium price. The demand curve, $DD$, in Chart 6 falls continuously to the right in one-unit steps, while the supply curve, $SS$, becomes perfectly inelastic at the price $4.00, well below the equilibrium price $10.75. The tentative hypothesis was that the large rent ($6.75) enjoyed by the marginal seller, with still larger rents for the intramarginal sellers, might prevent the theoretical equilibrium from being established. From the results it is seen that the earlier conjecture concerning the effect of a divergence between buyer and seller rent on the approach to equilibrium is confirmed. The approach to equilibrium is from below, and the convergence is relatively slow. However, there is no indication that the lack of marginal sellers near the theoretical equilibrium has prevented the equilibrium from being attained. The average contract price in trading period 4 is $10.90, only $0.15 above the predicted equilibrium.

At the close of trading period 4 in test 6A, the old buyer cards corresponding to $DD$ were replaced by new cards

---

[10] Note also that there was a small (one-unit) decrease in supply from $SS$ to $S'S'$. This was not planned. It was due to the inability of one subject (the seller with the $2.10 reservation price) in test 5A to participate in test 5B. Therefore, except for the deletion of this one seller from the market, the conditions of supply were not altered, that is, the sellers of test 5B retained the same reservation price cards as they had in test 5A.

# CHART 6

## TEST 6A AND TEST 6B

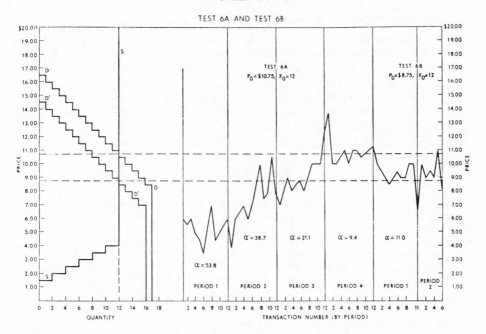

## CHART 7

## TEST 7

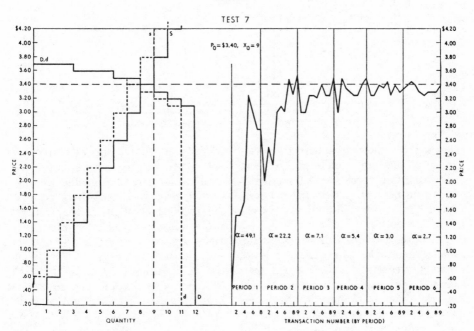

124                               VERNON L. SMITH

corresponding to $D'D'$ in Chart 6. Trading was resumed with the new conditions
of decreased demand (test 6$B$). There
was not sufficient time to permit two
full trading periods of market experience
to be obtained under the new demand
conditions. However, from the results
in Chart 6, it is evident that the maiket
responded promptly to the decrease in

(test 8$A$), only sellers were permitted
to enunciate offers. In this market, buyers
played a passive role; they could either
accept or reject the offers of sellers but
were not permitted to make bids. This
market was intended to simulate approximately an ordinary retail market.
In such markets, in the United States,
sellers typically take the initiative in

CHART 8

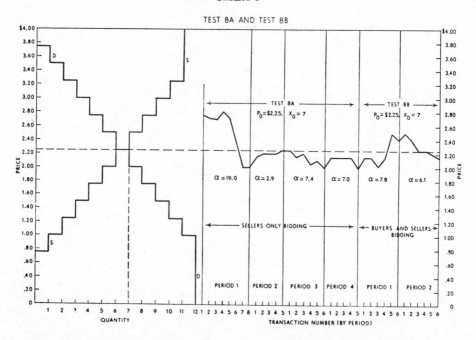

demand by showing apparent convergence to the new equilibrium. Note in
particular that there occurred no significant tendency for market prices to overshoot the new equilibrium as was observed in test 5$B$.

All of the above experiments were conducted under the same general rules of
market organization. Test 8 was performed as an exploratory means of testing the effect of changes in market organization on market price. In the first
four trading periods of this experiment

advertising their offer prices, with buyers
electing to buy or not to buy rather
than taking part in a higgling and bargaining process. Since sellers desire to
sell at the highest prices they can get,
one would expect the offer prices to be
high, and, consequently, one might expect the exchange prices to show a persistent tendency to remain above the
predicted equilibrium. The result was
in accordance with this crude expectation
in the first market period only (test 8$A$,
Chart 8). Since sellers only were making

EXPERIMENTAL STUDY OF COMPETITIVE MARKET BEHAVIOR 125

offers, the price quotations tended to be very much above equilibrium. Five of these offers were accepted at prices ranging from $2.69 to $2.80 by the five buyers with maximum reservation prices of $2.75 or more. This left only buyers with lower reservation prices. The competition of sellers pushed the offer prices lower and the remaining buyers made contracts at prices ($2.35, $2.00, and $2.00) near or below the equilibrium price. The early buyers in that first market period never quite recovered from having subsequently seen exchange prices fall much below the prices at which they had bought. Having been badly fleeced, through ignorance, in that first trading period, they refrained from accepting any high price offers in the remaining three periods of the test. This action, together with seller offer price competition, kept exchange prices at levels persistently below equilibrium for the remainder of test 8A. Furthermore, the coefficient of convergence increased from 2.9 per cent in the second trading period to 7.4 and 7.0 per cent in the last two periods. At the close of the fourth trading period, the market rules were changed to allow buyers to make quotations as well as sellers. Under the new rules (test 8B) two trading periods were run. Exchange prices immediately moved toward equilibrium with the closing prices of period 1 and opening prices of period 2 being above the equilibrium for the first time since period 1 of test 8A.

It would seem to be of some significance that of the ten experiments reported on, test 8 shows the clearest lack of convergence toward equilibrium. More experiments are necessary to confirm or deny these results, but it would appear that important changes in market organization—such as permitting only sellers to make quotations—have a distinctly disturbing effect on the equilibrating process. In particular the conclusion is suggested that markets in which only sellers competitively publicize their offers tend to operate to the benefit of buyers at the expense of sellers.

Turning to tests 9A and 10 (shown in Charts 9 and 10), it should be noted that the buyers and sellers in these tests received the same cards as their counterparts in test 7. The only difference was that the former entered the market to effect two transactions each, instead of one. Thus the three buyers with $3.70 cards could each buy two units at $3.70 or less in tests 9 and 10. This change in the design of test 7 resulted in a doubling of the maximum demand and supply quantities at each hypothetical price.

By permitting each buyer and seller to make two contracts per period, twice as much market "experience" is potentially to be gained by each trader in a given period. Each trader can experiment more in a given market—correcting his bids or offers in the light of any surprises or disappointments resulting from his first contract. In the previous experiments such corrections or alterations in the bargaining behavior of a trader had to await the next trading period once the trader had made a contract.[11]

[11] This process of correction over time, based upon observed price quotations and the actual contracts that are executed, is the underlying adjustment mechanism operating in all of these experiments. This is in contrast with the Walrasian *tâtonnement* or groping process in which "when a price is cried, and the effective demand and offer corresponding to this price are not equal, another price is cried for which there is another corresponding effective demand and offer" (see Leon Walras, *Elements of Pure Economics*, trans. William Jaffe [Chicago: Richard D. Irwin, Inc., 1954], p. 242). The Walrasian groping process suggests a centralized institutional means of trying different price quotations until the equilibrium is discovered. In our experiments, as in real markets, the groping process is decentralized, with all contracts binding whether they are at equilibrium or non-equilibrium prices.

Comparison of the results of the three trading periods in test 9*A* with the first three trading periods of test 7 shows that the tendencies toward equilibrium (as measured by *α*) were greater in test 9*A* during the first two periods and smaller in the third period. The same comparison between tests 7 and 10 reveals a stronger tendency toward equilibrium in test 10 than in the first three periods

of trade increased to the new equilibrium rate of twenty units per period. Note that the equilibrium tendency in the trading period of test 9*B* was greater than in any of the perious periods of test 9*A*. The increase in demand, far from destabilizing the market as was the case in test 5*B*, tended to strengthen its relatively weak equilibrium tendencies.

CHART 9

TEST 9A AND TEST 9B

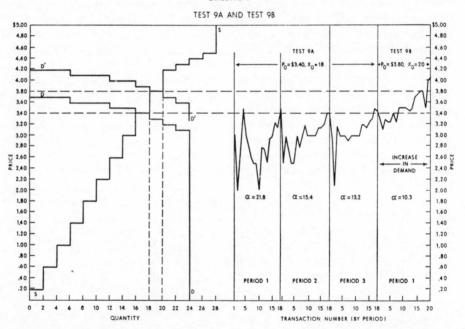

of 7. Hence an increase in volume appears to speed the equilibrating process. Indeed, the three trading periods of test 10 are roughly equivalent to the six trading periods of test 7, so that doubling volume in a given period is comparable to running two trading periods at the same volume.

In test 9*B* the consequences of an increase in demand were once again tested. Contract prices responded by moving upward immediately, and the volume

IV. EMPIRICAL ANALYSIS OF EXPERI-
MENTAL DATA: THE "EXCESS-
RENT" HYPOTHESIS

The empirical analysis of these ten experiments rests upon the hypothesis that there exists a stochastic difference equation which "best" represents the price convergence tendencies apparent in Charts 1–10. The general hypothesis is that

$$\Delta p_t = p_{t+1} - p_t = f[x_1(p_t), \quad x_2(p_t), \ldots] + \epsilon_t, \tag{1}$$

where the arguments $x_1$, $x_2$, ... reflect characteristics of the experimental supply and demand curves and the bargaining characteristics of individual test groups, and $\epsilon_t$ is a random variable with zero mean. For a given experimental test group, under the so-called Walrasian hypothesis $x_1(p_t)$ might be the excess demand prevailing at $p_t$, with $f = 0$ when $x_1 = 0$.

My first empirical investigation is concerned with the measuremet of the equilibrating tendencies in these markets and the ability of supply and demand theory to predict the equilibrium price in each experiment. To this end note that equation (1) defines a stochastic phase function[12] of the form $p_{t+1} = g(p_t) + \epsilon_t$. An equilibrium price $P_0$ is attained when $P_0 = g(P_0)$. Rather than estimate the phase function for each experiment, it was found convenient to make linear estimates of its first difference, that is,

$$\Delta p_t = a_0 + a_1 p_t + \epsilon_t .$$

The corresponding linear phase function has slope $1 + a_1$. The parameters $a_0$ and $a_1$ were estimated by linear regression techniques for each of the ten fundamental experiments and are tabulated in column 1 of Table 2.[13] Confidence

[12] See, for example, W. J. Baumol, *Economic Dynamics* (New York: Macmillan Co., 1959), pp. 257–65.

[13] The least squares estimate of $a_1$ in these experiments can be expected to be biased (see L. Hurwicz, "Least-Squares Bias in Time Series," chap. xv, in T. Koopmans, *Statistical Inference in Dynamic Economic Models* [New York: John Wiley & Sons, 1950]). However, since in all of the basic experiments there are twenty or more observations, the bias will not tend to be large.

CHART 10

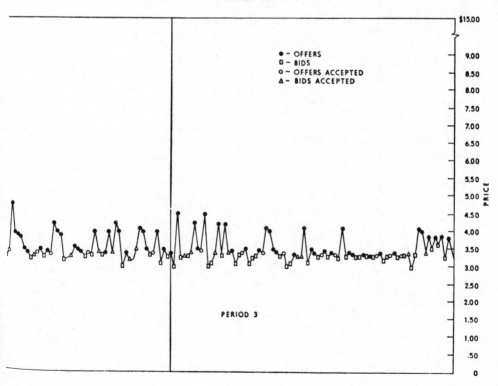

● – OFFERS
□ – BIDS
○ – OFFERS ACCEPTED
△ – BIDS ACCEPTED

PERIOD 3

TABLE 2

| Experiment | $(\Delta p_t = \alpha_0 + \alpha_1 p_t)$ | Walrasian $(\Delta p_t = \beta_{01} + \beta_{11} x_{1t})$ | Modified Walrasian $(\Delta p_t = \beta_{01} + \beta_{11} x_{1t} + \beta_{31} x_{3t})$ | Excess Rent $(\Delta p_t = \beta_{02} + \beta_{22} x_{2t})$ | Modified Excess Rent $(\Delta p_t = \beta_{04} + \beta_{14} x_{1t} + \beta_{24} x_{2t})$ |
|---|---|---|---|---|---|
| 1 | $0.933 - 0.474\, p_t$<br>$(\pm 0.329)$ | $-0.026 + 0.070\, x_{1t}$<br>$(\pm 0.042)$ | $-0.027 + 0.068\, x_{1t} - 0.0056\, x_{3t}$<br>$(\pm 0.015)\ (\pm 0.0220)$ | $-0.028 + 0.486\, x_{2t}$<br>$(\pm 0.322)$ | $-0.031 + 0.491\, x_{2t} - 0.0054\, x_{3t}$<br>$(\pm 0.104)\ (\pm 0.0215)$ |
| 2 | $1.904 - 0.560\, p_t$<br>$(\pm 0.250)$ | $.002 + .035\, x_{1t}$<br>$(\pm .015)$ | $-\ .170 + .042\, x_{1t} - .0693\, x_{3t}$<br>$(\pm .006)\ (\pm .0311)$ | $.008 + .141\, x_{2t}$<br>$(\pm .067)$ | $-\ .070 + .152\, x_{2t} - .0313\, x_{3t}$<br>$(\pm .024)\ (\pm .0649)$ |
| 3 | $2.275 - 0.647\, p_t$<br>$(\pm 0.292)$ | $.157 + .107\, x_{1t}$<br>$(\pm .045)$ | $.093 + .105\, x_{1t} + .0042\, x_{3t}$<br>$(\pm .014)\ (\pm .0317)$ | $.071 + .227\, x_{2t}$<br>$(\pm .097)$ | $-\ .022 + .225\, x_{2t} + .0064\, x_{3t}$<br>$(\pm .031)\ (\pm .0315)$ |
| 4A | $2.852 - 0.849\, p_t$<br>$(\pm 0.287)$ | $.761 + .168\, x_{1t}$<br>$(\pm .057)$ | $.794 + .169\, x_{1t} - .0007\, x_{3t}$<br>$(\pm .018)\ (\pm .0564)$ | $.145 + .129\, x_{2t}$<br>$(\pm .049)$ | $.139 + .130\, x_{2t} + .0017\, x_{3t}$<br>$(\pm .016)\ (\pm .0641)$ |
| 5A | $2.448 - 0.784\, p_t$<br>$(\pm 0.302)$ | $.031 + .023\, x_{1t}$<br>$(\pm .009)$ | $-\ .035 + .023\, x_{1t} - .0029\, x_{3t}$<br>$(\pm .003)\ (\pm .0043)$ | $-\ .007 + .205\, x_{2t}$<br>$(\pm .098)$ | $-\ .009 + .204\, x_{2t} - .0015\, x_{3t}$<br>$(\pm .032)\ (\pm .0048)$ |
| 6A | $1.913 - 0.220\, p_t$<br>$(\pm 0.174)$ | $-\ .675 + .243\, x_{1t}$<br>$(\pm .175)$ | $.010 + .285\, x_{1t} + .0211\, x_{3t}$<br>$(\pm .057)\ (\pm .0847)$ | $.309 + .038\, x_{2t}$<br>$(\pm .037)$ | $.305 + .034\, x_{2t} + .0146\, x_{3t}$<br>$(\pm .013)\ (\pm .0906)$ |
| 7 | $1.216 - 0.368\, p_t$<br>$(\pm 0.116)$ | $.102 + .074\, x_{1t}$<br>$(\pm .049)$ | $-\ .070 + .075\, x_{1t} + .0063\, x_{3t}$<br>$(\pm .009)\ (\pm .0738)$ | $.007 + .051\, x_{2t}$<br>$(\pm .021)$ | $.058 + .053\, x_{2t} + .0096\, x_{3t}$<br>$(\pm .007)\ (\pm .0750)$ |
| 8A | $0.225 - 0.121\, p_t$<br>$(\pm 0.226)$ | $-\ .040 + .020\, x_{1t}$<br>$(\pm .030)$ | $-\ .027 + .025\, x_{1t} - .0462\, x_{3t}$<br>$(\pm .011)\ (\pm .0487)$ | $-\ .036 + .051\, x_{2t}$<br>$(\pm .094)$ | $-\ .022 + .064\, x_{2t} - .0396\, x_{3t}$<br>$(\pm .035)\ (\pm .0505)$ |
| 9A | $1.653 - 0.554\, p_t$<br>$(\pm 0.273)$ | $-\ .450 + .061\, x_{1t}$<br>$(\pm .036)$ | $-\ .447 + .085\, x_{1t} + .0198\, x_{3t}$<br>$(\pm .012)\ (\pm .0423)$ | $-\ .209 + .071\, x_{2t}$<br>$(\pm .029)$ | $-\ .065 + .094\, x_{2t} + .0222\, x_{3t}$<br>$(\pm .009)\ (\pm .0356)$ |
| 10 | $1.188 - 0.356\, p_t$<br>$(\pm 0.233)$ | $-0.039 + 0.020\, x_{1t}$<br>$(\pm 0.014)$ | $-0.028 + 0.020\, x_{1t} + 0.0008\, x_{3t}$<br>$(\pm 0.004)\ (\pm 0.0199)$ | $-0.022 + 0.055\, x_{2t}$<br>$(\pm 0.032)$ | $-0.008 + 0.056\, x_{2t} + 0.0011\, x_{3t}$<br>$(\pm 0.014)\ (\pm 0.0194)$ |

## EXPERIMENTAL STUDY OF COMPETITIVE MARKET BEHAVIOR 129

intervals for a 95 per cent fiducial probability level are shown in parentheses under the estimate of $a_1$ for each experiment. With the exception of experiment 8A, the 95 per cent confidence interval for each regression coefficient is entirely contained in the interval $-2 < a_1 < 0$, which is required for market stability. Hence, of these ten experiments, 8A is the only one whose price movements are sufficiently erratic to prevent us from rejecting the null hypothesis of instability, and of the ten basic experiments this

$$t = \frac{a_0 + a_1 P_0}{S(a_0 + a_1 P_0)}$$

for the sample estimates on the assumption that $\Delta p_t = 0$ when $p_t = P_0$ in the population. These $t$-values are shown in column 1, Table 3, for the ten primary and the five "$B$" auxiliary experiments. Low absolute values of $t$ imply that, relative to the error in the prediction, the predicted equilibrium is close to the theoretical. The four lowest absolute $t$-values are for experimental designs with the smallest difference between equilibri-

TABLE 3

| EXPERIMENT | $t = (a_0 + a_1 P_0)/$ $[S(a_0 + a_1 P_0)]$ (1) | WALRASIAN | | | EXCESS RENT | | | DEGREES OF FREEDOM (8) |
|---|---|---|---|---|---|---|---|---|
| | | $|\beta_{01}|$ (2) | $S(\beta_{01})$ (3) | $t = \beta_{01}/S(\beta_{01})$ (4) | $|\beta_{02}|$ (5) | $S(\beta_{02})$ (6) | $t = \beta_{02}/S(\beta_{02})$ (7) | |
| 1......... | −0.673 | 0.026 | 0.019 | −1.36 | 0.028 | 0.021 | −0.66 | 21 |
| 2......... | 0.460 | .002 | .029 | 0.08 | .008 | .030 | 0.25 | 42 |
| 3......... | 1.008 | .157 | .055 | 2.88 | .071 | .046 | 1.56 | 57 |
| 4A........ | 4.170 | .761 | .137 | 5.57 | .145 | .048 | 3.05 | 30 |
| 4B........ | 3.219 | .391 | .284 | 1.37 | .161 | .052 | 3.08 | 16 |
| 5A........ | −0.333 | .031 | .008 | −3.72 | .007 | .006 | −1.16 | 33 |
| 5B........ | −0.230 | .002 | .034 | 0.05 | .013 | .026 | −0.51 | 20 |
| 6A........ | −1.412 | .675 | .362 | −1.87 | .309 | .311 | −0.99 | 42 |
| 6B........ | 2.176 | .299 | .314 | 0.95 | .179 | .290 | 0.62 | 13 |
| 7......... | −0.740 | .102 | .057 | −1.78 | .007 | .045 | 0.15 | 44 |
| 8A........ | −1.597 | .040 | .029 | −1.40 | .036 | .032 | −1.13 | 18 |
| 8B........ | −0.140 | .010 | .042 | −0.24 | .016 | .043 | −0.37 | 8 |
| 9A........ | −0.647 | .450 | .151 | −2.99 | .209 | .065 | −3.21 | 49 |
| 9B........ | −0.021 | .012 | .112 | 0.11 | .016 | .071 | −0.23 | 17 |
| 10........ | −0.731 | 0.039 | 0.033 | −1.19 | 0.022 | 0.028 | −0.80 | 47 |

is the one in which the trading rules were altered to permit only sellers to quote prices.[14]

The regressions of column 1, Table 2, and associated computation provide a means of predicting the adjustment pressure on price, $\Delta p_t$, for any given $p_t$. In particular, we can compute

[14] Three of the five auxiliary "$B$" experiments demonstrated a similar instability (in the fiducial probability sense), but the samples were considerably smaller than their "$A$" counterparts, they represented considerably fewer trading periods, and they had different and varying objectives. The unstable ones were 4B, 8B, and 9B.

um buyers' and sellers' rent. These results provide some additional evidence in favor of our conjecture in Part III, that the equilibrium is influenced by the relative sizes of the areas $A$ and $B$. However, from the $t$-values it would seem that the influence is small except for test 4, where $B = 0$. In this case, the null hypothesis ($\Delta p_t = 0$ when $p_t = P_0$) is rejected even at a significance level below .005.

Four specific forms for the difference equation (1) were studied in detail and tested for their ability to predict the theoretical equilibrium price. These will be referred to as the Walrasian, the excess-rent, the modified Walrasian, and the modified excess-rent hypotheses, respectively. The Walrasian hypothesis is $\Delta p_t = \beta_{01} + \beta_{11}x_{1t}$, where $x_{1t}$ is the excess demand prevailing at the price, $p_t$, at which the $t$th transaction occurred. Because of the conjecture that buyers' and sellers' rent might have an effect on individual and market adjustment, an excess-rent hypothesis was introduced. This hypothesis is $\Delta p_t = \beta_{02} + \beta_{22}x_{2t}$, where $x_{2t}$ is the algebraic area

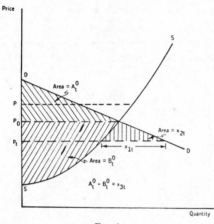

FIG. 1

between the supply and demand curves, and extends from the equilibrium price down to the price of the $t$th transaction, as shown in Figure 1. The modified Walrasian hypothesis is $\Delta p_t = \beta_{03} + \beta_{13}x_{1t} + \beta_{33}x_{3t}$, where $x_{3t} = A_t^0 - B_t^0$, the algebraic difference between the equilibrium buyers' rent, $A_t^0$, and the equilibrium sellers' rent, $B_t^0$. The motivation here was to introduce a term in the adjustment equation which would permit the actual equilibrium price to be biased above or below the theoretical equilibrium, by an amount proportional to the algebraic difference between buyers' and

sellers' rent at the theoretical equilibrium. It was believed that such a general hypothesis might be necessary to account for the obvious price equilibrium bias in experiment 4 and the slight apparent bias in experiments 3, 6$A$, 7, and 9$A$. A similar motivation suggested the modified excess-rent hypothesis, $\Delta p_t = \beta_{04} + \beta_{24}x_{2t} + \beta_{34}x_{3t}$.

Since the trading process in these experiments was such that transactions might and generally did take place at non-equilibrium prices, the supply and demand curves shift after each transaction. Hence, in generating observations on $x_{1t}$, $x_{2t}$, and $x_{3t}$, the supply and demand curves were adjusted after each transaction for the effect of the pairing of a buyer and a seller in reducing their effective demand and supply. Thus, in Chart 7, the first transaction was at \$0.50 between the seller with reservation price \$0.20 and a buyer with reservation price \$3.50. Following this trasaction the new effective demand and supply curves become $Dd$ and $ss$ as shown. The next transaction is at \$1.50. Our hypothesis is that the increase in price from \$0.50 to \$1.50 is due to the conditions represented by $Dd$ and $ss$ at the price \$0.50. Thus, for the first set of observations $\Delta p_1 = p_1 - p_0 = \$1.50 - \$0.50 = \$1.00$, $x_{11} = 11$, $x_{21} = 20.10$, and $x_{31} = -9.60$ as can be determined from Chart 7. The second transaction paired a \$3.70 buyer and a \$0.60 seller. The next set of observations is then obtained by removing this buyer and seller from $Dd$ and $ss$ to obtain $x_{12}$, $x_{22}$, and $x_{32}$ at $p_2 = 1.50$, with $\Delta p_2 = p_2 - p_1 = 0$, and so on.

Using observations obtained in this manner, regressions for the four different equilibrating hypotheses were computed for the ten fundamental experiments as shown in Table 2, columns 2–5. A 95 per cent confidence interval is shown in parentheses under each regression coefficient. With the exception of experiment $8A$, the regression coefficients for every experiment are significant under both the Walrasian and the excess-rent hypotheses. On the other hand, $\beta_{33}$ in the modified Walrasian hypothesis is significant only in experiment 2. In none of the experiments is $\beta_{34}$ significant for the modified excess-rent hypothesis. These highly unambiguous results seem to suggest that little significance can be attached to the effect of a difference between equilibrium buyers' and sellers' rent in biasing the price equilibrium tendencies.

On this reasoning, we are left with the closely competing Walrasian and excess-rent hypotheses, showing highly significant adjustment speeds, $\beta_{11}$ and $\beta_{22}$. In discriminating between these two hypotheses we shall compare them on two important counts: (1) their ability to predict zero price change in equilibrium, and (2) the standard errors of said predictions. Since $x_{1t}^0 = x_{2t}^0 = 0$, in equilibrium, this requires a comparison between the absolute values of the intercepts of the Walrasian and the excess-rent regressions, $|\beta_{01}|$ and $|\beta_{02}|$, and between $S(\beta_{01})$ and $S(\beta_{02})$. Under the first comparison we can think of $|\beta_{01}|$, shown in column 2, Table 3, as a "score" for the Walrasian hypothesis, and $|\beta_{02}|$, shown in column 5, as a "score" for the excess-rent hypothesis. A low intercept represents a good score. Thus, for experiment 1, in equilibrium, there is a residual tendency for price to change (in this case fall) at the rate of 2.6 cents per transaction by the Walrasian and 2.8 cents by the excess-rent regressions. A casual comparison of columns 2 and 5 reveals that in most of the experiments $|\beta_{01}| > |\beta_{02}|$, and in those for which the reverse is true the difference is quite small, tend-

ing thereby to support the excess-rent hypothesis. A more exact discrimination can be made by applying the Wilcoxon[15] paired-sample rank test for related samples to the "scores" of columns 2 and 5. This test applies to the differences $|\beta_{01}| - |\beta_{02}|$, and tests the null hypothesis, $H_0$, that the Walrasian and excess-rent alternatives are equivalent (the distribution of the differences is symmetric about zero). If applied to all the experiments, including the "$B$'s" ($N = 15$), $H_0$ is rejected at the $< .02$ significance level. The difference between our paired series of "scores" in favor of the excess-rent hypothesis is therefore significant. It is highly debatable whether all the experiments should be included in such a test, especially 4, which did not tend to the predicted equilibrium, 8, which represented a different organization of the bargaining, and possibly the "$B$" experiments, where the samples were small. Therefore, the test was run omitting all these experiments ($N = 8$), giving a rejection of $H_0$ at the .05 level. Omitting only 4 and 8 ($N = 11$) allowed $H_0$ still to be rejected at the $< .02$ level.

If we compare the standard errors $S(\beta_{01})$ and $S(\beta_{02})$ in Table 3, columns 3 and 6, we see that again the excess-rent hypothesis tends to score higher (smaller standard errors). Applying the Wilcoxon test to $S(\beta_{01}) - S(\beta_{02})$ for all the experiments ($N = 15$), we find that this difference, in favor of the excess-rent hypothesis, is significant at the $< .01$ level. The difference is still significant at the $< .01$ level if we omit 4 and 8 from the test, and it is significant at the .05 level if we also eliminate all the "$B$" experiments.

The $t$-values for the two hypotheses

[15] See, for example, K. A. Brownlee, *Statistical Theory and Methodology in Science and Engineering* (New York: John Wiley & Sons, 1960), pp. 196–99.

are shown in columns 4 and 7 of Table 3. They tend also to be lower for the excess-rent hypothesis.

Bearing in mind that our analysis is based upon a limited number of experiments, and that revisions may be required in the light of further experiments with different subjects or with monetary payoffs, we conclude the following: Of the four hypotheses tested, the two modified forms show highly insignificant regression coefficients for the added explanatory variable. As between the Walrasian and the excess-rent hypotheses, the evidence is sharply in favor of the latter.

## V. RATIONALIZATION OF THE EXCESS-RENT HYPOTHESIS

Having provided a tentative empirical verification of the hypothesis that price in a competitve (auction) market tends to rise or fall in proportion to the excess buyer plus seller rent corresponding to any contract price, it remains to provide some theoretical rationale for such a hypothesis. From the description of the above experiments and their results, the excess-rent hypothesis would seem to have some plausibility from an individual decision-making point of view. Given that a particular contract price has just been executed, it is reasonable to expect each trader to compare that price with his own reservation price, the difference being a "profit" or rent which he considers achievable, and to present a degree of bargaining resistance in the auction process which is greater, the smaller is this rent. Such resistance may tend to give way, even where the rents on one side or the other are very small, if it becomes clear that such rents are unattainable. Thus, if equilibrium buyers' rent exceeds sellers' rent, any early tendency for contract prices to remain above equi-

librium (and balance the rents achieved on both sides) might be expected to break down, as it becomes evident that the "paper" rents at those prices may not be attainable by all of the sellers. By this argument, it is suggested that the propensity of sellers to reduce their offers when price is above equilibrium is related to their attempts to obtain some—even if a "small"—amount of rent rather than to a direct influence of excess supply.

A particularly interesting aspect of the excess-rent hypothesis is that it leads naturally to an interesting optimality interpretation of the static competitive market equilibrium. The principle is this: in static equilibrium a competitive market minimizes the total virtual rent received by buyers and sellers. By "virtual rent" I mean the rent that would be enjoyed if all buyers and sellers could be satisfied at any given disequilibrium price. To see this optimality principle, let $D(p)$ be the demand function and $S(p)$ the supply function. At $p = P$, the sum of buyer and seller virtual rent is

$$R = \int_P^\infty D(p)\,dp + \int_0^P S(p)\,dp$$

and is represented by the area from $DD$ down to $P$ and from $SS$ up to $P$ in Figure 1. $R$ is a minimum for normal supply and demand functions when

$$\frac{dR}{dP} = -D(P) + S(P) = 0,$$

that is, when demand equals supply with $P = P_0$. Note particularly that there is nothing artificial about this conversion of the statement of an ordinary competitive market equilibrium into a corresponding minimum problem. Whether one desires to attach any welfare significance to the concepts of consumer and producer surplus or not, it is com-

EXPERIMENTAL STUDY OF COMPETITIVE MARKET BEHAVIOR 133

pletely plausible to require, in the interests of strict market efficiency, that no trader be imputed more rent than is absolutely necessary to perform the exchange mechanics. Hence, at price $P$ in Figure 1, virtual rent exceeds equilibrium rent, and if this price persists, some sellers get more rent than they "should."

It should perhaps be pointed out that the excess-rent and Walrasian hypotheses are close analogues in that both deal with virtual, unattainable quantities. Thus, under the Walrasian hypothesis the "virtual" excess supply at $P$ in Figure 1 is unattainable. Indeed, it is this fact that presumably causes price to fall. Similarly, at $P$, the excess rent area above $S$ and $D$ is unattainable, and leads to price cutting. Also note that the Walrasian hypothesis bears a gradient relationship, while the excess-rent hypothesis shows a global adjusting relationship, to the rent minimization principle. At $P > P_0$ the Walrasian hypothesis says that price tends to fall at a time rate which is proportional to the marginal rent, $dR/dP$, at that price. The excess-rent hypothesis states that price tends to fall at a time rate which is proportional to the global difference between total rent at $P$ and at $P_0$.

Samuelson has shown how one may convert the Cournot-Enke problem of spatial price equilibrium into a maximum problem.[16] The criterion to be maximized in a single market would be what he calls social payoff, defined as the algebraic area under the excess-demand curve. In spatially separated markets the criterion is to maximize net social payoff, defined as the sum of the social payoffs in all regions minus the total transport costs of all interregional ship-

ments. But, according to Samuelson, "this magnitude is artificial in the sense that no competitor in the market will be aware of or concerned with it. It is artificial in the sense that after an Invisible Hand has led us to its maximization, we need not necessarily attach any social welfare significance to the result."[17] I think the formulation of competitive market equilibrium as a rent minimization problem makes the "Invisible Hand" distinctly more visible and more teleological.[18] It also has great social (though not necessarily welfare) significance in relation to "frictionless" market efficiency. Rent is an "unearned" increment which literally cries out for minimization in an efficient economic organization. Furthermore, as we have seen with the excess-rent and Walrasian hypotheses, both the abstract teleological goal of the competitive market and the dynamics of its *tâtonnement* process are branches of the same market mechanism.

In view of the electrical circuit analogue so often mentioned in connection with spatially separated markets, a final bonus of the minimum rent formulation is the fact that it represents a more direct analogy with the principle of minimum heat loss in electric circuits.[19] Nature has devised a set of laws to govern the flow of electrical energy, which, it

[16] P. A. Samuelson, "Spatial Price Equilibrium and Linear Programming," *American Economic Review*, XLII (June, 1952), 284–92.

[17] *Ibid.*, p. 288.

[18] The discovery of the excess-rent hypothesis draws me nearer to the camp of "Invisible Hand" enthusiasts, but only because of the greater visibility of the Hand. I cannot quite carry my market metaphysics as far as does Samuelson. It is well known that any problem in economic equilibrium can be converted into a maximum (or minimum) problem, but I question the value of such a transformation (beyond technical advantages) if it is purely artificial without any meaningful interpretation; and if we work at it, such a meaningful transformation may often be found.

[19] Samuelson, *op. cit.*, p. 285.

can be shown, minimizes the inefficient, wasteful loss of heat energy from electrical systems. Similarly, the market mechanism provides a set of "laws" which minimizes the "wasteful" payment of excessive economic rent.

## VI. SUMMARY

It would be premature to asseit any broad generalizations based upon the ten experiments we have discussed. Yet conclusions are important for purposes of specifying the exact character of any findings, whether those findings are ultimately verified or not. In this spirit, the following tentative conclusions are offered concerning these experiments:

1. Even where numbers are "small," there are strong tendencies for a supply and demand competitive equilibrium to be attained as long as one is able to prohibit collusion and to maintain absolute publicity of all bids, offers, and transactions. Publicity of quotations and absence of collusion were major characteristics of these experimental markets.

2. Changes in the conditions of supply or demand cause changes in the volume of transactions per period and the general level of contract prices. These latter correspond reasonably well with the predictions of competitive price theory. The response to such changes may, however, produce a transient phase of very erratic contract price behavior.

3. Some slight evidence has been provided to suggest that a prediction of the static equilibrium of a competitive market requires knowledge of the shapes of the supply and demand schedules as well as the intersection of such schedules. The evidence is strongest in the extreme case in which the supply curve is perfectly elastic, with the result that the empirical equilibrium is higher than the theoretical equilibrium.

4. Markets whose institutional organization is such that only sellers make price quotations may exhibit weaker equilibrium tendencies than markets in which both buyers and sellers make price quotations—perhaps even disequilibrium tendencies. Such one-sided markets may operate to the benefit of buyers. A possible explanation is that in the price-formation process buyers reveal a minimum of information concerning their eagerness to buy.

5. The so-called Walrasian hypothesis concerning the mechanism of market adjustment seems not to be confirmed. A more adequate hypothesis is the excess-rent hypothesis which relates the "speed" of contract price adjustment to the algebraic excess of buyer plus seller "virtual" rent over the equilibrium buyer plus seller rent. This new hypothesis becomes particularly intriguing in view of the fact that a competitive market for a single commodity can be interpreted as seeking to minimize total rent.

## APPENDIX

In the course of this experimental study and its analysis several additional or peripheral issues were investigated, a discussion of which would not fit clearly into the main body of this report. Three such issues will be discussed briefly in this appendix for the benefit of readers interested in some of the numerous additional lines of inquiry that might be pursued.

### I. EVIDENCE OF INTER-TRADING-PERIOD LEARNING

In testing the various equilibrating hypotheses under investigation in this paper, no attempt was made to distinguish the effects of different trading periods. The sample of observations for each experiment embraced all the trading periods of that ex-

EXPERIMENTAL STUDY OF COMPETITIVE MARKET BEHAVIOR    135

periment with transactions running continuously from the first trading period through the last. It would appear, however, that learning occurs as the experiment progresses in such a way as to alter the parameters of each equilibrating hypothesis from one trading period to the next. To obtain some idea of the extent of these alterations, regressions for the excess-rent hypothesis were computed by individual trading period for tests 6A, 9A, and 10. These regression equations are summarized in Table 4. It is evident that there is a tendency for the intercepts of these regressions to converge toward zero as the number of trading periods increases. Convergence of the intercepts suggests that the later trading period regressions may be better equilibrating equations (better predictors of zero price change when excess rent is zero) than the earlier period regressions.

## II. CONVERGENCE OF BID, OFFER, AND CONTRACT PRICES

In experiments 9 and 10 a tape-recorder was used for the first time to obtain a record of all bid and offer prices as well as the contract prices. No analysis has as yet been attempted with these additional data. However, a graph of the bid, offer, and contract prices in their serial sequence of occurrence is suggestive. Such a sample graph is shown in Chart 11 for experiment 10. Perhaps the most interesting fact revealed in this

TABLE 4

EXCESS-RENT REGRESSIONS $\Delta p_t = \beta_{02} + \beta_{22} x_{2t}$ BY TRADING PERIOD

| Trading Period | Experiment 6A | Experiment 9A | Experiment 10 |
|---|---|---|---|
| 1....... | $-2.769+0.101\,x_{2t}$ | $-0.335+0.078\,x_{2t}$ | $-0.160+0.087\,x_{2t}$ |
| 2....... | $-2.876+0.216\,x_{2t}$ | $-0.148+0.061\,x_{2t}$ | $-0.053+0.408\,x_{2t}$ |
| 3....... | $0.273+0.029\,x_{2t}$ | $-0.191+0.093\,x_{2t}$ | $0.007+0.349\,x_{2t}$ |
| 4....... | $0.121+0.391\,x_{2t}$ | | |

CHART 11

BIDS, OFFERS, AND TRANSACTIONS ON TEST 10

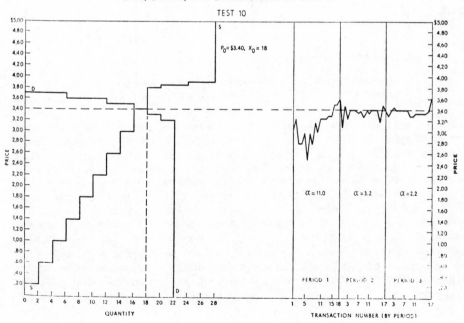

chart is the apparent tendency for the variance of the bids and offers to stabilize early,
with the contract prices continuing to converge within this variation in bids and offers.
Thus it is at the beginning of period 1,
up to about the eighth transaction, that the
bids and offers seem to show the most pronounced variation. This variation then remains reasonably steady to the very end
of the last trading period. Contract prices

## III. A PILOT EXPERIMENT IN "SHORT-RUN" AND "LONG-RUN" EQUILIBRIUM

An important characteristic of the ten
experiments discussed in this paper was
the absence of any quantity-adjusting decision-making behavior on the part of either
buyers or sellers. Such experiments represent the simulation of markets for commodities which do not have to be delivered or

CHART 12

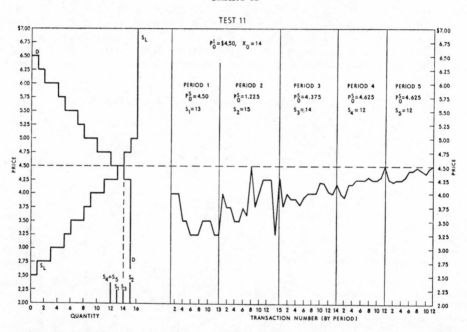

TEST 11

converge, but the traders continue to attempt to get better terms by making re-
peatedly high offers and low bids. In this
connection note that the unaccepted offers
are further above the contract prive level
than the unaccepted bids are below the
contract price level. Similar results were
evident in a corresponding chart (not shown)
for experiment 9. This, apparently, is the
auction market's way of compensating for
the fact that, in this particular experiment,
sellers were in a "softer" (higher rent) position than buyers.

even produced until after the sale contract
is executed. Hence, the possibility of distress
sales, leading to losses by sellers, is ruled
out by experimen.al design. In long-run
price theory we think of producers entering
or leaving an industry in response to the
profits or losses they expect to make. The
results of one pilot experiment to simulate
this process is shown in Chart 12. The
significant new element in this experiment
was giving all sellers the option at the
beginning of each trading period of entering
the market or remaining "out of produc-

EXPERIMENTAL STUDY OF COMPETITIVE MARKET BEHAVIOR      137

tion." It was understood that if they entered the market it was at a cost equal to the price on their card, and this cost was a net loss to any seller failing to make a sale. Also in this experiment some sellers were producers of two units and some of one unit. Specifically, there were six sellers with one unit and five with two units. Similarly, some buyers were two-unit buyers and some were one-unit buyers. It was not known to the traders generally how many or who were traders in one or in two units. This procedure was employed primarily to prevent traders from having exact knowledge of short-run supply by simply counting the number of sellers in the market in any trading period. Buyers in particular were thereby faced with some uncertainty to temper their knowledge that sellers were under strong selling pressure once they entered the market.

The experiment was conducted over five trading periods. In period 1 two sellers with a capacity to produce three units (the $4.75 and $3.00 sellers in Chart 12) elected to remain out of production. They were market observers only. Therefore the period 1 short-run theoretical supply was perfectly inelastic at $S_1 = 13$. In period 2 only the $4.50 seller, who sold at a loss the first time, remained out, giving $S_2 = 15$. In period 3 the $5.00 and $4.50 sellers remained out giving $S_3 = 14$, and in periods 4 and 5 production stabilized with the $5.00, $4.50, and $4.25 producers out of the market, giving $S_4 = S_5 = 12$.

From the results is it clear that this market approaches its "long-run" equilibrium price, $4.50, more slowly than was the case in the previous experiments. The approach is from below as might be expected by the "distress sale" characteristic of the market. The pressure on producers to sell seems to have had its strongest effect in period 1, in which market prices tended to decline from their opening. Prices moved erratically in period 2, and in the remaining periods climbed steadily in the direction of equilibrium.

## ERRATA

In the article, "An Experimental Study of Competitive Market Behavior," by Vernon L. Smith published in the April, 1962, issue of this *Journal*, Charts 10 and 11 (pp. 127 and 135) were inadvertently interchanged. The left half of Chart 11 (mislabeled Chart 10) was also omitted. For the convenience of readers, we reproduce the whole of Chart 11 here.

CHART 11

BIDS, OFFERS, AND TRANSACTIONS ON TEST 10

TEST 10

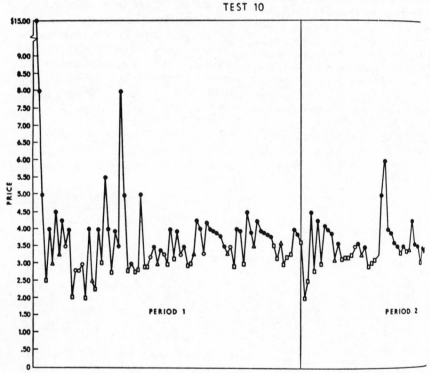

322

CHART 11—*Continued*

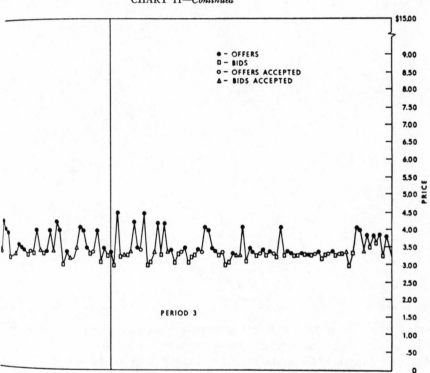

# [2]

## *Theoretical Formulation*

### THE EQUAL-STRENGTH CASE

Perhaps the most general bilateral monopoly situation is one in which neither party has a structural advantage. We report in Siegel and Fouraker (1960) the results of experiments conducted under such simulated conditions. Those results may be summarized as follows:

Let the seller of the commodity have an average cost of production represented by the linear function

$$\frac{C}{Q} = A' + B'Q \qquad (2.1)$$

## 12    Bilateral Monopoly

where   $Q$ = quantity produced
$C$ = total cost
$A'$ and $B'$ = parameters

Any contract which satisfies (2.1) will yield zero profits to the seller. Let the buyer's demand curve be represented by the linear function

$$\frac{R}{Q} = A - BQ \qquad (2.2)$$

where   $R$ = total revenue
$A$ and $B$ = parameters

Any contract which satisfies (2.2) will yield zero profit to the buyer. We assume that the buyer and seller attempt to maximize their respective profits $\pi_b$ and $\pi_s$.

Negotiations were conducted as follows: One party proposed a price and quantity contract; the other party would either accept the proposal or make a counteroffer. Most pairs of buyers and sellers succeeded in arriving at a contract after protracted negotiation. The central tendency of such contracts was to the quantity which maximized joint profits and to the price which divided those joint profits equally. This solution is shown in Figure 2.1.

Joint profits are defined as

$$\pi_b + \pi_s = R - C$$
$$= AQ - BQ^2 - A'Q - B'Q^2. \qquad (2.3)$$

This function is maximized by that value of $Q$ which makes the first derivative zero and the second derivative negative:

$$\frac{d(\pi_b + \pi_s)}{dQ} = A - 2BQ - A' - 2B'Q = 0$$

$$\frac{d^2(\pi_b + \pi_s)}{dQ^2} = -2B - 2B' < 0.$$

The resulting quantity, which maximizes joint payoff, is designated $Q_p$ and is

$$Q_p = \frac{A - A'}{2B + 2B'}. \qquad (2.4)$$

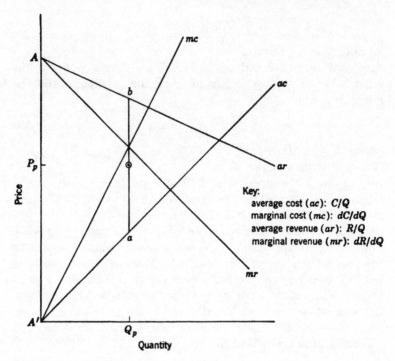

**FIGURE** 2.1   Central tendency $(P_p, Q_p)$ of contracts under equal-strength bilateral monopoly.

The set of prices between the average revenue and the average cost functions associated with this quantity is defined as the Paretian optima (line segment *ab* in Figure 2.1).   Any contract which is an element of this set has the following characteristic: It is impossible to move to any other contract and improve the profit position of both parties; indeed, any change will worsen the profit position of at least one of the parties.   Our observed central tendency was to the midpoint of the Paretian optimal set (contract $P_p$, $Q_p$ in Figure 2.1); price $P_p$ results in an equal division of the maximum joint profits and is defined

$$P_p = \frac{AB' + A'B}{B + B'}. \tag{2.5}$$

14    Bilateral Monopoly

## THE UNEQUAL-STRENGTH CASE:
## PRICE LEADERSHIP MODELS

In view of the results from the equal-strength bilateral monopoly models, the price leadership case suggested by Bowley (1928) is of particular interest. Under this structure one of the parties has the power to establish the price at which the exchange will take place; the other party has the power to choose the quantity which will be exchanged at the established price. The role of price leader is a privileged one: for normal linear functions the price leader will receive between two-thirds and all of the joint profits, according to the Bowley model. This asymmetric power relationship results in an equilibrium solution that is *not* an element of the Paretian optima.

Assume that both parties seek to maximize their individual profits and that the seller is the price leader. The buyer's profits are defined as

$$\pi_b = R - PQ$$
$$= AQ - BQ^2 - PQ \qquad (2.6)$$

where $P$ is the price set by the seller and $Q$ is the quantity selected by the buyer. The buyer's profits, within the constraints of the established price, are maximized when he selects a quantity so that the first derivative of Equation (2.6) is zero, provided the second derivative is negative. That is,

$$\frac{d\pi_b}{dQ} = A - 2BQ - P = 0$$
$$Q = \frac{A - P}{2B}. \qquad (2.7)$$

This adjustment equates the buyer's marginal revenue ($A - 2BQ$) with his marginal cost ($P$). The seller's profit is defined as

$$\pi_s = PQ - C$$
$$= PQ - A'Q - B'Q^2. \qquad (2.8)$$

It is assumed that the seller either knows or will discover that the buyer's quantity selection will be as indicated in Equation

(2.7). If we substitute this value for $Q$ in Equation (2.8), we may write the seller's profit as

$$\pi_s = \frac{1}{2B}\left( AP - P^2 - A'A + A'P - \frac{B'A^2}{2B} + \frac{AB'P}{B} - \frac{B'P^2}{2B}\right).$$
$$(2.9)$$

To derive the price choice which renders Equation (2.9) a maximum, take the first derivative of $\pi_s$ with respect to $P$, equate this function to zero, and solve for $P$ (noting that the second derivative is negative). That is,

$$\frac{d\pi_s}{dP} = \frac{1}{2B}\left( A - 2P + A' + \frac{AB'}{B} - \frac{B'P}{B}\right) = 0. \quad (2.10)$$

Since $1/2B > 0$, the Bowley price is

$$P_b = \frac{AB + A'B + AB'}{2B + B'}. \quad (2.11)$$

If the seller chooses this price, the buyer will respond with the Bowley quantity selection of

$$Q_b = \frac{A - A'}{2B' + 4B}. \quad (2.12)$$

The price and quantity strategies indicated by (2.11) and (2.12) are equilibrium strategies in the game-theory sense. If the seller chooses the price $P_b$ shown in (2.11), the buyer maximizes on that transaction by choosing the quantity $Q_b$ shown in (2.12). If the buyer is going to choose a maximizing quantity, the highest profit accrues to the seller when he chooses price $P_b$.

It follows that the Bowley quantity is less than the Pareto quantity:

$$Q_b = \frac{A - A'}{2B' + 4B} < Q_p = \frac{A - A'}{2B' + 2B}. \quad (2.13)$$

It would be possible for bilateral monopolists who had reached an agreement at the Bowley point to increase their profits by moving to some contract that was an element on a subset of the

## 16 Bilateral Monopoly

Paretian optima. This condition led Fellner (1947) to reject the Bowley solution in favor of some solution on the Paretian optima. Since we had established a tendency to the midpoint of the Paretian optimal set under equal-strength bilateral monopoly [Siegel and Fouraker (1960)], we took this contract $(P_p, Q_p)$ as the basis for an alternative hypothesis to the Bowley contract $(P_b, Q_b)$. We shall call the contract $(P_p, Q_p)$ the Pareto solution for purposes of simplicity.

These considerations may be summarized by means of Figure 2.2. The seller, in the role of the price leader, assumes that the

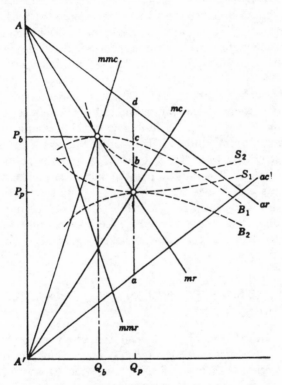

**FIGURE 2.2** The bilateral monopoly model for price leadership.

buyer will choose the quantity determined by the intersection of the established price and the buyer's marginal revenue function, according to the Bowley model. The seller considers $mr$ as the demand confronting his concern and maximizes by choosing the price $P_b$, since the resulting quantity $Q_b$ is associated with the intersection of his marginal cost and what he considers to be his marginal revenue $mmr$. (This function is marginal to the marginal revenue curve.) If the buyer always maximizes in response to a price quotation (i.e., chooses a contract that is on $mr$), the most favorable contract to the seller is $(P_b, Q_b)$, where $mr$ is tangent to the highest feasible isoprofit curve of the seller $S_2$. This solution results in a profit to the buyer associated with his isoprofit curve $B_1$. It would be possible for both buyer and seller to move to more favorable isoprofit curves if they could exchange $Q_p$ at some price in the subset $cb$ of the Paretian optimal set of prices $ad$.

An alternative solution is $(P_p, Q_p)$, the contract which yields an equal division of maximum joint profits, indicated by the intersection of the marginal functions in this example. This is a quasi-equilibrium point, for the isoprofit curves $S_1$ and $B_2$ are tangent at $(P_p, Q_p)$ and have slopes of zero at the point of tangency. If the seller quotes $P_p$, the buyer responds with $Q_p$, which is the best choice for both parties, given that $P_p$ has been chosen [see Fouraker (1957)]. Note that the minima of the seller's isoprofit curves generate his marginal cost function, while the maxima of the buyer's isoprofit curves generate his marginal revenue function.

## THE EXPERIMENTAL CONDITIONS AND STATEMENT OF HYPOTHESES

To obtain an experimental representation of an economic model, it is often necessary to incorporate variables which are not present in the original theory. From our previous work on bilateral monopoly and from our pilot work for the present experiments, it appeared that three experimental variables might affect the

## 18   Bilateral Monopoly

central tendency of contracts negotiated within the structure of price leadership. These variables were (1) amount of information, (2) form of the bidding, (3) incidence of culturally reinforced or prominent contracts, such as one involving an equal division of profits. It was decided to allow each of these variables to take on two states, one expected to be favorable to the Bowley solution and one expected to be favorable to the Paretian optimal solution.

In general we expected the Bowley solution to obtain because of its strong equilibrium properties. Relative to the information variable, it appeared that the condition of *incomplete* information (in which a participant knows only his own profit resulting from a contract) would tend to favor the Bowley solution. The equilibrium structure of the situation could be identified under incomplete information, while Pareto optimal nonequilibrium solutions could be identified only under *complete* information (in which the participant knows the profits accruing to both parties as the result of a contract). Therefore complete information does not favor the Bowley solution. Complete information makes it possible to identify some non-Bowley solution, such as $(P_p, Q_p)$, and conceivably to move toward it; so this condition is designated as favoring the Pareto solution.

The form of the negotiations might be either a single, once-and-for-all transaction or a sequence of price and quantity transactions having profits associated with each bid. The single transaction would seem to favor equilibrium behavior (and thus the Bowley solution), for there is no opportunity for effective communication in the market. Repeated bidding makes it possible for the parties to communicate [Luce and Raiffa (1957)] and possibly to achieve some nonequilibrium solution by a learning process. The probability of the parties' arriving at a Paretian optimal solution seems greater with repeated bidding.

Pigou (1908) and Schelling (1957) indicate that a contract involving an equal division of joint profits has an ethical appeal in our culture. If a feasible contract on the Paretian optima involves an equal division of profits, and the Bowley solution

TABLE 2.1  Combinations of Experimental Conditions and Related Hypotheses

| Experiment | Information | Form of bidding | Position of equal split | Predicted solution |
|---|---|---|---|---|
| 1 | $C$ | $S$ | $E_b$ | Bowley point |
| 2 | $C$ | $S$ | $E_p$ | Bowley point |
| 3 | $I$ | $R$ | $E_p$ | Bowley point |
| 4 | $C$ | $R$ | $E_b$ | Bowley point |
| 5 | $C$ | $R$ | $E_p$ | Pareto point |
| 6 | $I$ | $S$ | $E_b*$ | |
| 7 | $I$ | $S$ | $E_p*$ | |
| 8 | $I$ | $R$ | $E_b\dagger$ | |

\* Eliminated because $I$ and $S$ are incompatible.

† Unnecessary in that altering the position of the equal split (from experiment 3) should not affect the results under incomplete information.

Key: $I$ = incomplete information

$C$ = complete information

$S$ = single transaction

$R$ = repeated transactions

$E_b$ = equal-split payoff at Bowley point

$E_p$ = equal-split payoff on the Paretian optima

does not, the contract $(P_p, Q_p)$ will be favored.   If the profits are transformed so that the payoff at the Bowley point is in equal parts, while no such contract appears as an element of the (discrete) Paretian optimal set, the Bowley solution is favored.*

With three experimental variables, each taking on two states, $2^3 = 8$ possible experiments may be conducted.   These combinations of experimental variables are listed in Table 2.1.   Only five of the possible eight combinations were conducted as experiments.   The sixth and seventh were dropped because one-shot

---

\* There is always some price which would divide the maximum joint profits equally, but it does not have to be offered as a possible choice in an experiment if discrete prices are listed and interpolation is not permitted. All profit transformations to make the Bowley contract yield equal profits must, of necessity, make the implied revenue and cost functions nonlinear.

## 20    Bilateral Monopoly

price bids under incomplete information would be pointless: the situation would contain no guide to intelligent behavior. The eighth combination, $IRE_b$ (incomplete information, repeated bidding, equal-split at Bowley point), was dropped because it was hypothesized that $IRE_p$ would lead to the Bowley solution, and this expected result would not be changed by altering the equal-split position to favor the Bowley solution. Indeed, the incidence of the equal-split is unimportant under incomplete information, for the participants cannot identify which contract is thus ethically reinforced. Therefore, condition $E_p$ is likely to become effective only in conjunction with $C$; complete information enables the parties mutually to identify a specific non-Bowley contract. Even so, the parties may need some means, such as sequential bidding, to move toward such a contract once it is identified.

In the next chapter the procedures of the experiments are discussed in detail.

**CHAPTER 3**

# *Experimental Procedures*

To test the hypotheses of the research concerning bilateral monopoly, we conducted a series of five experiments. Each experiment in the series was designed to test one or more different hypotheses, and therefore each one had certain distinctive controls, distinctive procedures related to the various independent and dependent variables, and so forth. The common features of the experiments, however, loom larger than the differences among them. The purpose of this chapter is to describe those features of the experimental procedures which were common to all the experiments concerning bilateral monopoly. The distinc-

21

## 22    Bilateral Monopoly

tive procedures of particular experiments will be presented and discussed in later chapters, where the experiments are reported.

## SUBJECTS

In all, 106 individual subjects participated in the various bilateral monopoly experiments, serving in 53 different bargaining pairs. All subjects were male undergraduates from The Pennsylvania State University; at the time of recruitment, they were told only that they would be paid for participating in a research project. They were assured that they would not be exposed to noxious stimuli. The amount of money that could be earned was not specified, nor was the nature of their participation. Each experimental session was conducted with different subjects; no subject participated in more than one session.

## PROCEDURES

An experimental session began with the subjects coming to an assigned room, where they were met individually by the experimenters. Each subject was given a number corresponding to the order of his arrival. After all subjects for the session had arrived, each exchanged his number for a second one, randomly drawn. This second number identified the subject in the experiment. Thus, the order in which the various subjects arrived did not determine their identifying number in the experiment.

Before the subjects arrived at the experimental session, a list of numbers from 1 to $n$ was set up for that session. (The $n$'s in the various sessions varied from 20 to 24.) Then, by use of a table of random numbers, these numbers were paired. The paired numbers represented the various bargaining teams. On the basis of the toss of a coin, one of the numbers in each pair was designated as the buyer and the other as the seller.* For

* The price leadership role was not randomized over the buyer-seller conditions. From Siegel and Fouraker (1960) it was concluded that the buyer-seller classification did not exercise a significant influence on the

all experimental sessions in which information levels were to be compared, another toss of a coin determined whether the pair was assigned to have complete or incomplete information.

Reference to this prepared list determined whether each subject was a buyer or a seller, the identity of his bargaining partner, and whether, in the appropriate circumstances, he was to bargain under complete or incomplete information. That is, each of these subject assignments was determined by random procedures.

After the subjects had received their identifying numbers and the experimenter had determined their assignments by referring to the prepared sheet, the buyers were sent to one room and the sellers to another. When information level was varied, four rooms were used in order to separate the buyers and sellers with complete information from those with incomplete information. Once in their rooms, subjects were told whether they were buyers or sellers. Each subject was given printed instructions, a profit table,* and a sheet for recording the price and quantity bids and his profits. The instructions were read, and each subject had his own copy of them to use throughout the experimental session.

After hearing the instructions read, the subjects were given the opportunity to ask questions. Most of the questions centered on interpreting and using the profit tables. Specific examples were presented to clarify the use of the tables. The fact was emphasized that any profit earned during the session would become the subject's personal property.

The period of instructions lasted about 20 minutes. Then the

---

division of profits in the equal-strength case. In all the following experiments the seller was allowed to be the price leader because in our culture this is more often the case.

* The appendixes contain the various instructions and profit tables used by buyers and sellers in the different experiments. The functions on which the tables are based are presented in the following chapters in connection with discussions of specific hypotheses and their tests. References to specific sets of instructions and profit tables in the appendixes are made at appropriate places in the following chapters.

## 24  Bilateral Monopoly

subjects were taken individually into a large room containing separate cubicles, each furnished with a desk and a chair. These cubicles were formed by partitions extending about halfway to the ceiling. Once in his assigned cubicle, a subject could not see anyone except the research personnel; nor could he be seen by anyone but them. Negotiations were conducted in silence, with no communication permitted between the participants other than the written bids.

After all subjects had been directed to their assigned cubicles, a general announcement was made calling for the bargaining to begin. The seller, as price leader, initiated the process by writing a price bid on the sheet provided for that purpose. This price was recorded by a research assistant, who then informed the buyer of the price which would prevail for the transaction. In the light of this information, the buyer made his quantity selection, thus establishing the profit for himself and the seller.

When the bargaining was in the form of a single transaction, it was ended as soon as the buyer made his quantity choice and the seller was informed of this decision. After the transaction the buyers and sellers remained in their cubicles until they were paid the actual amounts they had negotiated; they were then dismissed from separate exits so that they would not come into contact with their bargaining opponent.

When the bargaining was in the form of repeated transactions, the bidding process was identical for each transaction in the series. The seller was always informed of the buyer's quantity choice before he was required to make the next price offer of the series. When repeated bidding was used, the first three transactions were practice trials and were provided to let the subjects become accustomed to the use of the profit table; the profit from these trials was not included in determining the cash payoff. After the practice trials, the sessions consisted of 19 regular transactions, an announced final trial, plus a special twenty-first trial, run under slightly different conditions. In a general announcement preceding the twentieth trial, all subjects were told that the following bid would be their final one; the objective was to hold end effects constant on both the twentieth and twenty-first trials.    After the twentieth trial, however, it was announced that an additional transaction was to be run under the condition that all entries in the profit table were to be tripled—i.e., all profits and losses for this one transaction were to be three times the amount shown on the table.    After this transaction was completed, the buyers and sellers were led to separate rooms where their profits were totaled, and each was paid in cash.

For each experiment in the series, each subject, upon being paid, was asked not to divulge the nature of the study or the amount of money earned, as doing so might affect the results of future experiments.    Subsequent analysis indicated that subjects were probably keeping this trust.

## THE PAYOFF MATRIX

The payoff tables given to the subjects showed the levels of profit corresponding to the various combinations of price and quantity choices.    Quantity choices ranged from 0 to 18, and price choices from 1 to 16.    The prices that the seller might select were listed along the left margin, while the top row consisted of possible quantity selections for the buyer.    Entered in the body of the table, at the intersection of each price row and quantity column, were the profits associated with these bids.    For subjects bargaining under complete information each entry in the profit table (see Appendix I) contained the payoff to both buyer and seller, while the bargaining pairs under incomplete information were furnished with tables which contained only the payoff to the subject making the decision, not showing the payoff to his rival (see Appendix III).

The payoff matrices were derived from hypothetical cost and revenue functions.    If the buyer chose a quantity of zero, it was assumed that he wished to maintain the status quo; such a contract was given the arbitrary value $\pi_b = 0$, $\pi_s = 0$ and held constant over the several experiments, regardless of the transformation involved.

26    Bilateral Monopoly

## DISCUSSION OF THE PROCEDURES

One purpose of the experimental procedures was to minimize interpersonal reactions between subjects.   Thus, the bargainers were physically separated, and they communicated only through an intermediary.   Subjects did not know the identities of their bargaining rivals.   The bargaining was conducted in silence, to preclude the possibility that a subject might identify his opponent by recognizing his voice.   Moreover, the buyers and sellers were given instructions in separate rooms so that they could not see their possible bargaining rivals during the instruction period.

This procedure eliminates certain variables which may well be important in bargaining—variables connected with interpersonal perceptions, prejudices, incompatibilities, etc.   It is our belief that such variables should be either systematically studied or controlled in the experimentation on bargaining.   It cannot be assumed that such variables may simply be neglected.   We have chosen to control these variables at this stage of our research program, with the intention of manipulating and studying them systematically in future studies.

Another purpose of our experimental procedures was to randomize the effects of certain variables which were not of interest to us at the present stage of our research.   We used randomization procedures to cancel any possible effects of arrival of subjects, thinking that early and late comers might differ in strength of motivation to participate, utility of money, compulsiveness, etc.—variables we did not wish to study systematically at this time.   We also used randomization procedures to control those preferences which may draw particular sellers and buyers together in the marketplace.

**CHAPTER 4**

# *Experimental Tests of*
# *Alternative Models*

The theoretical models presented in Chapter 2 offer two distinct solutions to the price leadership bilateral monopoly bargaining situation.   It was shown that if

$A$ = price axis intercept of average revenue function
$A'$ = price axis intercept of average cost function
$B$ = slope (negative) of average revenue function
$B'$ = slope of average cost function
$Q$ = quantity

then the price and quantity predicted by Bowley are

27

## 28    Bilateral Monopoly

$$P_b = \frac{AB + A'B + AB'}{2B + B'} \qquad (2.11)$$

$$Q_b = \frac{A - A'}{2B' + 4B} \qquad (2.12)$$

whereas the quantity which maximizes joint profits $Q_p$ is

$$Q_p = \frac{A - A'}{2B' + 2B}. \qquad (2.4)$$

When the even division of payoff appears explicitly on the Paretian optimal set the equal-split price $P_p$ is a feasible choice and is defined as

$$P_p = \frac{AB' + A'B}{B + B'}. \qquad (2.5)$$

This chapter presents the experiments which were designed to test the prediction that price leadership bilateral monopoly contracts would support either the Bowley or the Pareto solution, depending on the combination of three experimental variables. The three relevant variables—information conditions, form of the bidding, and position of the equal payoff—were experimentally manipulated in order to test the hypotheses.

The following combinations of experimental conditions were studied:

Experiment 1.    Complete information, single transaction, and equal-split payoff at the Bowley point: $CSE_b$

Experiment 2.    Complete information, single transaction, and equal-split payoff on the Paretian optima: $CSE_p$

Experiment 3.    Incomplete information, repeated transactions, and equal-split payoff on the Paretian optima: $IRE_p$

Experiment 4.    Complete information, repeated transactions, and equal-split payoff at the Bowley point: $CRE_b$

Experiment 5.    Complete information, repeated transactions, and equal-split payoff on the Paretian optima: $CRE_p$

The order of the experiments reported here starts with the set of conditions thought to most strongly favor the Bowley solution (experiment 1 above) and ends with the only set of conditions thought to be favorable to a Pareto solution (experiment 5 above).

In the studies reported below, the following set of parameters was used initially in deriving the expected values associated with the alternative theories: $A = 19$, $A' = -11$, $B = 0.5$, $B' = 0.5$. Thus, for each study, the operational statements of the Bowley point and the joint maximum (Paretian optimal set) in terms of the parameters are as follows:

The Bowley point:

$$P_b = \frac{AB + A'B + AB'}{2B + B'} = \frac{19(0.5) + (-11)(0.5) + 19(0.5)}{2(0.5) + 0.5} = 9$$

$$Q_b = \frac{A - A'}{2B' + 4B} = \frac{19 - (-11)}{2(0.5) + 4(0.5)} = 10.$$

The Paretian optimal set:

$$Q_p = \frac{A - A'}{2B' + 2B} = \frac{19 - (-11)}{2(0.5) + 2(0.5)} = 15.$$

For those studies for which the Pareto set $Q_p = 15$ includes an even division of joint payoff, the equal-split price $P_p$ is operationally defined as follows:

$$P_p = \frac{AB' + A'B}{B + B'} = \frac{19(0.5) + (-11)(0.5)}{0.5 + 0.5} = 4.$$

It should be noted that although the Bowley point ($P_b = 9$, $Q_b = 10$) and the joint maximum ($Q_p = 15$) do not vary from study to study, the payoffs to the bargainers cannot remain constant because they are affected by manipulation of the position of the equal-split, the form of the bidding, etc. Therefore, for each study, a linear transformation was applied to all payoffs resulting from the above parameters. This transformation, which did not change the quantity predictions, was used to (1) manipulate the equal-split point and (2) keep the total possible amount of joint profit equal for all studies.

30    Bilateral Monopoly

## EXPERIMENT 1: COMPLETE INFORMATION, A SINGLE TRANSACTION, AND EQUAL-SPLIT PAYOFF AT THE BOWLEY POINT

### Introduction

According to the theoretical formulation in Chapter 2, the set of conditions which should lead bargainers to show the greatest tendency to the Bowley solution is the $CSE_b$ combination. For all the experiments under consideration, this particular combination of conditions is unique in that it contains *two* forces favorable to the Bowley solution, whereas all other combinations contain only one. The two conditions favoring this solution are:

1. Single transaction: The lack of opportunity for communication through a series of transactions eliminates the possibility of using threat of punishment, or reward, in order to reach a solution on the Paretian optimal set.
2. Equal payoff at the Bowley point: Under this condition the Bowley point, besides being a strong equilibrium solution in itself, is given the added appeal of being an ethical or "fair" solution, in that the participants can divide joint profits equally at that point.

### The Experimental Test

**Subjects and Procedure.**    Twenty male undergraduate students (10 bargaining pairs) participated in this experiment. Each subject was given a double-entry profit table* containing both his own and his rival's payoffs, and a set of printed instructions.

---

\* Entries in the profit table are shown in dollars, the following transformations having been applied:

Seller's profits:        $\pi_s = .04\pi_s - 1.56$
Buyer's profits:        $\pi_b = .04\pi_b + 2.44.$

An exception to this transformation was the zero payoff to the buyer and seller for the contracts involving a zero quantity choice by the buyer, as noted above.

The profit table is shown in Appendix I.   The instructions were as follows:

## *Instructions*

The National Science Foundation and the Ford Foundation have provided funds for the conduct of research regarding economic decisions.   If you follow instructions carefully and make an appropriate decision, you will earn an appreciable amount of money.   *You may keep all the money you earn.*   You cannot lose your own money, but a poor choice can result in small or no profit to you.

You will be paired, at random, with another person.   You will not see this person or speak with him at any time.   You will never know the identity of your opponent, nor will he be aware of yours.

You and your anonymous partner will engage in a single transaction by means of a written bid.   Imagine that you and he are exchanging some commodity.   One of you will be selected (at random) to act as the seller of this commodity, the other will act as the buyer.   You must deal only with your unknown counterpart and he must deal only with you.

You will be furnished with a table showing the various levels of profit you can attain.   Prices are listed on the left hand side of the table, quantities across the top.   The upper figure in each box of the body of the table represents the profit the *buyer* will receive, depending upon the price and quantity selected.   The lower figure in each box represents the profit the *seller* receives for the associated price and quantity choices.   For example, at a price of 16 and a quantity of 8, the buyer's profit is $2.12 and the seller's profit is $5.80.   All figures in the body of the table are in dollars.

The *seller* will start the transaction by quoting a price.   He may select any one of the prices on the left hand side of the table.   The price he has selected will be recorded by an experimental assistant on a yellow sheet provided for that purpose.

The yellow sheet then is taken by the assistant to the *buyer*.   He sees the price which has been established for the transaction.   In the light of this information he selects the quantity to be exchanged at this price.   He may choose any of the quantities across the top of the table.   In other words, the seller chooses the price line, the buyer chooses the quantity column.   The box where these choices intersect indicates the amount of profit you receive for the transaction, the

## 32    Bilateral Monopoly

upper figure being the buyer's profit, the lower figure being the seller's profit.

After the buyer has made his quantity choice the seller will be informed of the decision and both buyer and seller will be paid the amount of money (profit) indicated in the table. This will be done in separate counting rooms, so you will not see the person with whom you have been bidding.

Are there any questions?

As was explained in Chapter 3, subjects were randomized into pairs and into the roles of buyer and seller and were taken individually to cubicles where they were isolated from all persons other than the experimenters and other research personnel. Each bargaining pair participated in a single transaction, the seller setting the price at which the exchange would take place, the buyer naming the quantity to be exchanged at this price. Negotiations were conducted in silence by means of written bids transmitted by the research personnel.

TABLE 4.1   Price and Quantity Agreed upon in Contracts
Reached by Bargaining Pairs
(Experiment 1, $CSE_b$)

| Bargaining pair | Price | Quantity | Observation supports, Bowley: $B$, Pareto: $P$ |
|---|---|---|---|
| 1 | 11 | 7 | $B$ |
| 2 | 9 | 10 | $B$ |
| 3 | 9 | 10 | $B$ |
| 4 | 9 | 10 | $B$ |
| 5 | 9 | 10 | $B$ |
| 6 | 9 | 10 | $B$ |
| 7 | 9 | 10 | $B$ |
| 8 | 9 | 11 | $B$ |
| 9 | 9 | 11 | $B$ |
| 10 | 7 | 12 | $P, B$ |
| Mean | 9.00 | 10.10 | |
| Median | 9 | 10 | |

*Experimental Economics*

**Results.**    Table 4.1 contains the price and quantity observations for the 10 bargaining pairs.

The hypothesis under test here is that contracts will support the Bowley solution ($P_b = 9$, $Q_b = 10$) rather than the Pareto solution ($Q_p = 15$, $7 < P_p < 8$).    If a bargaining pair negotiates a contract with both a price and a quantity closer to one of the solutions, it is counted as an observation in support of that solution; if the quoted price supports one model but the quantity selection supports the other, it is counted as one-half an observation in support of each solution.    Thus, the first nine bargaining pairs had contracts closer to the Bowley solution than to the Pareto solution; in the tenth pair the seller named a price closer to the Pareto solution, but the buyer chose a quantity closer to the Bowley solution.    With 9.5 observations in support of the Bowley prediction and .5 in support of the Pareto alternative, it is apparent that the first experiment supports the Bowley model.    The incidence is significant against the null hypothesis (one-tailed binomial test, $p < .01$).    The null hypothesis in this situation would be that each model had an equal chance of being supported by an observation.

This conclusion is supported by the sample averages: the mean and median prices are 9, the Bowley prediction; the mean quantity is 10.10, only .10 units from the Bowley prediction but 4.9 units from the Pareto amount.    The median quantity is precisely the Bowley amount.

## Discussion

The data are consistent with the hypothesis drawn from the Bowley model that, with the parameters used, contracts will tend to be negotiated at a price of 9 and a quantity of 10.    It is interesting to note that while 8 of 10 sellers named exactly the Bowley price, only 6 of 10 buyers chose the Bowley quantity.    Two cooperative buyers chose quantities of 11 rather than the maximizing quantity of 10; thus, by imposing only a 2-cent loss on themselves, they gave their unknown opponent an extra 38 cents. Additional discussion of these data will be given in Chapter 6.

## 34    Bilateral Monopoly

## EXPERIMENT 2: COMPLETE INFORMATION, A SINGLE TRANSACTION, AND EQUAL–SPLIT PAYOFF ON THE PARETIAN OPTIMA

### Introduction

In the second experiment, as in the first, subjects bargained under complete information, and the negotiations consisted of a single transaction. Experiment 2 differed from experiment 1 in the location of the equal-split payoff; in experiment 2 the equal-split payoff was located on the Paretian optima. Although it is true for this experiment that a "fair," "ethical," or "prominent" solution exists on the Paretian optima, it is also true that a seller would prefer a Bowley contract, for at the Bowley solution he makes a larger profit than at the equal-split price of 4. The set of conditions contains only one condition specifically favorable to a Bowley solution: the single transaction condition, which eliminates the possibility of "communication" between bargainers such as can be achieved in repeated transactions. The hypothesis guiding the experiment is that this force alone would be strong enough to produce results consistent with the Bowley solution.

### The Experimental Test

**Subjects and Procedure.** The subjects whose contracts provided a test of the hypothesis were 20 male undergraduates (none of whom participated in previous studies), serving in 10 bargaining pairs. Instructions and a double-entry profit table* containing the profits to both buyer and seller were given to each subject (see Appendix II). Subjects were randomized into pairs and into buyer and seller roles. Buyers were given instructions in one room and sellers in another, to preserve the anonymity of

---

* Buyer and seller profit entries, shown in dollars, were arrived at by means of the following transformations (except for the arbitrary value assigned to zero buyer responses):

$$\pi_b = 0.04\pi_b + 0.44$$
$$\pi_s = 0.04\pi_s + 0.44.$$

TABLE 4.2   Price and Quantity Agreed upon in Contracts
Reached by Bargaining Pairs
(Experiment 2, $CSE_p$)

| Pair | Price | Quantity | Observation supports |
|------|-------|----------|----------------------|
| 11 | 9 | 7 | B |
| 12 | 9 | 8 | B |
| 13 | 11 | 8 | B |
| 14 | 10 | 9 | B |
| 15 | 9 | 10 | B |
| 16 | 9 | 10 | B |
| 17 | 9 | 10 | B |
| 18 | 9 | 10 | B |
| 19 | 9 | 10 | B |
| 20 | 10 | 10 | B |
| Mean | 9.40 | 9.20 | |
| Median | 9 | 10 | |

the pairs. Subjects were taken individually to their assigned
cubicles, where they participated in a single transaction. No
communications other than the written bids were permitted
between the participants.

**Results.** Table 4.2 presents the data relevant to the research
hypothesis. The price and quantity contracts agreed upon by
all bargaining pairs are shown in this table.

The hypothesis under test here is that contracts will support
the Bowley solution ($P_b = 9$, $Q_b = 10$) rather than the Pareto
solution ($P_p = 4$, $Q_p = 15$). All 10 pairs negotiated contracts
closer to the Bowley point, providing strong support for this
solution. The difference from the null hypothesis is significant
(one-tailed binomial test, $p < .001$).

Again the median price and median quantity have exactly the
Bowley values; the mean price and quantity are closer to the
Bowley than to the Pareto predictions, as expected.

### Discussion

The data of the experimental test offer strong support for the
Bowley hypothesis.

**36    Bilateral Monopoly**

The buyers, in general, indicated displeasure upon being informed of the seller's price choices, but most of them chose quantities to maximize their own profits. Several buyers, however, chose to punish the sellers by taking a loss for themselves in such a manner that they would inflict even greater losses on their anonymous counterparts. In pair 11, for example, the buyer cut his own profit by 18 cents when he chose a quantity of 7 instead of 10, but in so doing he reduced his seller's profit by $1.38. Only one buyer took a loss so that the seller could earn more; the buyer in pair 20 chose a quantity of 10 rather than 9, reducing his profits by 2 cents but increasing the seller's profits by 46 cents (see Appendix II). Additional discussion of these data will be given in Chapter 6.

## EXPERIMENT 3: INCOMPLETE INFORMATION, REPEATED TRANSACTIONS, AND EQUAL-SPLIT PAYOFF ON THE PARETIAN OPTIMA

### Introduction

In the first two experiments, negotiations consisted of a single transaction. In experiment 3, in contrast, repeated transactions were used. Bargainers negotiated under incomplete information, and the equal-split payoff was on the Paretian optima.

It is hypothesized that the incomplete-information condition in experiment 3 would dominate the other two conditions, and that the contracts therefore would stabilize at the Bowley solution. The significance of the condition of incomplete information is that neither party can identify the equal-split price $P_s$ nor the fact that a "fair" solution exists along the Paretian optima. For that matter, neither can even identify the joint maximizing quantity. Thus it seemed unlikely that a contract would be reached along this optimal set, especially since a strong equilibrium is available as an alternative. In the light of the information afforded them, the buyer and seller have no a priori reason for not being satisfied with Bowley strategies.

## The Experimental Test

**Subjects and Procedure.** The subjects of the third experimental session were 22 male undergraduate students (11 bargaining pairs).* None of them had participated in any of the previous bargaining experiments.

Subjects were randomized into pairs and into buyer and seller roles and were given sets of instructions and profit tables† (see Appendix III). The profit table furnished to each buyer showed only the profits to a buyer; a seller's profit table showed only the profits to a seller. After the instruction period the buyers and sellers were led individually to their assigned cubicles. The experimental session consisted of a total of 24 transactions; the seller first named a price, and the buyer then named a quantity for each transaction. The 24 transactions consisted of 3 practice trials, 19 regular transactions, an announced final regular transaction, and a special transaction which will be considered later.

**Results.** The last regular transaction, number 19, is taken to represent the relevant statistic,‡ and contracts from this trans-

---

* Although 22 subjects (11 pairs) started the experiment, 2 pairs had to be dropped since 1 person in each of 2 bargaining pairs indicated that he did not understand the instructions; these pairs therefore are not included in the analysis.

† Profit table entries are in hundredths of a cent and were arrived at by means of the following transformations:

$$\pi_b = 20\pi_b + 220$$
$$\pi_s = 20\pi_s + 220.$$

‡ Inspection of the data revealed, in general, few differences among the average results of transactions 18, 19, and 20. The number of transactions to be used was decided prior to the collection of data on the basis of pilot studies which indicated that 20 transactions would be sufficient for the average subject to reach equilibrium behavior.

The determination of the proper length for such an experiment is difficult. Some subjects need more transactions to approach equilibrium behavior—they are still engaged in a learning process when the experiment is terminated. If the experiment continues too long, however, subjects are likely to grow bored and begin to amuse themselves with unusual choice patterns. This is particularly true for some subjects who quickly identify and follow some equilibrium strategy. The termination point is an attempt at compromise between these two sources of variation.

## 38   Bilateral Monopoly

TABLE 4.3   Price and Quantity Agreed upon for the Nineteenth Transaction

(Experiment 3, $IRE_p$)

| Pair | Price | Quantity | Observation supports |
|------|-------|----------|----------------------|
| 21 | 8 | 11 | B |
| 22 | 8 | 12 | B |
| 23 | 8 | 11 | B |
| 24 | 10 | 10 | B |
| 25 | 8 | 11 | B |
| 26 | 8 | 11 | B |
| 27 | 7 | 12 | B |
| 28 | 14 | 5 | B |
| 29 | 5 | 14 | P |
| Mean | 8.44 | 10.78 | |
| Median | 8 | 11 | |

action were used to test the hypothesis that the Bowley price of 9 and quantity of 10 would be supported. The results of this transaction are presented in Table 4.3. Complete protocols for all nine bargaining pairs are presented in Appendix III.

The hypothesis under test here is that contracts resulting from the nineteenth transaction will support the Bowley solution ($P_b = 9$, $Q_b = 10$) rather than the Pareto solution ($P_p = 4$, $Q_p = 15$). Eight of the nine pairs performed in accordance with this expectation. These results provide strong support for the Bowley model. The variation from the null prediction is significant (binomial test, $p < .02$). However, one pair, 29, did approximate the Pareto solution as a result of some rivalrous signals on the buyer's part.* This tendency to defect from the Bowley point is continued on the twentieth transaction, which includes end effects. There, seven of the nine pairs supported

---

* A rivalrous signal by a buyer would take the form of a quantity response which fell short of the amount required to maximize the buyer's profit. This action reduces the buyer's profits, but it generally reduces the seller's profits by an even larger amount. Further discussion is presented in Chapter 6.

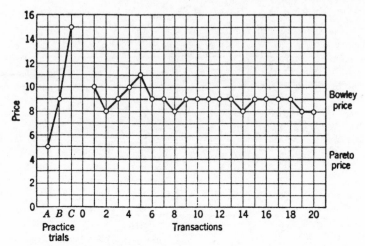

**FIGURE** 4.1   Median price bid for each transaction in experimental session 3: $IRE_p$.

the Bowley prediction, while two pairs (28 and 29) negotiated contracts closer to the Pareto solution.

The averages continue to support the Bowley values, however. The median price is 8, the median quantity 11.   This is true on the twentieth transaction as well as the nineteenth.   The mean contract of $\bar{P} = 8.44$, $\bar{Q} = 10.78$ on the nineteenth transaction supports the Bowley point; on the twentieth transaction the mean values are even closer: $\bar{P} = 8.78$, $\bar{Q} = 10.22$.   Median price and quantity bids are shown in Figures 4.1 and 4.2.   Note that after the fifth transaction the median prices never deviate by more than one unit from the Bowley prediction.

## Discussion

The variability of price and quantity bids in this experiment was greater than in the studies reported earlier, probably because of the limited information possessed by the subjects.   Toward the end of the session, the quantity chooser was generally content to maximize his profits on each trial by choosing his optimal quantity.   (This is reflected in the median choices shown in

**40    Bilateral Monopoly**

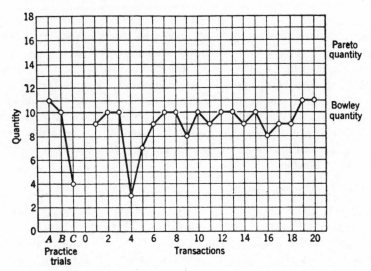

FIGURE 4.2    Median quantity bid for each transaction in experimental session 3: $IRE_p$.

Figure 4.2.)    From these choices, the price leader seemed able to behave as though he could discern the nature of the demand curve facing him and tended toward maximizing his own profits by approaching the Bowley point.    Additional discussion of these data will be given in Chapter 6.

## EXPERIMENT 4: COMPLETE INFORMATION, REPEATED TRANSACTIONS, AND EQUAL-SPLIT PAYOFF AT THE BOWLEY POINT

### Introduction

In experiment 4, subjects again negotiated via repeated transactions.    This experiment differs from the third, however, in two important respects: bargainers had complete information, and the equal-split payoff was at the Bowley point.    It seems that the Bowley solution is somewhat weaker for experiment 4 than for the first three, since both complete information and repeated transactions allow the possibility of communication by means of punishment and reward. However, even though both buyer and seller might prefer some contract along the Paretian optimal set, the absence of a discrete "prominent" solution (i.e., an equal division of profits) along this set makes agreement difficult. Thus, while it was hypothesized that the Bowley solution should still obtain, it was recognized that the prediction was a weak one since the pull of the possibility for greater profits along the Paretian optima might offset somewhat the strength of the Bowley solution.

## The Experimental Test

**Subjects and Procedure.** The hypotheses concerning the fourth experimental session were tested with 20 male undergraduate subjects (10 bargaining pairs), none of whom participated in previous studies. Subjects were randomly assigned into pairs and randomly designated as buyers or sellers. Buyers and sellers were instructed in separate rooms, where each received a double-entry profit table, * containing the profits of both buyer and seller, and a set of printed instructions (see Appendix IV). The bargaining session consisted of 24 transactions (3 practice trials, 19 regular trials, a final trial, and a special final trial); the same procedure was used as in the third experimental session, and it is outlined in Chapter 3.

**Results.** Table 4.4 contains the prices and quantities resulting from the nineteenth transaction in the fourth experimental session. Complete protocols for all 10 bargaining pairs are presented in Appendix IV.

The hypothesis under test is that the Bowley solution ($P_b = 9$, $Q_b = 10$) will be supported. Of the 10 contracts, 6.5 were closer

---

\* Buyer and seller profit entries, in hundredths of a cent, were arrived at by means of the following transformations:

$$\pi_s = 20\pi_s - 780$$
$$\pi_b = 20\pi_b + 1220.$$

Again the buyer's quantity choice of zero was assigned the payoff of $\pi_b = 0$, $\pi_s = 0$.

42 Bilateral Monopoly

TABLE 4.4  Price and Quantity Agreed upon for the Nineteenth Transaction

(Experiment 4, $CRE_b$)

| Pair | Price | Quantity | Observation supports |
|------|-------|----------|----------------------|
| 30 | 9 | 9 | B |
| 31 | 7 | 11 | P, B |
| 32 | 9 | 9 | B |
| 33 | 16 | 1 | B |
| 34 | 8 | 11 | P, B |
| 35 | 8 | 13 | P |
| 36 | 13 | 3 | B |
| 37 | 7 | 16 | P |
| 38 | 8 | 12 | P, B |
| 39 | 9 | 10 | B |
| Mean | 9.4 | 9.5 | |
| Median | 8.5 | 10.5 | |

to the Bowley solution than to the Pareto solution, while 3.5 were closer to the Pareto solution. These results do not differ significantly from the null prediction; according to the binomial test, $p < .38$.

As expected, the model tendency is still toward the Bowley solution, but there is much more variability among the contracts than was the case in the first three experiments, suggesting that the strength of the Bowley solution is diminished under the conditions of experiment 4.

This tendency continues through the twentieth transaction, in which the support for the two theories is evenly divided.

The sample averages reflect the same considerations. The median contract for the nineteenth transaction was at a price of 8.5 and a quantity of 10.5; for the twentieth transaction, the comparable figures were 8 and 11.5. The mean contract for the nineteenth transaction was $\bar{P} = 9.4$, $\bar{Q} = 9.5$, amounts which are close to the Bowley amounts. For the twentieth transaction, the means moved toward the Pareto amounts: $\bar{P} = 7.4$, $\bar{Q} = 12.0$.

Figures 4.3 and 4.4 display the median price and quantity bids on each of the transactions in experiment 4.

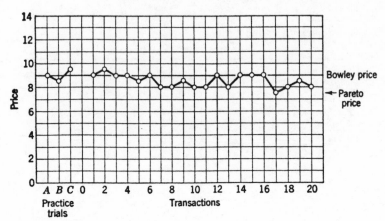

**FIGURE 4.3**    Median price bid for each transaction in experimental session 4: $CRE_b$.

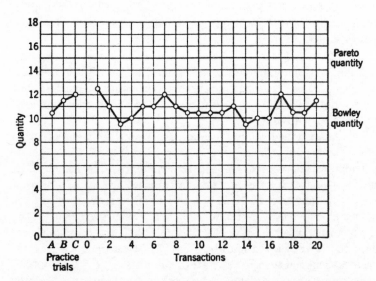

**FIGURE 4.4**    Median quantity bid for each transaction in experimental session 4: $CRE_b$.

**44    Bilateral Monopoly**

Discussion

While these results, on balance, support the Bowley solution, the support is not strong. The repeated transactions, in conjunction with complete information, tended to induce an increased attempt on the part of buyers to communicate by their quantity choices. The absence of a prominent Pareto optimal contract made it difficult to communicate effectively, however. Three pairs (35, 37, and 38) did manage to approximate the Pareto point; they created three different patterns in moving away from the Bowley point. Additional discussion of these data will be given in Chapter 6.

## EXPERIMENT 5: COMPLETE INFORMATION, REPEATED TRANSACTIONS, AND EQUAL–SPLIT PAYOFF ON THE PARETIAN OPTIMA

### Introduction

If the Paretian optimal solution is to obtain for any experimental situation of bilateral monopoly with price leadership, it should obtain when negotiators have complete information, when they negotiate via repeated transactions, and when the equal-split payoff is located on the Paretian optima. These were the circumstances in experiment 5, and thus the experiment was a test of the prediction that bargainers would negotiate contracts on the joint optimal solution. The condition of complete information allows both the buyer and the seller to identify the "fair," equal division of profits associated with the Pareto solution, while repetitive bidding gives the buyer an opportunity to communicate through punishment and reward—to "teach" the seller which price he considers acceptable.

### The Experimental Test

**Subjects and Procedure.** Twenty-four male undergraduates (twelve bargaining pairs), none of whom participated in previous studies, served as subjects for the fifth experimental session.

Experimental Tests of Alternative Models    45

TABLE 4.5   Price and Quantity Agreed upon for the Nineteenth Transaction
(Experiment 5, $CRE_p$)

| Pair | Price | Quantity | Observation supports |
|------|-------|----------|----------------------|
| 40 | 9 | 10 | $B$ |
| 41 | 9 | 10 | $B$ |
| 42 | 11 | 4 | $B$ |
| 43 | 4 | 15 | $P$ |
| 44 | 5 | 14 | $P$ |
| 45 | 5 | 0 | $P, B$ |
| 46 | 5 | 0 | $P, B$ |
| 47 | 4 | 15 | $P$ |
| 48 | 4 | 15 | $P$ |
| 49 | 4 | 15 | $P$ |
| 50 | 4 | 8 | $P, B$ |
| 51 | 9 | 14 | $B, P$ |
| Mean | 6.08 | 10.00 | |
| Median | 5.00 | 12.00 | |

The procedures followed in the execution of this session were precisely the same as those followed in the immediately previous two sessions (described earlier). Randomly paired buyers and sellers were isolated and given instructions and a double-entry profit table* containing the profits both to the buyer and to the seller (see Appendix V). Negotiations were conducted in silence, with each bargaining pair participating in 24 transactions by means of written bids. As in the immediately previous two sessions, there were 3 practice trials, 19 regular trials, a final trial, and a special final trial.

**Results.** Table 4.5 shows the price and quantity bids resulting from the nineteenth transaction. Complete protocols for all 12 bargaining pairs are presented in Appendix V.

* Profit entries, in hundredths of a cent, were arrived at by means of the following transformations:

$$\pi_b = 20\pi_b + 220$$
$$\pi_s = 20\pi_s + 220.$$

## 46    Bilateral Monopoly

The hypothesis under test here is that contracts resulting from the nineteenth transaction will support the Pareto contract $(P_p = 4, Q_p = 15)$ rather than the Bowley solution $(P_b = 9, Q_b = 10)$.

Of the 12 contracts, 5 support the Bowley prediction and 7 support the Pareto prediction. This is the only experiment of the five which yielded a preponderance of contracts closer to the Pareto solution. While this result is not significant against the null hypothesis (according to the binomial test, $p < .4$), it does indicate the direction of change resulting from the altered state of the control variables.

This conclusion is reinforced when the contracts negotiated on the twentieth trial are examined. Only 2.5 observations support the Bowley prediction, while the remaining 9.5 support the Pareto prediction. According to the binomial test, this result is significant against the null hypothesis at $p < .08$.

The averages support no simple interpretation. On the nineteenth transaction, the mean price $\bar{P} = 6.08$ is nearer the Pareto value $P_p = 4$ than the Bowley value $P_b = 9$. The median price, 5, also supports the Pareto prediction. The mean quantity on the

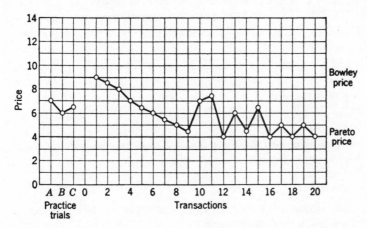

FIGURE 4.5 Median price bid for each transaction in experimental session 5: $CRE_p$.

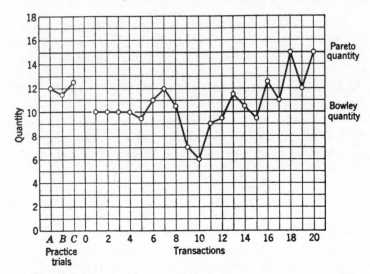

FIGURE 4.6   Median quantity bid for each transaction in experimental session 5: $CRE_p$.

nineteenth transaction, however, is $\bar{Q} = 10$, precisely the Bowley amount.    This mean is perhaps not representative since it is distorted by the fact that two of the values were zero (see Table 4.5). The median quantity, 12, falls between the Pareto and the Bowley predictions.

On the twentieth transaction, the mean contract supported the Pareto prediction more closely: $\bar{P} = 5.00$, $\bar{Q} = 13.91$.   The medians were also closer to the Pareto prediction: the median price 4 was precisely the Pareto value, as was the median quantity 15.

Median price and quantity bids for each transaction are shown in Figures 4.5 and 4.6.

### Discussion

Examination of the individual protocols contributes to the interpretation of these results.

The protocols of two pairs, 40 and 41, provide clear support for

**48    Bilateral Monopoly**

the Bowley solution. The bargaining conducted by pair 42, in contrast, was quite erratic, producing a pattern which does not provide support for either theory.

The next eight pairs, 43 through 50, conducted negotiations which seem to provide support for the Pareto solution. Either the bargainers had identified the equal-profit contract at the outset, as was the case for pair 43, or the buyer engaged in considerable "teaching activity" to induce the seller to lower his price. Among these pairs, there were five price bids of 4 and three of 5 on the nineteenth transaction. The quantity responses were optimal in all but three of these eight cases. The exceptions were pairs 45, 46, and 50; in these cases each buyer was still trying to induce the seller to lower his price.

The final pair, 51, oscillated between a contract with a price of 9 and a quantity of 14, yielding high profits to the seller, and a contract with a price of 1 and a quantity of 18, yielding high profits to the buyer. This seemingly irrational behavior was clarified by a postexperimental interview with the subjects concerned; they indicated that they were trying to split maximum joint profits and somehow felt this strategy would be most profitable.

The results of experiment 5 suggest that when a prominent Pareto optimal contract is available, many buyers are able to use repeated bids under complete information to force the sellers (the price leaders) away from the Bowley point to a more mutually advantageous contract.

## GENERAL DISCUSSION

The purpose of the experiments reported in this chapter was to investigate the effect of various combinations of three experimental conditions—amount of information, form of bidding, and position of the equal-split payoff—and to test specific predictions of the results of experiments involving combinations of these conditions. The general hypothesis underlying these experiments was that either the Bowley or the Pareto solution would obtain,

*Experimental Economics*

TABLE 4.6   Observations Supporting the Bowley or Pareto Solutions
(Summary of the Experiments)

| Experiment | Conditions | I | | II | |
|---|---|---|---|---|---|
| | | *Bowley* | *Pareto* | *Bowley* | *Pareto* |
| 1 | $CSE_b$ | 9.5 | 0.5 | | |
| 2 | $CSE_p$ | 10.0 | 0.0 | | |
| 3 | $IRE_p$ | 8.0 | 1.0 | 7.0 | 2.0 |
| 4 | $CRE_b$ | 6.5 | 3.5 | 5.0 | 5.0 |
| 5 | $CRE_p$ | 5.0 | 7.0 | 2.5 | 9.5 |

Note: I represents observations for the single-transaction experiments and on the nineteenth transaction for the repeated-transaction experiments; II represents observations on the twentieth transaction for the repeated-transaction experiments.

depending on the particular combination of conditions.   The results of the experiments are summarized in Table 4.6.

It was suggested initially that four out of the five experimental sessions involved conditions that would favor the Bowley solution, but that the sessions would differ predictably in their strength of support for this solution.   These experiments were presented in the order of the strength of their predicted tendency toward the Bowley point, starting with the set of conditions most strongly favoring a Bowley solution and ending with those least strongly favoring that solution.   Since a trend toward a particular solution was predicted, it was thought appropriate to perform an overall test on the data.   Toward that end, the Jonckheere test (1954), a nonparametric test for ordered alternatives, was applied to the differences between the observed contracts and the predicted Bowley contract.   The hypothesis was that the size of these differences would tend to be smallest for the $CSE_b$ combination of conditions, larger for the $CSE_p$ combination, larger for the $IRE_p$, and larger still for $CRE_b$.

Table 4.7 presents the absolute differences between each contract and the Bowley quantity for the four experimental sessions

## 50    Bilateral Monopoly

TABLE 4.7   Differences in Absolute Value between Observed
Quantity Contracts and the Bowley Quantity
(Four Combinations of Conditions)

| $CSE_b$ | $CSE_p$ | $IRE_p$ | $CRE_b$ |
|---------|---------|---------|---------|
| 3 | 3 | 1 | 1 |
| 0 | 2 | 2 | 1 |
| 0 | 2 | 1 | 1 |
| 0 | 1 | 0 | 9 |
| 0 | 0 | 1 | 1 |
| 0 | 0 | 1 | 3 |
| 0 | 0 | 2 | 7 |
| 1 | 0 | 5 | 6 |
| 1 | 0 | 4 | 2 |
| 2 | 0 |   | 0 |

under discussion.   The results of the Jonckheere test on the data
in Table 4.7 permit rejection of the null hypothesis in favor
of the hypothesis that the difference scores show this trend:
$CSE_b < CSE_p < IRE_p < CRE_b$.   (In performing this statistical test, we were faced with the problem created by ties.   If every
single tie is counted against the hypothesis, surely a conservative
procedure, the probability level yielded by the Jonckheere test is
$p < .12$.   If one-half the ties are counted against the hypothesis
and one-half for it, perhaps a more sensible procedure, then
$p < .005$.)

This finding may be interpreted to mean that when bargainers
have single-shot bids and when the equal-split payoff is at the
Bowley point, there is considerable force toward a Bowley solution.   Contracts deviate little from this point when the equal-
split payoff is at the Paretian optima, however.   Indeed, the
difference between the results of the first and second experiments
appears insignificant by any standards.   However, the support
for the Bowley solution is weakened when repeated bids are
allowed, rather than a single-shot bid, since with repeated bids
the bargainer in the weaker position (here, the quantity chooser)
can communicate by means of his choices and attempt to influ-

ence the choices of his opponent.   The use of repeated bids forces
a movement of the contracts away from the Bowley point.   This
tendency is particularly strong under complete information, as
opposed to incomplete information.

In the chapter which follows, attention is given to comparisons
across conditions.   Analysis is focused on the effect each of the
following has on the bargaining outcome: amount of information,
form of the bidding, and location of the prominent contract.

**CHAPTER 5**

# *Comparison of Treatments*

We concluded in Chapter 4 that the Bowley model is a reasonably good predictor of contracts negotiated under conditions of price leadership bilateral monopoly, except in experiment 5.   In that experiment we chose the states for the three treatment variables that favored the Pareto solution and saw that this combination of forces was sufficient to shift the incidence of the observations away from the Bowley point.   It is our purpose in this chapter to assess the relative strength of these forces by means of cross comparisons of experiments.   For example, the first two experiments involved complete information and one transaction; they

53

**54**     Bilateral Monopoly

TABLE 5.1    Summary of Experimental Results

| Experiment | Conditions | Number of observations closer to | | | |
|:---:|:---:|:---:|:---:|:---:|:---:|
| | | *Bowley price* | *Pareto price* | *Bowley quantity* | *Pareto quantity* |
| 1 | $CSE_b$ | 9 | 1 | 10 | 0 |
| 2 | $CSE_p$ | 10 | 0 | 10 | 0 |
| 3 | $IRE_p$ | 8 (7) | 1 (2) | 8 (7) | 1 (2) |
| 4 | $CRE_b$ | 5 (4) | 5 (6) | 8 (6) | 2 (4) |
| 5 | $CRE_p$ | 4 (2) | 8 (10) | 6 (3) | 6 (9) |

Note: Figures in parentheses are the count on the twentieth transaction and include end effects; other figures are for the nineteenth transaction for repeated-bid experiments.

differed only in the location of the prominent contract. A comparison between the data from experiments 1 and 2 should indicate the influence of this treatment variable. Further, experiments 4 and 5 also differed only in the location of the prominent contract, so a replication is available.

The results of the experiments are summarized in Table 5.1. This table differs from the summary (Table 4.6) in the last chapter; here we have separated the decisions made by the buyers and sellers and recorded the number of price observations closer to the Bowley or the Pareto price and the number of quantity observations closer to the Bowley or the Pareto quantity. The major purpose of this finer classification is to obtain data in integer form so the cross comparisons may be made by the Fisher exact probability test [Siegel (1956)].

## EFFECT OF THE LOCATION OF A PROMINENT CONTRACT

The first comparisons concern the importance of the location of the equal-split contract. The hypothesis is that state $E_b$, an equal division of profits at the Bowley point, will favor the Bowley solution; state $E_p$, a discrete Pareto optimal equal-split

TABLE 5.2 Effect of Variables $E_p$ and $E_b$

| Experiment | Conditions | Price | | Quantity | |
|:---:|:---:|:---:|:---:|:---:|:---:|
| | | *Bowley* | *Pareto* | *Bowley* | *Pareto* |
| 1 | $CSE_b$ | 9 | 1 | 10 | 0 |
| 2 | $CSE_p$ | 10 | 0 | 10 | 0 |

contract, will favor the Pareto parameters. Table 5.2 shows the results of the first comparison, between experiments 1 and 2.

It is apparent that the hypothesis is not supported by the data: there is not a significant shift in the observations as a result of the changed state of $E$ (for price, $p < .5$; for quantity, $p < 1.0$ by the Fisher test). Indeed, the only difference between the experiments is in the opposite direction from that predicted by the hypothesis: the price observations provide stronger support for the Bowley model in experiment 2 than they do in experiment 1.

Another comparison regarding the effect of the prominent contract is possible, however. Experiments 4 and 5 involve complete information and repeated bids and differ only with respect to $E$. The results are shown in Table 5.3 for the nineteenth transaction.

Again the result is not significant (for price, $p < .4$; for quantity, $p < .16$). However, the changes are in the direction predicted by the hypothesis for both price and quantity, and the probabilities have been reduced. This trend is continued on the

TABLE 5.3 Effect of Variables $E_p$ and $E_b$
(A Replication)

| Experiment | Conditions | Price | | Quantity | |
|:---:|:---:|:---:|:---:|:---:|:---:|
| | | *Bowley* | *Pareto* | *Bowley* | *Pareto* |
| 4 | $CRE_b$ | 5 | 5 | 8 | 2 |
| 5 | $CRE_p$ | 4 | 8 | 6 | 6 |

## 56    Bilateral Monopoly

twentieth transaction, where the probability that $E$ exercises no influence on price is reduced to $p < .25$, and for quantity, $p < .12$. It must be concluded, however, that the location of the prominent contract is not a powerful experimental condition; such influence as it does have on the results is activated by the repeated form of bidding.

## EFFECT OF THE FORM OF THE BIDDING

The first and the fourth experiments provide an opportunity to test for the influence of the form of bidding since the experiments are similar in other respects. The hypothesis is that single bids will tend to favor the Bowley solution (because of its strong equilibrium properties), while repeated bids will tend to favor the Pareto solution (for they provide a means for communication regarding non-Bowley contracts). The results are shown in Table 5.4 for the nineteenth transaction.

The changes in the supporting observations are in the predicted direction; however, the probabilities that such changes resulted from chance, rather than the altered form of bidding, are still fairly large ($p < .07$ for price, $p < .24$ for quantity). The twentieth transaction (experiment 4), which the subjects knew to be the last, reduced these probabilities rather sharply ($p < .033$ for price, $p < .044$ for quantity).

It is possible, with experiments 2 and 5, to make another comparison of the form of the bidding. These results, for the nineteenth transaction, are shown in Table 5.5.

TABLE 5.4    Effect of Variables $R$ and $S$

| Experiment | Conditions | Price | | Quantity | |
|:---:|:---:|:---:|:---:|:---:|:---:|
| | | *Bowley* | *Pareto* | *Bowley* | *Pareto* |
| 1 | $CSE_b$ | 9 | 1 | 10 | 0 |
| 4 | $CRE_b$ | 5 | 5 | 8 | 2 |

TABLE 5.5  Effect of Variables $R$ and $S$
(A Replication)

| Experiment | Conditions | Price | | Quantity | |
|---|---|---|---|---|---|
| | | *Bowley* | *Pareto* | *Bowley* | *Pareto* |
| 2 | $CSE_p$ | 10 | 0 | 10 | 0 |
| 5 | $CRE_p$ | 4 | 8 | 6 | 6 |

Once more the changes are in the expected direction; the probabilities that they resulted from chance are quite small (for price, $p < .002$; for quantity, $p < .012$). These probabilities are reduced even further if the relevant observations are assumed to occur on the twentieth transaction ($p < .0001$ for price and quantity).

It would seem to follow from these considerations that the form of the bidding is an important experimental condition. Single-shot bids provide strong support for the Bowley contract—there is little chance for other institutional factors to interfere with the equilibrium properties of that solution. Repeated bidding permits exchange of information, and there is some tendency to move away from the Bowley solution toward the Paretian optima; this tendency is greatly strengthened when the Paretian optima contain a prominent contract as a discrete element.

## EFFECT OF THE AMOUNT OF INFORMATION

Since we conducted only one experiment under conditions of incomplete information (number 3), we can make only one comparison; this is shown in Table 5.6, for the nineteenth transaction. This comparison is between experiments 3 and 5, which differed only in the amount of information available to the bargainers. The hypothesis is that incomplete information will act as noise in the channel of communication and thus will tend to support the Bowley solution; complete information will enable the parties to use the repeated bids more effectively as a communication device and will tend to assist the Pareto solution.

58    Bilateral Monopoly

TABLE 5.6   Effect of the Variables *I* and *C*

| Experiment | Conditions | Price | | Quantity | |
|---|---|---|---|---|---|
| | | *Bowley* | *Pareto* | *Bowley* | *Pareto* |
| 3 | $IRE_p$ | 8 | 1 | 8 | 1 |
| 5 | $CRE_p$ | 4 | 8 | 6 | 6 |

The observed changes are in the expected direction and, quite probably, are a result of the altered experimental circumstance ($p < .02$ for price; $p < .08$ for quantity). Once again these probabilities are contracted when based on the twentieth transaction (for price, $p < .01$; for quantity, $p < .025$). This conclusion is reinforced by Figure 5.1, which shows the pattern of median price bids on each transaction for the third and fifth experiments.

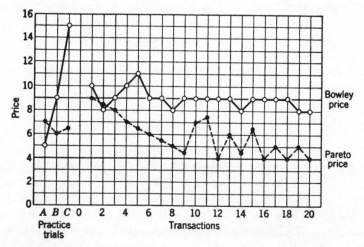

**FIGURE 5.1**   Median price bid for each transaction under incomplete information ($IRE_p$) and complete information ($CRE_p$). White circles represent incomplete information; black circles represent complete information.

It seems appropriate to conclude that the amount of information is a significant experimental variable, falling between the form of the bidding and the location of the prominent contract in the degree of its importance.

## SUMMARY

We conclude that the following experimental variables do influence (in the order listed) the results of negotiations under price leadership bilateral monopoly:

1.  Form of bidding
2.  Amount of information
3.  Location of a prominent (equal-split) contract

The states $S$, $I$, and $E_b$ favor the Bowley solution; in fact, the Bowley solution is so robust that the presence of any one of these states in an experiment tended to produce Bowley results. The states $R$, $C$, and $E_p$ favor the Pareto solution. However, the Pareto solution is contingent upon these three favorable conditions being brought together in concert.

# [3]

# *The* SOUTHERN ECONOMIC JOURNAL

VOLUME XXXIII          January 1967          NUMBER 3

## THE STABILITY OF AN EXPERIMENTAL MARKET
## WITH A SUPPLY-RESPONSE LAG

JOHN A. CARLSON[1]

*Purdue University*

The words 'stability' and 'instability' frequently crop up in theoretical discussions of markets. In context the meanings are usually clear enough, but what would happen in an actual market if the preconditions for instability were met? Would prices, for example, go through increasingly large fluctuations, or might the early manifestations of instability lead to a change in expectations and, hence, alter or negate the preconditions themselves? If subjects were put into a simulated market, could existing theoretical models be used to explain the prices and quantities observed over a sequence of periods?

The foregoing questions suggest the motivation behind this paper. Our interest here will focus on theoretical models that have assumed a *supply-response lag*. In other words, these models characterize markets in which an interval of time elapses between the date at which suppliers decide how much to produce or make available for sale and the date at which the supply actually becomes available. The models to be considered also assume that once the supply comes onto the market the price adjusts immediately to the existing demand so as to clear the market. The key difference between the different theoretical formulations arises in the assumption about the current supply response to what has occurred in the past.

[1] The author is grateful to Vernon Smith for comments on an earlier draft of this paper and to members of a workshop on experimental economics sponsored by the Ford Foundation at Carnegie Institute of Technology, August 1964. Portions of the research have been supported by the National Science Foundation (GS 370).

The first part of this paper deals with a number of models in the literature. The second part presents and discusses some pilot experiments in which subjects were asked to decide on a quantity to supply before the selling price was known. In the third part the experimental data are used to test hypotheses taken from the theoretical literature.

## I. THEORETICAL MODELS

Most of the recent theoretical literature presents supply and demand functions in algebraic form with quantity written as a function of price. Since we shall be dealing only with linear functions, the basic equations will be:

(1) $\quad S_t = c + dP_t^e \quad$ (Supply)

(2) $\quad D_t = a - bP_t \quad$ (Demand)

(3) $\quad S_t = D_t \quad$ (Market-clearing condition)

where:

$S_t$ = quantity supplied,

$D_t$ = quantity demanded,

$P_t^e$ = price expected by the suppliers,

$P_t$ = market price,

$a, b, c, d$, are parameters, and the subscript $t$ denotes the time period. One further simplification will be the assumption of a positively sloped supply curve and a negatively sloped demand curve, i.e., $d > 0$, $b > 0$.

Equilibrium will occur when $P_t = P_t^e = \bar{P}$ and there is no further change in expected price. The equilibrium price $\bar{P}$ satisfies the condition:

JOHN A. CARLSON

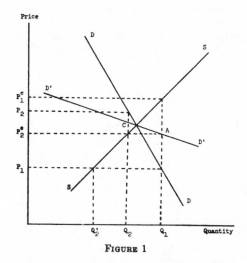

FIGURE 1

$$c + d\bar{P} = a - b\bar{P},$$

or

$$(4) \qquad \bar{P} = \frac{a - c}{b + d}$$

and the equilibrium quantity supplied $\bar{S}$ becomes

$$(5) \qquad \bar{S} = \frac{ad + bc}{b + d}.$$

1. *The Cobweb Theorem.* The expectation function assumed in the cobweb theorem [3] is:

$$(6) \qquad P_t^e = P_{t-1}.$$

Equations (1), (2), (3), and (6) reduce to the first-order difference equation:

$$bP_t + dP_{t-1} = a - c,$$

and the solution in terms of $P_t$ is:

$$(7) \quad P_t = \bar{P} + [-(d/b)]^t (P_0 - \bar{P})$$

where $P_0$ is some initial price.

If $d/b < 1$, then price converges to its equilibrium value and the market is said to be stable. If $d/b > 1$, the fluctuations around equilibrium become larger and larger and the market is said to be unstable.

To bridge the gap between the foregoing

formulation and the usual diagrammatic approach, equations (1) and (2) can be rewritten:

$$(8) \qquad P_t^e = \frac{c}{d} = \frac{1}{d} S_t,$$

and

$$(9) \qquad P_t = \frac{a}{b} - \frac{1}{b} D_t.$$

The slope of the supply curve (labeled $SS$ in Fig. 1) is $1/d$ and the slope of the demand curve ($DD$ in Fig. 1) is $-(1/b)$. The condition for stability is often stated as the requirement that the demand curve be less steep (in absolute value) than the supply curve, i.e., that $1/b < 1/d$. This is equivalent to the stability condition,

$$(10) \qquad d/b < 1.$$

2. *Adaptive Expectations.* Nerlove [11] introduced an alternative model in which he assumed that suppliers might only gradually change their expectations about price. He postulated that expected price is adjusted according to a function of how wrong the expected price was in the last period. Specifically, he used the function:

$$(11) \quad P_t^e - P_{t-1}^e = \beta (P_{t-1} - P_{t-1}^e)$$

$$\text{with} \quad 0 \leqq \beta \leqq 1.$$

$\beta$ will be called the "adaptive coefficient of expectation".

Nerlove manipulated his model into a first-order difference equation and solved for $P_t$. In this model the condition for stability becomes:

$$(12) \qquad d/b < 2/\beta - 1.$$

If $\beta = 1$, then $P_t^e = P_{t-1}$ and condition (12) reduces as it should to the same condition (10) for stability as in the cobweb theorem. As $\beta$ grows smaller, the range of relative slopes of the supply and demand curve that will produce stability is increased.

We shall present a geometric interpretation of this model. Those familiar with the cobweb theorem may find this approach helpful in understanding condition (12). Consider Figure 1 in which the demand curve $DD$ is steeper than the supply curve $SS$. The "adaptive expectations" hypothesis (11) can be rewritten:

$$P_t{}^e = \beta P_{t-1} + (1 - \beta)P_{t-1}^e.$$

Thus, the new expected price is a weighted average of the most recent actual price and the last expected price, with the weights summing to one.

In Figure 1, if the quantity $Q_1$ were supplied in anticipation of price $P_1{}^e$, the actual price would be $P_1$. In the cobweb theorem, the new expected price would be $P_1$ and the quantity would be $Q_2'$. In Nerlove's model, however, the new expected price $P_2{}^e$ differs from $P_1{}^e$ by $\beta$ times the distance from $P_1{}^e$ to $P_1$. With this expected price, suppliers will decide on a quantity $Q_2$. As a result price must rise to $P_2$. The next expected price will then be above $P_2{}^e$ by $\beta$ times the distance from $P_2{}^e$ to $P_2$, and the same sort of process repeats itself. Points $A$ and $C$ in Figure 1 relate quantity outcomes $Q_1$ and $Q_2$, respectively, with subsequent expected prices. Through these points, we generate a curve $D'D'$, which divides the angle between $SS$ and $DD$ in the ratio $\beta$ to $(1 - \beta)$.

As the foregoing discussion indicates, the slope of $D'D'$ influences the degree of stability in the market. A decrease in $\beta$ has the effect of rotating $D'D'$ counterclockwise. Thus, any potentially explosive market can become stable if $\beta$ is sufficiently small and $D'D'$ has been rotated to the extent that its slope is less (again in absolute value) than that of the supply curve.

The equivalence between this geometric interpretation and stability condition (12) can be seen by noting that $D'D'$ is a weighted average of $DD$ and $SS$. It can readily be shown that the slope of $D'D'$ is:

$$\beta\left(-\frac{1}{b}\right) + (1 - \beta)\frac{1}{d}.$$

So long as $D'D'$ does not slope downward at

a rate any greater than $-(1/d)$, then by the cobweb theorem the price will converge to equilibrium. Algebraically, we require for stability:

$$\beta\left(-\frac{1}{b}\right) + (1 - \beta)\frac{1}{d} > -\frac{1}{d}.$$

Multiply through by $-d$ to get:

$$\beta(d/b) - 1 + \beta < 1.$$

Add $(1 - \beta)$ to both sides, divide through by $\beta$, and stability condition (12) results.

3. *An Extrapolative Approach.* Somewhat earlier, Goodwin [5] worked out the consequences of assuming that all producers expect price to change by some constant factor times the most recent change in price. In terms of our notation, Goodwin's expectation hypothesis is:

$$(13) \quad P_t{}^e - P_{t-1} = -\rho\,(P_{t-1} - P_{t-2})$$

where $-\rho$ denotes the constant factor. Metzler [7] has called $-\rho$ the "coefficient of expectation." To distinguish this concept from the $\beta$ associated with Nerlove's model, we shall call $\rho$ the "extrapolative coefficient of expectation," a designation employed by Muth [10].

With the assumed sequence of events in this model, prices in periods $t - 1$ and $t - 2$ determine the expected price $P_t{}^e$, which in turn determines a quantity supplied; once the quantity is given, the demand function determines $P_t$. Thus, $P_{t-2}$ and $P_{t-1}$ lead to $P_t$, and the time path for price can be characterized by a second-order difference equation. The conditions for stability in this model are ([5], p. 195, [10], p. 272):

$$(14) \quad \begin{aligned} &\frac{d}{b} < \frac{1}{\rho} \qquad \text{for } \rho \geq \tfrac{1}{3}; \\[2mm] &\frac{d}{b} < \frac{1}{-2\rho + 1} \quad \text{for } \rho \leq \tfrac{1}{3}. \end{aligned}$$

As an example with $\rho = \tfrac{1}{2}$, a demand curve, such as $DD$ in Fig. 1, could be almost two times as steep as the supply curve and price would still converge to equilibrium. Note that this model cannot produce market stability whenever the demand curve is more than three times as steep as the supply curve.

4. *An Induced-Caution Hypothesis.* Another variant of this model was proposed by Hooton [6]. He discussed the possibility that large fluctuations in price can have two effects. Supply becomes less elastic owing to the cautiousness of suppliers; and demand becomes more elastic as speculators enter the market. Both effects are in the direction of contributing to greater stability. Since our experiments do not include the holding of inventories or any possibility of speculative buying, we shall concentrate here on the supply considerations.

Our assumed supply equation (1) tells us that given an expected price a certain quantity will be supplied. Suppose, however, that suppliers do not know exactly what price to expect since prices have been fluctuating in the past. Hooton suggested that the relevant supply response might not be a curve such as $SS$ but one he labeled $S_r$ to stand for supply with risk. He contended that the shape and position of an $S_r$ curve depends upon both the average price in the past and the degree of price fluctuations. His assertion (pp. 71–72, with italics added here for emphasis) was:

*The $S_r$ schedules are always less elastic than the guaranteed schedule, their elasticity decreasing as risk increases.* Other things being equal, they are likely to become extremely inelastic at very high prices which are well beyond the average fluctuations. At these prices the producer, even though he may not have reason to *expect* a lower price, nevertheless recognizes that the risk of a lower price is increased.

Hooton's assertion confuses the risk of large price changes in either direction with the risk of a fall in prices. If prices are believed to be unusually high, there may be an awareness or feeling that they should come down and, hence, a tendency *to expect* a lower price. The expectation of a one-way change in prices is quite a different situation from the one in which there is a possibility of a large increase in price as well as the chance of a large decrease. Why not turn Hooton's position 180 degrees and argue that the greater the past fluctuations in price the *more* each producer will supply in hopes of being lucky enough to hit upon an upswing in prices?

Hooton drew a "risky" supply curve as a shift to the left and a slight counterclockwise rotation of the "guaranteed" schedule. A leftward shift of the supply curve is neither a necessary nor a sufficient condition for increasing elasticity of supply; but Hooton drew his curves that way and reasoned that the higher the expected price, the greater would be the leftward shift.

We can relate these claims to utility theory by means of the following conjecture. Given: a cost function with increasing marginal cost, a utility function for money, a subjective probability distribution of price, and the objective of maximizing expected utility. Then:

1. With a utility function that is concave from below,
   a. the quantity supplied will be less than the quantity at which marginal cost equals expected price, and
   b. the greater the dispersion of the subjective probability distribution of price, the smaller will be the quantity supplied.
2. With a utility function that is convex from below,
   a. the quantity supplied will be greater than the quantity at which marginal cost equals expected price, and
   b. the greater the dispersion of the subjective probability distribution for price, the greater will be the quantity supplied.[2]

---

[2] It can be demonstrated that this conjecture holds in the case of a quadratic cost function, a quadratic utility function, and a uniform probability distribution. The demonstration is too involved to warrant reproducing here. With a convex function, however, there is the possibility that the second-order condition is not satisfied.

Hooton's hypothesis is equivalent to the claim that 1.a. and 1.b. will be the most prevalent type of supply response in a market situation. This hypothesis will be examined in Section III in terms of our experimental data. Attempts that have been made to measure utility functions experimentally would suggest that no such generalization is warranted, at least when small amounts of money are at stake [1], [9].

## II. THE EXPERIMENTS

Models of the type discussed in Section I can be transformed into an experimental setting in which subjects form their own price expectations and make supply decisions. Supply-response behavior can then be studied within a controlled environment. The structure and results of a few such experiments are described in this section.[3] Analysis of the results is deferred until Section III.

In each session, every subject was given information about the cost of supplying different quantities of some fictitious commodity. A subject was asked to make a decision about how much to supply knowing only what the price had been in the past or on the basis of some expectation of what the price was going to be. Marginal cost was an increasing linear function of quantity supplied. Thus, the supply curve would have the form of equation (1), an upward-sloping straight line, if subjects always chose a quantity at which marginal cost equaled expected price.

The actual price was determined by the total quantity supplied, the price adjusting so as to clear the market in accordance with

a demand function not revealed to the participants. The process of having the subjects make supply decisions and then determining price was repeated for a sequence of periods.

The experiments were run in pairs. The procedure adopted was to select two groups of undergraduate students taking the same course, a practice followed by Smith [15], [16], [17]. For one group the demand curve was made flatter than the supply curve and with the other, steeper. By the cobweb theorem, one market should have been stable and the other unstable. Since it was not obvious beforehand what sort of results could be expected, these sessions are best described as pilot experiments.

1. *The First Pair of Experiments.* For ease of reference, we shall refer to Group A as the one with the flatter demand curve and to Group B as the one with the steeper demand curve. Twenty subjects comprised each group. A subject was given the cost schedule shown in Table I and a form to fill out. On the form he recorded his estimate of what the price was going to be, his quantity decision, and the corresponding cost. He was told that the actual price depended upon the total production by all producers, i.e., that the more produced by all of them the lower would be the price and the fewer units produced the higher would be the price. After the actual price was announced he computed his current profit and went on to make his decisions for the next period.

In order to get a feeling for the procedure there was a trial period in which the subjects were told what to record on their form. Each subject was to supply 5 units. For Group A the resulting price was .20 and for Group B the price was .24. In effect this provided them with a knowledge of one point on the market demand curve. After that they were on their own to make individual decisions on the basis of their appraisals of the market. They were also told that each of them would be paid half of his cumulative profit at the end of the experiment.

Under those circumstances, in the special case considered, the supplier would produce as much as possible at all times and any greater expected variation in price would have no effect. This possibility seems of little practical consequence.

[3] The first pair of experiments were conducted at Purdue University with two senior level classes of Industrial Management majors taking a course in Government Regulation of Business. The second pair used two introductory economics classes in the 1964 summer session at Purdue.

JOHN A. CARLSON

TABLE I

COST SCHEDULE SUPPLIED TO SUBJECTS IN FIRST
SET OF EXPERIMENTS

| Number of units produced each period | Total cost | Marginal cost |
|---|---|---|
| 0 | $0.00 | |
| 1 | .02 | .02 |
| 2 | .06 | .04 |
| 3 | .12 | .06 |
| 4 | .20 | .08 |
| 5 | .30 | .10 |
| 6 | .42 | .12 |
| 7 | .56 | .14 |
| 8 | .72 | .16 |
| 9 | .90 | .18 |
| 10 | 1.10 | .20 |
| 11 | 1.32 | .22 |
| 12 | 1.56 | .24 |
| 13 | 1.82 | .26 |
| 14 | 2.10 | .28 |
| 15 | 2.40 | .30 |
| 16 | 2.72 | .32 |
| 17 | 3.06 | .34 |
| 18 | 3.42 | .36 |
| 19 | 3.80 | .38 |
| 20 | 4.20 | .40 |
| 21 | 4.62 | .42 |
| 22 | 5.06 | .44 |

During each session a subject made six decisions. The total quantities supplied in each period and the resulting prices are shown in Table II. A detailed array of the individual decisions is given in Table III. Both groups, quite by accident, hit the intended market equilibrium quantity of 160 units in the first period. The optimism of a few was apparently offset by a cautiousness on the part of the others. Only two subjects in Group A and one in Group B supplied exactly 8 units, the intended individual equilibrium quantity.

Out of a comparison of the two groups, the similarity of the decisions despite different demand curves emerges as the most notable result. The subjects apparently had the training to sense the degree of inelasticity of the demand curve from the information given in the trial period. One subject in Group B had plotted, on scratch paper, a demand curve through the initial point and only slightly steeper than the actual curve used. Providing both quantity and price information is evidently an artificial obstacle to instability.

Another point to note is that production decisions may vary as much or more when prices have hardly changed as they do when prices have had sizeable changes. This suggests that the demand curves can be made much more elastic or much more inelastic without having much effect on the speed with which all quantity decisions converge to a common equilibrium value.

If we measure degree of convergence of individual suppliers by the sample variances of quantity decisions, recorded in Table II, then Group B showed a stronger tendency to converge. In other words, the suppliers in the potentially explosive market seemed to be closing in on an equilibrium faster than

TABLE II

AGGREGATE QUANTITIES ($Q$), PRICES ($P$), MEANS ($\bar{q}$) AND SAMPLE VARIANCES ($S_q^2$) OF INDIVIDUAL QUANTITY DECISIONS, AND NUMBER OF SUBJECTS CHANGING QUANTITY DECISIONS Experiments 1 and 2

| Period | $Q$ | $P$ | $\bar{q}$ | $S_q^2$ | No. of changes |
|---|---|---|---|---|---|
| Group A | | | | | |
| 0 | 100 | 20 | | | |
| 1 | 160 | 16 | 8.00 | 4.70 | — |
| 2 | 167 | 16 | 8.35 | 3.73 | 16 |
| 3 | 192 | 14 | 9.60 | 7.34 | 14 |
| 4 | 158 | 16 | 7.90 | 4.39 | 16 |
| 5 | 152 | 16 | 7.65 | 1.34 | 14 |
| 6 | 147 | 17 | 7.35 | 0.93 | 7 |
| Group B | | | | | |
| 0 | 100 | 24 | | | |
| 1 | 160 | 16 | 8.00 | 5.40 | — |
| 2 | 171 | 14 | 8.55 | 8.16 | 15 |
| 3 | 146 | 18 | 7.30 | 2.71 | 14 |
| 4 | 150 | 17 | 7.50 | 2.75 | 13 |
| 5 | 157 | 16 | 7.85 | 0.83 | 12 |
| 6 | 151 | 17 | 7.55 | 0.85 | 11 |

TABLE III

DISTRIBUTION OF INDIVIDUAL QUANTITY DECISIONS

Experiments 1 and 2

| Period | Quantity | | | | | | | | | | | | | | | | | | | |
|---|---|---|---|---|---|---|---|---|---|---|---|---|---|---|---|---|---|---|---|---|
| | 1 | 2 | 3 | 4 | 5 | 6 | 7 | 8 | 9 | 10 | 11 | 12 | 13 | 14 | 15 | 16 | 17 | 18 | 19 | 20 |
| **Group A** | | | | | | | | | | | | | | | | | | | | |
| 1 | | | 1 | | 2 | 2 | 3 | 2 | 4 | 5 | | | 1 | | | | | | | |
| 2 | | | | 1 | | 3 | 2 | 5 | 2 | 5 | 1 | | 1 | | | | | | | |
| 3 | | | | | | 1 | 3 | 4 | 5 | 4 | 1 | | 1 | | | 1 | 1 | | | |
| 4 | | | | 1 | | 4 | 6 | 4 | 1 | 2 | 1 | | 2 | | | | | | | |
| 5 | | | | | | 3 | 7 | 6 | 2 | 2 | | | | | | | | | | |
| 6 | | | | | | 3 | 10 | 5 | 1 | 1 | | | | | | | | | | |
| **Group B** | | | | | | | | | | | | | | | | | | | | |
| 1 | | | | 1 | 1 | 4 | 3 | 1 | 7 | 2 | | | | | 1 | | | | | |
| 2 | | | | | 1 | | 6 | 5 | 6 | 1 | | | | | | | | | | 1 |
| 3 | | | | 1 | 1 | 3 | 5 | 7 | 2 | 1 | | | | | | | | | | |
| 4 | | | | | | 4 | 5 | 7 | 3 | 1 | | | | | | | | | | |
| 5 | | | | | | 2 | 4 | 11 | 4 | | | | | | | | | | | |
| 6 | | | | | | 3 | 6 | 8 | 3 | | | | | | | | | | | |

those in the market which ought to converge to equilibrium by the stability condition (10) of the cobweb theorem.

There were a number of minor difficulties with the design. The equilibrium price was .16 and the equilibrium quantity was 8. From an individual's viewpoint, however, a quantity of 7 was equally profitable. If all produced 7 units, price would rise, but a few individuals could be at 7 without affecting price. Hence equilibrium for total quantity was not unique.

Subjects continued to produce over a range from 6 to 10 units. This is probably attributable to the very small opportunity cost associated with certain non-optimal quantity decisions. With a price of .16, the profit when producing 6 or 9 units is only .02 less than at 7 or 8 units. At 5 or 10 units it is .06 less. Since the cash payoff was only half the profit, the incentive to be more precise is the marginal utility of only .01 or .03. The marginal utility of other considerations, such as for variability, must have outweighed the profit incentive for many subjects (Siegel, [14]).

One thing that took extra time was the making of profit calculations. The cost schedule included a column with the marginal cost, and classes had been selected in which marginal cost would be a familiar concept. Nevertheless many of the subjects filled an entire page calculating the relative profits associated with alternative situations. The next experiments were designed in an attempt to overcome some of the shortcomings of the original design.

2. *The Second Pair of Experiments.* The second pair of experiments was run with 25 subjects in each group. A Profit Table was substituted for the cost schedule. The Table was a matrix with 21 rows and 37 columns. Each row represented a quantity supplied from 1 to 21, and each column was headed by a price from 2 to 38 cents. Each element within the matrix showed the profit that would be realized by a quantity decision and a market price. The cost function was the same as that shown in Table I, so the profit entry was simply total revenue less total cost. This enabled the subjects to consider what they thought the price was going to be

TABLE IV

AGGREGATE QUANTITIES $(Q)$, PRICES $(P)$, MEANS $(\bar{q})$ AND SAMPLE VARIANCES $(S_q{}^2)$ OF INDIVIDUAL QUANTITY DECISIONS, AND NUMBER OF SUBJECTS CHANGING QUANTITY DECISIONS Experiments 3 and 4

| Period | $Q$ | $P$ | $\bar{q}$ | $S_q{}^2$ | No. of Changes |
|---|---|---|---|---|---|
| | | | Group A | | |
| 0 | | .12 | | | |
| 1 | 189 | .18 | 7.56 | 10.25 | |
| 2 | 233 | .15 | 9.32 | 3.90 | 22 |
| 3 | 213 | .16 | 8.52 | 8.25 | 22 |
| 4 | 217 | .16 | 8.68 | 9.02 | 13 |
| 5 | 233 | .15 | 9.32 | 9.42 | 12 |
| 6 | 204 | .17 | 8.16 | 2.05 | 19 |
| 7 | 210 | .16 | 8.40 | 2.80 | 13 |
| 8 | 206 | .17 | 8.24 | 2.02 | 11 |
| 9 | 216 | .16 | 8.64 | 2.15 | 8 |
| | | | Group B | | |
| 0 | | .12 | | | |
| 1 | 158 | .23 | 6.32 | 3.18 | |
| 2 | 273 | .07 | 10.92 | 10.23 | 24 |
| 3 | 206 | .17 | 8.24 | 7.14 | 25 |
| 4 | 193 | .18 | 7.72 | 9.88 | 22 |
| 5 | 198 | .17 | 7.92 | 9.91 | 21 |
| 6 | 193 | .18 | 7.72 | 2.82 | 14 |
| 7 | 196 | .18 | 7.84 | 1.57 | 12 |
| 8 | 193 | .18 | 7.72 | 2.20 | 10 |
| 9 | 198 | .17 | 7.92 | 1.43 | 10 |

and to look up the profit that would be realized at any quantity supplied if their expectations about price were correct. It was hoped that the Profit Table would eliminate computation time and make apparent the risks associated with extreme quantity decisions.

Both groups were supplied with identical initial information. They had the same Profit Table; the same instructions were read aloud; and in both cases they were told that the price in the period prior to period 1 had been .12. The demand curves were constructed so as to achieve a unique equilibrium at a quantity of 8 units per subject and a market price of .17.

The actual demand functions used to relate price to quantity, written in the form of equation (9) to correspond to a diagrammatic presentation, were:

$$P_t = .31 - .0007\, D_t \text{ for experiment 3,}$$

and

$$P_t = .45 - .0014\, D_t \text{ for experiment 4.}$$

The supply curve, while actually occurring in steps, can be approximated by the formula:

$$P_t{}^e = .01 + .0008\, S_t.$$

According to the cobweb criterion for stability, the market in experiment 3 should experience gradual convergence. For experiment 4, the structure suggests potential instability. As before we shall denote the subjects with the seemingly more stable market structure as Group A. Hence the subjects in experiment 4 become Group B for this pair of experiments.

Each of these sessions lasted nine periods. The results are summarized in Tables IV and V. In Table V for period 1, the quantity decisions of Group B appear generally lower than those of Group A. This impression, however, is not supported by a Chi-square test. (See [13], p. 110.) At a ten-per cent significance level, we cannot reject the hypothesis that the differences were purely random.

The price sequence was much more striking for Group B. The price jumped to .23 in the first period, fell to .07 in the second period, and apparently hit the equilibrium value of .17 in the third period.[4] Thereafter, the price was always either .17 or .18 and the mean quantity response stayed within the range 7.7 to 8.1. With the exception of one maverick who produced 20 units in period 4, 21 in period 5, and 3 in period 8, all the subjects in Group B made reasonably profitable decisions from the fourth period on.

[4] A minor recording error kept the third-period price from being the .16 that the demand function calls for when total quantity is 206.

TABLE V

DISTRIBUTION OF INDIVIDUAL QUANTITY DECISIONS

Experiments 3 and 4

| Period | Quantity | | | | | | | | | | | | | | | | | | | | |
|---|---|---|---|---|---|---|---|---|---|---|---|---|---|---|---|---|---|---|---|---|---|
| | 1 | 2 | 3 | 4 | 5 | 6 | 7 | 8 | 9 | 10 | 11 | 12 | 13 | 14 | 15 | 16 | 17 | 18 | 19 | 20 | 21 |
| **Group A** | | | | | | | | | | | | | | | | | | | | | |
| 1 | | | 1 | | 6 | 5 | 4 | 2 | 1 | 3 | 1 | | | 1 | | | | 1 | | | |
| 2 | | | | 1 | | 1 | 1 | 6 | 1 | 10 | 3 | 1 | | 1 | | | | | | | |
| 3 | | | | 1 | | 4 | 6 | 6 | 1 | 4 | | 1 | | | 1 | | | 1 | | | |
| 4 | | | | | | 3 | 7 | 8 | | 4 | | 1 | | | 1 | | | | 1 | | |
| 5 | | | | | | | 4 | 12 | 1 | 5 | | | | 1 | 1 | | | | | | 1 |
| 6 | | | | | | 1 | | 9 | 7 | 3 | 2 | 3 | | | | | | | | | |
| 7 | | | | | | 1 | 1 | 4 | 10 | 4 | 3 | | 1 | 1 | | | | | | | |
| 8 | | | | | | 1 | | 4 | 15 | 2 | 3 | | | 1 | | | | | | | |
| 9 | | | | | | | 1 | 17 | 3 | 2 | | 1 | | 1 | | | | | | | |
| **Group B** | | | | | | | | | | | | | | | | | | | | | |
| 1 | | | 1 | 2 | 5 | 9 | 2 | 2 | 2 | 2 | | | | | | | | | | | |
| 2 | | | | | 2 | | | 2 | 1 | 4 | 3 | 2 | 1 | 4 | 2 | | | 1 | | | |
| 3 | | 1 | | | 2 | 2 | 4 | 5 | 4 | 5 | 1 | | | | | | 1 | | | | |
| 4 | | | | | 6 | 5 | 4 | 1 | 5 | 1 | 2 | | | | | | | | 1 | | |
| 5 | | | | | 3 | 7 | 4 | 2 | 4 | 4 | | | | | | | | | | | 1 |
| 6 | | | | | 2 | 4 | 5 | 6 | 4 | 4 | | | | | | | | | | | |
| 7 | | | | | 1 | 2 | 7 | 8 | 4 | 3 | | | | | | | | | | | |
| 8 | | 1 | | | 3 | 6 | 7 | 6 | 2 | | | | | | | | | | | | |
| 9 | | | | | 1 | 2 | 5 | 9 | 6 | 2 | | | | | | | | | | | |

Group A observed only moderate price changes, in the range .15 to .18. The first period price of only .18, compared with .23 for Group B, can be explained partly by the larger initial quantity response and partly by the flatter demand curve. As in the first pair of experiments there seems to be a greater willingness to try moderately wild decisions when the price variations have not been so great. As a result, the convergent market shows little if any tendency to converge faster than the potentially unstable market.

### III. THE ANALYSIS

The pairs of experiments described in the preceding section were designed primarily with the cobweb theorem in mind, with one market convergent and the other potentially divergent. Contrary to the cobweb hypothesis, both converged fairly rapidly. The

behavior of subjects in experiment 4 suggested a cobweb pattern for two periods; yet the exuberant and ill-fated leap in supply during period 2 was not followed by unduly pessimistic decisions in period 3. Even more was supplied than in period 1. The process of convergence had begun by a simple interpolation of previous decisions.

There are, of course, other hypotheses about how expectations might be formed or how suppliers might react to certain market situations when there exists a lag in the supply response. The remainder of this section is devoted to the utilization of our experimental data to test the hypotheses discussed in Section I.

1. *The Induced-Caution Hypothesis.* The subjects never knew for certain what the price was going to be. Hence, the supply response was subject to what Hooton has called "risk." His claim, it will be recalled,

was that with "risk" the supply "schedules are always less elastic than the guaranteed schedule, their elasticity decreasing as risk increases."

Operationally, we shall interpret this to mean that (a) suppliers will produce less than the quantity at which marginal cost equals expected price and (b) if price expectations are the same, suppliers will produce less in markets in which price fluctuations have been greater in the past.

In the experiments, the subjects were instructed for each period to record "your estimate, or guess, of what the price is going to be that period. This figure will not affect the actual price. You are asked simply to try to make as accurate a forecast as you can on the basis of the information available at that time." In retrospect those instructions were clearly inadequate. The results are therefore highly tentative.

For each stated expected price, there are some quantity decisions that will yield a maximum profit or at least come within a penny of the maximum profit if that price materializes. If those quantities are taken as "consistent" decisions, then each subject's quantity decisions can be classified into one of four categories:

(i) perfectly consistent or displayed slight random inconsistencies.
(ii) generally consistent or a bit low.
(iii) generally consistent or a bit high.
(iv) too inconsistent to believe.

In terms of utility theory, categories (i), (ii), and (iii) correspond to utility functions of money that are linear, concave from below, and convex from below, respectively (if the conjecture in Section I 4 is correct).

For the first part of Hooton's claim to be substantiated, there should be a noticeable preponderance of subjects whose decisions fall into category (ii), i.e., they tend to produce less than if they had tried to maximize profit on the basis of stated expected price. While the process of classification required a few somewhat arbitrary decisions, the following figures are indicative of the

degree of individual consistency with respect to stated price expectations:

| | Experiments 1 and 2 | | | Experiments 3 and 4 | |
|---|---|---|---|---|---|
| | Group A | Group B | | Group A | Group B |
| (i) | 10 | 12 | (i) | 15 | 11 |
| (ii) | 3 | 4 | (ii) | 2 | 5 |
| (iii) | 5 | 3 | (iii) | 7 | 6 |
| (iv) | 2 | 1 | (iv) | 1 | 3 |

There was certainly no overwhelming tendency to underproduce (category *ii*). In fact, looking at category (*iii*), we find a number of subjects who were inclined to produce more than an expected-profit maximizer.

Disregarding misunderstandings and possible irrationalities of individual participants, we took all the stated price expectations at face value and averaged over an entire group. These average expected prices are shown in Table VI for Experiments 3 and 4. The functional relationship between aggregate supply and expected price is given in Section II 3. This can be rewritten as $S_t = (P_t^e - .01)/.0008$. Taking this supply function and the average expected price, an optimum aggregate was computed for each period. These figures are recorded in the second column of Table VI as $S_t^*$. For purposes of comparison the actual total quantities ($S_t$) are recorded in the third column.

A surprising result is the degree of rationality for each group as a whole in terms of the average of the stated expectations. The differences between the two groups in the quantity responses for periods 1 and 2 are almost wholly explainable by stated expectations.

For use in the next section, the fourth column of Table VI records the implicit expected price. This would be the expected price consistent with the actual total quantity. In other words, if this had been the expected price then the actual total quantity would have been optimal according to our supply function.

There is little evidence here that the

presence of uncertainties about the actual price causes the supply to be less than it would be when based only on expected price. Group B's quantity decisions were very close to what would be predicted if the average expected price were guaranteed. With Group A, the quantity decisions were contrary to Hooton's hypothesis. The supply response was greater, not less, than the optimum supply given the price expectations.

The second part of Hooton's hypothesis, however, has not been contradicted by the data. We could rephrase that part by saying, *"ceteris paribus,* the greater the past fluctuations in price, the less will be the quantity supplied." Throughout the final four periods, Group A exhibited an average stated expected price less than or equal to that of Group B. At the same time Group A which had experienced the milder price fluctuations, tended to supply the greater quantity.

We shall turn now to hypotheses about the formation of price expectations. Since there is reason to doubt the validity of the stated price expectations, our procedure will be to assume that the subjects acted as maximizers of expected profit. It is then possible to assign to each quantity decision an implicit expected price. In what follows "expected price" will be the price for which the actual quantity supplied would maximize expected profits.

2. *The Adaptive-Expectations Hypothesis.* Equation (11), which expresses the adaptive-expectations hypothesis, is a linear equation constrained to pass through the origin of the two-dimensional space $(P_{t-1} - P_{t-1}^e,$ $P_t^e - P_{t-1}^e)$. The relevancy of this constraint to our data was examined by plotting the observations for a number of subjects and for each group. In many cases, the fit could be improved substantially by relaxing the constraint. We shall, therefore, postulate a linear function of the form:

(11a)
$$P_t^e - P_{t-1}^e$$
$$= \alpha + \beta (P_{t-1} - P_{t-1}^e) + \eta_t$$

TABLE VI

AVERAGE STATED EXPECTED PRICE $(\bar{P}_t^e)$, "OPTIMAL" SUPPLY $(S_t^*)$, ACTUAL SUPPLY $(S_t)$, AND IMPLICIT EXPECTED PRICE $(P_t^e)$

Experiments 3 and 4

| $t$ | $\bar{P}_t^e$ | $S_t^*$ | $S_t$ | $P_t^e$ |
|---|---|---|---|---|
| Group A | | | | |
| 1 | 15.1 | 176 | 189 | 16.12 |
| 2 | 19.1 | 226 | 233 | 19.64 |
| 3 | 16.8 | 198 | 213 | 18.04 |
| 4 | 16.7 | 196 | 217 | 18.36 |
| 5 | 18.2 | 215 | 233 | 19.64 |
| 6 | 16.1 | 189 | 204 | 17.32 |
| 7 | 16.5 | 194 | 210 | 17.80 |
| 8 | 16.2 | 190 | 206 | 17.48 |
| 9 | 16.4 | 193 | 216 | 18.28 |
| Group B | | | | |
| 1 | 13.0 | 150 | 158 | 13.64 |
| 2 | 22.1 | 264 | 273 | 22.84 |
| 3 | 15.4 | 180 | 206 | 17.48 |
| 4 | 16.5 | 194 | 193 | 16.44 |
| 5 | 16.7 | 196 | 198 | 16.84 |
| 6 | 16.6 | 195 | 193 | 16.44 |
| 7 | 16.5 | 194 | 196 | 16.68 |
| 8 | 17.2 | 203 | 193 | 16.44 |
| 9 | 16.7 | 196 | 198 | 16.84 |

where $\eta_t$ is a random variable, independently and identically normally distributed with a zero mean and a finite variance. These assumptions are to be implied whenever $\eta_t$ appears subsequently.

The constant term $\alpha$ can be readily interpreted as a "bias" parameter.[5] A subject might alter his price expectations adaptively, but still retain either an optimistic or a

[5] In an article devoted to criticizing Hooton's argument, Newman [12] introduced an "imagined" demand curve to show that incorrect expectations could promote stability. Though viewed from a different perspective, this "imagined" demand curve comes to the same thing as our modified adaptive-expectations equation. Since the spirit of his article was essentially negative, however, Newman was unwilling to take an interesting idea seriously. He commented that he was "not much impressed with the practical use" of his own model and that he was "concerned with theoretical, and not empirical possibilities" (p. 340).

316                                   JOHN A. CARLSON

## TABLE VII
### Group A, Experiment 3
### Results of Fitting the Equation
$$P_t^e - P_{t-1}^e = \alpha + \beta \ (P_{t-1}^e - P_{t-1})$$

| (1) Subject number | (2) $\alpha$ | (3) $\beta$ | (4) $s_\beta$ | (5) $r^2$ | (6) Sum squared residuals | (7) Residual reduction ratio |
|---|---|---|---|---|---|---|
| 1 | 1.02 | 1.084 | .113 | .939 | 7.33 | .00 |
| 2 | .82 | 1.261 | .208 | .859 | 15.46 | 1.37 |
| 3 | 0 | 1.000 | .170 | .852 | 8.00 | .00 |
| 4 | 3.38 | 1.281 | .240 | .826 | 28.89 | 3.95 |
| 5 | .11 | 1.284 | .109 | .959 | 7.26 | .29 |
| 6 | 1.68 | 1.091 | .318 | .663 | 53.27 | .27 |
| 7 | 4.63 | .479 | .229 | .422 | 122.34 | .62 |
| 8 | 10.38 | .848 | .414 | .412 | 414.13 | .25 |
| 9 | 4.64 | .878 | .304 | .582 | 108.56 | .00 |
| 10 | 1.05 | .785 | .107 | .900 | 9.55 | 15.19 |
| 11 | .85 | .731 | .190 | .712 | 5.62 | .88 |
| 12 | −.25 | 0 | .382 | 0 | 3.50 | — |
| 13 | .05 | .563 | .081 | .890 | 1.70 | .83 |
| 14 | .55 | .200 | .150 | .229 | 2.70 | .19 |
| 15 | −.52 | .678 | .397 | .327 | 111.76 | 6.87 |
| 16 | .60 | .881 | .229 | .712 | 22.49 | 8.15 |
| 17 | −.59 | .891 | .104 | .493 | 2.96 | .67 |
| 18 | .08 | .842 | .116 | .898 | 3.05 | .15 |
| 19 | .49 | .979 | .278 | .674 | 21.98 | .03 |
| 20 | .25 | .833 | .140 | .855 | 2.84 | .31 |
| 21 | 1.60 | 1.092 | .338 | .635 | 785.77 | .01 |
| 22 | .50 | 1.079 | .254 | .750 | 29.53 | .33 |
| 23 | 5.79 | .964 | .440 | .444 | 259.71 | 7.65 |
| 24 | 1.40 | .717 | .281 | .521 | 68.04 | .27 |
| 25 | .76 | 1.046 | .158 | .879 | 11.34 | 1.54 |
| Average | 1.57 | .859 | | | | |
| Group | 1.60 | .737 | .140 | .823 | 3.982 | .00 |

pessimistic bias. For example, if he over-estimated price in one period, $(P_{t-1} - P_{t-1}^e)$ would be negative. Within certain ranges he might not change his expectations and so $\alpha$ would be positive indicating an optimistic bias. Whenever a subject's decision indicated some such bias, the plots generally show that he maintained this bias consistently throughout the experiment.

The results of estimating $\alpha$ and $\beta$ by the method of least squares are presented in columns (2) and (3) respectively of Tables VII and VIII. The standard errors of the $\beta$ coefficients are in column (4) and the $r^2$ terms are in column (5). At the bottom of the tables where the row is labeled average there

is an arithmetic mean for the coefficients $\alpha$ and $\beta$. The last row presents the estimates derived as if a single supplier were basing the market supply on adaptive price expectations.

A number of observations follow from an inspection of these estimates. For one thing, the coefficients based on aggregate market behavior do not differ markedly from the coefficients obtained by a simple average of individual coefficients.

In no case in either section does an estimate of $\beta$ fall significantly outside of the postulated range from zero to one. The estimates of $\beta$ do, however, appear generally larger for Group A. This impression was sub-

## TABLE VIII
### Group B, Experiment 4
### Results of Fitting the Equation
$$P_t^e - P_{t-1}^e = \alpha + \beta \ (P_{t-1} - P_{t-1}^e)$$

| (1) Subject number | (2) $\alpha$ | (3) $\beta$ | (4) $s_\beta$ | (5) $r^2$ | (6) Sum squared residuals | (7) Residual reduction ratio |
|---|---|---|---|---|---|---|
| 1 | 5.05 | .672 | .340 | .395 | 962.62 | .00 |
| 2 | .99 | .486 | .153 | .628 | 40.95 | .65 |
| 3 | 1.12 | .368 | .185 | .399 | 62.24 | .61 |
| 4 | −.14 | .712 | .234 | .607 | 311.34 | .13 |
| 5 | −.33 | .618 | .145 | .752 | 57.53 | .27 |
| 6 | .22 | .141 | .381 | .022 | 218.49 | 30.79 |
| 7 | 4.70 | .823 | .207 | .726 | 236.95 | .01 |
| 8 | −3.75 | .750 | .055 | .969 | 4.50 | 2.88 |
| 9 | 1.10 | .709 | .205 | .666 | 176.46 | .01 |
| 10 | .55 | .603 | .167 | .686 | 55.34 | 4.62 |
| 11 | .176 | .507 | .076 | .880 | 10.49 | 4.61 |
| 12 | .08 | .538 | .204 | .537 | 148.00 | 1.08 |
| 13 | 1.84 | .613 | .157 | .718 | 65.37 | .68 |
| 14 | −1.29 | .685 | .142 | .795 | 61.56 | 11.99 |
| 15 | .42 | .348 | .122 | .574 | 23.00 | 7.24 |
| 16 | 1.41 | .564 | .072 | .911 | 9.29 | 1.23 |
| 17 | 1.51 | .432 | .332 | .220 | 517.91 | 3.22 |
| 18 | −.44 | .397 | .080 | .805 | 10.06 | .11 |
| 19 | .53 | −.100 | .132 | .088 | 14.59 | 9.07 |
| 20 | 0 | .500 | .239 | .422 | 74.00 | 10.51 |
| 21 | 2.22 | .626 | .180 | .668 | 113.68 | .00 |
| 22 | .32 | .184 | .199 | .125 | 54.26 | 12.10 |
| 23 | 1.72 | .970 | .068 | .971 | 15.02 | .42 |
| 24 | −1.07 | .393 | .051 | .910 | 3.43 | .20 |
| 25 | −.20 | .400 | .118 | .657 | 24.00 | .06 |
| Average | .73 | .518 | | | | |
| Group | .45 | .498 | .115 | .757 | 27.62 | .06 |

jected to a median test ([13], pp. 104–116). The median value of $\beta$ is about .70 for both groups combined. 20 in group A and only 5 in group B exceeded this value. Under the null hypothesis that these estimates were drawn from populations with the same median, the probability of obtaining this or a more unequal split between the two groups is below .001.

This result, together with the experience of rapid convergence in both sessions, suggests two tentative hypotheses:

1. *The greater the fluctuations in prices, the smaller will be the coefficient of adaptive expectations.*
2. *The coefficient will always adapt sufficiently to assure stability.*

We are postulating that the reaction coefficient for an individual or a group is not independent of experience in a particular market. The greater the past gyrations in price, the less faith will a supplier have in the most recent price. Thus, if a market is potentially unstable, the manifestations of that instability would be increasingly large price changes; but the larger the changes the relatively more conservative will be the suppliers in adjusting their expectations. This conservatism should lead to the convergence of market price to its equilibrium value.

Our point estimates of $\beta$ can be compared with the stability conditions (12) under the hypothesis of adaptive expectations. The following tabular presentation gives the ratio of $d/b$ for each of the two experiments and the corresponding restriction that $\beta$ would have to satisfy to assure stability. The least-squares estimates $\hat{\beta}$ taken from Tables VII and VIII are seen to satisfy these conditions in both cases.

|         | $d/b$ | *For Stability* | $\hat{\beta}$ |
|---------|-------|-----------------|---------------|
| Group A | .875  | $\beta < 1.067$ | .737          |
| Group B | 1.750 | $\beta < .727$  | .498          |

Tentative hypothesis 2 states that such a relationship will hold in other experiments of this type.

There is one more question to be considered with regard to the adaptive-expectations hypothesis. How much better would an unrestricted linear function of last period's expected price and last period's actual price explain the observations of current expected price? In other words, we shall consider the following maintained hypothesis:

(11b)   $P_t^e = \alpha + \beta_1 P_{t-1}^e + \beta_2 P_{t-1} + \eta_t.$

(11b) reduces to (11a) when $\beta_1 + \beta_2 = 1$.

Therefore, we shall test:

$$H_0 : \beta_1 + \beta_2 = 1, \quad \text{against}$$

$$H_1 : \beta_1 + \beta_2 \neq 1.$$

The sum of the squared residuals is one measure of how well a regression equation fits the observations of the dependent variable. If some linear function of independent variables improves the fit substantially, then the residuals would be generally smaller. Column (6) in Tables VII and VIII gives the sum of squared residuals under $H_0$.

Column (7) is a measure of how much the residuals were reduced when $H_0$ was not imposed. It is a ratio of the reduction in sum of squared residuals over the unrestricted mean square error. This is analogous to the $F$ ratio used in analyzing the significance of a new independent variable added to a multiple regression equation. Large values of such a ratio indicate significant improvement in fit and call for rejection of the null hypothesis that the new variable is unrelated to the dependent variable given the other independent variables.

In looking at the residual reduction ratios in column (7) of Tables VII and VIII, we see a number of fairly large values (4 or greater) and a few that are very large. These individual functions, however, do not add up to any consistent pattern in the aggregate. For each of the groups as a whole the improvement in fit was negligible. $H_0$ is unquestionably acceptable for both groups.

3. *The Extrapolative-Expectations Hypothesis.* Graphs of the observations of a number

TABLE IX

GROUP A, EXPERIMENT 3

Results of Fitting the Equation

$$P_t{}^e - P_{t-1} = \alpha - \rho \ (P_{t-1} - P_{t-2})$$

| (1) Subject Number | (2) $\alpha$ | (3) $\rho$ | (4) $s_\rho$ | (5) $r^2$ | (6) Sum squared residuals | (7) Residual reduction ratio |
|---|---|---|---|---|---|---|
| 1 | .91 | −.140 | .153 | .123 | 7.018 | .15 |
| 2 | .52 | −.366 | .207 | .343 | 12.822 | .00 |
| 3 | 0 | 0 | .164 | 0 | 8.000 | .00 |
| 4 | 2.40 | −.566 | .255 | .451 | 19.499 | .04 |
| 5 | −.01 | −.416 | .151 | .557 | 6.867 | .01 |
| 6 | 1.22 | −.451 | .383 | .188 | 43.850 | 1.06 |
| 7 | 8.51 | 1.218 | .716 | .325 | 153.504 | .45 |
| 8 | 12.59 | .546 | 1.169 | .035 | 408.612 | .08 |
| 9 | 5.20 | −.075 | .610 | .003 | 111.218 | 1.75 |
| 10 | 1.31 | .501 | .108 | .783 | 3.469 | 2.11 |
| 11 | 1.20 | −.075 | .155 | .038 | 7.218 | 3.25 |
| 12 | 4.97 | .356 | .063 | .842 | 1.183 | — |
| 13 | −.28 | .351 | .114 | .614 | 3.860 | 2.47 |
| 14 | 3.93 | .296 | .193 | .281 | 11.138 | 3.12 |
| 15 | −.19 | 1.303 | .362 | .683 | 39.288 | .08 |
| 16 | .45 | −.486 | .198 | .502 | 11.709 | .01 |
| 17 | −.67 | .125 | .096 | .224 | 2.717 | .12 |
| 18 | .10 | .160 | .095 | .321 | 2.717 | 1.44 |
| 19 | .48 | −.030 | .271 | .002 | 21.955 | .50 |
| 20 | .34 | .145 | .090 | .301 | 2.446 | .01 |
| 21 | 1.28 | .045 | 1.630 | .000 | 795.398 | .02 |
| 22 | .51 | .010 | .317 | .000 | 29.995 | .10 |
| 23 | 7.15 | 1.845 | .549 | .653 | 90.296 | .08 |
| 24 | 1.76 | .015 | .515 | .000 | 79.489 | .63 |
| 25 | .62 | −.206 | .177 | .183 | 9.393 | .67 |
| Average | 2.17 | .164 | | | | |
| Group | 2.17 | .164 | .129 | .213 | 4.978 | 1.71 |

of subjects disclosed that the extrapolative-expectations hypothesis should be modified, as was the adaptive-expectations hypothesis, to remove the constraint forcing the equation through the origin. Consequently, we estimated the coefficients $\alpha$ and $\rho$ of the following equation:

$$(13a) \quad P_t{}^e - P_{t-1} = \alpha - \rho \ (P_{t-1} - P_{t-2}) + \eta_t \ .$$

The results of estimation by the method of least squares are presented for Group A in Table IX and for Group B in Table X. These tables have the same format as Tables VII and VIII.

In this case the average and group esti-

mates of the coefficients were identical. Goodwin, [5], p. 192, demonstrated that the appropriate coefficients for the market as a whole will be the weighted average of differing individual coefficients. His starting point was the assumption that each supplier, or group of suppliers, forms his price expectations according to a linear extrapolative function where the coefficients can differ from one supplier to another. This assumption is questionable here in view of the poor fits obtained for many of the subjects.

An identical value for the average and aggregate estimates, however, is not a chance occurrence. Sufficient conditions in fact exist for perfect aggregation, a concept

TABLE X

GROUP B, EXPERIMENT 4

Results of Fitting the Equation

$$P_t{}^e - P_{t-1} = \alpha + \rho \ (P_{t-1} - P_{t-2})$$

| (1) Subject number | (2) $\alpha$ | (3) $\rho$ | (4) $s_\rho$ | (5) $r^2$ | (6) Sum squared residuals | (7) Residual reduction ratio |
|---|---|---|---|---|---|---|
| 1 | 7.62 | −.180 | .620 | .014 | 1096.13 | 9.66 |
| 2 | 1.86 | .486 | .045 | .951 | 5.78 | .73 |
| 3 | 2.01 | .346 | .211 | .310 | 126.59 | 13.29 |
| 4 | −.18 | .423 | .327 | .218 | 305.04 | 9.86 |
| 5 | −.71 | .391 | .134 | .587 | 51.24 | .00 |
| 6 | −2.40 | .799 | .188 | .752 | 100.32 | 10.69 |
| 7 | 5.74 | .322 | .276 | .185 | 216.77 | .07 |
| 8 | −4.85 | .193 | .028 | .890 | 2.20 | 1.44 |
| 9 | 1.57 | .420 | .231 | .355 | 151.80 | .06 |
| 10 | .51 | .352 | .130 | .549 | 48.50 | 2.31 |
| 11 | 3.03 | .371 | .079 | .785 | 17.99 | 10.63 |
| 12 | −.14 | .477 | .241 | .396 | 165.63 | 1.61 |
| 13 | 3.17 | .227 | .194 | .186 | 107.47 | 2.30 |
| 14 | −1.80 | .265 | .166 | .298 | 78.61 | .01 |
| 15 | .55 | .399 | .140 | .574 | 55.98 | 41.26 |
| 16 | 2.71 | .280 | .100 | .564 | 28.80 | 4.31 |
| 17 | 4.18 | .911 | .363 | .512 | 375.70 | 1.03 |
| 18 | −1.21 | .393 | .107 | .694 | 32.46 | 11.48 |
| 19 | −4.86 | .514 | .142 | .686 | 57.78 | 75.03 |
| 20 | .26 | .341 | .160 | .657 | 72.81 | 7.22 |
| 21 | 3.43 | .243 | .242 | .144 | 167.44 | 4.26 |
| 22 | −.03 | .629 | .079 | .913 | 17.99 | 8.48 |
| 23 | 1.76 | .018 | .073 | .010 | 15.35 | .77 |
| 24 | −3.19 | .410 | .046 | .930 | 6.03 | 3.20 |
| 25 | .57 | .432 | .116 | .697 | 38.69 | .13 |
| Average | 0.78 | .378 | | | | |
| Group | 0.78 | .378 | .129 | .590 | 47.24 | 3.62 |

analyzed by Theil [18]. The special feature here is that the independent variables take on exactly the same values for each individual decision function as they do for the assumed aggregate function.[6]

The estimates $\hat{\rho}$ of the extrapolative coefficient of expectations also satisfy stability conditions (14):

|         | $d/b$  | For Stability        | $\rho$ |
|---------|--------|----------------------|--------|
| Group A | .875   | $-.07 < \rho < 1.14$ | .164   |
| Group B | 1.750  | $.21 < \rho < .57$   | .378   |

The individual estimates of $\rho$ generally fall within the hypothesized range from 0 to 1 for Group B. With Group A, however, two-fifths of the subjects display negative coefficients. A negative value of $\rho$ implies a

------

[6] Let

$$Y_i = Xa_i + u_i \qquad i = 1, \cdots, m$$

characterize the assumed decision process for $m$ individuals. If there are $T$ periods of observations and $s$ independent variables, then:

$Y_i$ = a $(T \times 1)$ vector of observations of the dependent variable,

$X$ = a $(T \times s)$ matrix of observations of independent variables,

$a_i$ = an $(s \times 1)$ vector of parameters and,

$u_i$ = a $(T \times 1)$ vector of random variables.

Let $Y = \Sigma_{i=1}^{m} w_i Y_i$ = a $(T \times 1)$ vector of observations of the aggregate dependent variable. $w_i$ is the weight assigned to the $i$th individual in obtaining the aggregate. The macro-hypothesis states:

$$Y = Xa + u$$

and the least-squares estimate of $a$ is:

$$\hat{a} = (X'X)^{-1}X'Y$$

The estimates for individuals are:

$$\hat{a}_i = (X'X)^{-1}X'Y_i \qquad i = 1, \cdots, m$$

If these individual estimates are weighted by $w_i$ and summed, the result can be seen to be exactly $\hat{a}$ by means of elementary matrix algebra:

$$\sum_{i=1}^{m} w_i (X'X)^{-1} X'Y_i = (X'X^{-1}) X' \sum w_i Y_i$$

$$= (X'X)^{-1} X'Y$$

In our case, expected price is the $Y$ value and the weights are $1/m$, i.e., equal for all suppliers. Therefore, no matter how badly the assumed equations fit the data, the aggregate coefficient of expectations will coincide with the mean of the individual estimates.

tendency to extrapolate observed price changes in the same direction as the most recent change. The willingness of subjects to experiment with their quantity decisions when price changes are only moderate, noted in Section II, has shown up here as a negative $\rho$ for many subjects when this form of expectation function is assumed. Part of the difficulty may be our use of an implicit expected price rather than some better measure of what the subjects really thought might happen to price.

We next considered an unrestricted linear function of prices over the past two periods. The maintained hypothesis becomes:

$$(13b) \quad P_t^e = \alpha + \rho_1 P_{t-1} + \rho_2 P_{t-2} + \eta_t .$$

Acceptance of the extrapolative hypothesis (13a) would require acceptance of the following null hypothesis:

$$H_0: \rho_1 + \rho_2 = 1, \quad \text{against}$$

$$H_1: \rho_1 + \rho_2 \neq 1.$$

We again computed a residual reduction ratio, presented in column (7) of Tables IX and X. With Group B (Table X), quite a number of the ratios are substantial. The figure of 3.62 for the group as a whole does not appear negligible, but we do not have a value for this statistic that would define the critical region.

There is, however, an appropriate $t$-test. ([4], p. 178). Let $q = \hat{\rho}_1 + \hat{\rho}_2$ where $\hat{\rho}_1$ and $\hat{\rho}_2$ are the least-squares estimates of $\rho_1$ and $\rho_2$, respectively. Under the null hypothesis $H_0$ and the assumptions about the distribution of the random variable $\eta_t$, the following statistic has a $t$-distribution with five degrees of freedom:

$$t = (q - 1)/s_q$$

where $s_q$ is a sample standard deviation of $q$.

Using a symmetric two-tailed test such that the probability under $H_0$ is .05 that $t$ will fall in one tail or the other, the acceptance region with five degrees of freedom is:

$$-2.57 < t < 2.57$$

For Group B, $s_q = .323$ and the unrestricted estimates of the regression coefficients are:

$$\hat{\rho}_1 = .203, \qquad \hat{\rho}_2 = -.007.$$

From these figures,

$$t = \frac{.196 - 1.000}{.323} = \frac{-.804}{.323} = -2.49$$

$H_0$ may not be rejected for Group B, although $t$ is close to the critical region.

A similar calculation was performed for Group A. The results:

$$s_q = .792, \quad \hat{\rho}_1 = .168, \quad \hat{\rho}_2 = -.204$$

$$t = \frac{-.036 - 1.000}{.792} = \frac{-1.036}{.792} = -1.31.$$

$H_0$ is evidently acceptable for Group A, a conclusion supported by the relatively small ratios in column (7) of Table IX.

### IV. CONCLUDING REMARKS

The experiments reported in this paper were originally designed to see if it would be possible to observe cobweb-type behavior in an experimental setting. Such behavior did not materialize, and so the data were analyzed with other hypotheses in mind. These analytical efforts have been characterized by an inability to reject hypotheses. Part of Hooton's hypothesis was not borne out experimentally, but the reliability of the *ex ante* expectations data is so tenuous that even these results are far from decisive.

The main accomplishments of this project to date have been in uncovering problems in the design and administration of this sort of experiment, in developing a few new tentative hypotheses, and in devising tests of some hypotheses appearing in the literature.

The failure of these experimental markets to exhibit anything approaching cobweb-type behavior may be attributable to the compressed time span in which the sequence of decision periods were completed. Interviewers of farmers occasionally gain the impression that price expectations are formed on the basis of the most recent prevailing price. (Cf. Williams [19], p. 23.) In such real-life situations any changes occur over relatively long periods; in the experimental situation subjects are very much aware of all recent price changes. Undoubtedly, the vivid recollection of prices over a number of periods into the past contributed to the stability of these experimental markets. If so, better information about the typical effects of unusually high or low prices would be likely, as Dean and Heady ([2], p. 859) have suggested, to cause a decrease in the elasticity of the supply response and contribute to greater stability in agricultural markets.

Finally, our results provide some support for the rational-expectations hypothesis ([8], [10]) within a simple and unchanging market structure. While Tables III and V reveal a variety of individual responses to the same stimuli, the average response soon corrected for prior forecasting errors. Our hypothesis that the coefficient of adaptive expectations itself adapts to the market situation provides one theoretical reason for expecting rapid convergence no matter what the relative slopes of the supply and demand curves.

### REFERENCES

1. D. Davidson, P. Suppes, and S. Siegel, *Decision Making, An Experimental Approach* (Stanford Calif.: Stanford University Press, 1957).
2. G. W. Dean and E. O. Heady, "Changes in Supply Response and Elasticity for Hogs," *Journal of Farm Economics*, Vol. 40 (1958), pp. 845–860.
3. M. Ezekiel, "The Cobweb Theorem," *Quarterly Journal of Economics*, Vol. 52 (1938), pp. 255–280.
4. A. S. Goldberger, *Econometric Theory* (New York: John Wiley and Sons, 1964).
5. R. M. Goodwin, "Dynamical Coupling with Especial Reference to Markets Having Production Lags," *Econometrica*, Vol. 15 (1947), pp. 181–204.
6. F. G. Hooton, "Risk and the Cobweb Theorem," *Economic Journal*, Vol. 60 (1950), pp. 69–80.
7. L. A. Metzler, "The Nature and Stability of

Inventory Cycles," *Review of Economic Statistics*, Vol. 23 (1941), pp. 113–129.

8. E. S. Mills, *Price, Output and Inventory Policy* (New York: John Wiley, 1962).

9. F. Mosteller and P. Nogee, "An Experimental Measurement of Utility," *Journal of Political Economy*, Vol. 59 (1951), pp. 371–404.

10. J. F. Muth, "Rational Expectations and the Theory of Price Movements," *Econometrica*, Vol. 29 (1961), pp. 315–335.

11. M. Nerlove, "Adaptive Expectations and Cobweb Phenomena," *Quarterly Journal of Economics*, Vol. 73 (1958), pp. 227–240.

12. P. K. Newman, "A Note on 'Risk and The Cobweb Theorem'," *Economic Journal*, Vol. 61 (1951), pp. 334–341.

13. S. Siegel, *Nonparametric Statistics* (New York: McGraw-Hill, 1956).

14. S. Siegel, "Theoretical Models of Choice and Strategy Behavior: Stable State Behavior in the Two-Choice Uncertain Outcome Situa-

tion," *Psychometrika*, Vol. 24 (1959), pp. 303–316.

15. V. L. Smith, "An Experimental Study of Competitive Market Behavior," *Journal of Political Economy*, Vol. 70 (1962), pp. 111–137.

16. V. L. Smith, "Effect of Market Organization on Competitive Equilibrium," *Quarterly Journal of Economics*, Vol. 78 (1964), pp. 181–201.

17. V. L. Smith, "Experimental Auction Markets and the Walrasian Hypothesis," *Journal of Political Economy*, Vol. 73 (1965), pp. 387–393.

18. H. Theil, *Linear Aggregation of Economic Relations* (Amsterdam: North-Holland Publishing Company, 1954).

19. D. B. Williams, "Price Expectations and Reaction to Uncertainty by Farmers in Illinois," *Journal of Farm Economics*, Vol. 33 (1951), pp. 20–39.

# [4]

## SYMPOSIUM ON EXPERIMENTAL ECONOMICS

# On Experimental Research in Oligopoly[1,2]

### 1. INTRODUCTION

Economics has not generally been regarded as an experimental science, although in recent years this view has changed a little. The first experiment in economics of which this writer is aware was conducted by E. H. Chamberlin [2] and appeared in 1948 in the *Journal of Political Economy*. The next effort, appearing in the same journal several years later, is the utility experiment of Mosteller and Nogee [12]. In the past decade the amount of experimental research in economics has increased markedly, although the volume could by no means be called large. Some examples are the experiments in competitive markets of V. L. Smith [15, 16, 17], the utility experiments of Davidson, Suppes and Siegel [3], Dolbear [4] and Yaari [18], the bilateral monopoly experiments of Fouraker and Siegel [6, 14], and the oligopoly experiments of Hoggatt [10, 11], Fouraker and Siegel [6] and Friedman [7, 8, 9].

This paper is concerned with a detailed review and discussion of a group of oligopoly experiments (Hoggatt [10, 11], Fouraker and Siegel [6] and Friedman [7]). These experiments are all concerned with the same economic question: does standard oligopoly theory (e.g., Cournot's) predict behaviour in markets in which the usual textbook assumptions are met? Though this may seem a useless enterprise (why worry about whether an " unrealistic " theory predicts behaviour in an " unrealistic " situation?), it is far from being so. Indeed all theory is unrealistic by nature. Its value lies in organizing the mind in an insightful way and in giving manageable, comprehensible models which can predict behaviour in a complex world. Oligopoly theory is very hard to test empirically, not only because of the complexities of modern industry, but also because much useful data is owned by firms who cherish their right to privacy.

Experimental testing of oligopoly theory is of interest for several reasons. First, in the laboratory an artificial market may be created which satisfies the assumptions of standard theory (e.g. each firm has only its own quantity as a decision variable, no randomness enters the profit functions, a firm knows its own cost and demand functions, etc.). Surely if theory fails to predict behaviour in a market meeting these assumptions, one has strong evidence the theory is not valid. Second, there is an interaction between theoretical and empirical research. Perhaps experimental results which cannot be explained by existing theory are suggestive of new lines of theoretical development. Finally, as a social scientist, the economist has a general interest in understanding decision making by individuals. Experiments involving human subjects making decisions are relevant to this end.

[1] This research was supported by a Junior Faculty Fellowship from Yale University and also by a grant from the National Science Foundation.
[2] I wish to thank Professor William Brainard, Michael Farrell, Lawrence Fouraker, Austin Hoggatt and an anonymous referee for helpful comments. None of them, however, can be assumed to approve the final result.

2 C

The several experiments reviewed below deal with " non-cooperative " oligopoly, that is, oligopoly where the subjects have no verbal or written communication with one another. The only information a subject has when he makes a decision are the previous decisions he and his rivals have made. He is informed of his rivals' decisions for the current period only after he has made his own.

In discussing the experiments, attention will, of course, focus on the economic hypotheses which they test; however, the experimental procedures will also come under close scrutiny. The procedures are of interest because they bear on the validity of the results, and because experimental techniques are not familiar to most economists.

## 2. DESCRIPTION OF AND COMMENTS ON THE EXPERIMENTS

### 2.1. *General Characteristics*

There are a few general characteristics which are identical in all the experiments, and certain others which differ in very specific ways. Concerning the former: (*a*) Each subject represented a single firm in a market with two, three or four firms. (*b*) Each firm

TABLE I

|  | Hoggatt 1 | F-S | Friedman | Hoggatt 2 |
|---|---|---|---|---|
| **Were subjects paid their actual profits?** | No | Yes | Yes | No |
| **How many games did each subject play?** | 1 | 1 | 6 or 9 sequentially | 2 simultaneously |
| **In what form was profit information given?** | Algebraic profit function | Payoff matrix | Payoff matrix | Algebraic profit function |
| **What information known on profits?** | Incomplete | Some complete, some incomplete | Complete | Complete |

had exactly one decision variable. In some experiments this was price, in some, output level. (*c*) Demand functions were always linear, as were marginal cost curves. (*d*) In all the experiments, subjects played in " games " which lasted for many " periods ".[1] In each period, subjects would make their decisions (choose price or output, as the case may be), each in ignorance of what his rivals were choosing. After all had chosen, each would be informed of the decisions taken by the rivals, and the next period would commence. During a single game, a subject knew that his rivals would be the same identical individuals, and the payoff matrix (or other information) he received would be unchanged. Subjects did not know the identity of their rivals. (*e*) There was no communication allowed between subjects. (That is, no written messages or conversations.) The only information to accumulate to a subject in the course of a game was the past decisions of the rivals.

Systematic differences between experiments were: (*a*) whether subjects were paid their actual profits, (*b*) the length of time subjects spent in the experiment, (*c*) the form in which market information was given and (*d*) the information state. The two information states are " complete " and " incomplete ". Complete information is the case in which the subject knows the profits to each firm in the industry, corresponding to a given set of choices. Incomplete information describes the condition in which the subject knows only the profits to himself. Table I summarizes these differences. Thus, for example, F-S subjects were paid their actual game earnings, each subject was in only one game, information was provided in the form of a payoff matrix, and both complete and incomplete information states were used in their experiments.

[1] Fouraker and Siegel did have some " one shot games " in which subjects had only one decision period which they played for real stakes. None of these is reviewed in the present paper.

ON EXPERIMENTAL RESEARCH IN OLIGOPOLY                401

## 2.2. *Hoggatt* 1

2.2.1. *Description.* Hoggatt's first experiment [10] employed nine of his University of California (Berkeley) business school colleagues, in three triopolies, as subjects. The games were played under incomplete information with each subject being given the industry demand curve and his own cost curve. The demand and total cost functions had the form:

$$p_t = \alpha_0 - \alpha_1(q_{1t} + q_{2t} + q_{3t}) - \alpha_2(q_{1,t-1} + q_{2,t-1} + q_{3,t-1}) - \alpha_3(q_{1,t-2} + q_{2,t-2} + q_{3,t-2}),$$

$$C_{it} = \beta_{i0} + \beta_{i1}q_{it} + \beta_{i2}q_{it}^2, \quad i = 1, 2, 3,$$

where:

$p_t$ is the industry price in period $t$,

$q_{it}$ is the output of the $i$th firm in period $t$,

$\alpha_0 > 0, \alpha_1 > \alpha_2 > \alpha_3 > 0, \beta_{ij} > 0, i = 1, 2, 3, j = 0, 1, 2.$

Thus demand is modelled in a way which causes an increase in the output of period $t$ to have a depressing effect on the prices of the next two periods ($p_{t+1}$ and $p_{t+2}$) as well as on the current price ($p_t$).

The three yardsticks against which the behaviour of the firm is measured are [10, page 106]:

*Generalized Cournot Behaviour Assumption I:* The Manager of each firm assumes on day $t$ that the combined outputs of other firms will be the same in the current period as they were in the previous period. Output is set so that profit on day $t$ will be maximized if the assumption is correct.

*Generalized Cournot Behaviour Assumption II:* The Manager of each firm assumes that the combined outputs of the other firms will be the same in the current and the next two future periods as they were in the previous period. Output level is set on day $t$ so that if it is constant for two future periods, and if the assumption of fixed opponents' outputs is correct, then profit on day $t+2$ will be maximized.

The third yardstick is joint industry profit maximization.

The three games ran, respectively, for 13, 16 and 20 periods, and the firms chose output levels tolerably close to the short-run Cournot levels (Cournot I, above). This experiment is of great interest because it is the first oligopoly experiment to be reported and it is the only one to date in which there is a behavioural hypothesis in which explicit consideration is given to profits in a future period.

2.2.2. *Comments.* The prime weaknesses of the experiment relate to experimental control and the motivation of the subjects. Concerning the first, subjects were not confined to a laboratory and isolated from one another during the experiment; rather, they made decisions every day or few days, leaving them in a mailbox and picking up their results from another mailbox. As a result there is no experimental control insuring that the subjects did not discuss the experiments with one another, although the results are hardly those one would expect from collusion. Even without collusion, the mere fact that subjects *could* talk to one another, and assorted others, during the course of the experiment adds an uncontrolled element (*a*) the importance of which is very difficult to assess and (*b*) which could have been easily controlled by a different design.

These subjects were not paid money in proportion to their profits, which raises the question of what objectives they might have had in the game. Under incomplete information, the subject lacks opportunity to formulate an objective function involving the profits of rivals. Furthermore, with their training as professional economists, they are aware of the more popular oligopoly formulations. Both these influences should incline them toward a simple, Cournot-type of behaviour.

In general, to refrain from paying subjects their actual profits is to refrain from building into the experiment a real-world incentive which is easily duplicated in the laboratory. The unwanted effects on behaviour which may result are best illustrated by considering complete information oligopoly—where subjects know their rival's profit functions. Where profits are not paid, the subject will not cherish a marginal " dollar " of profit as if it were a dollar in his pocket. Indeed the absolute level of his profits is without meaning. The subject will be in a parlour game situation where success is judged by how well he does in relation to his rivals. Compare the subject whose profits are low, but are greater than those of any rival, with the subjects whose profits are twice as high, but lower than those of any rival. The first will regard himself a success, the second a failure. Giving real money payoffs to subjects will moderate, perhaps completely over-shadow, this parlour game influence.[1]

Generally the behaviour which maximizes profit does not maximize the extent to which one's profit exceeds his rivals'. Indeed pursuit of the latter objective requires a sacrifice of one's profit level.

The experimental situation should speak for itself. As the intent of the experiment is to see whether and in what manner subjects react to a profit incentive in an oligopoly setting, the best experiment is one which provides a real profit incentive in its basic design. Then, subjects are merely given instructions which describe the features of the experiment without reference to how they *should* behave; and the experimenter records and analyzes the resulting behaviour.

The " long-run " Cournot behaviour, designed to maximize profits in the second period hence, is a bothersome notion. It appears highly arbitrary and hard to defend. Why maximize tomorrow's profit and pay no attention to today's? A much more natural notion would be that of maximizing the sum of profits over the current and next two periods, with the firm assuming his rivals will continue indefinitely their outputs of the preceding period, and choosing his current and next two output levels so as to accomplish this maximization (with the firm *not* required to assume it must hold its output constant for three periods).[2]

In summary, it is difficult to guage the success of this experiment. In part, its success depends upon how its purpose is viewed. As a demonstration that experimental research is possible in oligopoly, it is surely successful despite the shortcomings which have been noted. The importance of paying profits to subjects is minimized by the incomplete information state, and the problem that subjects could have colluded because they were not confined to a laboratory is not of concern here because Hoggatt's subjects were his colleagues, whom he could surely trust. These results form the first experimental support of the hypothesis that the Cournot solution is typical of behaviour in incomplete information games.

### 2.3. *Fouraker-Siegel*

2.3.1. *Description*. Fouraker and Siegel (F-S) performed ten oligopoly experiments and half a dozen bilateral monopoly experiments which are described in their second book [6]. Their first book [14] was concerned only with bilateral monopoly. Their experiments are characterized by the virtues of extreme simplicity of design, a high degree of control and excellent documentation of their procedures and results. The subjects were college undergraduate students, who were paid their actual earnings for participating in the experiment.

Among the 10 oligopoly experiments were eight which exhaust all possible com-binations of (*a*) complete and incomplete information, (*b*) duopoly or triopoly and (*c*)

----

[1] No doubt the desired tradeoff between absolute income and one's position *vis-à-vis* rivals will vary from one person to another. This relationship would be a most interesting one to explore experimentally with the aid of a psychologist.

[2] More sensible still is the assumption that the firm seeks to maximize a discounted stream of profits extending from the current period until the firm will cease to operate.

## ON EXPERIMENTAL RESEARCH IN OLIGOPOLY     403

Cournot or Bertrandesque market. The crucial difference between Cournot and Bertrand markets is that the latter have discontinuities in demand for the output of a firm and the former do not.[1] Only the four standard Cournot experiments will be discussed here. All the F-S experiments are based on demand functions of the form:

$$p_t = \alpha_0 - \alpha_1(q_{1t} + q_{2t} + q_{3t}) \quad \text{for triopoly,}$$
$$p_t = \alpha_0 - \alpha_1(q_{1t} + q_{2t}) \quad \text{for duopoly.}$$

Costs are nil, so profit for a firm is

$$\pi_{it} = p_t q_{it} \quad i = 1, 2 \quad \text{for duopoly,}$$
$$i = 1, 2, 3 \quad \text{for triopoly.}$$

Information was given to the subjects in the form of payoff matrices which afforded each a choice of 25 output levels (the integers from 8 to 32). Under incomplete information, payoff matrices gave profit to the subject corresponding to any output he might choose and any total output the rivals might choose. Under complete information, the subject's matrix also gave total profit to the rivals corresponding to the choices which might be made.[2]

There were 16 incomplete information duopoly games, 11 triopoly, 16 complete information duopoly and 11 triopoly. The precise demand functions were, in cents:

$$p_t = 2 \cdot 4 - 0 \cdot 04(q_{1t} + q_{2t}) \quad \text{for duopoly,}$$
$$p_t = 2 \cdot 4 - 0 \cdot 04(q_{1t} + q_{2t} + q_{3t}) \quad \text{for triopoly.}$$

Costs were assumed nil.

F-S singled out three solution concepts as being of special interest. There are (a) the " Cournot solution " which is found by assuming each firm seeks to maximize its own profit with respect to its own decision variable

$$\frac{\partial \pi_i}{\partial q_i} = 0, \quad i = 1, ..., n;$$

(b) the " joint maximum " which is found by assuming each firm seeks to maximize total industry profits with respect to its decision variable

$$\frac{\partial \Sigma_j \pi_j}{\partial q_i} = 0;$$

and (c) the " rivalistic solution " which is found by assuming the firm seeks to maximize the excess of its profit over the average profit of its rivals

$$\frac{\partial}{\partial q_i}\left(\pi_1 - \frac{1}{n-1}\sum_{j \neq i}\pi_j\right) = 0.$$

---

[1] In the Cournot experiments, quantities are the decision variables; however, in the Bertrand case prices are chosen by the firms, with the following understanding: (1) Only the firm charging the lowest price has any sales, (2) his sales are given by the industry demand relationship, and (3) if two or three firms tie for low price they share industry sales equally. Obviously for a firm, a discontinuity in the profit function occurs where its price is equal to the lowest of the rivals. At prices above this level, sales are zero and profit equals zero. At the rival's price, profit jumps to half the profit previously enjoyed by the low priced rival and, if price is lowered just below the rival's profit doubles. The original hint for this model is found in Bertrand [1], and further analysis appears in Edgeworth [5] and Shubik [13]. The Bertrand games will not be discussed further.

[2] There were two additional duopoly experiments which are of a very strange nature. In one of them the subjects are told that he who makes more profit than his rival shall win an extra $8.00, over and above his regular game winnings. This extra prize so greatly overshadowed the potential ordinary game winnings that a subject interested in simply maximizing his own gain would behave in the game as if he (apart from the $8.00 prize) wished to maximize the excess of his profit over the profit of his rival. The second experiment of the pair is intended to induce cooperative behaviour by giving a prize of $4.00 to each subject if the pair attain a joint profit of approximately the joint maximum. Like the other experiment, this induces the desired behaviour in only the most trivial sense—by making it become indistinguishable from non-cooperative behaviour.

Table II gives the output levels which correspond to these solutions for the models used by F-S. All games in the four experiments ran for 25 periods of which the first three were designated " practice ", and for which subjects were paid no profits.

The principal hypotheses tested by F-S in these experiments are: (*a*) industries and individuals under incomplete information will tend to choose the Cournot solution output levels (40 and 20 for duopoly, and 45 and 15 for triopoly), and (*b*) the variability of responses under complete information is greater than under incomplete.[1]  Apparently the rationaliza-

TABLE II
*Output quantity*

|  | Duopoly | | Triopoly | |
|---|---|---|---|---|
|  | Firm | Industry | Firm | Industry |
| Rivalistic (R) | 30 | 60 | 20 | 60 |
| Cournot (M) | 20 | 40 | 15 | 45 |
| Joint maximum (C) | 15 * | 30 | 10 * | 30 |

* The joint maximum is achieved so long as total industry output is 30, irrespective of how the total is allocated among the firms.

tion for the latter is that under incomplete information, those subjects with a rivalistic or cooperative bent are prevented from exercising it due to ignorance of their rival's profit functions.

The hypothesis (*a*) is confirmed.  Using as data the output decisions for the penultimate period, the mean observed output levels are: 20·9 for individual duopolists, 16·0 for individual triopolists, 41·8 for duopoly games, and 48·1 for triopoly games.  Also a tabulation was made, reproduced in Table III, in which each individual and each game

TABLE III
*Observed cooperativeness*

|  | Individual | | | Game | | |
|---|---|---|---|---|---|---|
|  | R | M | C | R | M | C |
| Complete information duopoly | 9½ | 12½ | 10 | 3½ | 7½ | 5 |
| Complete information triopoly | 15 | 15 | 3 | 6 | 5 | 0 |
| Incomplete information duopoly | 4 | 26 | 2 | 2 | 14 | 0 |
| Incomplete information triopoly | 9 | 20 | 4 | 2 | 9 | 0 |

was classified as *R*, *M* or *C* according to whether the decision of the next to last period was nearest the *R*, *M* or *C* output level.

The specific hypotheses on Cournot behaviour (item *a*) were two: (1) As the individual Cournot output for duopoly (20) exceeds that for triopoly (15), while the joint Cournot output for duopoly (40) is less than triopoly (45); it was hypothesized that the observed individual mean for duopoly (20·9) would be significantly larger than the triopoly mean (16·0), and the joint duopoly mean (41·8) would be significantly less than the joint triopoly mean (48·1).  These hypotheses were confirmed by Student " t " tests. (2) The second hypothesis is that, in the absence of systematic preferences by subjects, there would be a

---

[1] F-S also tested hypotheses, not reviewed below, relating to subjects' propensity to prefer outcomes in which all have equal profits.  These are discussed under the heading " Level of Aspiration " [6, pp. 151-154].

## ON EXPERIMENTAL RESEARCH IN OLIGOPOLY

probability of 1/2 that a given game will (in the next to last period) exhibit total output nearer the Cournot level than either the rivalistic or cooperative. At significance levels of 0·002 for duopoly and 0·035 for triopoly (or greater) it is concluded that observed behaviour is not due to chance, and therefore systematic preference is indicated for the Cournot output.[1]

A fault common to both the preceding tests is that they employ the wrong data. The analysis is based on the assumption that Cournot maximizing behaviour by an individual is the same as choosing the Cournot equilibrium point output. This is only so if rivals are expected to choose Cournot equilibrium output also. The same applies to rivalistic and cooperative behaviour. For example, consider Cournot maximizing behaviour for firm 1 in a duopoly. His profit function is

$$\pi_{1t} = q_{1t}(2\cdot4 - 0\cdot04q_{1t} - 0\cdot04q_{2t}),$$

and his estimate of his profit for period $t$ is

$$\pi^e_{1t} = q_{1t}(2\cdot4 - 0\cdot04q_{1t} - 0\cdot04q^e_{2t}),$$

where $q^e_{2t}$ is his estimate of the output level his rival will choose in period $t$. His estimated profit is maximized when:

$$\frac{\partial \pi^e_{1t}}{\partial q_{1t}} = 2\cdot4 - 0\cdot08q_{1t} - 0\cdot04q^e_{2t} = 0$$

$$= 60 - 2q_{1t} - q^e_{2t}$$

or, equivalently, when

$$q_{1t} = 30 - 0\cdot5q^e_{2t}.$$

Thus, the for Cournot maximizer, the appropriate output level depends on the expected output level of the rival, and, it is the Cournot equilibrium output of 20 if, and only if, the rival is also expected to choose 20.

The F-S procedure for classifying the decisions of individuals implies that whatever type of behaviour a subject decides to exhibit, he expects his rival to do the same *in the current period*. This makes sense if a subject is first presumed to estimate the behaviour he expects his rivals to exhibit and then mimic that behaviour himself. The latter appears an absurd way to behave, unless the subjects are assumed to have an obsession of making equal profits.

One alternative is to assume the subject takes the preceding period output levels of its rivals as his estimate of what they will do in the current period. Then a Cournot response is one which is nearer the Cournot level than the rivalistic or cooperative, with the three points calculated under the relevant output assumptions. Under this procedure Cournot behaviour for duopoly is given by:

$$q_{1t} = 30 - 0\cdot5q_{2,t-1}.$$

Rivalistic behaviour is given by:

$$\frac{\partial(\pi_{1t} - \pi_{2t})}{\partial q_{1t}} = 2\cdot4 - 0\cdot08q_{1t} = 0,$$

or

$$q_{1t} = 30,$$

[1] F-S did not follow the usual procedure of selecting a significance level in advance of performing tests. Instead, they reported, for each test, the significance level for which the null hypothesis would be marginally accepted.

and co-operative by:

$$\frac{\partial(\pi_{1t}+\pi_{2t})}{\partial q_{1t}} = 2\cdot4 - 0\cdot08q_{1t} - 0\cdot08q_{2,t-1} = 0,$$

or

$$q_{1t} = 30 - q_{2,t-1}.$$

Table IV contains the same information as Table III for individual responses, with the classification made on this basis. A marked increase in Cournot behaviour and decrease in cooperative behaviour is seen in Table IV, as compared with Table III.

To test the hypothesis (*b*), F-S first calculate the standard deviation of total game output, for the next to last period, across all games of an experiment. They then test whether the standard deviation for complete information duopoly exceeds that of incomplete information duopoly, and similarly for triopoly. The hypothesis is confirmed that standard deviations are greater for complete information.

TABLE IV

*Alternative classification of observed cooperativeness*

|  | Individual | | |
|---|---|---|---|
|  | R | M | C |
| Complete information duopoly | $9\frac{1}{2}$ | $15\frac{1}{2}$ | 7 |
| Complete information triopoly | 14 | 19 | 0 |
| Incomplete information duopoly | 4 | 26 | 2 |
| Incomplete information triopoly | 9 | 23 | 1 * |

\* This observation is ambiguous. While the output choice of eight units is nearer M than C, it was the lowest available output level.

2.3.2. *Comments.* Many issues are raised by reflecting on the F-S experiments: (*a*) They make little use of their data. (*b*) Are students appropriate as subjects? (*c*) Can relevant, useful, results be gotten when subjects participate in only one game each? (*d*) Their behavioural hypotheses are quite crude. These will be discussed in turn.

(*a*) In each game some twenty-five observations are generated. Most hypotheses used only the next to last. This procedure naturally raises questions: How many periods of play are necessary before a " learning phase " is over and some sort of stable-state equilibrium behaviour begins? Could the experiment shed light on the learning phase? Are there characteristics peculiar to an individual which may be seen in the learning phase and which give an indication of how he will behave in the stable state?

Of course, knowing the length of the learning phase suggests a minimum length for the game if one wants observations on settled behaviour. The minimum differences to be expected between learning phase and later behaviour are: (i) The random component in learning behaviour is likely to be larger because the subject's aims are not as well defined as they will eventually become. (ii) To the extent that learning phase behaviour has regular features, one would expect these to change over time as learning proceeds. One characteristic of stable equilibrium behaviour should be that it is characterized by features which remain constant over time. For example, the quantity choice of firm 1 of a duopoly might be described by a reaction function:

$$q_{1t} = f(q_{2,t-1}, \xi_t).$$

The reaction function gives the decision of firm 1, in the current period, as a function of his rival's decision in the preceding period and a random variable. One would expect, as the learning phase proceeds, that the function, $f$ will change, and the role of $\xi_t$ will diminish in importance.

It would be most interesting to see experiments which distinguished the two phases and tested hypotheses relevant to each.

F-S did not include learning hypotheses among those which they sought to test. As a research strategy, it does make sense to attempt first an understanding of equilibrium behaviour because that is probably the easier task and its solution facilitates the study of learning.

(b) The obvious questions about the student sample (or about Hoggatt's faculty sample) is whether they are drawn randomly and from the " right " population. F-S generally sought male volunteer subjects who were told they " could make some money by participating in a research project." [1]  Are students drawn in this way typical of the male student population or are they different because they wanted to earn money or be in a research project? Perhaps these volunteers are more hard working.  Are students typical of the population of businessmen?  They are both younger and more uniform in age and education.  Perhaps there are relevant, singular traits which are typical of business-men and not of students.  Does the businessman's years of experience change him in ways relevant to this sort of experiment?  It would be a mistake to pretend to answer these questions here.  They are empirical questions to be answered by appropriate, well-designed studies.  All the studies reviewed here retain interest, whether or not different samples reveal different behaviour, as studies of human decision making.

(c) Each subject participated in only one game, probably of an hour's duration.  As businessmen may be assumed quite familiar and accustomed to their usual circumstances, the appropriate thing is to have data from subjects who are used to theirs—who have got a feeling for the game, as a businessman has a feeling for his business.  The experience of the present writer suggests that for games of the approximate complexity of these reviewed here, two to four hours of play must elapse before a subject gets fully accustomed to his circumstances.  Striking evidence in [8] shows behaviour changing for approximately three hours and stable for the next seven in an experiment which consisted of two five hour sessions on consecutive nights with the same subjects.  The experimenter ought consciously to decide whether he wishes to study the behaviour of novice subjects or subjects who have some feel for the particular experimental environment in which they are placed.

Considering the comments of paragraph (a), above, raises the question whether there may be two sorts of learning relevant to the subject who plays many games.  The first is that which gives him general understanding of and feel for the experimental situation, and the second is that which gives him a sense of how his particular rivals of the moment make their decisions.  These may be termed " experimental " learning and " within game " learning.  Surely that latter proceeds more quickly, the more experimental learning the subject has experienced.  Loosely speaking, experimental learning is like acquiring general business experience, while within game learning is like gaining experience in a particular new market.

(d) They admit of three types of behaviour, $R$, $M$ and $C$.  $R$ and $M$ are polar extremes of cooperativeness, while $M$, in between, is non-cooperative.  Below, in section 2.4, a somewhat less rigid alternative is suggested.

On balance, the F-S experiments are exciting, disappointing and very suggestive. After the very great care with which they designed their experiments, chose and handled their subjects, and reported all they have done, it is a let-down to see the very crude and indirect nature of the hypotheses they test, and to see how little use they make of their

---

[1] See [6], pages 22 and 14.

data as well as how little attention they pay to determining which data they really want. To call down F-S for these shortcomings is, perhaps, to criticize them for not seeing before they ran their experiments certain things which are much more clearly perceived after seeing what they have done.

Whether or not their experiments are ideal, they are designed to facilitate testing the hypotheses they set out to test in simple and uncluttered ways. Their results provide a further corroboration of the hypothesis that the Cournot solution will prevail under incomplete information. The great dispersion of results under complete information suggests that personal characteristics may play a role in determining equilibrium behaviour, and that the most appropriate solution concept may be one for which the outcome is not unique.

### 2.4. *Friedman*

2.4.1. *Description.* The Friedman experiments [7] were designed and executed after F-S and with a knowledge of their work. In many respects F-S techniques and procedures were copied: Student subjects were used and were paid their actual profit. Subjects entered and left the laboratory singly so they would not see fellow subjects. Instructions were given in written form so that the precise instruction each subject received could be fully reported in the research report. Subjects were in single decision variable games which could be represented by payoff matrices.

These experiments differed from F-S in several important respects. They are confined to oligopoly and, although price was the decision variable, the models were not Bertrandesque, so there were no discontinuities in the demand relations. All games were the complete information variety, as F-S seemed to have strong results for the incomplete case.

The Friedman experiments were designed to have each subject play in many (6 or 9) games. The games were sequential with the payoff matrices and grouping of subjects into games varying from game to game. While a subject never knew who his rivals were, he did know that he had the same rivals all through a game, and that he would have new ones from game to game. The original intent of having a subject play in many games was to provide sufficient data so that the behaviour of each subject, as a function of the behaviour exhibited by his rivals, could be characterized individually.

The payoff matrices were derived from the following demand and total cost relations:

demand:

$$q_{it} = \alpha_0 - \alpha_1 p_{it} + \frac{\alpha_2}{n-1} \sum_{j \neq i} p_{jt} \quad i = 1, ..., n;$$

total cost:

$$C_{it} = \beta_0 + \beta_1 q_{it} + \beta_2 q_{it}^2,$$

$$\alpha_0, \alpha_1, \alpha_2, \beta_1, \beta_2 > 0, \quad \alpha_1 > \alpha_2,$$

$$\pi_{it} = p_{it} q_{it} - C_{it} = \pi_i(p_{it}, \sum_{j \neq i} p_{jt}).$$

Thus, as with F-S, the firms were symmetric (if each makes the same decision, profits are identical for all). $n$, the number of firms, was 2, 3 or 4.

The principal analysis was based on an index of cooperativeness: Consider the following for the $i$th firm:

$$F_{it} = \pi_{it} + \rho_i \sum_{j \neq i} \pi_{jt}.$$

If a firm chose its price so as to maximize $F_{it}$, $\rho_i$ could be regarded as its index of co-operativeness. An index of zero corresponds to a Cournot, or non-cooperative, maximizer.

## ON EXPERIMENTAL RESEARCH IN OLIGOPOLY                           409

Values greater than zero show a positive degree of cooperativeness, with $\rho_i = 1$ corresponding to a firm seeking to maximize industry profits. Negative values correspond to various degrees of rivalistic behaviour, with $\rho_i = \dfrac{-1}{n-1}$ being the rivalistic behaviour notion of F-S. When $\rho_i = \dfrac{-1}{n-1}$, the firm seeks to maximize the excess of its own profit. over average profit of its rivals.[1]

If it is assumed that a firm believes its rivals will repeat in the current period the prices they charged in the preceding period, then the price the firm should charge in period $t$ is implicitly defined by:

$$\frac{\partial \pi_i(p_{it}, \sum_{j \neq i} p_{j,t-1})}{\partial p_{it}} + \rho_i \sum_{j \neq i} \frac{\partial \pi_j(p_{j,t-1}, p_{it} + \sum_{k \neq i, j} p_{k,t-1})}{\partial p_{it}} = 0.$$

Friedman assumed that the firm might have a different value of $\rho_i$ in each period and that $\rho_{it}$ depended on the $\rho_{j,t-1}$ ($j \neq i$). The degree of cooperativeness exhibited by a subject in period $t$ was assumed to depend on the cooperativeness shown by his rivals in period $t-1$. Clearly, if the $\rho_{j,t-1}$ ($j \neq i$) are known, and it is assumed the firm maximizes in the way described, $\rho_{it}$ is given by:

$$\rho_{it} = \frac{-\partial \pi_i(p_{it}, \sum_{j \neq i} p_{j,t-1})/\partial p_{it}}{\sum_{j \neq i} \partial \pi_j(p_{j,t-1}, p_{it} + \sum_{k \neq i, j} p_{k,t-1})/\partial p_{it}}.$$

The relationship, whose parameters were estimated separately, for each subject, is a variant of:

$$\rho_{it} = \alpha_i + \frac{\beta_i}{n-1} \sum_{j \neq i} \rho_{j,t-1} + \varepsilon_{it}.$$

Where $\varepsilon$ is a random disturbance term with zero mean.

The data used were from the ten periods preceding the final period of each game. Earlier periods (the first ten to fifteen) were not used on the premise that the subjects required this time to get used to each new game. The latter assumption appears inconsistent with the validity of the estimated relationship, because it is assumed the parameters $\alpha_i$ and $\beta_i$ do not depend on how the rivals choose their $\rho$ values. If the $\alpha$ and $\beta$ of a subject were thought to depend on the $\alpha$'s and $\beta$'s of the rivals, one might wish to exclude the early periods of each game when subjects would be assumed to be sizing up one another and deciding on appropriate parameter values. Thus consistency would appear to demand that Friedman either (a) assume $\alpha$ and $\beta$ for a subject depend on the $\alpha$'s and $\beta$'s of rivals, and estimate a different $\alpha$ and $\beta$ for each subject for each game (which justifies using only the later periods of each game to estimate the behavioural relationships) or (b) assume $\alpha$ and $\beta$ are not dependent on the behaviour of rivals, in which case there is no reason to assume the values of $\alpha$ and $\beta$ should differ early in a game from their later values. Friedman made the assumption (b), yet did not use the data from the early part of the games.

The justification for Friedman's formulation is not that one firm really cares about the profits accruing to its rival, but, rather, that the firm believes it will make more profits in the long run if it allows its cooperativeness index to be higher, the higher are the indices of its rivals. This could be valid if the firm believed the rivals' indices were positively related to its own. Then it would seem likely that a firm would select its $\alpha$ and $\beta$ as some function of the $\alpha$'s and $\beta$'s of its rivals.

---

[1] If $\rho_i = \dfrac{-1}{n-1}$ for all $i$, the oligopoly game with the $F_i$ as payoff functions would be a zero sum $n$-person game. I point this out because zero sum games do not often arise naturally in economics.

The questions raised above about Friedman's analysis are too much for his data to bear. Its proper settlement would require a new, and well thought out, experiment. In part this is because in his experiments, certain parameters of the profit functions, as well as the grouping of subjects into games, were changing from game to game. Thus it is impossible to tell whether $\alpha$ and $\beta$ for a subject change from game to game due to changes in game parameters or due to differences in the $\alpha$'s and $\beta$'s exhibited by rivals. If $\alpha$ and $\beta$ did not change from game to game, weak support would be gained for the hypothesis that neither rival behaviour nor game parameters affect the $\alpha$ and $\beta$ of a subject. This strange conclusion is not borne out, however. Game parameters were introduced in the regression by means of dummy variables, and it was found that they cannot, in general, be removed without significant effect.[1] For each game and each subject, in both experiments, the $\beta$'s were usually between zero and one.

Friedman's first experiment involved only duopoly games, with six subjects playing in six games each.[2] The second utilized nine subjects in 2, 3 and 4 person games. Eight of them were in 3 duopolies, 3 triopolies and 3 four person games, with the ninth subject in 6 duopolies and three triopolies.

A second type of information coming out of his experiments concerns the number of games that eventually reach the joint maximum and, once attained, stay there until the end of the game. In the first experiment it is 6 out of 18 duopolies. In the second, it is 6 out of 15 duopolies, 2 out of 9 triopolies and 0 out of 6 four-person games. The proportion of joint-maximum games appears to decline rapidly as the number of players increases.

*2.4.2. Comments.* In comparing the F-S complete information games to Friedman's, one difference that stands out is the frequency of joint maximum games. There were none among their 16 duopolies or 11 triopolies; while 12 of 33 of Friedman's duopolies were joint maximum, and 2 of 9 triopolies. Only one of these games occurs when subjects were in their first game. It was a duopoly and was among 5 duopoly games which were the first played by subjects. This information is summarized below in Table V. The evidence is not conclusive, but it suggests that there are differences between the mode of play of a subject in his first game, as compared with later games. Additional, and stronger evidence may be found in an experiment not reviewed here [8].

TABLE V

*Frequency of joint maximum games*

|          | First game | Later games |
|----------|------------|-------------|
| Duopoly  | 1 of 5     | 11 of 28    |
| Triopoly | 0 of 12    | 2 of 8      |

Another side to the question of subjects participating in many games is that casual empiricism suggests some may become bored after a while. Boredom may lead to random choices, choices designed to shock one's rivals, mechanical repetition of some pattern of play while the mind dwells on other things, etc. Perhaps the real world of business

---

[1] F tests were performed comparing, for each subject, a regression with several dummy variables present to represent game parameters and a regression with all dummy variables removed in which only two parameters were estimated. For nearly all subjects in the second experiment the two regressions were significantly different at the 5 per cent level. While the reverse was true in the first experiment, there was considerably less data available per subject.

[2] Actually eight subjects were hired, one quit in the middle of the experiment resulting in complete participation for only six subjects. The seventh was played against dummy strategies in every game after the eighth quit.

involves stakes so large or an environment so interesting and varied that boredom is rare. In any case, it is really not known when and how boredom sets in to the experimental scene, much less whether it occurs in a way different from or similar to the real business world. In the progress of an experiment, a stable equilibrium phase may give way to a boredom phase.

Friedman tried to do too much in his experiments and, as a consequence, somewhat muddied his results. Clearly the more variables one wishes to examine, the more observations are required for good analysis. Friedman gave in to the temptation to let vary almost anything he could, given the number of games and subjects he used. The result is that when all variables are accounted for, nearly none seems significant; however, if, say, half the variables are excluded nearly all the remainder are significant. The half to be used may be chosen arbitrarily.

It was also noted earlier that the theoretical underpinnings of the regression are shaky. The behavioural hypotheses embodied in it do not arise from any well-defined optimization process. They are supported by (somewhat contradictory and fuzzy) *ad hoc* reasoning.

### 2.5. *Hoggatt 2*

2.5.1. *Description.* Hoggatt has done a second experiment [11], after those reported earlier in this section, which is, in certain ways, a notable improvement in design over its predecessors; however, it also fails to utilize certain important lessons learned or demonstrated in them. The weak points in this experiment are: (1) using unpaid subjects, and (2) having subjects play only a small number of periods (two games of between 13 and 21 periods each).

Hoggatt had 12 subjects for this duopoly experiment, all of whom were researchers in the School of Engineering of the University of Chile. Like the F-S and Friedman experiments, this one is concerned with the cooperativeness of subjects; however, it is nearer in approach to the latter than the former. The fundamental F-S hypothesis was that behaviour is more uniformly non-cooperative, the less information the subjects possess. Friedman used the index of cooperativeness, $\rho$, to characterize the behaviour of a subject and estimated the relationship between the index of a subject and that of his rivals' in the preceding period. Hoggatt's hypothesis is the higher the $\rho$ value of the rival, the higher is one's own $\rho$ value.

His experiment is designed in a very simple, yet very powerful and sensible way. His subjects each played in two games simultaneously. They were told they sold in two completely isolated and independent markets with a distinct rival in each. The rivals were in fact robot players, whose modes of play were previously determined by the experimenter. The strategy against which the subject played in one market was $\rho = -0 \cdot 6$ and in the other $\rho = +0 \cdot 6$. The precise hypothesis is that in a game with fixed $\rho$ for the robot, the series of $\rho_{it}$ chosen by the subject will go to a limit $\rho_i^*$. The higher is the value of the robot, the higher is equilibrium value $\rho_i^*$ of the subject.

The precise statement of Hoggatt's hypothesis is [11, pp. 118-119]:

, . . . we shall split each time series of outputs by the subject into a " first half " and a " last half," discarding the central term in the event that the number of terms is odd. Similarly, we divide the series of first differences with respect to time into a first half and second half. We say that the path of a particular market shows a tendency toward stability if:

(*a*) The mean of the absolute deviations of the last half series of outputs is less than the mean of the absolute deviation of the first half series of outputs for that market and;

(*b*) the mean of the first difference with respect to time of the last half series of output is less than the mean of the first difference with respect to time of the first half series of output.

Seven of the games with robot $\rho$ of $-0.6$ and eleven with robot $\rho$ of $+0.6$ pass tests (*a*) and (*b*) for stability. Table VI below shows the contingency table for the 12 subjects concerning the passing of the tests (*a*) and (*b*). A $\chi^2$ test for independence of the entries of Table VI is accepted at the 95 per cent level. On this basis, one cannot conclude for stability.

While one cannot conclude formally for stability, a glance at the data leaves the impression that $\rho$ is higher for a subject, the higher is the $\rho$ played against him. In six of the 12 cases the $\rho$ a subject plays is never lower against the $\rho = 0.6$ robot than the corresponding move against the $\rho = -0.6$ robot. In four cases there are a few instances (6 out of 68 periods) where a lower $\rho$ is played against the 0.6 robot than the $-0.6$. The remaining two cases are less clearcut; however, the overall effect leaves the strong impression that Hoggatt's hypothesis concerning the happy effect of cooperation is correct.

TABLE VI

| | | Does behaviour tend toward stability (pass test (*a*), (*b*)) in games where the robot strategy is $+0.6$ | |
|---|---|---|---|
| | | Yes | No |
| Does behaviour tend toward stability (pass tests (*a*) and (*b*)) in games where the robot strategy is $-0.6$ | Yes | 7 | 0 |
| | No | 4 | 1 |

2.5.2. *Comments.* Like all the experiments discussed in the present paper, this one is interesting because of some novel insights of design, as well as because the results, themselves, are suggestive. Using unpaid subjects and not allowing them enough experience to get fully used to the game situation has been commented on before. The experimental design is excellent for its simplicity. The parameters allowed to vary are kept down to a reasonable few. The analysis itself utilizes techniques calling for a minimum of underlying statistical assumptions, in contrast with Friedman, who uses ordinary least squares regression.

The really novel feature of this experiment is the use of pre-programmed strategies. The obvious advantages are that subjects may be paired with many types of rival players, and, as the experimenter *knows* the parameters of the robot players, any statistical analysis is simplified. Instead of having a set of parameters to estimate for each subject, with interdependence between the values for them, causality runs only one way. The parameters of a subject are never affected by those of another subject.

Like most good things, the robots come at a price. If their behaviour is very singular and unlike the behaviour of people, it is possible the subjects play against them in ways they would never play with other subjects. For example, Hoggatt's robots have no learning phase. It is possible that the response of a subject to this learning phase may affect the final, stable equilibrium behaviour of his rival. In these circumstances, one could not predict subjects' behaviour in games with other subjects on the basis of their performance with robots. Clearly the ideal is to have robots which behave like people.

Hoggatt's robot strategies were of the form

$$x_{rt} = a + bx_{s, t-1}$$

where $x_{rt}$ is the *t*th period output of the robot and $x_{st}$ is the *t*th period output of the subject. Such a simple, rigid pattern may be easily detected by subjects, and spotted as a mechanical strategy. It may be possible to make the robot appear more human by adding a random element to its behaviour rule. In any case, the robot strategies, while potentially very useful, must be understood better and handled carefully.

## 3. FURTHER COMMENT ON THE EXPERIMENTS

### 3.1. *Motivation of Subjects*

The first question concerns whether the subjects are likely to have a relevant sort of motivation. All the experiments reported above are aimed at a simple modelling of business behaviour, thus the subjects are supposed to be actuated by the most important forces operating on real businesses. A common list of business motivations would probably include: (*a*) profit, (*b*) sales, (*c*) rate of growth of profit or sales or assets, (*d*) power, (*e*) relative share of industry sales going to the firm, (*f*) level of profit, sales, or growth rate relative to rivals.

Traditionally, economists would argue for (*a*) and claim that (*b*) and (*c*) might be regarded as proxies for future profits while (*d*), (*e*) and (*f*) either play no role or are of secondary importance next to profit. It remains an empirical question of importance to determine whether there are motivations more important than profit, and if there are, after determining what they are, to reconstruct economic theory with these new, correct, motivations in such a way that it gives more insight into and explanation of economic realities than the presently accepted theory. For those who, like the author, believe that profit is unlikely to be dethroned, the experiments which have been described focus on the principal motivation.

### 3.2. *On the Hypotheses Which are Tested*

A number of behavioural hypotheses have been put forward in the oligopoly literature. In each of the experiments reviewed here, a few of the alternatives are singled out and the experiment is used to choose among them, or a relationship is sought between the mode of behaviour displayed by a subject and the behaviour of his rivals.

Hoggatt's first experiment featured standard Cournot behaviour and a misconceived notion of long-run Cournot behaviour. The F-S experiments focussed on Cournot, rivalistic and joint profit maximizing behaviour. The Friedman and Hoggatt 2 experiments assume firms seek to maximize a weighted sum of their own and their rivals' profits.

All of these modes of behaviour assume single period profit maximization, which is a rather naïve objective for oligopolists. They are presumably aware that their actions will affect the behaviour of their rivals and that there will be many decision periods after the current one. Surely maximizing a discounted profit stream is more sensible. Another difficult assumption is that a firm assumes its rivals will repeat in period $t$ their decisions of period $t-1$. Generally this assumption will be contradicted by the facts, so its maintenance by rational economic agents is untenable.

### 3.3. *Concluding Comments*

On balance the experiments discussed here are pioneering efforts which go far to demonstrate the usefulness of experimental methods for economic research. They contain much information on and insight into the problems of good experimental design, and they test interesting hypotheses in fruitful ways.

The extreme care with which F-S wrote instructions and handled subjects was a contribution from experimental psychology, and it helped to launch experimental economics at a high level. Perhaps the individual choice circumstances characteristic of oligopoly, bilateral monopoly and utility may require a much longer period of familiarization than the psychologists' subjects need. A longer time is needed than was at first recognized.

Paying subjects is an important piece of realism. When this is done, decisions are not hypothetical. Profit to the subject actually depends on his behaviour, and he need not be asked to pretend it does. Chances are most people are poor at guessing how they would behave in situations with which they are not thoroughly familiar, so anything that can be done to make an experiment real instead of hypothetical is very important.

414                    REVIEW OF ECONOMIC STUDIES

The advantages of experimental research, when adapted to the needs of economics, are striking. Compared to traditional empirical research in economics the experimenter has considerable control over the design of the markets within which his economic agents operate, and he can exclude some influences from which he wishes to abstract while concentrating on others he wishes to study. Anyone questioning results within the experimental framework is able to replicate an experiment performed by someone else and analyze entirely new and independent data. On the other hand, the world of the experimenter is artificial and of his own design; so the extent to which experimental results may be taken as a clue to behaviour in real life markets is uncertain.

The two conclusions on oligopolistic behaviour which emerge from these studies are: the Cournot solution characterizes behaviour in incomplete information situations, and, under complete information, a subject is more cooperative, the more cooperative is his rival. It is not obvious whether these conclusions will obtain under more intensive examination, or how more comprehensive experiments will find them modified; however, they are interesting results and suggestive of what might be done experimentally.

*University of Rochester*                                          J. W. FRIEDMAN

*First version received* 8.4.68; *final version received* 25.10.68

REFERENCES

[1]  Bertrand, Joseph. " Review of Walras' *Theorie Mathematique de la Recherche Sociale* and Cournot's *Recherches Sur les Principles Mathematiques de la Theorie des Richesses* ", *Journal des Savants*, **68** (1883), 449-508.

[2]  Chamberlin, Edward H. " An Experimental Imperfect Market ", *Journal of Political Economy*, **56** (1948), 95-108.

[3]  Davidson, Donald, Suppes, Patrick and Siegel, Sidney. *Decision Making: An Experimental Approach* (Stanford: Stanford University Press, 1957).

[4]  Dolbear, F. Trenery. " Individual Choice Under Uncertainty: An Experimental Study ", *Yale Economic Essays*, **3** (1963), 419-470.

[5]  Edgeworth, Francis Y. *Papers Relating to Political Economy, I* (London: Macmillan, 1925), pp. 111-142.

[6]  Fouraker, Lawrence E. and Siegel, Sidney. *Bargaining Behavior* (New York: McGraw-Hill, 1963).

[7]  Friedman, James W. " Individual Behaviour in Oligopolistic Markets: An Experimental Study ", *Yale Economic Essays*, **3** (1963), 359-417.

[8]  Friedman, James W. " An Experimental Study of Cooperative Duopoly ", *Econometrica* (October 1967), pp. 379-397.

[9]  Friedman, James W. " Equal Profits as a Fair Division ", to appear in *Beitrage Zur Experimentellen Wirtschaftsforschung*, Vol. II (ed. Professor Heinz Sauermann).

[10]  Hoggatt, Austin C. " An Experimental Business Game ", *Behavioral Science*, **4** (1959), 192-203.

[11]  Hoggatt, Austin C. " Measuring Behavior in Quantity Variation Duopoly Games ", *Behavioral Science*, **12** (1967), 109-121.

[12]  Mosteller, Frederick and Nogee, Philip. " An Experimental Measurement of Utility ", *Journal of Political Economy*, **59** (1951), 371-401.

[13]  Shubik, Martin.  *Strategy and Market Structure* (New York: Wiley, 1959).

[14]  Siegel, Sidney and Fouraker, Lawrence E.  *Bargaining and Group Decision Making*: *Experiments in Bilateral Monopoly* (New York: McGraw-Hill, 1960).

[15]  Smith, Vernon L.  " An Experimental Study of Competitive Market Behavior ", *Journal of Political Economy*, **70** (1962), 111-137.

[16]  Smith, Vernon L.  " Effect of Market Organization on Competitive Equilibrium ", *Quarterly Journal of Economics*, **77** (1964), 181-201.

[17]  Smith, Vernon L.  " Experimental Auction Markets and the Walrasian Hypothesis ", *Journal of Political Economy*, **73** (1965), 387-393.

[18]  Yaari, Menahem E.  " Convexity in the Theory of Choice Under Risk ", *Quarterly Journal of Economics*, **79** (1965), 278-290.

# [5]

# Income Distributions in Two Experimental Economies

## Raymond C. Battalio, John H. Kagel, and Morgan O. Reynolds

*Texas A&M University*

Data on individual labor earnings are reported from two experimental economies where the primary factors responsible for income differences were differences in tastes for market income versus leisure and differences in abilities working manual job tasks. Measured income dispersion under these conditions was strikingly similar to that in the United States and other market economies, indicating that these two factors alone are sufficient to generate such income differences. Further, in tests of the functional form of the distributions of income, the hypothesis of lognormality fit better than the hypothesis of normality, just as it does in national data.

> Differences in incomes that are associated with differences in effort are generally regarded as fair. If everyone were offered the same hourly wage rate and the opportunity to work as many hours as he or she chose, the resulting discrepancies on payday would be understandable. In fact, it would seem unfair for the person who takes more leisure to get just as much income. [ARTHUR OKUN 1975]

Judging by recent literature it appears that professional interest in income distribution and inequality has rarely been higher. A key question continues to be why reported income distributions have their apparent similarity in general shape, dispersion, and positive skewness. Economists

Battalio and Kagel received research support from NSF grant GS 32057 and Reynolds thanks the Earhart Foundation for its support. We thank C. G. Miles for making the data for the Cannabis Economy available and R. L. Basmann for first suggesting that we look at income distributions in the experimental economies and for helpful comments on an earlier draft of this paper. Roy Gilbert, Tom Saving, and Bill Brown provided several helpful suggestions and comments. Responsibility for errors remains ours alone.
[*Journal of Political Economy*, 1977, vol. 85, no. 6]

have not had to look far to find a host of factors which might be responsible for the observed differences in income, although it has proven difficult to discriminate empirically among various hypotheses with available data. Special attention has focused on isolating differences in ability and effort because of a common belief that, if these were the only factors involved in earnings differences, incomes would be more evenly distributed than they currently are. Naturally, many would find it very agreeable if this were the case.

The purpose of this paper is to analyze data on individual labor earnings from two economies in which many of the alleged sources of unequal incomes in national economic systems were greatly reduced and in some cases entirely eliminated. Sufficient experimental control was maintained so that the primary factors reponsible for differences in individual incomes were differences in individual tastes for market income and differences in individual abilities to perform relatively simple job tasks. In other words, each individual could vary his or her level of earnings, subject, of course, to corresponding reductions in leisure time. Under these conditions empirical measures of income dispersion were remarkably similar to comparable figures for the United States and other market economies.

Since this paper describes earnings behavior observed under laboratory-type conditions—an unusual area for economists—we make a few remarks about the relevance of the data. The fact that income dispersion is similar in the experimental and national economies demonstrates that prevailing differences in effort and productivity among relatively homogeneous people (by demographic characteristics) are sufficient to generate differences in earnings as large as those in the U.S. economy, a point which has been seriously questioned (Fair 1971; Blinder 1974). However, this is not the same thing as asserting that the U.S. distribution of income is created solely by individual differences in ability and effort. There are obvious differences between the institutional structure and population characteristics of experimental and national economies which prevent such generalizations. But our results falsify the contention that incomes necessarily will be more evenly distributed in a world where all sources of income differences, except ability and tastes for leisure, are eliminated. In this respect our analysis serves the traditional function of experimentation in the biological and behavioral sciences—to isolate basic relationships under controlled conditions, a technique now receiving a somewhat more respectful hearing in economics (Rivlin 1974; Smith 1976). Moreover, even if it were pronounced impossible to draw reliable inferences about the behavior of a more general population from experiments, we surely would want to know if the empirical regularities reported in national data also occurred under seemingly special conditions.

Section I below describes the experimental economies, Section II describes the variation in individual earnings which occurred under these conditions, Section III presents statistical tests for normality and log-normality in the distribution of earnings, and the last section concludes the discussion.

## I. The Experimental Economies

Stigler (1966) provides a representative discussion of factors generating differences in labor incomes, which can be summarized in the following list: (1) luck (personal factors—health, accidents; employer factors—weather, fire, flood, bankruptcy; market factors—general business conditions, finding best job and best pay within a job); (2) direct occupation expenses; (3) costs of occupational training and education; (4) lifetime concavity of earnings with respect to experience; (5) variability or instability of earnings (risk preferences, progressive income tax); (6) differences in cost of living; (7) occupational prestige and social esteem; (8) fringe benefits, like insurance, etc.; (9) monopoly power and restrictions; (10) inability to borrow investment funds for training; (11) imperfect foresight; (12) discrimination and nepotism; (13) relative desire for market income versus leisure; and (14) ability or productive capacity.

The first factor is stochastic; factors 2–8 are the compensatory or equalizing principles of Adam Smith which would exist in full competitive markets and cause wage incomes to differ even among workers of similar ability and taste for income. Factors 9–12 describe divergencies from a perfectly competitive economy which can create additional income differences. The institutional structure of the experimental economies analyzed here permitted factors 1–12 to play, at most, a minor role in accounting for the observed nonuniformity of earnings in these economies. That is, economic conditions were such that differences in ability and preferences for income over leisure were the primary factors responsible for income differences.

Both economies were planned economic environments in the sense that they were organized systems in which individuals lived for continuous, extended time periods and received tokens or points for work performed which were exchangeable for present or future consumption goods.[1] The first was a therapeutic token system established in a female ward for chronic psychotics at the Central Islip State Hospital in New York. The second was an experimental economy (Cannabis Economy) established at the Addiction Research Foundation in Ontario to study the socio-economic effects of marijuana consumption among volunteer subjects.[2]

In the Central Islip economy income was earned primarily in janitorial

---

[1] For a discussion of the use of planned economic environments as laboratories for analysis of economic behavior, see Kagel (1972).

[2] Detailed descriptions of the institutional structures, measurement procedures, and studies of individual consumption and saving behavior in these two economies are available in Battalio et al. (1973) and Kagel et al. (1975).

chores such as sweeping and mopping floors, sorting laundry, and washing dishes, although income could also be earned from self-care activities (straightening up a bed) or activities designed to teach social skills. Each token earning behavior was clearly defined and available at regularly scheduled intervals at a specified token wage rate. Wage rates were structured to approximately clear the labor market, avoiding excess demand or supply in each job activity. Patients did not have fixed job assignments, and the staff allocated janitorial activities among those willing to work on a day-to-day basis. In principle, all patients had the requisite skills to perform any of the jobs, but of course some did higher-quality work than others. Individual patients generally volunteered to perform a given job on a fairly regular basis, and the staff relied upon these patients to perform these jobs. Most patients worked a variety of jobs as well as working the same job more than once a week. However, there was no fixed maximum on the amount of work that an individual was allowed to perform or minimum amount of work required.

With respect to consumption opportunities, all patients were supplied with an assured bundle of goods normally provided by a hospital, such as a bed in a public dormitory room, meals, and medical care, independent of token earning activities. Tokens were used to purchase additional goods like cigarettes, coffee, candy, cookies, soda, and milk at the token store, rent a private room or locker, obtain a grounds pass, or purchase clothing and dance tickets. An important feature of consumption behavior in this economy was that the individual distribution of consumption expenditures coincided very closely with the distribution of labor earnings. Examination of saving and consumption behavior in this economy has demonstrated that these consumers conform to standard principles of economic behavior (Battalio et al. 1973; Kagel et al. 1975).

The second economy (Cannabis Economy) consisted of three groups of volunteer subjects, two male groups and one female group, which entered the experiment on different dates. Subjects ranged from 20 to 28 years of age, typically used marijuana (or other derivatives of the cannabis plant) regularly for at least 2 years, were unemployed at the time of volunteering, and had 12 or more years of schooling. The structure of the economic system was the same for all groups except for availability and conditions of marijuana consumption. These differences are ignored here because they did not affect the distribution of output per hour, hours worked, or earnings.[3]

Income-earning activity in the Cannabis Economy consisted of weaving

[3] Measures of dispersion in earnings during the predrug phase of each experiment, when subjects did not know which treatment condition they would be assigned to and no cannabis was available, did not differ in any important respect from the measures reported in the text. It appears that the primary effect of cannabis conditions on individual economic behavior lies in the rearrangement of the sequence of daily activities (see Kagel, Battalio, and Miles 1976).

woolen belts on small portable hand looms. Standards for acceptable belts were established and subjects received $2.50 (Canadian currency) for each acceptable belt submitted. The material used in weaving belts was provided free of charge and was always available in the work area. Subjects were free to work anywhere in the ward, during any desired time period, and for as long or as little as they wished. Records of output, earnings, and consumption were maintained by the experimenters, and a record of each subject's activity was made every half-hour.[4]

The consumer goods provided free of charge during the 98-day experimental period consisted of assignment, in pairs, to semiprivate rooms with heat, lights, and cleaning services. All other goods had to be purchased from production earnings. A store on the premises offered canteen items, including alcoholic beverages; recreation facilities were available for small rental fees; and meals were available at the hospital cafeteria or snack bar, as well as from food-to-go outlets outside the hospital. A staff member was regularly available to purchase other retail items outside the hospital at market prices, while all unspent earnings could be taken home at the end of the experiment. Consumption and saving behavior in this economy also corresponded to standard principles of economic behavior (Kagel et al. 1975).

## II. Differences in Individual Earnings

The data in table 1 provide descriptive measures of the distribution of individual earnings within the two experimental economies. Weekly distributions and individual income totals over 5 weeks are reported for the Central Islip economy.[5] Total earnings for the 3-month experimental

---

[4] An independent check of data accuracy compared the amount of money subjects received upon leaving the economy with what they should have left with on the basis of income and consumption records. Using data from group 3, the differences between these two measures of saving taken as a percentage of individual subject income range from 0 to 6 percent with an average value of 2.4 percent. Independent checks for data accuracy were also maintained in Central Islip by recording total tokens disbursed by weeks and comparing this measure with total earnings. The discrepancy of these two measures over 5 weeks averaged 3.6 percent of the average value of the two measures.

[5] While income is often estimated over a 1-year interval, weekly income distributions are appropriate for the Central Islip economy. Contracting for jobs was daily rather than monthly or annually. Major adjustments to changes in the relative prices of consumption goods were completed within 1 week, as were adjustments to changes in wage rates, a common pattern in token economies. Week-to-week correlations between individual earnings were about 0.9, which are similar to those for annual earnings for national economies. Therefore, it appears that a week is sufficient in a steady-state token economy such as Central Islip to assess the persistent differences among individual earning behaviors. Income is reported for the top 25 earning individuals who were present for all weeks of the study. The rationale for selection was to eliminate patients whose income was primarily earned in self-care activities, i.e., subjects who effectively were nonparticipants in the general labor market. Note also that money wage rates were constant during the reported weeks, but large systematic changes in prices of groups of goods occurred (see Battalio et al. 1973).

## TABLE 1

### Income Distribution in Two Experimental Economies

| Economy | Sex | N | Median | Mean | Min/Max | C.V. | Var. Logs. | Gini Coefficient | Share of Earnings | | Pearson's Coefficient 3 (Mean-Median) / SD | Pareto Function $\lvert \alpha \rvert$ |
|---|---|---|---|---|---|---|---|---|---|---|---|---|
| | | | | | | | | | Lowest* Fifth | Highest* Fifth | | |
| Central Islip: | | | | | | | | | | | | |
| Week 1 ......... | F | 25 | 42 | 47.6 | 11–157 | .80 | .51 | .406 | 5.9 | 45.5 | .15 | 1.13 |
| Week 2 ......... | F | 25 | 36 | 47.5 | 12–133 | .72 | .53 | .400 | 5.8 | 43.1 | .34 | 1.98 |
| Week 3 ......... | F | 25 | 44 | 47.7 | 13–139 | .65 | .40 | .353 | 6.6 | 40.4 | .12 | 1.90 |
| Week 4 ......... | F | 25 | 35 | 42.7 | 11–170 | .87 | .44 | .402 | 6.6 | 47.1 | .21 | 1.07 |
| Week 5 ......... | F | 25 | 32 | 37.9 | 12–150 | .76 | .31 | .346 | 8.5 | 42.5 | .20 | 1.21 |
| 5 weeks ......... | F | 25 | 184 | 223.3 | 70–689 | .68 | .34 | .344 | 7.4 | 41.2 | .26 | 1.38 |
| Cannabis Economy: | | | | | | | | | | | | |
| Group 1 ......... | M | 19 | 1,857 | 1,753 | 720–3,347 | .42 | .23 | .249 | 9.5 | 33.1 | −.42 | 3.56 |
| Group 2 ......... | M | 19 | 2,385 | 2,852 | 1,114–5,397 | .45 | .22 | .264 | 9.8 | 35.8 | 1.06 | 5.93 |
| Group 3 ......... | F | 18 | 1,507 | 1,600 | 282–3,747 | .60 | .56 | .358 | 6.4 | 42.9 | .29 | 4.12 |
| Groups 1 and 2 ... | M | 38 | 2,105 | 2,302 | 720–5,397 | .51 | .28 | .285 | 8.8 | 38.5 | .50 | 3.04 |
| Groups 1, 2, and 3 | M-F | 56 | 1,977 | 2,077 | 282–5,397 | .56 | .41 | .310 | 6.6 | 37.2 | .25 | 3.10 |

Note.—C.V. = coefficient of variation; var. logs. = variance of the logarithm of income.
* Lowest and highest 20% rounded to nearest whole number for Cannabis Economy.

period are reported for the three groups in the Cannabis Economy.

Students of income distribution will note some familiar features about the dispersion and skewness shown in table 1. In the Central Islip economy there was considerable dispersion in earnings among individuals in the economy regardless of which index of variability is chosen. The highest earner received over 10 times as much as the lowest earner, the coefficient of variation was about 0.75, the variances of the logarithm of income averaged 0.42, and the Gini coefficient was about 0.375.[6] The absolute value for the slope of the Pareto function was around 1.5, the value which Pareto found long ago. In addition, the Central Islip income distributions all exhibited positive skewness, as indicated by the consistent positive sign for Pearson's coefficient.

The distributions of income from the Cannabis Economy are generally more compact than those for Central Islip. If we consider the combined distribution for all 56 subjects, the coefficient of variation (0.56) and Gini ratio (0.310) were somewhat smaller than those in Central Islip, although the maximum income was over 10 times as large as the minimum income and the variances of the log of income were similar. However, differences in dispersion emerge among the three subgroups comprising this total. Each male group had a maximum income only about five times as large as its minimum income. In addition, coefficients of variation, log variances, and Gini ratios were smaller for the male groups than those reported for the women in table 1. The income distributions in the Cannabis Economy, with the exception of the first group of men, also exhibited positive skewness. The Pareto slopes for the top 20 percent of the Cannabis Economy all exceeded 3.0, indicating that income was distributed more evenly among high income earners in the Cannabis Economy than in Central Islip.[7]

The numerical measures of dispersion reported for the experimental

---

[6] The Gini coefficient is defined as the mean difference divided by twice the mean income. In the discontinuous case (individual data) two formulas arise because the mean difference can be calculated with or without repetition. Ours was calculated without repetition, which means that the deviations of each value from itself, which add nothing to the sum of deviations, are not taken, so the number of pairs is $N(N-1)$ rather than $N^2$ (see Kendall and Stuart 1969, pp. 46–51). Geometrically the Gini coefficient is the ratio of the area between the Lorenz curve and the diagonal of perfect equality to the total area under the diagonal. The Gini ratio ranges from 0, when incomes are equal (the Lorenz curve coincides with the diagonal), to 1 at the other extreme. Atkinson (1975) offers the following description: Suppose we choose two people at random from the income distribution, and express the difference between their incomes as a proportion of the average income, then this difference turns out to be on average, twice the Gini coefficient: a coefficient of 0.4 means that the expected difference between two people chosen at random is 80 percent of the average income (p. 45).

[7] A Chow test shows that the probability is less than 5 percent that the Pareto value reported from Central Islip for week 2 (the largest Pareto value reported for that economy) is equal to the Pareto value reported for groups 1 and 2 in the Cannabis Economy (the smallest Pareto value reported for that economy).

economies fall within the range of comparable measures reported for the United States and other national economies. This is substantiated in table 2, where a sampling of Gini ratios for income distributions in national data is shown. Obviously, no single distribution constitutes *the* correct comparison because representations of income dispersions always depend upon definitions of income recipient unit, income period, and data accuracy, as well as the statistical methods used to summarize and interpret the data. As illustrated in table 2, however, the general tendency in these data is for income to be more evenly distributed the more homogeneous the group of income recipients and the narrower the occupational classifications covered. Gini ratios often exceed 0.40 when distributions include all sources of money income (before personal taxes) for all types of households. However, it is not unusual for Gini ratios of relatively homogeneous groups of workers to be considerably smaller, often falling below 0.30. The Gini indexes for the experimental data fall within these extremes—the Cannabis Economy, which had a single source of earnings and a more homogeneous population of workers, had a smaller Gini ratio than the Central Islip economy, which had multiple sources of earnings and a somewhat more heterogeneous population of income earners.

Comparisons of income dispersion should, however, not rely on any single summary measure, especially since Lorenz curves may cross. But other statistical comparisons suggest the same general conclusion as the Gini index. For instance, the highest fifth of U.S. full-time craftsmen received 32 percent of total earnings in 1970, as did the highest fifth of operatives (Henle 1972). By comparison, the highest fifth of earners in the experimental economies always received more than 32 percent of total earnings, indicating as much dispersion of income in the experimental economies as for manual occupations in the national economy. Similarly, Lydall (1968) reported coefficients of variation in labor earnings for all U.S. males of 0.52, 0.36, and 0.37 in 1939, 1949, and 1959, respectively, which are generally smaller than coefficients of variation in the experimental economies.

In summary, data from the experimental economies show that differences in abilities to perform simple manual jobs and differences in preferences for market income among relatively similar individuals (by demographic characteristics) are *sufficient* to generate income dispersions like those observed in national economies. It bears emphasis, however, that this does not imply that these two factors *necessarily* account for all income differences in national data. This issue receives more attention in the conclusion.

## III. Functional Form in Distributions

In addition to an interest in dispersion, economists have devoted a great deal of research to determining what the shape of the income distribution

TABLE 2

SELECTED GINI RATIOS FOR INCOME DISTRIBUTIONS IN NATIONAL AND EXPERIMENTAL ECONOMIES

| Country or Experiment | Income Concept | Recipient Unit | Gini Ratio |
|---|---|---|---|
| 1. United States | IRS adjusted gross income | Individual tax returns | .46 |
| 2. Central Islip | Labor earnings (no personal tax) | Female workers | .41 (max) |
| 3. United States | Pretax money income | Families and unattached individuals | .40 |
| 4. United States | Pretax money income | Female-headed families | .40 |
| 5. United States | Income after taxes and transfers | Families and unattached individuals | .36 |
| 6. United States | Pretax money income | Families | .35 |
| 7. Central Islip | Labor earnings (no personal tax) | Female workers | .34 (min) |
| 8. Cannabis | Pretax labor earnings | All workers | .31 |
| 9. United States | Consumption expenditures | Families and unattached individuals | .31 |
| 10. India | Consumption expenditures | Individuals | .31 |
| 11. United States | Pretax labor earnings | Household heads, age 25–34 | .29 |
| 12. Cannabis | Pretax labor earnings | Male workers, age 20–28 | .29 |
| 13. United States | Pretax wages and salaries | Male workers, full time, all industry | .28 |
| 14. United States | Pretax wages and salaries | Male workers, full time, manufacturing | .26 |
| 15. United Kingdom | Pretax wages and salaries | Male workers, full time employees | .21 |

SOURCES.—For national estimates, line 1: Gastwirth 1972; line 3: U.S. Bureau of the Census 1974*a*; line 4: Danziger and Plotnik 1975; lines 5 and 11: Taussig 1973; line 6: U.S. Bureau of the Census 1974*b*, also see Paglin 1975 and Taussig 1976; line 9: Reynolds and Smolensky 1977; line 10: Paukert 1973; lines 13 and 14: Henle 1972; line 15: Hill 1959.

is like, especially since this could provide the basic datum which a theory of income distribution must explain. Three functional forms for the distribution of income have been especially prominent: the Pareto distribution, the normal distribution, and the lognormal distribution (Lydall 1968, p. 13). The Pareto distribution provides a reasonably adequate characterization of earnings for the top 20 percent of the income distribution in the experimental economies, with simple correlation coefficients ranging from .87 to .98 for the Pareto functions reported in table 1. This is typically the case for national data as well, although the Pareto distribution fits overall distributions poorly.

The hypothesis of normality in the distribution of earnings has been a candidate to fit the overall distribution because of the possibility that human earning capacities are normally distributed, just as some other variates in nature are. The second major candidate has been the lognormal distribution, which has a long history based upon statistical models like the law of the proportionate effect or the multiplicative interaction among abilities relevant to producing earnings. The $W$-statistic (Shapiro and Wilk 1965) was used to test the hypothesis that earnings were distributed normally (or lognormally) in the experimental economies, as Monte Carlo studies have shown it to be quite powerful for small sample sizes relative to other common tests (Shapiro, Wilk, and Chen 1968).

The hypothesis of lognormality in the distribution of earnings was accepted at the 1 percent confidence level for each week and for incomes totaled over 5 weeks in the Central Islip economy. By contrast, the hypothesis of normality was rejected at this confidence level.

The Cannabis data did not conform quite so clearly to only one functional form. Lognormality was accepted for the distribution of income in all three experimental groups, but normality was also accepted at the 1 percent level. To resolve this ambiguity we reorganized the data to see if one functional form would dominate. When the earnings for all men were pooled (experiments 1 and 2), lognormality was accepted and normality rejected. Similarly, in pooling the data for all subjects, lognormality was accepted and normality rejected at the 1 percent level.

The results of our tests for normality and lognormality are reasonably similar to those using data from national economies (Lydall 1968). The hypothesis of normality is usually in poor agreement with national data but provides a somewhat better characterization in more narrowly defined manual occupations. Similarly, normality did not fit as badly in the Cannabis groups as in Central Islip, which had a more heterogeneous job structure. As with most national data, the hypothesis of lognormality was in better agreement with the data from both experimental economies than the hypothesis of normality.

We note one more striking similarity between the Cannabis data and national data, namely, the difference between male and female earnings. Lydall (1968, p. 242), among many others, has puzzled over this ancient difference between the sexes: "For full-period workers in the developed countries, the median earnings of women seem to be mostly between a half and two-thirds of the earnings of men; and the question which arises is whether this ratio is an accurate reflection of the differences of average effective abilities of men and women, or whether it is partly institutionally or sociologically determined." Remarkably enough, female mean earnings in the Cannabis experiment were 69.5 percent of the mean earnings for all males, a statistically significant difference at the 1 percent level. Many explanations might account for the observed difference—differences between the sexes in physical stamina or desire for leisure—but, given the structure of the Cannabis Economy, it cannot be accounted for by sex bias or segregation of the sexes into different jobs.

## IV. Conclusions

We have analyzed data on the distribution of incomes in two experimental economies in which many of the factors commonly cited as responsible for generating income differences were absent. Nonetheless, measured income dispersion and functional form of the distributions in these simple economies is not very different from those in the United States and other market economies.

Since the bulk of empirical work on the distribution of incomes generally does not derive from analytical models in which the income distribution is either an important dependent or independent variable, much of the interest appears to be motivated ideologically. Some might be tempted to use our results on behalf of various opinions about the fairness of the existing distribution of income. We make only two points. The first is that this study provides evidence for the proposition that measures of dispersion in income and earnings reveal virtually nothing about the socioeconomic structure in which the observed distribution was generated. We considered two institutional structures and populations that were quite different from national economic systems and from each other, yet the empirical measures of income dispersion were not dramatically different. This draws attention to the fact, sometimes overlooked, that particular individuals occupying a given income rank may be quite different under alternative economic structures although the overall distribution remains unchanged. Thus, in an economic system where factors such as 9 and 12 (monopoly power, nepotism, discrimination) are important factors generating a particular distribution of income, removal of these factors need not change the empirically measured Gini coefficient or coefficient of variation but certainly can change the income position of individuals.

The second point is that our study provides evidence for the importance of differences in individual tastes for market income and abilities as major determinants of the income distribution. For instance, our evidence certainly throws doubt upon the empirical relevance of the theoretical model which led Fair (1971, p. 575) to conclude that "it is thus apparent that one has to make rather extreme assumptions about the variation of the productivity and industriousness of people before the optimal Gini coefficient approaches 0.35." But even if preferences and productive abilities play a dominant role in creating the income dispersion observed in the U.S. economy, it does not follow that the distribution of income is immutable. To the extent that tastes and abilities are formed by environmental experience, changes in these variables potentially can modify the equilibrium distribution of income.

### References

Atkinson, A. B. *The Economics of Inequality*. London: Oxford Univ. Press, 1975.

Battalio, R. C.; Kagel, J. H.; Winkler, R. C.; Fisher, E. B., Jr.; Basmann, R. L.; and Krasner, L. "A Test of Consumer Demand Theory Using Observations of Individual Consumer Purchases." *Western Econ. J.* 11 (December 1973): 411–28.

Blinder, A. S. *Toward an Economic Theory of Income Distribution*. Cambridge, Mass.: M.I.T. Press, 1974.

Danziger, S., and Plotnik, R. "Demographic Change, Government Transfers, and the Distribution of Income." *Monthly Labor Rev.* 100, no. 4 (April 1977): 7–11.

Fair, R. C. "The Optimal Distribution of Income." *Q.J.E.* 85 (November 1971): 551–79.

Gastwirth, J. L. "The Estimation of the Lorenz Curve and Gini Index." *Rev. Econ. and Statis.* 54 (August 1972): 306–16.

Henle, P. "Exploring the Distribution of Earned Income." *Monthly Labor Rev.* 95, no. 12 (December 1972): 16–27.

Hill, T. P. "An Analysis of the Distribution of Wages and Salaries in Great Britain." *Econometrica* 27 (July 1959): 355–81.

Kagel, J. H. "Token Economies and Experimental Economics." *J.P.E.* 80, no. 4 (July/August 1972): 779–85.

Kagel, J. H.; Battalio, R. C.; and Miles, C. G. "The Effects of Cannabis Consumption on Production, Hours Worked, and Efficiency: An Experimental Investigation." Mimeographed. College Station: Texas A&M Univ., 1976.

Kagel, J. H.; Battalio, R. C.; Winkler, R. C.; Fisher, E. B., Jr.; Basmann, R. L.; and Krasner, L. "Income Consumption and Saving Behavior in Controlled Environments: Further Economic Analysis." In *Experimentation in Controlled Environment*, edited by C. G. Miles. Toronto: Addiction Res. Found., 1975.

Kendall, M. G., and Stuart, A. *The Advanced Theory of Statistics*. New York: Hafner, 1969.

Lydall, H. *The Structure of Earnings*. London: Oxford Univ. Press, 1968.

Okun, A. M. *Equality and Efficiency: The Big Trade-off*. Washington: Brookings Inst., 1975.

INCOME DISTRIBUTIONS                                                  1271

Paglin, M. "The Measurement and Trend of Inequality: A Basic Revision."
    *A.E.R.* 65 (September 1975): 598–609.
Paukert, F. "Income Distribution at Different Levels of Development: A Survey
    of Evidence." *Internat. Labour Rev.* 108 (August/September 1973): 97–125.
Reynolds, M. O., and Smolensky, E. *Public Expenditures, Taxes, and the U.S.
    Distribution of Income.* New York: Academic Press, 1977.
Rivlin, A. M. "How Can Experiments Be More Useful?" *A.E.R., Papers and
    Proc.* 64 (May 1974): 346–54.
Shapiro, S. S., and Wilk, M. B. "An Analysis of Variance Test for Normality
    (Complete Samples)." *Biometrika* 52 (December 1965): 591–611.
Shapiro, S. S.; Wilk, M. B.; and Chen, H. J. "A Comparative Study of Various
    Tests for Normality." *J. American Statis. Assoc.* 63 (December 1968): 1343–72.
Smith, V. L. "Experimental Economics: Induced Value Theory." *A.E.R., Papers
    and Proc.* 66 (May 1976): 274–79.
Stigler, G. J. *The Theory of Price.* 3d ed. New York: Macmillan, 1966.
Taussig, M. K. *Alternative Measures of the Distribution of Economic Welfare.* Princeton,
    N.J.: Princeton Univ. Press, 1973.
———. "Trends in Inequality of Well-Offness in the United States since World
    War II." Mimeographed. New Brunswick, N.J.: Rutgers—The State Univ.,
    1976.
U.S. Bureau of the Census. *Current Population Reports.* Series P-60, no. 89. Wash-
    ington: Government Printing Office, 1974. (*a*)
———. *Current Population Reports.* Series P-60, no. 90. Washington: Government
    Printing Office, 1974. (*b*)

# [6]

# An Experimental Examination of Two Exchange Institutions

CHARLES R. PLOTT
*California Institute of Technology*

and

VERNON L. SMITH
*University of Arizona*

## 1. INTRODUCTION

Economists have shown increasing interest in the analysis of information and organization in decentralized price adjustment processes. This interest is most frequently manifested at the theoretical level (summaries of the relevant literature, concepts, and methodologies have been provided by Hurwicz [3] and Rothschild [4]), but it also has found expression through several laboratory experimental studies. These latter have unusual appeal because they can serve as a " proving ground " for the former. If well-formulated theories consistently fail to predict simple laboratory behaviour, then one would be hesitant to trust their predictions in richer environments. Furthermore, when replicable laboratory behaviour can be demonstrated, one should seek those extensions of accepted theory which explain why it occurs.

The laboratory studies have attempted to measure the effect of different forms of market organization on the efficiency, performance, convergence pattern and equilibrium level of prices. The variables of market organization examined have been the mechanisms or rules under which prices are communicated and contracts are executed. The focus on these particular variables has been motivated by the more prominent features of certain observed exchange institutions rather than formal models based on pre-scientific, casual observations of the kind that form the basis of embryonic modelling. We view the present work as providing a rigorous empirical foundation for a more formal development of theory.

## 2. TRADING INSTITUTIONS

The experiments we report here are based on two modes of trading organization.

(a) The one-sided oral auction in which buyers (sellers) make repeated oral price bids (offers) for the exchange of many units, one unit at a time. This form of market organization has been studied by Smith [6] for the case in which each of many traders has a capacity to exchange a single unit of the commodity per trading period. This process has the important informational characteristic that traders obtain sequential price observations as binding contracts are formed. The " country auction " for livestock and machinery is typically organized in this manner.

(b) The posted-price institution in which the price quotations cannot be altered (at least not without considerable cost) during the exchange period. Williams [9] studied the case in which buyers (sellers) of multiple units each post one price bid (offer) and sellers (buyers) respond with quantity offers which are then accepted in whole or in part by the buyers (sellers). Williams' [9] objective was to adapt the one-sided studies of Smith [6] specifically to ordinary retail markets and other price-posting markets, in which there is a price commitment extending over several transactions. This modification of the experimental design, we argue, is of considerable substance and is not simply a minor variation on trading mechanics.

In order to help understand the divergence of experimental results under these two forms of market organization, we will need to refer to the sealed-bid auction. In this institution, studied by Smith [7] and Belovicz [1], in each market period a single seller offers a quantity, $Q$, and invites buyers to submit independent bids at stated prices for stated. quantities of the good. The bids are arranged from highest to lowest and the first $Q$ bids are accepted. There are two variations:

(i) In the *discriminative auction* all the accepted bids are filled at the stated bid prices. The best-known continuing market with this structure is the weekly auction of US Treasury bills.

(ii) In the *competitive auction* all the accepted bids are filled at the price represented by the lowest of the accepted bids. The French auction of new stock issues corresponds approximately to this paradigm.

## 3. DIVERGENT EXPERIMENTAL RESULTS

The principal result in Smith's [6] experiments with oral auctions incorporating one-unit incentives is for contract prices beyond the first trading period to be executed to the disadvantage of the side making the quotations. Thus, when only sellers are permitted to make offers, contract prices tend to be significantly below the contract prices resulting when both buyers and sellers make quotations, which in turn are below contract prices occurring when only buyers can make bids.

Williams [9] modified Smith's experiment in two respects.

1. Smith's subjects could each trade only one unit, i.e. buyers had a total revenue " schedule " consisting of a single point, and sellers a total cost " schedule " consisting of one point. Williams' subjects were given total revenue and total cost schedules for multiple units. Thus Williams induces a demand or supply schedule for each subject, rather than a demand or supply point, for each subject.

2. Price quotations were made orally in the Smith experiment and could be revised during a trading period if no acceptance occurred. Thus the market was an auction where each buyer (seller) orally quoted a bid (offer) to sellers (buyers) *en masse* and could change his bid (offer) if no one accepted. Williams, in contrast required each subject buyer (seller) to submit a single price bid (offer). Each price was posted and a seller (buyer), selected at random, then chose a buyer (seller) and offered to sell (buy) a stated quantity. The buyer (seller) then accepted all or any part (but at least one unit) of the quantity offered. If the buyer (seller) accepted the entire quantity, the next seller (buyer), again chosen at random, could attempt to sell (buy) to (from) that same buyer (seller) before choosing another buyer (seller).

Williams reports results which are the exact opposite of those reported by Smith [6]. That is, when buyers post bids Williams finds that contracts, beyond an initial learning period, tend to be *below* the theoretical supply and demand equilibrium and when sellers post offers, he finds that contracts tend to *exceed* this theoretical price. The cumulative distribution of trades for two of Williams' experiments are shown on Figure 1. These distributions, which indicate for each price $p^*$ the total volume of trades which occurred at prices $p \geqq p^*$, are typical of his results in general.

We regard the second modification as the crucial treatment variable that explains the results reported by Williams. Our suspicions about the importance of this second treatment variable arise from the institutional similarities between the discriminative sealed-bid and posted-bid processes and also from the results which have emerged from sealed-bid experiments.

In both the posted-bid and sealed-bid institutions a price bid must be made before the

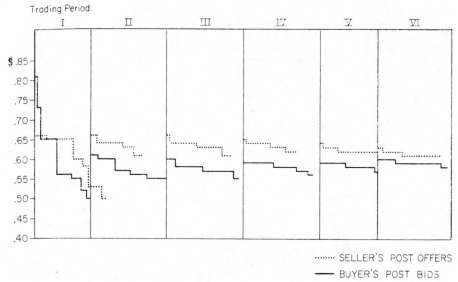

SELLER'S POST OFFERS
BUYER'S POST BIDS

FIGURE 1

Williams' results: cumulative distribution of trades with multi-unit incentives. The figure represents for each price $p^*$, the volume of trades which took place at a price $p \geq p^*$

beginning of a period and without the knowledge of the bids made by other people. In the sealed-bid discriminative auction buyers know only the highest and lowest bids from previous periods and the total quantity to be sold, whereas in the posted-bid case all previous bids are known. Thus, if this informational difference proves to be minor, the information on market conditions is approximately the same under both institutions at the time of decision and the mode of price expression is identical.[1]

Smith's [7] study of the sealed-bid auction shows that expected utility-maximizing buyers will tend to bid less in a discriminative auction than in a competitive auction. In the competitive sealed-bid auction, all bids are filled at the lowest of the accepted bids, while in the discriminative auction you pay what you bid. Hence, in the competitive auction there is no profit penalty in bidding above the low accepted bid, and so bidding one's true maximum willingness to pay (or limit price) maximizes the chance of being among the accepted bids. In the discriminative auction the ideal bid is epsilon above the bid one believes will be the lowest one to be accepted, and is therefore likely to be below one's true maximum willingness to pay. These theoretical predictions are supported by the experimental results of Smith [7] and are reinforced and considerably extended in the definitive study of sealed-bid auctions by Belovicz [1]. The same theory applies to the sealed-offer auction and leads to the prediction that sellers will tend to submit higher offer prices in a discriminative auction than in a competitive auction. Consequently, one should expect prices in a sealed-offer discriminative auction to dominate those in the sealed-bid discriminative auction. From this conjecture and the close similarity between the posted-price and discriminative auctions the Williams [9] experimental results are to be expected.

This argument suggests that there is no contradiction between Smith's [6] oral auction results and Williams' [9] posted-price results because Williams' examination of the multi-unit case was executed within institutions which are substantially different from those examined by Smith [6]. On this interpretation Williams' results take on an added dimension of significance.

A natural way to test our interpretation of the divergent results of Smith and Williams is to conduct new experiments comparing the multiunit oral-bid auction with the multiunit posted-bid organization. *A priori* we expected the distribution of prices in the oral-bid auction to dominate the distribution of posted-bid contracts. This was because in [7] Smith showed that expected utility-maximizing bidders would bid their true marginal valuations (limit prices) in a competitive sealed-bid auction. This implies that the competitive sealed-bid auction should yield results very close to that of the oral double auction. But from [6] it is known that the distribution of prices in the oral-bid auction dominates the distribution of prices in the double auction. Hence, we expect prices in the oral-bid auction to dominate those in the discriminative sealed-bid auction, and *pari passu* those in the similar posted-bid institution.

## 4. EXPERIMENTAL DESIGN

A total of four experimental sessions were conducted. Each of the four sessions involved four buyers and four sellers. Figure 2 shows the individual (marginal cost) induced supply, and (marginal revenue) induced demand functions implied by the total cost and total revenue schedules given to each subject. In each experiment two buyers (sellers) received schedules corresponding to $D_1(S_1)$, and two buyers (sellers) received schedules corresponding to $D_2(S_2)$. No subject participated in both experiments. All subjects were undergraduate students at Caltech who volunteered to participate in a " decision-making experiment " in which they would be paid US currency in amounts that would depend upon their decisions.

Experiments 1 and 3 are posted-bid procedures for buyers. The purpose of these experiments is to check the extension of the Williams results to our subject pool, experimental procedures, etc. Without such replication we cannot be sure that our research results are attributable to the treatment variable. Experiments 2 and 4 apply the oral-bid institution procedure used by Smith to the multiunit supply and demand conditions of experiments 1 and 3.

Experiments 1 and 2 differ from 3 and 4 in four important ways. First, in experiments 1 and 2 no commissions were paid for trading. This conformed with the incentive structure used by Williams. In experiments 3 and 4 a five-cent commission was paid for each trade. As will be explained below, this allowed greater accuracy in the efficiency comparisons between the two trading institutions. The remaining three differences are in the instructions, reproduced in Appendix 1. These differences reflect some evolution of experimental design in general since the Williams' experiment. First the format of the incentives differs. In experiments 1 and 2 buyers and sellers were given tables which contained the total and marginal costs and redemption values. Detailed forms for recording trades and profits were not used. Second, the time limit mentioned in experiment 4 was not used in experiment 2. Actually the time limit was not binding after the first trading period in experiment 4. The final difference is in the way bids were offered. In experiment 2 the experimenter called (in a rotating fashion) upon bidders who simultaneously signalled (by raising a hand) they wanted to bid. In experiment 4 bidders did not need to be recognized. They simply called out the bid—and the bid of the highest bidder was taken when ties in calling out occurred.

No economic sophistication on the part of the subjects was assumed. Indeed, two experimental sessions (experiment 0 and a first attempt at experiment 4) were discarded because of the failure of subjects, a seller in one case and a buyer in the other, to understand the incentive structure. In experiment 0 a seller sold triple the number of units that would have been profitable in the first trading period. This so depressed the market that several trading sessions were required for it to recover. This invalidated session was useful as a pilot test of our procedures and resulted in a decision to reduce the number of buyers and sellers by one-half and make the institutional and procedural changes indicated above. From extensive experience with these kinds of experiments we have learned that very small numbers with approximately equal power yield competitive market outcomes. A buyer

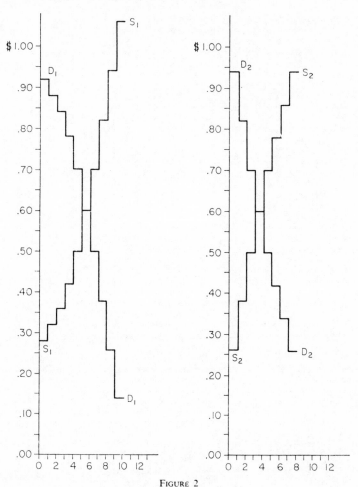

FIGURE 2

Induced individual supply and demand functions

in our first attempt to run experiment 4 purchased many more units than would have been profitable during the first period. The experiment was immediately terminated and later conducted with a new group of subjects.

## 5. EXPERIMENTAL RESULTS: PRICE COMPARISONS[2]

Our hypothesis is that the mode of organization chosen by Williams is a major treatment variable. This claim is supported by Figures 3 and 4 which report the cumulative distribution of contract prices for all four experiments.

Although we induced somewhat steeper supply and demand schedules than Williams [9, p. 10], the price distributions for our experiments 1 and 3 are very similar to those he reports for his buyer bidding sessions 2, 4 and 6. Through the first six to ten trading periods, the bids in all four of Williams' experiments appear to converge toward the

138 REVIEW OF ECONOMIC STUDIES

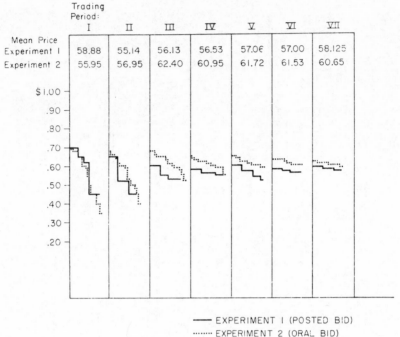

FIGURE 3

Cumulative distribution of trades. For the posted-bid institution this cumulative distribution is also the sequence of trades

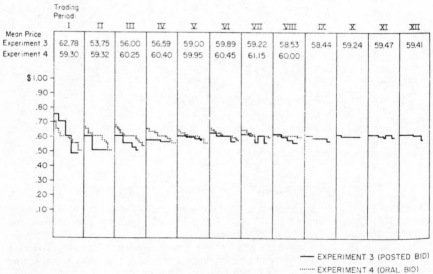

FIGURE 4

Cumulative distribution of trades. For the posted-bid institution this cumulative distribution of trades is also the sequence of trades in every period except XI. For period XI we report the sequence of trades

equilibrium price from below. However, Williams' session 6, which was conducted for twenty trading periods, reached equilibrium in the tenth period, but was below the equilibrium in the thirteenth to twentieth period. This suggests that some downward bias in bid prices may persist indefinitely.

It seems undeniable that we have replicated the research results of Williams' experiments with our subjects. The average price is below equilibrium in every period for both replications except period six in experiment 3, and prices appear to be converging to equilibrium from below. The quantity exchanged also tends to be below equilibrium.

In the oral bid experiments (2 and 4) for every period except the first, prices tend to be above the prices in the posted-bid institution. In addition there is a tendency for contracts to rise above the equilibrium price in the oral-bid auction. Hence, the Smith result generalizes, within this institution, to the multiunit case.

Williams' results appear to be a natural feature of " take-it-or-leave-it " pricing within which the sealed-bid and posted-bid institutions are special cases. The behaviour of sellers in the posted-bid institution is almost identical to the mechanistic response in the sealed-bid arrangement. Sellers respond to posted bids as pure competitors. They do not try to withhold supply, give preferential treatment or otherwise collude among themselves. They are evidently faced with a particularly difficult prisoner's dilemma. Of the eighty-one supply responses in the two experiments made by individual suppliers, only twenty were not the exact competitive response, and of these twenty only four can be interpreted as restrictions of supply (most of the remaining twenty offers exceed the competitive response with such subjects revealing a willingness to trade for less than the five-cent commission).

## 6. EXPERIMENTAL RESULTS: EFFICIENCY

Both the posted-bid and the oral-bid institutions are remarkably efficient (recall that no participant knows anything other than his own incentives), but the oral-bid auction is more efficient than is the posted-bid institution. One might suspect this from viewing Figures 3 and 4: volume in the oral-bid case is always greater than in the posted-bid case. This suggests that not all gains from trade are exhausted in the posted-bid institution.

These markets are perfectly efficient if and only if the maximum amount of money is extracted by the participants from the experimenter. If trades resulted in less than the maximum profit and commissions for the group as a whole, gains from trade would still be possible. The maximum total amount participants could receive in a period in experiments 1 and 2 is $7.12, and in experiments 3 and 4 it is $9.12, the difference, $2.00, being due to commissions paid in experiments 3 and 4.

Where commissions are paid, it is easy to show that a market is efficient in a given period if and only if the following are true:

(i) All buyers (sellers) exchange all units with redemption values (marginal cost) above (below) the competitive equilibrium price. These are called the *intra marginal demand (supply) units*.

(ii) All buyers (sellers) exchange all units with redemption values (marginal cost) equal to the competitive equilibrium price. These are called *marginal demand (supply) units*.

(iii) No buyers (sellers) exchange any units with redemption values (marginal cost) below (above) the competitive equilibrium price. These are called *extra-marginal demand (supply) units*.

The reader can get a good idea of the meaning of inefficiency and why inefficient trades occur in the posted-price institution by studying Figure 5. This is a sketch of the trading which occurred in period five of experiment 3. Buyers 17, 18, 19, 20, respectively, posted prices of 0·60, 0·59, 0·58, 0·57. Suppliers were ordered (by reference to a random number table) with 21 first, then 24, 23 and 22.

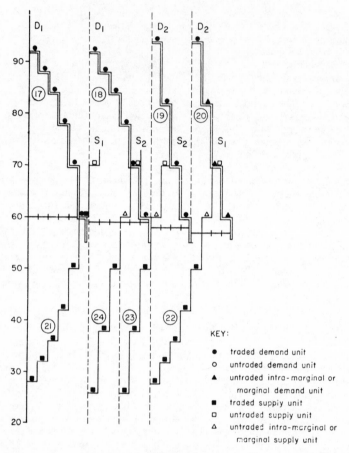

FIGURE 5

Contracts, Experiment 3, period V

Trading proceeded as follows. Seller 21 offered his competitive response of six units to the highest priced buyer, number 17, who purchased all six, his demand, and retired from the market. Next, seller 24 offered his competitive response of three units to buyer 18 who took them all. Then seller 23 offered his competitive response of three units to buyer 18 who purchased them all, then retired from the market. Seller 22, last in line, offered his competitive response of five units to buyer 19 who had bid 0·58. Buyer 19 purchased four of the five units offered, his quantity demanded, and then retired from the market. Seller 22, having sold five of his six units, then offered one unit to buyer 20 who took it.

The inefficiencies that resulted are as follows: Sellers 24, 23 and 22 failed to trade marginal units. Buyer 20 failed to trade two intramarginal units and one marginal unit. Profits amounted to $6.80 for the period. Commissions came to $1.70. Total return to participants was thus $8.50, which is 93 per cent of the maximum.

Tables I and II summarize the effectiveness of these institutions to exhaust the gains from trade. Efficiency of the posted-bid institution averages 95 per cent across periods in experiments 1 and 3. Not bad, we would say, after considering the magnitude of the

TABLE I

*Exchange efficiency of posted-bid institutions by period: Experiments 1 and 3*

| Trading period | Type of inefficiency by subject number | | | Efficiency measure |
| | (i) Untraded intramarginal units | (ii) Untraded marginal units | (iii) Traded extra-marginal units | |
|---|---|---|---|---|
| **Experiment 1** | | | | |
| I | 8 | 2, 3, 4, 5, 6, 8 | 7 | 0·97 |
| II | 4, 4, 4, 5, 7 | 2, 3, 4, 5, 6, 7, 8 | — | 0·92 |
| III | 4, 4, 4, 7 | 4, 5, 6, 7 | — | 0·94 |
| IV | 2, 2 | 2, 5, 6, 7 | — | 0·96 |
| V | 3, 3 | 3, 5, 7, 8 | — | 0·96 |
| VI | 2, 2 | 2, 3, 5, 6, 7, 8 | — | 0·99 |
| VII | 3, 3, 3 | 3, 5, 6, 7, 8 | — | 0·95 |
| VIII | 4, 4 | 4, 5, 6, 8 | — | 0·96 |
| **Experiment 3** | | | | |
| I | 18, 22, 23 | 17, 18, 22, 23 | 20, 21, 24 | 0·91 |
| II | 20, 20, 20, 22 | 17, 20, 21, 22, 24 | 19 | 0·83 |
| III | 19, 19 | 19, 20, 21, 22, 23, 24 | — | 0·92 |
| IV | 17, 17 | 17, 22, 23, 24 | — | 0·94 |
| V | 20, 20 | 20, 22, 23, 24 | — | 0·93 |
| VI | — | 17, 20, 22, 24 | — | 0·98 |
| VII | 18 | 18, 21, 22 | — | 0·97 |
| VIII | 18, 18 | 18, 21, 23, 24 | — | 0·94 |
| IX | 19 | 19, 22, 24 | — | 0·97 |
| X | 17 | 17, 19, 22, 23, 24 | — | 0·96 |
| XI | — | 20, 22 | — | 0·99 |
| XII | 20, 20 | 20, 22, 23, 24 | — | 0·93 |

TABLE II

*Exchange efficiency of oral-bid institution by period: Experiments 2 and 4*

| Trading period | Type of inefficiency by subject number | | | Efficiency measure |
| | (i) Untraded intramarginal units | (ii) Untraded marginal units | (iii) Traded extra-marginal units | |
|---|---|---|---|---|
| **Experiment 2** | | | | |
| I | — | 11, 12, 13, 14 | — | 1·00 |
| II | 9 | 9, 11, 13, 14, 15 | — | 0·99 |
| III | — | 9, 11, 13, 16 | — | 1·00 |
| IV | — | 10, 16 | — | 1·00 |
| V | — | 9, 11, 13, 16 | — | 1·00 |
| VI | — | 9, 10, 11, 13, 15, 16 | — | 1·00 |
| VII | — | 9, 10, 11, 13, 15, 16 | — | 1·00 |
| **Experiment 4** | | | | |
| I | — | 26 | 25 | 0·99 |
| II | — | 26, 32 | — | 0·99 |
| III | — | — | — | 1·00 |
| IV | — | — | — | 1·00 |
| V | — | — | — | 1·00 |
| VI | — | — | — | 1·00 |
| VII | — | — | — | 1·00 |
| VIII | — | — | — | 1·00 |

problem. But relative to the oral bid, the posted bid is strictly second class. In both experiments 2 and 4 the oral-bid auction is over 99 per cent efficient in the first two periods and always 100 per cent efficient in the subsequent periods. An important implication is that the price bias in one-sided oral auctions affects income distribution but not resource allocation.

Of considerable interest, especially from a methodological point of view, is the importance of commissions in bringing trading in " tight " around the equilibrium. This can be seen by comparing the untraded marginal units in experiments 3 and 4 and reflects the possible importance of transactions costs in market environments (Smith [8]).

## 7. EXPERIMENTAL RESULTS: PRICE DYNAMICS

We have not yet formulated a satisfactory model of our experimental results. One cannot yet simply appeal to those laws of economics which account for the behaviour exhibited by these two institutions, but we will provide a detailed description of the contracting process.

The pattern of contracts is easy to summarize: in the oral-bid auctions prices rise to levels that are to the disadvantage of the side with price initiative and fall to levels that are advantageous to this side in the posted-bid case. Why should this be? If we look at the first-period contracts on Figures 3 and 4 we see there is a great deal of similarity between the behaviour of the two institutions. Since this similarity is not preserved in later periods, it is clear that a fundamental difference in the two institutions is in the dynamics of adjustment.

### 1. *Oral Bid*

Figures 6 and 7 present the pricing and bidding dynamics of oral-bid experiments 2 and 4. These patterns, when compared with the data reported by Smith [6, pp. 192-193], demonstrate the generality of the dynamics seen in experiments of this type. In each period prices tend to start below the equilibrium, rise above, then decline to equilibrium near the end of the period. In period 1 buyers, having no information as to prices that might be acceptable to sellers, start probing with bids below equilibrium. Sellers, not knowing that later bids may be better or whether they will succeed in contracting at later bids, accept some of these initial low bids. (Since there is excess demand at these bids not all of them *can* be accepted.) This may induce buyers to try still lower bids, which are not accepted (observe bids 3-5 in Figure 6; bid 8 in Figure 7). When bids stand unaccepted, buyers are likely to raise their bids to induce sales. Once this occurs, sellers are alerted to the effect that their " waiting " has in raising prices. Thereafter contract prices rise and go above equilibrium with many bids standing unaccepted (thirteen in Figure 6 before the peak at 70 and seven in figure 7 before the peak, also at 70). This price rise is arrested because with bids much above equilibrium there is excess supply and " waiting " sellers tend to break their silence with two- and three-way ties to accept bids. Buyers, sensing seller eagerness as revealed by tied acceptances, now lower their bids, and the final few contracts are closer to the equilibrium. This pattern tends to repeat itself in each period except that (1) the first contracts occur at higher prices in successive periods (the time sequence of opening contract prices is 40, 40, 52, 55, 59, 59, 62 in Figure 6; and is 50, 50, 55, 55, 55, 57, 59, 59 in Figure 7), and (2) the price rise peaks out at lower prices in successive periods (70, 68, 68, 65, 65, 63, 62 in Figure 6; 70, 66, 65, 65, 64, 65, 64, 61 in Figure 7).

We are fortunate in experiment 4 to have the opportunity to observe the process when very few unaccepted bids occur. From period three on, notice that rising price sequences occur without unaccepted bids. This was a particularly active oral auction, and buyers may have been competitively raising bids to avoid the non-acceptance experienced in the first two periods or simply to avoid bid congestion. Also it may mean that some vehicle in addition to unaccepted bids is operating to express the excess demand. The tendency to overshoot

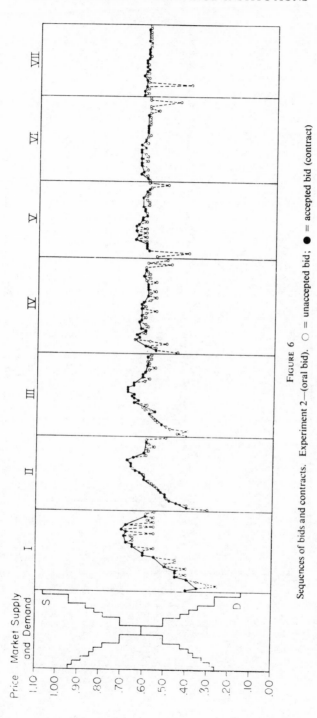

FIGURE 6

Sequences of bids and contracts. Experiment 2—(oral bid). ○ = unaccepted bid; ● = accepted bid (contract)

144         REVIEW OF ECONOMIC STUDIES

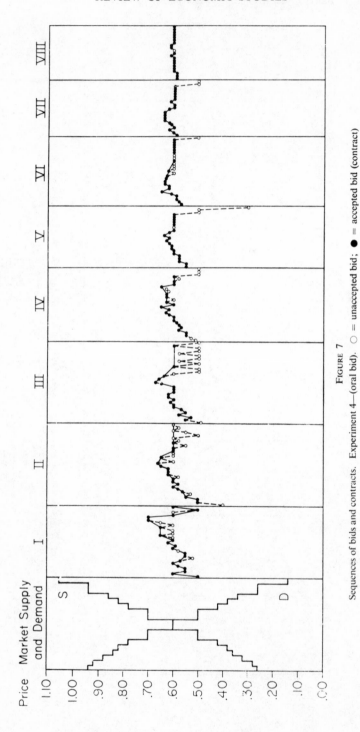

FIGURE 7

Sequences of bids and contracts. Experiment 4—(oral bid). ○ = unaccepted bid). ○ = unaccepted bid; ● = accepted bid (contract)

is lower in the absence of the unaccepted bids, thereby suggesting the importance of unaccepted bids as a partial explanation of the overshooting phenomenom.

### 2. *Posted Bid*

Figures 8 and 9 graph the sequence of bids entered by individual buyers in the two posted-bid experiments. In neither experiment is there a tendency for buyers to use changes in profits *alone* as a cue to future pricing decisions, so any model of the dynamics based on such a behavioural postulate would be suspect at best. For example, in experiment 1,

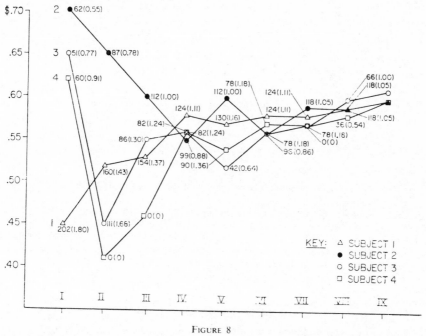

FIGURE 8

Buyer bids, profits, percentage of equilibrium profit by trading period. Experiment 1.

subject 1 increases prices for the first three periods even though it *seems* to produce reduced profits. He then lowers his price and experiences an increase in profits and raises prices for the rest of the experiment even though his profits continue to fall. Bidders experience two types of posterior errors in the announced price. It may be too high *or* too low. If it is the highest bid, then profits are lost if the bid is more than an epsilon above the next highest bidder. For example, in Figure 8 the high bidder always receives a smaller proportion of his potential profit than at least one other bidder. Subject 2 is severely penalized the first three periods by bidding too high. If a bid is the lowest, then, depending upon the distribution of remaining bids, sellers may satisfy all or most of their sales at the higher bids so that the volume for the low bidder is too small to yield a good profit (cf. Figure 9, period V). In experiment 1 the low bidder makes no purchases in periods II, III and VII, and only one in periods V and VIII.

The tendency for high and low bids to yield unsatisfactory profits has the expected effect on bid sequence as bidders begin to consider the actions of each other as well as their profits in formulating a bid strategy. In almost all periods of both experiments, the high

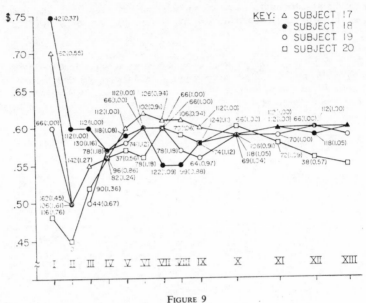

FIGURE 9

Buyer bids, profits, percentage of equilibrium profit by trading period. Experiment 3.

(low) bidder in period $t$ lowers (raises) his bid in period $t+1$. An exception occurs in periods XI, XII and XIII during experiment 3. Subject number 20 continues to lower his bid even in the face of greatly reduced profits. This, it seems, is a clear attempt at price leadership or tacit collusion. Most of our experience with these markets suggests that he will not have much success even though we suspect that the posted-bid institution provides a more favourable environment for co-operation than does the oral-bid auction.

## 8. SUMMARY AND CONCLUSIONS

We have studied two exchange institutions under experimental controls designed so that the experimental sessions were alike in all respects except that (1) experiments 1 and 3 (the " control " sessions) were conducted under irrevocable posted-bid exchange rules, while experiments 2 and 4 (the " treatment " sessions) were conducted under oral-bid rules (in each case only buyers made quotations), and (2) the subjects were different in the two sessions, but were obtained from the same population (Caltech undergraduates).

Experiments 1 and 3 replicated the findings of Williams in a multiunit posted-bid exchange experiment while experiments 2 and 4 replicated in the multiunit case the results Smith isolated for single-unit oral-bid auctions. We conclude that Williams' result—contract prices below equilibrium when buyers post bids—is due to the posted-bid institution and has nothing to do with individual traders' having a capacity to trade a single or several units in each trading period. We conclude that the Smith result—contract prices above equilibrium when buyers make oral bids—extends in its general pattern where subjects have a capacity to trade multiple units per trading period. Our explanation of the robust results of Williams is that the effect of seller discrimination causes buyers to bid lower than in the oral auction. Therefore, the posted-price institution is related analytically to sealed-bid auctions in which discrimination causes a lowering of bids, as demonstrated by the experimental results of Smith [7] and Belovicz [1].

Both the posted-price and the oral-bid markets reveal a high degree of efficiency. The oral bid, however, is consistently near 100 per cent efficiency. Both models of organization have implications about the distribution of income. Income tends to be distributed in *favour* of the side which posts a price bid (offer) and *against* the side which makes an oral price bid (offer).

A single unifying theory which explains all the observed regularities does not yet exist. We attempt to describe the dynamics and offer these results as an empirical challenge for those interested in price adjustment processes.

## APPENDIX: INSTRUCTIONS AND PAYMENT SCHEDULES

A.

### TABLE III
*Subject identification number*

| Subject number | Demand or supply based on revenue or cost conditions assigned to subject (see figure 2) | Experiment in which subject participated |
|---|---|---|
| 1 | $D_1$ | 1 |
| 2 | $D_1$ | 1 |
| 3 | $D_2$ | 1 |
| 4 | $D_2$ | 1 |
| 5 | $S_1$ | 1 |
| 6 | $S_1$ | 1 |
| 7 | $S_2$ | 1 |
| 8 | $S_2$ | 1 |
| 9 | $D_1$ | 2 |
| 10 | $D_1$ | 2 |
| 11 | $D_2$ | 2 |
| 12 | $D_2$ | 2 |
| 13 | $S_1$ | 2 |
| 14 | $S_1$ | 2 |
| 15 | $S_2$ | 2 |
| 16 | $S_2$ | 2 |
| 17 | $D_1$ | 3 |
| 18 | $D_1$ | 3 |
| 19 | $D_2$ | 3 |
| 20 | $D_2$ | 3 |
| 21 | $S_1$ | 3 |
| 22 | $S_1$ | 3 |
| 23 | $S_2$ | 3 |
| 24 | $S_2$ | 3 |
| 25 | $D_1$ | 4 |
| 26 | $D_1$ | 4 |
| 27 | $D_2$ | 4 |
| 28 | $D_2$ | 4 |
| 29 | $S_1$ | 4 |
| 30 | $S_1$ | 4 |
| 31 | $S_2$ | 4 |
| 32 | $S_2$ | 4 |

## B. INSTRUCTIONS: EXPERIMENTS 1 AND 2

The instructions used for these two experimental sessions are divided into five parts: General, Specific Instructions to Sellers, Specific Instructions to Buyers, Market Organization, Payoff Tables. The General section was identical for both sessions. The Specific Instructions for Sellers sections and the Specific Instructions for Buyers sections are almost the same[3] for both experiments, and the payoff formats were identical. The only major difference occurs in the Market Organization section, and the differences here reflect the changes in the treatment variable.

148           REVIEW OF ECONOMIC STUDIES

## INSTRUCTIONS

**General**

This is an experiment in the economics of market decision mak:.ng. Various research foundations have provided funds for the conduct of this research. The instructions are simple, and if you follow them carefully and make good decisions you might earn a considerable amount of money which will be paid to you in cash after the experiment.

In this experiment we are going to simulate a market in which some of you will be buyers and some of you will be sellers in a sequence of market days or trading periods. Two kinds of sheets will now be distributed—information for buyers and information for sellers. The sheets are identified and numbered. The number is only for data-collecting purposes. If you have received sellers' information, you will function only as a seller in this market. Similarly, if you have received buyers' information, you will function only as a buyer in this market. The information you have received is for your own private use. **Do not reveal it to anyone.**

This is a one commodity market in which there is no product differentiation. That is, each seller produces a product which is similar in all respects to the products offered by the other sellers. A seller is free to sell to any buyer or buyers. Likewise, a buyer may purchase from any seller or sellers.

**Specific Instructions for Sellers**

During each market period you are free to produce and sell any of the amounts listed on your information sheet. Assume that you produce only for immediate sale—there are no inventories. The dollar amounts listed in column 2 on your information sheet are your costs of producing that quantity.

Your payoffs are computed as follows: At the beginning of the experiment you will receive starting capital of $0.30. If you are able to make any sales, you will receive the difference between your sales revenue and your cost. For example, if you were to sell two units at $100 each, total revenue would be $200. Suppose your information sheet indicated that the cost of producing two units was $190. Your total profit would then be $200 − $190 = $10 for the trading period. If you sold two units for less than $190 you would incur a loss. Column 3 will be useful to a seller in deciding at any time during a given trading period whether to sell an additional unit. Suppose a seller has already sold one unit at a profit, and wants to know if he should sell a second unit. If the additional cost of producing the second unit is $10, then he will lose money on that unit if he sells it at any price below $10. Obviously, these figures are illustrative only and should not be assumed to apply to the actual sellers in this experiment.

All of your profits will be added to your starting capital, and any losses you might incur will be subtracted. Your total payoffs will be accumulated over several trading periods and the total amount will be paid to you after the experiment.

**Specific Instructions for Buyers**

During each market period you are free to purchase any of the quantities listed on your information sheet. Assume that you are buying this commodity for the purpose of reselling it in an entirely different market. The dollar amounts listed beside each quantity are the total value of that quantity. That is, they are the amounts you can sell that quantity for in the other market.

Your payoffs are computed as follows: You will receive starting capital of $0.30. If you are able to make any purchases, you will receive the difference between the total value as shown on your information sheet and the total amount you paid for the purchases. For example, if you were to purchase one unit for $105 and another for $95, you would obviously have paid a total of $200 for the two units. Suppose your information sheet indicated that the revenue from two units was $210. Your profit for the market period would then be $210 − $200 = $10. If you had paid more than $210 for the two units, you would have incurred a loss. Column 3 will be useful to a buyer in deciding at any time during a given period whether to buy an additional unit. Suppose a buyer has already bought two units at a profit, and wants to know if he should buy a third unit. If the additional revenue he gets from the third unit is $7, then he will lose money on that unit if he buys it at any price above $7. Obviously, these figures are illustrative only and should not be assumed to apply to the actual buyers in this experiment. All of your profits will be added to your starting capital, and any losses you might incur will be subtracted.

Your total payoffs will be accumulated over several trading periods and the total amount will be paid to you after the experiment.

**Market Organization** (included in Exp. 1 instructions but not Exp. 2)

The market for this commodity is organized as follows: we open the market for each trading day. Each buyer decides on a purchase price which he will write on one of the cards provided. The buyers will be given two minutes to submit their prices. The cards will be collected and the prices written on the blackboard. Sellers will then be free to make offers to sell whatever quantities they desire and to specify the buyer to whom they wish to sell. Offers will be made as follows: a seller will raise his hand and, when called upon, will state the quantity he wishes to sell and the buyer to whom he wishes to sell. The buyer will then accept any part of the seller's offer by stating the quantity he wishes to buy. However, when a buyer posts a price,

## TABLE IV

*Incentive schedules: Experiments 1 and 2*

Seller Number......

### SELLER'S COST SCHEDULE

| Quantity of commodity Q in each trading period | Total cost of producing Q units of commodity | Additional cost of producing the last or Qth unit of commodity |
|---|---|---|
| 0 | $0.00 | |
| | | $0.26 |
| 1 | 0.26 | |
| | | 0.38 |
| 2 | 0.64 | |
| | | 0.50 |
| 3 | 1.14 | |
| | | 0.60 |
| 4 | 1.74 | |
| | | 0.70 |
| 5 | 2.44 | |
| | | 0.78 |
| 6 | 3.22 | |
| | | 0.86 |
| 7 | 4.08 | |
| | | 0.94 |
| 8 | 5.02 | |

Seller Number......

### SELLER'S COST SCHEDULE

| Quantity of commodity Q in each trading period | Total cost of producing Q units of commodity | Additional cost of producing the last or Qth unit of commodity |
|---|---|---|
| 0 | $0.00 | |
| | | $0.28 |
| 1 | 0.28 | |
| | | 0.32 |
| 2 | 0.60 | |
| | | 0.36 |
| 3 | 0.96 | |
| | | 0.42 |
| 4 | 1.38 | |
| | | 0.50 |
| 5 | 1.88 | |
| | | 0.60 |
| 6 | 2.48 | |
| | | 0.70 |
| 7 | 3.18 | |
| | | 0.82 |
| 8 | 4.00 | |
| | | 0.94 |
| 9 | 4.94 | |
| | | 1.06 |
| 10 | 6.00 | |

Buyer Number......

### BUYER'S REVENUE SCHEDULE

| Quantity of commodity Q in each trading period | Total revenue from Q units of commodity | Additional revenue from the last or Qth unit of the commodity |
|---|---|---|
| 0 | $0.00 | |
| | | $0.92 |
| 1 | 0.92 | |
| | | 0.88 |
| 2 | 1.80 | |
| | | 0.84 |
| 3 | 2.64 | |
| | | 0.78 |
| 4 | 3.42 | |
| | | 0.70 |
| 5 | 4.12 | |
| | | 0.60 |
| 6 | 4.72 | |
| | | 0.50 |
| 6 | 5.22 | |
| | | 0.38 |
| 8 | 5.60 | |
| | | 0.26 |
| 9 | 5.86 | |
| | | 0.14 |
| 10 | 6.00 | |

Buyer Number......

### BUYER'S REVENUE SCHEDULE

| Quantity of commodity Q in each trading period | Total revenue from Q units of commodity | Additional revenue from the last or Qth unit of the commodity |
|---|---|---|
| 0 | $0.00 | |
| | | $0.94 |
| 1 | 0.94 | |
| | | 0.82 |
| 2 | 1.76 | |
| | | 0.70 |
| 3 | 2.46 | |
| | | 0.60 |
| 4 | 3.06 | |
| | | 0.50 |
| 5 | 3.56 | |
| | | 0.42 |
| 6 | 3.98 | |
| | | 0.34 |
| 7 | 4.32 | |
| | | 0.26 |
| 8 | 4.58 | |

he must be prepared *to buy at least one unit* if any seller wishes to sell to him. If a number of sellers desire to make simultaneous offers, one of them will be selected at random and he will then make his desired sales. If the first buyer will not purchase all units the seller wants to sell, the seller is free to make contracts with another buyer or buyers.

When the first seller has made all his contracts, another seller will be selected at random and he will make his desired purchases. The process will be continued until there are no offers to sell. This completes the trading day. We will reopen the market for a new trading day by having buyers submit new prices and the process will be repeated.

Are there any questions?

### Market Organization (included in Exp. 2 instructions but not Exp. 1)

The market for this commodity is organized as follows: we open the market for a trading day. Any buyer is free at any time to raise his hand and make a verbal bid to buy one unit of the commodity at a specified price. Any seller is free to accept or not accept the bid of any buyer but sellers cannot make counter offers. If a bid is accepted a binding contract has been closed for a single unit between that buyer and seller.

This process continues for a period of time. You will be warned in advance before the market closes and more bids will be called for before actually closing. This completes a market " day ". We will then reopen the market for a new trading period. The cost and revenue tables apply to each new trading period, and represent cost or revenue per period.

Are there any questions?

### C. INSTRUCTIONS: EXPERIMENTS 3 AND 4

Instructions used in Experimental Sessions 3 and 4 are identical with the exception of the section entitled " Market Organization ". The Market Organization sections outline the change in the treatment variable. Both forms are included below.

INSTRUCTIONS

### General

This is an experiment in the economics of market decision making. Various research foundations have provided funds for this research. The instructions are simple and if you follow them carefully and make good decisions you might earn a considerable amount of money which will be paid to you in cash.

In this experiment we are going to simulate a market in which some of you will be buyers and some of you will be sellers in a sequence of market days or trading periods. Attached to the instructions you will find a sheet, labelled Buyer or Seller, which describes the value to you of any decisions you might make. **You are not to reveal this information to anyone.** It is your own private information.

### Specific Instructions to Buyers

During each market period you are free to purchase from any seller or sellers as many units as you might want. For the first unit that you buy *during a trading period* you will receive the amount listed in row (1) marked *1st unit redemption value*; if you buy a second unit you will receive the additional amount listed in row (5) marked *2nd unit redemption value; etc.* The profits from each purchase (which are yours to keep) are computed by taking the difference between the redemption value and purchase price of the unit bought. *Under no conditions may you buy a unit for a price which exceeds the redemption value.* In addition to this profit you will receive a 5 cent commission for each purchase. That is

[your earnings = (redemption value) − (purchase price) + 0·05 commission].

Suppose for example that you buy two units and that your redemption value for the first unit is $200 and for the second unit is $180. If you pay $150 for your first unit and $160 for the second unit, your earnings are:

$$\text{\$ earnings from 1st} = 200 - 150 + 0·05 = 50·05$$
$$\text{\$ earnings from 2nd} = 180 - 160 + 0·05 = 20·05$$
$$\text{total \$ earnings} = 50·05 + 20·05 = 70·10$$

The blanks on the table will help you record your profits. The purchase price of the first unit you buy during the first period should be recorded on row (2) *at the time of purchase.* You should then record the profits on this purchase as directed on rows (3) and (4). At the end of the period record the total of profits and commissions on the last row (41) on the page. Subsequent periods should be recorded similarly.

### Specific Instructions to Sellers

During each market period you are free to sell to any buyer or buyers as many units as you might want. The first unit that you sell *during a trading period* you obtain at a cost of the amount listed on the attached sheet in the row (2) marked *cost of 1st unit*; if you sell a second unit you incur the cost listed in the row (6) marked *cost of the 2nd unit; etc.* The profits from each sale (which are yours to keep) are computed by

| Unit Sold | | Trading Period Number | 1 | 2 | 3 | 4 | 5 | 6 | 7 | 8 | 9 | 10 | 11 | 12 | 13 | 14 | 15 |
|---|---|---|---|---|---|---|---|---|---|---|---|---|---|---|---|---|---|
| 1 | 1 | 1st unit redemption value | .92 | .92 | .92 | .92 | .92 | .92 | .92 | .92 | .92 | .92 | .92 | .92 | .92 | .92 | .92 |
|  | 2 | Purchase price | | | | | | | | | | | | | | | |
|  | 3 | Profit (row 1 − row 2) | | | | | | | | | | | | | | | |
|  | 4 | Profit + 5 cents commission | | | | | | | | | | | | | | | |
| 2 | 5 | 2nd unit redemption value | .88 | .88 | .88 | .88 | .88 | .88 | .88 | .83 | .88 | .88 | .88 | .88 | .88 | .88 | .83 |
|  | 6 | Purchase price | | | | | | | | | | | | | | | |
|  | 7 | Profit (row 5 − row 6) | | | | | | | | | | | | | | | |
|  | 8 | Profit + 5 cents commission | | | | | | | | | | | | | | | |
| 3 | 9 | 3rd unit redemption value | .84 | .84 | .84 | .84 | .84 | .84 | .84 | .84 | .84 | .84 | .84 | .84 | .84 | .84 | .84 |
|  | 10 | Purchase price | | | | | | | | | | | | | | | |
|  | 11 | Profit (row 9 − row 10) | | | | | | | | | | | | | | | |
|  | 12 | Profit + 5 cents commission | | | | | | | | | | | | | | | |
| 4 | 13 | 4th unit redemption value | .73 | .78 | .78 | .78 | .78 | .78 | .78 | .78 | .78 | .78 | .78 | .78 | .78 | .78 | .78 |
|  | 14 | Purchase price | | | | | | | | | | | | | | | |
|  | 15 | Profit (row 13 − row 14) | | | | | | | | | | | | | | | |
|  | 16 | Profit + 5 cents commission | | | | | | | | | | | | | | | |
| 5 | 17 | 5th unit redemption value | .70 | .70 | .70 | .70 | .70 | .70 | .70 | .70 | .70 | .70 | .70 | .70 | .70 | .70 | .70 |
|  | 18 | Purchase price | | | | | | | | | | | | | | | |
|  | 19 | Profit (row 17 − row 18) | | | | | | | | | | | | | | | |
|  | 20 | Profit + 5 cents commission | | | | | | | | | | | | | | | |
| 6 | 21 | 6th unit redemption value | .60 | .60 | .60 | .60 | .60 | .60 | .60 | .60 | .60 | .60 | .60 | .60 | .60 | .60 | .60 |
|  | 22 | Purchase price | | | | | | | | | | | | | | | |
|  | 23 | Profit (row 21 − row 22) | | | | | | | | | | | | | | | |
|  | 24 | Profit + 5 cents commission | | | | | | | | | | | | | | | |
| 7 | 25 | 7th unit redemption value | .50 | .50 | .50 | .50 | .50 | .50 | .50 | .50 | .50 | .50 | .50 | .50 | .50 | .50 | .50 |
|  | 26 | Purchase price | | | | | | | | | | | | | | | |
|  | 27 | Profit (row 25 − row 26) | | | | | | | | | | | | | | | |
|  | 28 | Profit + 5 cents commission | | | | | | | | | | | | | | | |
| 8 | 29 | 8th unit redemption value | .38 | .38 | .38 | .38 | .38 | .38 | .38 | .38 | .38 | .38 | .38 | .38 | .38 | .38 | .38 |
|  | 30 | Purchase price | | | | | | | | | | | | | | | |
|  | 31 | Profit (row 29 − row 30) | | | | | | | | | | | | | | | |
|  | 32 | Profit + 5 cents commission | | | | | | | | | | | | | | | |
| 9 | 33 | 9th unit redemption value | .26 | .26 | .26 | .26 | .26 | .26 | .26 | .26 | .26 | .26 | .26 | .26 | .26 | .26 | .26 |
|  | 34 | Purchase price | | | | | | | | | | | | | | | |
|  | 35 | Profit (row 33 − row 34) | | | | | | | | | | | | | | | |
|  | 36 | Profit + 5 cents commission | | | | | | | | | | | | | | | |
| 10 | 37 | 10th unit redemption value | .14 | .14 | .14 | .14 | .14 | .14 | .14 | .14 | .14 | .14 | .14 | .14 | .14 | .14 | .14 |
|  | 38 | Purchase price | | | | | | | | | | | | | | | |
|  | 39 | Profit (row 37 − row 38) | | | | | | | | | | | | | | | |
|  | 40 | Profit + 5 cents commission | | | | | | | | | | | | | | | |
|  | 41 | Total per period earnings | | | | | | | | | | | | | | | |
|  | 42 | Damages | | | | | | | | | | | | | | | |
|  | 43 | Net income | | | | | | | | | | | | | | | |
|  | 44 | Capital payment | | | | | | | | | | | | | | | |

Name_____ Soc. Sec. No._____ Total Payment_____

Address_____

FIGURE 10

Record of Purchases and Earnings, Buyers No. 1 & 2

taking the difference between the price at which you sold the unit and the cost of the unit. *Under no conditions may you sell a unit at a price below the cost of the unit.* In addition to this profit you will receive a 5 cent commission for each sale. That is

[your earnings = (sale price of unit) − (cost of unit) + (0·05 commission).]

Your total profits and commissions for a trading period, which are yours to keep, are computed by adding up the profit and commissions on sales made during the trading period.

Suppose, for example, your cost of the 1st unit is $140 and your cost of the second unit is $160. For illustrative purposes we will consider only a two-unit case. If you sell the first unit at $200 and the second unit at $190, your earnings are:

$$\text{\$ earnings from 1st} = 200 - 140 + 0·05 = 60·05$$
$$\text{\$ earnings from 2nd} = 190 - 160 + 0·05 = 30·05$$
$$\text{total \$ earnings} = 60·05 + 30·05 = 90·10$$

The blanks on the table will help you record your profits. The sale price of the first unit you sell during the 1st period should be recorded on row (1) *at the time of sale*. You should then record the profits on this sale as directed on rows (3) and (4). At the end of the period record the total of profits and commissions on the last row (41) on the page. Subsequent periods should be recorded similarly.

**Market Organization** (included in instructions for Exp. 3 but not Exp. 4)

The market for this commodity is organized as follows: we open the market for each trading day. Each buyer decides on a purchase price which he will write on one of the cards provided. The buyers will be given two minutes to submit their prices. The cards will be collected and the prices written on the blackboard. Sellers will then be free to make offers to sell whatever quantities they desire and to specify the buyer to whom they wish to sell. Offers will be made as follows: a seller will be chosen using random numbers, and will state the quantity he wishes to sell and the buyer to whom he wishes to sell. The buyer will then accept any part of the seller's offer by stating the quantity he wishes to buy. However, when a buyer posts a price, he must be prepared *to buy at least one unit*. If the first buyer will not purchase all units the seller wants to sell, the seller is free to choose a second buyer, and so on.

When the first seller has made all his contracts, another seller will be selected at random and he will make his desired purchases. The process will be continued until there are no offers to sell. This completes the trading day. We will reopen the market for a new trading day by having buyers submit new prices and the process will be repeated. Except for the offers and their acceptance you are not to speak to any other subject. You are free to make as much profit as you can.

Are there any questions?

**Market Organization** (included in instructions for Exp. 4 but not Exp. 3)

The market for this commodity is organized as follows: we open the market for a trading period (a trading "day"). The period lasts for      minutes. Any buyer is free at any time during the period, to raise his hand and make a verbal bid to buy one unit of the commodity at a specified price. Any seller is free to accept or not accept the bid of any buyer but *sellers cannot make counter offers*. If a bid is accepted a binding contract has been closed for a single unit and the buyer and seller will record the contract price to be included in their earnings. Any ties in bids or acceptances will be resolved by a random choice of buyer or seller. Except for the bids and their acceptance you are not to speak to any other subject. There are likely to be many bids that are not accepted, but you are free to keep trying, and as a buyer or a seller you are free to make as much profit as you can.

Are there any questions?

*First version received July* 1975; *final version accepted May* 1976 (*Eds.*).

We are grateful for National Science Foundation financial support for this research.

NOTES

1. The behaviour on the supply side could be a point where the analogy fails. In the case of a discriminative sealed-bid auction the bidder states the maximum quantity he will accept along with his price bid. Then the supplier, following the institutional convention, sells to the highest bidder the amount the bidder desires and moves on to the next highest bidder, etc. This continues until the total quantity offered is exhausted. There is no attempt on the part of the supplier to act strategically by failing to supply all that is requested at a price (and thus influence prices) or by favouring in quantity those buyers who have historically offered higher prices. The reader may recognize this lack of strategic behaviour as the competitive supply response. Indeed, if we can depend upon competitive responses by suppliers in the posted-bid auction, the analogy between the two institutions would appear to be close.

2. Data regarding all bids, offers and individual contracts are available from the authors.

3. The instructions are those used in experimental session 2. Those used in experiment 1 are identical to these after the following sentences are deleted. In the Specific Instructions to Sellers section delete: " Column 3 will be useful to a seller deciding at any time during a given trading period whether to sell an additional unit. Suppose a seller has already sold one unit at a profit and wants to know if he should sell a second unit. If the additional cost of producing the second unit is $10, then he will lose money on that unit if he sells it at any price below $10." In the Specific Instructions to Buyers section delete: " Column 3 will be useful to a buyer in deciding at any time during a given period whether to buy an additional unit. Suppose a buyer has already bought two units at a profit, and wants to know if he should buy a third unit. If the additional revenue he gets from the third unit is $7, then he will lose money on that unit if he buys it at any price above $7."

REFERENCES

[1]   Belovicz, Mayer W. " The Sealed-Bid Auction: Experimental Studies " (PhD dissertation, Purdue University, August 1967).
[2]   Hess, Alan C. " Experimental Evidence on Price Formation in Competitive Markets ", *Journal of Political Economy*, **80**, 2 (March/April 1972), 375-385.
[3]   Hurwicz, Leonid. " The Design of Mechanism for Resource Allocation ", *American Economic Review*, **63**, 2 (May 1973), 1-30.
[4]   Rothschild, Michael. " Models of Market Organization with Imperfect Information: A Survey ", *Journal of Political Economy*, **81**, 6 (November/December 1973), 1283-1308.
[5]   Smith, Vernon L. " An Experimental Study of Competitive Market Behavior ", *Journal of Political Economy*, **70**, 2 (April 1962), 111-137.
[6]   Smith, Vernon L. " Effect of Market Organization on Competitive Equilibrium ", *Quarterly Journal of Economics*, **78**, 94 (May 1964), 181-201.
[7]   Smith, Vernon L. " Experimental Studies of Discrimination Versus Competition in Sealed-Bid Auction Markets ", *Journal of Business*, **40**, 1 (January 1967), 56-84.
[8]   Smith, Vernon L. " Experimental Economics: Induced Value Theory ", *American Economic Review*, **66**, 2 (May 1976).
[9]   Williams, Fred. " Effect of Market Organization on Competitive Equilibrium: The Multiunit Case ", *Review of Economic Studies*, **40** (January 1973), 97-113.

# [7]

# Relevance of Laboratory Experiments to Testing Resource Allocation Theory

*VERNON L. SMITH*

DEPARTMENT OF ECONOMICS
UNIVERSITY OF ARIZONA
TUCSON, ARIZONA

## 1. Introduction

Microeconomics, including the study of individual choice and of group choice in market and nonmarket processes, has generally been considered a field science as distinct from an experimental science. Hence microeconomics has sometimes been classified as "nonexperimental" and closer methodologically to meteorology and astronomy than to physics and experimental psychology (Marschak, 1950, p. 3; Samuelson, 1973, p. 7). But the question of using experimental or nonexperimental techniques is largely a matter of cost, and generally the cost of conducting the most ambitious and informative experiments in astronomy, meteorology, and economics varies from prohibitive down to considerable. The cost of experimenting with different solar system planetary arrangements, different atmospheric conditions, and different national unemployment rates, each under suitable controls, must be regarded as prohibitive. On a more feasible scale, cloud-seeding experiments, Jupiter–Saturn scientific space probes, and field experiments in negative income taxes and education vouchers, while costly, are not prohibitive. But these more grandiose experiments are of recent occurrence, and basic scientific development in the cases of astronomy and meteorology has depended upon small-scale laboratory experiments in the physics of mass motion, thermodynamics, and nuclear reactions.

In this paper we try to develop a foundation for the study of resource allocation mechanisms entirely in terms of propositions that are testable, and

**345**

tested, by means of controlled laboratory experiments. The question implicit throughout the paper is What can we, and do we, know with high credibility about allocative mechanisms? The statement "high credibility" means that the propositions have been tested under controls that can be evaluated and scrutinized, and the results replicated, by other researchers. Specifically, we can reject the hypothesis that the researcher and his subjects are themselves a significant treatment variable and become as sure as we please of the propositions by repeated replication. Although the measurement and verification of hypotheses about individual behavior, e.g., Slutsky–Hicks demand theory (Battalio *et al.*, 1973), are of coequal importance in experimental economics, the discussion here will be limited to experimental studies of resource allocation mechanisms.

## 2. Some Preceptual Foundations of Experimental Economics

Three precepts are offered to constitute a foundation for the use of laboratory experimental methods in testing hypotheses about the behavior of allocation mechanisms.[1]

**Precept 1:** *Nonsatiation* (Smith, 1976a). Given a *costless* choice between two alternatives which differ only in that the first yields more of the reward medium (e.g., currency) than the second, the first will always be chosen (preferred) over the second by an *autonomous* individual, i.e., utility $U(M)$ is a monotone increasing function of the reward medium.

In credible economics experiments real people must make real decisions about objects or activities that have real value. Since control is the essence of experimental methodology, it is critically important that the experimenter be able to control or specify individual values to a degree that allows one to state that as between two experiments individual values either do or do not differ in a specific way. Precept 1 allows such control to be achieved by using a reward structure to *induce value* on the objects traded, or the actions taken, in a particular experimental setting.

EXAMPLE 1. The simplest example of the application of Precept 1, and one that is used frequently in market mechanism experiments, is that of inducing a demand for units of an abstract commodity. Let subject buyers, $i = 1, 2, \ldots, n$, each be given a function (in graphical or tabular form) listing increasing concave currency receipts $R_i(q_i)$ to be provided by the experi-

---

[1] Also see Fiorina & Plott (1975) and Plott (1978) for further discussion of methodological aspects of laboratory decision experiments.

menter for $q_i$ units purchased in an experimental market. Neoclassical demand is defined as the set of alternative quantities that would be purchased contingent upon corresponding given prices prevailing in the market. Assuming differentiability, at price $p$ the utility to $i$ of purchasing $q_i$ units is $U_i[R_i(q_i) - pq_i]$, which is a maximum for $q_i > 0$ if and only if $[R_i'(q_i) - p] U_i'[\cdot] = 0$ for $U_i$ concave in $q_i$. Since $U_i' > 0$, the $i$th individual induced demand is $q_i = R_i'^{(-1)}(p)$. Hence the induced market demand for $n$ individuals is $Q = \sum_{i=1}^{n} R_i'^{(-1)}(p)$.

EXAMPLE 2. Subject agents are each given a function (in graphical or tabular form) listing quasi-concave total currency receipts, $V^i(y_i, X)$ to be paid to $i$ if $i$ retains $y_i$ units of a private good and the collective of agents agrees on the quantity $X$ of a public good. Then $i$'s unknown utility for money $U_i(\cdot)$ induces the utility $U_i[V^i(y_i, X)]$ on any point $(y_i, X)$. Induced on each subject is the experimentally controlled indifference map given by the level contours of $V^i(y_i, X) = $ constant, independent of a particular subject's utility of money. That is, each $i$'s marginal rate of substitution of $y_i$ for $X$ is given by

$$\frac{dy_i}{dX} \equiv -\frac{U_i'V_2^i}{U_i'V_1^i} = -\frac{V_2^i}{V_1^i}, \quad \text{if} \quad U_i' > 0.$$

It is assumed that $V^i$ is increasing in $y_i$ for all $i$, but $V^i$ could be increasing or decreasing in $X$ depending on whether $X$ is a "good" or a "bad" for any particular agent. The experimenter need not be constrained to impose the condition that the common outcome variable $X$ be a good for every agent.

It might be supposed that using currency to induce value on abstract experimental choices is an artificial procedure peculiar to the methodology of laboratory decision studies. But this interpretation is incorrect. Economic systems produce countless examples of intangible property on which value is induced by virtue of the specification of conditions under which the holder of the intangible item may claim money or goods. All financial instruments such as shares, bonds, options, futures contracts, and indeed fiat money itself have value induced upon the instruments by the bundle of rights they convey. Experimental instructions define the rights of subject agents, and specify the institutions of decision making in the experiment. In Example 1, subject buyer $i$ is given the unabridged right to claim $R_i(q_i)$ units of money (less any specified costs) from the experimenter in return for the acquisition of $q_i$ units of "commodity" under the trading rules of the exchange institution. Without such a right a subject need have no more motivation to purchase the experimental commodity than would an investor who had no claim to the earnings and assets of Chrysler Corporation as a result of purchasing the company's stock.

VERNON L. SMITH

At least three important qualifications to the theory of induced valuation based upon Precept 1 must be recognized because these qualifications constitute potential pitfalls to the routine, casual, or mechanical interpretation of experimental results. These qualifications stem from the adjectives "costless" and "autonomous" in the statement of Precept 1 and will be summarized in the following precept.

**Precept 2:** *Complexity.* In general individual decision makers must be assumed to have multidimensional values which attach nonmonetary subjective cost or value to (1) the process of making and executing individual or group decisions, (2) the end result of such decisions, and (3) the rewards (and perhaps behavior) of other individuals involved in the decision process.

This precept covers the phenomenon of subjective transaction cost or the cost of thinking, calculating, and acting (cf. Marschak, 1968), the possible commodity value of decision outcomes, and interpersonal utilities. Since the subjects in an economics experiment are a sample drawn from the socioeconomic system, they can be expected to exhibit the behavioral characteristics of economic agents in that system.

One such characteristic is the attachment of subjective cost (or value) to the making and execution of market or other social decisions. In an auction market experiment a subject may find it arduous to monitor quotations, make his own quotations, and execute transactions. In a voting experiment a subject may see the process of agenda discussion, thinking about alternatives, and voting as toilsome activities. If such considerations are not negligible, they may be an important source of uncontrolled individual valuation of actions. Hence the utility function for $i$ becomes $U^i(M, E)$ where $M$ is monetary reward, and $E$ is the "transactional effort" required to obtain this reward (cf. Leibenstein, 1976, for an analysis of the effect of such nonmonetary disutilities on traditional microeconomic theory). If $E$ depends on the level of the rewarded activity, such as $q_i$ in Example 1, then there is some inevitable loss of control over the value induced on that activity. This is why a very small transaction commission is usually paid in auction market experiments, and why one tries to design experiments so that the reward is large relative to the mechanical complexity of the decision task (see Smith (1976a)). In the strict sense such nonmonetary utilities or disutilities give rise to a fundamental "principle of indeterminacy" of induced value,[2] although practically, at least in many laboratory experiments, the problem can be finessed by simple experimental design procedures.

---

[2] That is, we use a reward medium to induce *gross* value, but *net* value is indeterminant because we do not observe the subjective costs of transaction, decision and calculation that are implicit in the task.

As with their counterparts in the economy, experimental subjects may attach subjective "game value" to experimental outcomes. Thus a make-believe profit $R_i(q_i) - pq_i$ may have subjective value $S_i[R_i(q_i) - pq_i]$. If $S_i$ is monotone increasing, then such gaming utilities create no methodological problems since they reinforce rather than distort the effect of an explicit monetary reward structure. Using instructions to induce role-playing behavior (i.e., acting as if profits were real) can be useful and informative, but the results are more likely to be sensitive to particular experimenters, subject groups, task complexity, and other sources of variability.

Another characteristic of economic agents, and therefore experimental subjects, is that they may not be autonomous own-reward maximizers. Interpersonal utility criteria may upset the theory of induced value as contained in Precept 1 by allowing equity, altruistic, or invidious comparisons to influence subjective realized value. This distorting interdependence is usually controlled satisfactorily by the condition of "incomplete information" (Fouraker & Siegel, 1963) wherein subject monetary rewards are only known privately during an experiment. Since such rewards are for the purpose of inducing utility on outcomes, and such utility is not observable in economic agents, this privacy condition is relevant to capturing "realism" in most experimental designs.

It is natural and important to inquire as to the relevancy of the results obtained from laboratory experiments to the behavior of economic agents in the economic system at large. This leads us to

**Precept 3:**   *Parallelism.*   Propositions about the behavior of individuals and of markets and other resource allocation mechanisms that have been tested in laboratory environments apply also to nonlaboratory environments where similar *ceteris paribus* conditions prevail.

This precept is not unique to social science but has relevance to all experimental methods.

We apply the term "parallelism" to the proposition suggested by Harlow Shapley (1964, p. 43) that "as far as we can tell, the same physical laws prevail everywhere." A science of astronomy or meteorology would scarcely have been possible without the maintained hypothesis that the physical laws of mass motion and the thermodynamics of gases, verifiable in small-scale laboratory experiments, had application to the stars and the climate. Furthermore, since nonexperimental measurements in astronomy and meteorology have not yet contradicted these physical laws, one has accepted this parallelism as having been confirmed.

This concept has important application to the study of microeconomic behavior. Two important research implications follow whenever replicable laboratory behavior has been firmly demonstrated. First, one should seek those extensions or modifications of existing theory that explain why it occurs, and second, one should seek field tests of the hypothesis that the behavior is also manifest in other, ostensibly "richer," environments.[3] The robustness of a behavioral "law" across different environments can only be determined empirically. Theories normally abstract from all those characteristics which lead one to apply the adjective "richer" to a given environment, and hence represent statements about behavior that are hypothesized to be independent of the environment. But this indepondence hypothesis may not be correct, and by comparing behavior in different environments one may establish a basis for important extensions in theory.

Experiments are sometimes criticized for not being "realistic", i.e., parallelism is questioned. There are two appropriate responses to this criticism: First, if the purpose of the experiment is to test a theory, are the elements of alleged unrealism in the experiment parameters of the theory? If not, then the criticism must be directed to the theory as much as to the experiment. Laboratory experiments are normally as "rich" as the theories they test. Second, are there field data to support the criticism, i.e., data suggesting that there may be differences between laboratory and field behavior. If not, then the criticism is pure speculation; if so, then it is important to parametrize the theory to include the behavior in question.

What is important about an experiment is that it be relevant to its purpose, not that it be realistic in the sense that it be "real-world-like" in some subjective sense. Indeed, the best experiment is the *crucial* experiment whose outcome clearly distinguishes between competing theories. But the conditions of the crucial experiment may rarely, if ever, occur in nature.

For example, one of the crucial experiments of relativity theory is to determine if stars behind the edge of the sun appear to be displaced from their known positions during a total solar eclipse (i.e., whether or not light signals "bend" in gravitational fields). One does not object to such experimental observations because solar eclipses are not "realistic," i.e., not commonly observed; rather one marvels at this scientific exploitation of an unusual event. Similarly in particle physics, experimentalists synthesize unnatural conditions to produce particles predicted by theory but unobservable in the natural order. Fouraker & Siegel (1963) have studied duopoly and triopoly price competition under the homogeneous product condition. This is "unrealistic" in the sense that such perfect oligopoly conditions are rarely, if ever, encountered in the field. A major Fouraker and Siegel finding is a strong

---

[3] See Plott & Levine (1974) for an interesting field experiment in the effect of agenda on majority rule group decision. Following the field experiment the authors designed similar laboratory experiments to test the replicability of their field results and to vary the agenda as a treatment variable in their model of group decision.

tendency for triopolies and even duopolies to converge to the Bertrand competitive price solution. These results can be interpreted as providing an important explanation of *why* one so rarely observes homogenous product competition among the few. It is unprofitable; hence there are strong incentives for product differentiation. So is the experiment "unrealistic," or does it provide a relevant explanation of why the conditions of the experiment are not likely to survive in "nature"? How does one acquire an understanding of why institutions and their outcomes are as we observe them? I know of no way other than to experiment with alternative institutions and observe the consequent outcomes.

## 3. Dynamic Market Adjustment Hypotheses

Two sets of experiments designed to test hypotheses about the dynamic adjustment behavior of oral double auction markets are reported in this section.

### 3.1. Two Experimental Markets with Growing Demand

Hess (1972) has studied the effects of period-by-period changes in both supply and demand in an experimental double auction market. However, the subjects did not receive cash profit rewards, and as indicated above, this may affect outcomes in market experiments. The sequence of changed supply and demand was designed to create and reinforce the expectation that price rises a fixed amount (10 cents) each period. The effect of this expectation on the subsequent empirical observations was determined in each of four different experimental sessions. This price expectation "treatment" was found to bias actual prices away from their theoretical values.

Arrow (1960) and Arrow & Capron (1959) have discussed price–quantity adjustments in competitive markets with rising demands. Assuming a linear demand function increasing linearly with time and a linear Walrasian adjustment process, Arrow proves several propositions briefly paraphrased as follows:

1. The shortage (defined as excess demand) increases from the initial value of 0 toward an asymptotic limit.
2. Prices rise, and the increase approaches a constant rate depending only on supply and demand conditions.
3. Actual price is always below the price that would clear the market.

These propositions also hold under the hypothesis of adaptive expectations, i.e., where the economic agent compares actual price with his previous expectation of it and then forms a new expectation by revising his previous expectation in the direction of the actual price.[4]

Two experiments designed to approximate the conditions of the preceding propositions are used to test their validity. In each experiment demand rises linearly with time, where "time" is measured in terms of trading periods, and the experimental supply and demand conditions are approximately linear.

Twenty-seven subjects participated in the first experiment and forty-seven in the second. The instructions were those of the double auction (Smith, 1964, pp. 199–201 where both buyers and sellers are permitted to make oral quotations (bids or offers). Each buyer (seller) received a 5 cent commission in addition to the profit from exchange. Profit was equal to buyer value or limit price minus purchase price (for sellers, price minus cost).

Experiment 1 consisted of six trading periods. At the end of each of the first four trading periods the buyers' cards were collected, and a new set of buyer limit prices, corresponding to an increase in demand, were distributed randomly among the buyers. Consequently, the highest limit buyer in period 1 would not be, except by accident, the highest limit buyer in period 2. The first five trading periods were characterized by the five demand arrays exhibited on the left of Fig. 1. At the end of the fifth trading period the buyer limit cards were collected, just as in the previous periods, except that this time the new cards that were distributed corresponded to a repeat treatment of the period 5 demand condition. Hence the subjects did not know at any time that the demand had increased in periods 2 through 5, nor that it had not increased in the case of period 6. They knew only what was obvious—that buyers were receiving new limit price cards. Subject information consisted only of their private limit prices, the sequence of verbal bids, offers, and contract prices that prevailed in each trading period.

Experiment 2 used approximately the same supply and demand conditions as in 1, except that seven trading periods were conducted with the six demand schedules shown on the left of Fig. 2. The first experiment used undergraduates at Stanford, the second used public school teachers in a summer program at Purdue.

The response of contract prices in experiments 1 and 2 is graphed on the right in Figs. 1 and 2. Contract prices tend to be equal to or below the theoretical equilibrium in the first three periods of each experiment. In experiment 1 (2), only one (three) of the fifteen contracts in periods 1 to 3 were above equilibrium. But in period 5 of experiment 1 only one contract is below the theoretical equilibrium, and in experiment 2, period 6, only three of thirteen

---

[4] See Arrow (1960, pp. 8–13) for a rigorous derivation of these propositions and their extension using adaptive (trend) expectations.

RELEVANCE OF LABORATORY EXPERIMENTS                              **353**

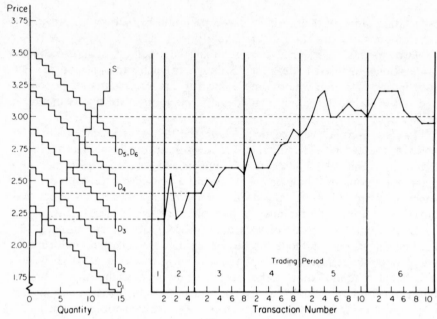

**Fig. 1.**

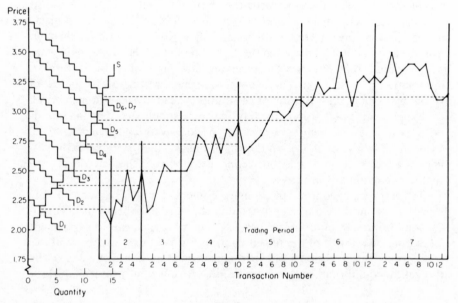

**Fig. 2.**

TABLE 1

PRICE–QUANTITY BEHAVIOR WITH GROWING DEMAND

| | Experiment 1 | | | | Experiment 2 | | | |
|---|---|---|---|---|---|---|---|---|
| Period | Theoretical price | Mean price | Increase in mean price | Shortage | Theoretical price | Mean price | Increase in mean price | Shortage |
| 1 | 2.20 | 2.20 | | 0 | 2.175 | 2.10 | | 2 |
| 2 | 2.40 | 2.36 | .16 | 1 | 2.375 | 2.34 | .24 | 2 |
| 3 | 2.60 | 2.53 | .17 | 2 | 2.50 | 2.40 | .06 | 4 |
| 4 | 2.80 | 2.73 | .20 | 2 | 2.725 | 2.73 | .33 | 0 |
| 5 | 3.00 | 3.05 | .32 | −1 | 2.925 | 2.90 | .17 | 0 |
| 6 | 3.00 | | | | 3.125 | 3.22 | .32 | −3 |
| 7 | | | | | 3.125 | | | |

contracts are below equilibrium. Proposition 3 fails to be supported in period 5 of experiment 1 and period 6 of experiment 2. Using a $t$ test on the contract prices in these two periods, we reject the hypothesis (Proposition 3) that the data came from populations with a mean equal to $3.00 ($t = 2.86$) in experiment 1 and equal to $3.125 ($t = 2.81$) in experiment 2. In each experiment the experience of rising prices eventually produced expectations that caused sellers to raise their offers (and buyers to accept) above the theoretical equilibrium.

Evidence contrary to Proposition 1 is shown in Table 1. The "shortage" is interpreted, i.e., measured, as initial excess demand prevailing at the mean contract price. The proposition is violated in period 5 of experiment 1 and periods 4, 5, and 6 of experiment 2.

Also in Table 1 it is seen that the mean price rises in successive periods, but, at least for the limited number of periods observed, the increase in price does not appear to be approaching a constant[5] (Proposition 2).

## 3.2. SPECULATION AND INTERTEMPORAL EQUILIBRIUM

Samuelson (1957) has provided an extension to intertemporal markets of the assumption sometimes made for stationary markets, that economic agents have "perfect" knowledge in the sense of foreknowledge of market supply and demand. Experiments such as those reported in the next sec-

[5] See Carlson (1967) for an experimental test of the cobweb theorem in dynamic markets with a lagged supply response. Carlson reports convergence in such markets even in the so-called "unstable" case. Both Carlson's experiments and those reported here suggest that conventional dynamic theory does not provide satisfactory models of price adjustment behavior.

tion make it obvious that such assumptions are not necessary to yield convergence to competitive equilibria under the oral double auction exchange mechanism. A recent experimental study (Miller, Plott, & Smith, 1977) has examined the hypothesis that, under incomplete information, speculation will narrow seasonal price differences significantly below the theoretical price differences in the absence of speculation. Williams (1977) has replicated this work and extended it to test the hypothesis that speculation will narrow actual, as well as theoretical, seasonal price differences.

In these two studies the intertemporal experimental paradigm is one in which (unknown to the subjects) demand cycles from $D_b$ in the "blue" (B) season to $D_y$ in the "yellow" (Y) season in each period, while the supply $S$ is stationary from one season to the next. These demand and supply configurations are shown on the left of Figs. 3 and 4. Again the double oral auction price mechanism was used in each season of trading. Six buyers each had a capacity to buy two units at specified limit prices that were different in each season. These limit prices defined demands $D_b$ and $D_y$ for up to twelve units per season as shown. Six sellers each had a capacity to sell two units at specified limit (cost) prices which did not differ between seasons. These limit prices defined the supply $S$ shown in Figs. 3 and 4.

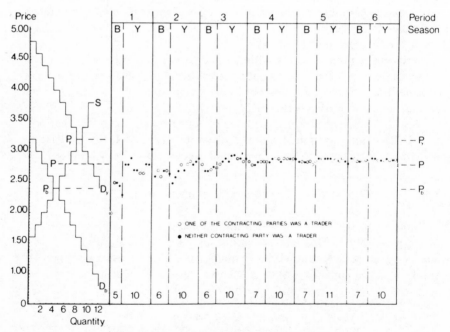

Fig. 3. [From Miller, Plott, & Smith (1977).]

VERNON L. SMITH

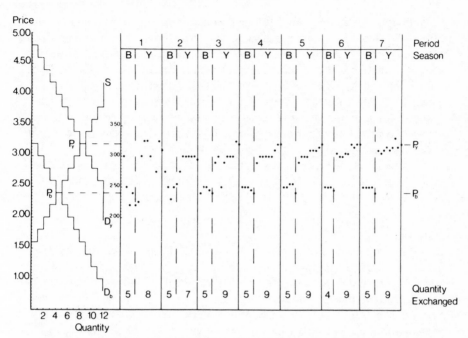

**Fig. 4.** [Reprinted from V. L. Smith (Ed.), *Research in Experimental Economies*, Volume 1, JAI PRESS INC., 1979.]

Finally, in each experiment two "traders" were given the power to buy any number of units in a B season. Any units thus purchased could be carried over (at zero cost) for resale only in the subsequent Y season. Since it was possible for these traders to make losses they were each given a $3 initial capital endowment. No subject had *any* information on market demand or supply, but all subjects could observe the bids, offers, and contracts as they occurred.

In Fig. 3 (from Miller *et al.* 1977), during period 1 two purchases were made by traders in *B*, and resold in *Y*. In periods 2 and 3 traders carried over three units, and in the subsequent periods they carried over five units. Effectively, market prices were very near the intertemporal equilibrium by period 3. The optimal trader carry-over was four units, but they consistently carried over five units in periods 4 to 6. This was because in each of these periods at least one seller, able to make a profit at these prices, failed to negotiate a sale before the trading season ended (seasons were timed, 5 minutes in length). In each case either a seller quoted offers too high to be accepted, or the offer lost to another seller. This reduced effective supply in the yellow season and permitted the unit of excess demand to be filled in by a trader carrying over an additional unit.

Williams (1977) replicated this experiment with different subjects, and obtained essentially the same results. He also designed and executed an autarky (i.e., no speculating traders participated) experiment with the same parameters and procedure. His results are reproduced in Fig. 4. Note the tendency of contract prices to lag behind the cyclical shifts in demand which is to be expected in view of the similar "hysteresis" effects in Figs. 1 and 2 for growing demand. But in successive trading periods the gap between contract prices widens. Comparing Figs. 3 and 4 it is clear that speculation is a significant treatment variable.

The null hypothesis that the prices observed in the B and Y seasons of the final trading period came from populations with means equal to the autarky prices in these seasons is tested with the $t$ statistic

$$t(n_1 + n_2 - 2) = \bar{p}_y - \bar{p}_b - (p_y^* - p_b^*)/s\sqrt{(1/n_1) + (1/n_2)}.$$

$\bar{p}_i$ is the sample mean of $n_i$ prices for $i = $ b, y, and $p_i^*$ is the autarky price for $i = $ b, y. $s^2$ is the pooled estimate of the population variance for the combined B and Y seasons. In the Miller, Plott, Smith experiment, $t = -59.8$, and in the Williams replication $t = -19.5$ both significant with better than a .001 confidence level. Williams (1977) compared his speculation market and autarky market mean prices giving $t = -10.72$. Consequently, the null hypothesis that "speculation" is an ineffective treatment variable is still rejected at better than a .001 level of confidence. In this sense we know with "high credibility" that speculation is effective in providing an intertemporal equilibrium.

## 4. Effect of Information on Price Convergence in Competitive Markets

One of the most prominent, replicable, empirical properties of the double auction competitive price mechanism is its rapid convergence to the supply and demand equilibrium under the condition of incomplete information, or privacy, where each agent knows only his own marginal valuation or marginal cost function (Smith, 1976b). It might be supposed that under complete information, where each agent is informed of the value and cost functions of other agents, market convergence would improve, or at minimum not be worse. As briefly reported earlier (Smith, 1976a, p. 278), there is at least one class of crucial experiments for which this proposition must be rejected, namely the class in which all the exchange surplus is obtained by the buyers (or sellers) at the equilibrium price. Precept 2 provides a possible explanation of why this is the case: when agents know each other's payoffs, it provides scope for interpersonal utility considerations to impinge upon behavior.

The supply and demand curves on the left of Figs. 5 and 6 have the characteristic that at the equilibrium price the entire exchange surplus of $1.10 (plus a 5 cent "commission") per transaction is captured by the buyers. Sellers receive only the 5 cent commission. In Fig. 5 the excess supply for all feasible transaction prices is five units, while for Fig. 6 excess supply is eight units. The panels in each figure plot successive transaction prices for independent groups of subjects, i.e., no subject participated in more than one of the eight experimental sessions. In each figure the (a) and (b) experiments were conducted under the incomplete information condition, the (c) experiments applied complete information, and the (d) experiments applied incomplete information initially for two (or three)

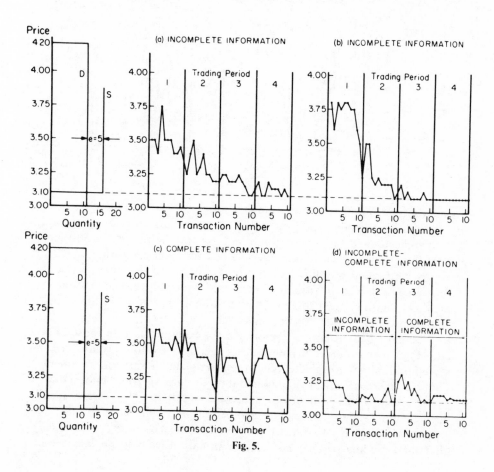

Fig. 5.

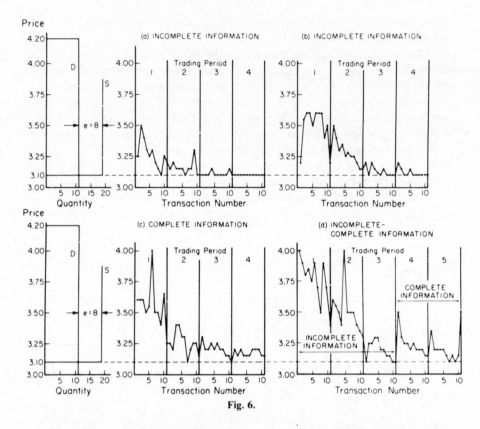

Fig. 6.

periods, then complete information was provided, and trading resumed for two additional trading periods. In all experimental sessions except 5(d) each subject could buy (or sell) one unit per trading period. In 5(d) there were three sellers, each of whom could sell six units per period, and two buyers who could buy five and six units respectively per trading period. Providing "complete information" meant informing all subjects that buyers each had limit prices $4.20 and sellers $3.10 and that up to 11 units could be purchased and up to 16 (19) units sold.

Comparing the results of the (a) and (b) experiments with those of (c), both Figs. 5 and 6 make it plain that convergence is more pronounced or more rapid in the incomplete than in the complete information treatments. That the differences are attributable to the treatment variable "information" is reinforced by the "switchover" experiments 5(d) and 6(d). In 5(d) introducing complete information after two periods of trading leads to a distinct "jump" in the level of contract prices, and similarly, in experiment 6(d) after three trading periods, complete information leads to an increase in the level of prices. But in each case the increase in prices is unable to persist in the final trading period as sellers compete to avoid forgoing sales.

Shubik (1959, pp. 169–170) long ago surveyed and incisively criticized what various authors have said about the alleged importance of "perfect knowledge" in driving competitive equilibria. Shubik's main point was that more information *increases* the likelihood that combinations will result. Although formal combinations were not allowed in the above experiments, a type of short-lived tacit collusion occurred under complete information which does indeed retard convergence to competitive equilibria.

## 5. Sealed-Bid Mechanisms for Private Goods

Sealed-bid auctions are an important and widely employed mechanism of exchange in construction, land, securities, and many other markets. This section will report on two previously unpublished experiments with sealed-bid auctions, summarize some previously published experiments, and relate these earlier experiments to recent field experiments in the auctioning of new securites. These latter developments are especially significant in attempting to evaluate parallelism in bidding behavior as between laboratory and field environments.

### 5.1. First, Second, and Seller Price Auctions

When a unique indivisible commodity, such as a piece of land or a contract to build a bridge, is sold by sealed bidding, the rules normally call for the item to be awarded to the highest bidder at a price equal to the amount bid. Vickrey (1961) has suggested another rule, namely, that the item be awarded to the highest bidder at a price equal to the next highest bid. This rule is incentive compatible, or demand revealing, in that it is optimal for each bidder to enter a bid equal to his valuation (the maximum price he is willing to pay for the item). This is because each buyer's surplus, if he is awarded the items, is independent of his bid provided that his bid is above that of the next highest bidder. Any bid below a buyer's actual valuation will therefore reduce the probability of the award, and be an inferior strategy. Marschak (see Smith (1979)) had suggested, prior to Vickrey's important contribution, a mechanism with the same property. Marschak's mechanism was to ask the seller to write down privately a "bid" for the item and put it in an envelope. The item is then awarded to the highest bidder provided the high bid exceeds that of the seller, otherwise the seller retains the item. This is equivalent to Vickrey's rule, since in effect the seller is being allowed to bid for his own item (which, by the way, is not permitted in some auctions). Marschak's rule has the advantage that it would apply even when there is only one buyer for the item. These three different mechanisms will be referred to as the first, second, and seller price auctions.

A pilot experiment was conducted as follows: each of six subjects bid on each of three auctioned "items," I, II, III, in each of 11 successive auction periods. The first period was a practice trial, while in each of the next ten periods the winning bidder on each item was paid the difference between that person's "resale" valuation price for the item and the price paid in that auction. Auction I was a first price auction, Auction II used the second price rule, while Auction III used Marschak's seller price rule. The subjects were naïve in the sense that they were not given any training or "coaching" on how one might bid. But ten "money" trials were run following the first trial with the idea of providing adequate scope for learning. The award rules for each of the three types of auctions were explained in written instructions, repeated verbally, and questions were answered. After the bids were collected in each period, the highest bid was posted on the blackboard for Auction I, the highest and second highest for Auction II, and the highest bid and the seller's bid for Auction III. The subjects' private "resale" valuations were chosen so that the highest value would be between $4 and $9, with the next highest subject valuation chosen at random among numbers that were $.50, $1.00, and $1.50 below the highest valuation for that auction. The remaining four valuations were chosen at arbitrary values lower than the second highest value.

Figure 7 plots by period the value—bid gap $(V_i - B_i)$, i.e., the difference between the resale value and the bid submitted by each subject for each auction. The above theory suggests the hypothesis that subjects will tend to bid so as to yield a higher $V_i - B_i$ in Auction I than in II or III. Ideally, according to the theory, subjects would bid their valuations in Auctions II and III so that $V_i - B_i = 0$, but we expect real people to perceive this with differing degrees of error and perhaps exhibit some learning conditioned by experiences.

From Fig. 7 it will be observed that subjects 2, 3, 4, and 6 either perceived immediately, or learned within the first several trials, that it was in their interest to bid $B_i = V_i$ in Auctions II and III. Subject 5 did this in Auction III but not II. Since subject 5 happened to have the winning bid for Auction II on three occasions in spite of having bid $B_5 < V_5$, no failure was experienced. Subject 1 is the only case of exceptionally slow learning if indeed it can be said that there was any learning.

The nonparametric paired-sample sign test was applied to the period-by-period bids of all subjects comparing Auction I with Auction II bids. The null hypothesis that the bids in II are as likely to be above as below those in

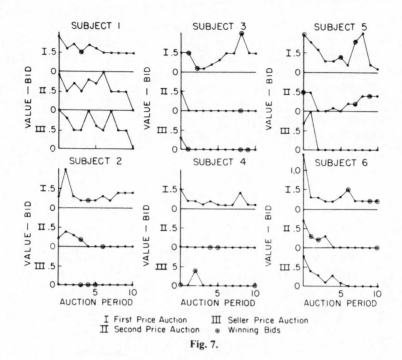

I   First Price Auction     III   Seller Price Auction
II   Second Price Auction     ⊚   Winning Bids

**Fig. 7.**

I is tested against the one-sided alternative that the bids in II are above those in I. By this test the null hypothesis is rejected at a level of significance $p < .001$. Similarly, comparing Auction I with Auction III we reject the null hypothesis at $p < .001$.

## 5.2. SEALED BIDDING FOR MULTIPLE UNITS: MONOPOLY PRODUCTION

Vickrey (1961) argues that some of the incentive characteristics of the First and Second Price auctions for a single item generalize to the case of multiple units offered for sale. When there are multiple units the analogue of the First Price auction has been called the discriminative auction (Smith, 1967) in which all accepted bids are filled at their respective bid prices. The analogue of the Second Price auction is the competitive or uniform-price auction wherein all accepted bids are filled at the lowest accepted bid price (Smith, 1967), or strictly, as noted by Vickrey, at the highest rejected bid price. But unless the offering is quite small one would not expect lowest accepted, versus highest rejected, bid rules to make more than an epsilon of behavioral difference.

RELEVANCE OF LABORATORY EXPERIMENTS                                    **363**

A pilot experiment was conducted using one subject as a monopoly producer and five subjects as buyers. The seller could produce up to twelve units at zero fixed cost and at marginal cost MC shown on the left of Fig. 8. Buyers each had marginal valuations for two units such that the five buyers together provided the demand $D$ shown in Fig. 8. Again the seller did not know the marginal valuations of any buyer and no buyer knew the valuations of other buyers nor the marginal cost situation of the seller. The theoretical monopoly price and quantity is $(P_m, Q_m) = (\$1.10, 5)$, while the competitive is $(P_c, Q_c) = (\$.80, 8)$.

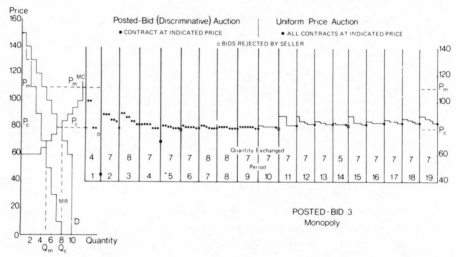

**Fig. 8.**

Initially in this experiment buyers independently select bids which are then posted by the experimenter from highest to lowest. The seller then selects a buyer (the highest bidder of course) and makes a quantity offer. The buyer responds with an acceptance of any part of that quantity except that the buyer is required to accept at least one unit. This specific take-it-or-leave-it pricing process has been referred to as the Posted-Bid institution and has been demonstrated (Plott & Smith, 1978) to operate to the advantage of buyers. This is because the incentive of individual buyers to understate or underreveal their demand supports buyer "cooperative" efforts to coordinate with low bids. In view of this a question of substance is whether or not the Posted-Bid institution might serve as a means of decentralized control over monopoly pricing.

In Fig. 8 the first nine trading periods were under the Posted-Bid form of discriminative auction. In periods 1–9 the bids plotted were also contract

VERNON L. SMITH

prices. The seller stabilized early in the delivery of seven or eight units against the bids tendered in each period while bid prices gradually converged toward the competitive price $.80. At the beginning of trial 10 it was announced that henceforth the seller could no longer sell units at different prices. When the bids were posted the seller first announced a cut-off bid price, then made offers successively to the buyers (in order) as before, but with the understanding that each would pay a price equal to the lowest bid accepted (indicated by the dot in periods 10–19 of Fig. 8) by the seller. As displayed in Fig. 8, the immediate effect of this change in the bidding institution produced an increase in the bids, and a gradual upward drift of the price level. It appears that the bids were converging slowly to the quantity-conditional competitive price $.90, i.e., the competitive price given that the seller was delivering seven units per period.

## 5.3. LABORATORY AND FIELD STUDIES OF SEALED-BID SECURITIES MARKETS

An earlier experimental study (Smith, 1967) of the effect of discriminative and competitive pricing rules on bidding behavior was patterned after procedures used, and procedures proposed, in the auctioning of U.S. Treasury bills. In the experimental paradigm subjects bid for 18 units of a commodity whose resale price was determined, after the bids were tendered, by a drawing from a rectangular probability mass function whose parameters were known to the subjects. There were two experimental treatment conditions: the award rules and the number of bidders. Under the discriminative (D) award treatment the highest 18 bids were accepted at the bid prices specified. Under the competitive (C) treatment the highest 18 bids were accepted at the bid price specified by the lowest or 18th bid. The number of subjects were 13, 15, and 17 in each of three pairs of experiments. Since each subject could tender two bids, and the offer quantity was always 18 units, the number of rejected or excess bids was 8, 12, and 16 in the three pairs of experiments. Hence the study consisted of six experiments in a 2 × 3 design with two levels for the bidding institution (D, C) and three levels for the number of rejected bids (8, 12, 16). In each experiment up to 10 successive auctions were performed to allow for learning and to study convergence under stationary conditions. Five independent subject groups participated in the six experiments. The D group with 13 subjects (8 rejected bids) participated in 8 auction periods, then the instructions for the C rules were introduced, and eight more auctions were performed. Hence the group wih 8 rejected bids participated in a D–C "switchover" experiment.

Figure 9 displays the bid distributions for each paired (D, C) set of experiments for trading periods 1, 3–5. The tendency for the C bid distributions to stochastically dominate the D bid distributions in the accepted

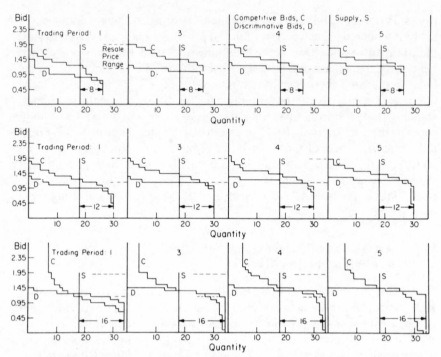

**Fig. 9.** [From Bidding and auctioning institutions: Experimental results by V. L. Smith. In Y. Ahimud (Ed.), *Bidding and auctioning for procurement and allocation*. New York: New York University Press, 1976. Chart 10, p. 61. Copyright © 1976 by New York University.]

bid range is obvious. Several hypotheses were tested leading to the following conclusions:

1. The variance of C bids is significantly greater than the variance of D bids, and this discrepancy increases as the number of rejected bids increases.

2. The distribution of *accepted* C bids is significantly higher than the distribution of *accepted* D bids for all rejected bid treatments. The proposition holds for *all* bids for C and D comparisons when there are 8 and 12, but not 16, rejected bids.

3. The total receipts of the seller are greater in a C than in a D auction for 8 and 12, but not for 16, rejected bids. This suggests that the advantage to the seller of the C over the D bidding rules may disappear if there is a large enough number of rejected bids.

4. D auctions with a larger number of rejected bids tend to stochastically dominate D auctions with a smaller number of rejected bids. The proposition does not hold for C auctions. This is consistent with the theoretical hypothesis that C auctions provide incentives for demand revelation while D auctions provide incentives to strategically underbid depending upon risk and ex-

**366**                                                          VERNON L. SMITH

pectations which in turn can be supposed to be affected by the volume of rejected bids.

5. The total receipts of the seller are greater, the greater the number of rejected bids in a D auction. The proposition does not hold for C auctions.

6. An interesting behavioral characteristic of the C auctions is observable in Fig. 9. In every C experiment, for many auction periods, one or more subjects entered bids equal to or greater than the highest possible resale price in the domain of the resale distribution. Clearly, these subjects are bidding in excess of their marginal valuation for the item in order to be very sure of having their bid or bids accepted. This is a safe risk only if no more than 17 such bids are tendered.

Belovicz (1979) has replicated and considerably extended the preceding experimental research. Generally, his results and conclusions are consistent with the preceding ones, including the observation that C auction subjects sometimes bid in excess of marginal valuation.

At least three important developments in the marketing of securities have occurred since the above laboratory experiments were initiated. A modified version of the uniform-price competitive auction was adopted beginning in 1964 in the French marketing of new equity issues (McDonald & Jacquillat, 1974). Beginning in January 1973 the Treasury auctioned six long-term bond issues using the low-bid uniform-price rule (Baker, 1976, p. 147). Finally in November, 1976, and again in April, 1977, Exxon Corporation took the unprecedented step of bypassing the normal underwriting institutions and marketing bond issues directly to registered broker-dealers using the low-bid uniform-price rule (*Wall Street Journal*, April 19, 1977). These developments are worthy of closer examination since they allow some comparisons to be made between the results of the laboratory experiments and the results of these "experiments" with new securities marketing institutions.

The French sealed-bid auction of new equity issues appears (by one criterion) to be a very successful institution. As of 1974 (McDonald & Jacquillat, 1974, p. 40) no initial equity issue since 1964 had failed to receive sufficient bids to clear the quantity offered at the minimum price or higher. In this auction the issuing company states a minimum acceptable price in advance. When the bids are tendered a committee of company directors, their bankers, and officials of the Paris Bourse examine the computer printout of bids ranked from highest to lowest. Since orders to bid "at market" are not admissible, the committee rejects bids above some arbitrary level as "disguised market orders." It then allocates shares on a pro rata basis so that the offering is exhausted at a bid price slightly below that which they think can be sustained by free trading in the aftermarket (McDonald & Jacquillat, 1974, pp. 41–42). The key point is that on a typical offering many

French investors tender bids that are obviously more than their marginal valuations just as do their counterparts in the experimental laboratory. Stand-out behavioral characteristics such as this provide important evidence on parallelism (McDonald & Jacquillat, 1974, p. 39, also note this similarity between investor and subject behavior).

In reporting on the results of the Treasury uniform-price auctions, Baker (1976) emphasizes the difficulty of being sure that differences in auction results are attributable to the auction form when the issues are of differing maturities and of different sizes. Considering all this, Baker (1976, p. 150) reports tentatively that there does appear to be some outward shift in the demand curve and the possibility of a small cost saving to the Treasury by pricing with the uniform-price auction.

Tsao & Vignola (1977) have written a preliminary report of their study comparing the U.S. Treasury's auctioning of ten long-term bond issues under discriminative rules, with the auctioning of six long-term issues under the uniform-price rules. Table 2 provides some evidence on parallelism between laboratory and field experiments by comparing the preliminary results of Tsao & Vignola (1977) for Treasury bond auctions with the results of the laboratory experiments reported by Smith (1967) and Belovicz (1979).

TABLE 2

COMPARISON OF COMPETITIVE AND DISCRIMINATIVE
AUCTION RESULTS USING LABORATORY AND TREASURY DATA

| Null hypothesis | Test results, laboratory experiments | Test results,[a] nondealer bids, Treasury's 6 competitive and 10 discriminative bond auctions |
|---|---|---|
| A. Variance of bids same under C and D | Reject in favor of $V_c > V_D$ | Reject in favor of $V_C > V_D$ |
| B. Mean bid same under C and D | Reject in favor of $\bar{B}_C > \bar{B}_D$ | Reject in favor of $\bar{B}_C > \bar{B}_D$ |
| C. Mean bid independent of volume of rejected bids under C | Cannot reject | Reject |
| D. Mean bid independent of volume of rejected bids under D | Reject | Cannot reject |
| E. Seller revenue same under C and D | Reject in favor of $R_C > R_D$ in 5 of 15 paired comparisons | Reject in favor of $R_C > R_D$ in 6 C auctions and 10 D auctions |

[a] Based on preliminary report of Tsao and Vignola (1977).

Conclusion 1 that the variance of C bids exceeds the variance of D bids holds also in the Treasury bond data. Conclusion 2 that the mean of C bids exceeds the mean of D bids holds for *all* bids, not just the subset of accepted bids, and for all proportions of rejected bids in the Treasury data. Conclusion 3 that seller receipts are greater in C than in D auctions holds for all proportions of rejected bids in the Treasury data. Finally, conclusion 4 is strangely reversed in the Treasury data, i.e., C auctions with a larger proportion of rejected bids tend to stochastically dominate C auctions with a smaller proportion of rejected bids. The proposition does not hold for D auctions. This reversal is directly contrary to what one would expect from the theory and suggests the need for further replication of the laboratory experiments to determine if there is anything artifactual about the original results.

Apparently the management of Exxon Corporation is satisfied that the uniform-price auction yields a net savings to the corporation's financing operations. In May 1977 Exxon guaranteed a $250 million issue of 30 year tax exempt bonds offered by the city of Valdez, Alaska, the proceeds to be used by Exxon Pipeline Co. This is the second such offering of Exxon guaranteed bonds under the uniform-price auction, and the company indicated that it may soon offer its own debt obligations by this procedure (*Wall Street Journal*, April 19, 1977, p. 31). The results of the second issue provided bid tenders for over one billion dollars, or about four times the quantity offered, giving a price of $985.82 per $1000 face amount of bonds, with a coupon rate of $5\frac{1}{2}\%$, to yield 5.598%. The yield equivalent of all the bids ranged from 5% to 5.88% (Rickert, 1977).

## 6. Choice Mechanisms for Public Goods

In this section we shall review one laboratory and two field experiments designed to test or compare decentralized decision mechanisms for public goods.

### 6.1. THE AUCTION MECHANISM FOR PUBLIC GOODS

The first set of experiments to be reviewed applies the Auction Mechanism (Smith, 1979) to a collective's choice of the quantity of a pure public good. The experimental design is based on a partial equilibrium (no income effects) version of the mechanism. In this mechanism, let $V_i(X)$ be the dollar value to $i$ of $X$ units of a common outcome public good that can be purchased by a collective of $I$ members at a price $q$. Let each $i$ submit a two-tuple

$(b_i, X_i)$, where $b_i$ represents member $i$'s contribution per unit of the public good toward its purchase, and $X_i$ is the quantity of the public good that $i$ proposes for collective purchase. In the experimental setting $V_i(X)$ is used to induce value on $X$ for each $i$. If $i$'s utility of money is $U_i(\cdot)$, and we let $u_i$ be $i$'s final outcome utility, then the Auction Mechanism yields

$$
u_i = \begin{cases}
U_i\left[ V_i(\bar{X}) - \left( q - \sum_{j \neq i} b_j \right) \bar{X} \right] & \text{if } b_i = q - \sum_{j \neq i} b_j \\
& \text{and} \\
& X_i = \bar{X} = \sum_{k=1}^{I} X_k/I \quad \text{for all } i, \\
U_i(0) = 0 & \text{if } b_i \neq q - \sum_{j \neq i} b_j \\
& \text{or} \\
& X_i \neq \bar{X} \quad \text{for any } i.
\end{cases} \tag{1}
$$

The collective's proposed quantity of the public good is defined as the mean, $\bar{X}$, of the individual proposals, while the collective's allocation of unit cost to $i$ is $q - \sum_{j \neq i} b_j$. Collective agreement occurs if every $i$ agrees to accept his share of cost by bidding $b_i = q - \sum_{j \neq i} b_j$ and agrees to accept the group's proposal by proposing $X_i = \bar{X}$. Otherwise none of the public good is purchased and no $i$ enjoys the potential surplus from the public good.

That the mechanism defined by (1) provides incentives for optimal collective decision is shown by selecting $(b_i, X_i)$ to maximize $U_i$. Maximization requires $i$ to choose $(b_i, X_i)$ so that $U_i'(\cdot)[(1/I)V_i'(\bar{X}) - (q - \sum_{j \neq i} b_j)(1/I)] = 0$, but also to choose $b_i = q - \sum_{j \neq i} b_j$ and $X_i = \bar{X}$ to avoid vetoing the arrangement. If $U_i' > 0$, then $V_i'(\bar{X}) = q - \sum_{j \neq i} b_j = b_i$, and since $b_i + \sum_{j \neq i}^{I} b_j = \sum_{k=1}^{I} b_k = q$, summing over all members gives $\sum_{i=1}^{I} V_i'(\bar{X}) = q$. Hence $X = X^0$, where $X^0$ is the Lindahl (and Pareto) optimal quantity of the public good.

Two comments on this mechanism refer respectively to its *relevancy* and its *behavioral interpretation*:

(1)   This mechanism is simply a generalization of a very common private institution for the provision of a public good. Whenever a religious, art, or music society attempts to obtain a new church, museum, or music hall by canvassing its members (and, often, nonmembers) for contributions, the society is effectively using a discrete version of the Auction Mechanism. That is, the new facility is purchased if and only if contributions equal or exceed the cost of the facility.

(2)   The Auction Mechanism has important behavioral similarities to the Vickrey-Marschak Second Price auction and to the uniform-price multi-unit auction. In these auctions the price paid by the buyer is determined directly by the actions of other buyers. One is awarded a unit only if his bid "beats" the first rejected bid. Similarly, in the Auction Mechanism for public goods agent $i$'s unit cost allocation $q - \sum_{j \neq i} b_j$ is determined by all $j \neq i$. If $i$ can and does bid high enough to accept this share of cost, then $i$ is able to enjoy the surplus attainable from the public good.

Twelve experiments (Smith, 1979) have been conducted using the mechanism described above (see Table 3). The experimental process consisted of a series of trials with a specified upper limit $T$ to the number of trials allowable. The stopping rule for determining collective agreement was for each subject to bid his share of cost on two successive trials $(t^* - 1, t^*)$, and to accept the group's proposal on the final "stop" trial $(t^*)$. Each trial began with each subject privately choosing $(b_i, X_i)$, and ended with the public posting of $\sum_{k=1}^{I} b_k$ and $\bar{X}$ which enables each subject to compute $q - \sum_{j \neq i} b_j = q - (\sum_{k=1}^{I} b_k - b_i)$ and determine his "profit" $V_i(\bar{X}) - (q - \sum_{j \neq i} b_j)\bar{X}$ on that trial.

Table 3 summarizes the results of three experimental sessions (A1) with $I = 5$, five sessions (A2) with $I = 4$, and four sessions (A3) with $I = 8$. The A3 sessions were a replication of the A2 but with two subjects rather than one having the valuation functions $V_i(X)$, $i = 1, 2, 3, 4$, and with the price of the public good twice its level in A2. This permitted an examination of the effect of doubling the size of the collective while keeping constant the relative structure of taste and cost. Table 3 records the Lindahl prices and quantity for each experimental design[6] and the actual final bids and quantities for each experimental session. Only session A3.2 failed to reach agreement for reasons clearly attributable to incentive incompatibility (or "free riding"). Four of the sessions (A1.2, A2.1, A2.3, and A3.2) encountered coordination problems associated with the stopping rule. That is, in these sessions the cost of the public good was either overbid or agreement was within one bid unit with one or more subjects hesitant to fill in the bid gap for fear of an overbid. (In recent experiments this problem has been solved by rebating any overbid to each subject in proportion to his bid and modifying the process to allow the collective simply to vote at the end of each trial for which the cost of the public good is covered. Agreement then requires a unanimous vote in favor of finalizing the outcome of that trial.)

By estimating the parameters of the regression equation $b_i = \beta_0 + \beta p_i$ where $p_i$ is the Lindahl price and $b_i$ the final bid for subject $i$ one may test

---

[6] See Smith (1979) for a complete presentation of the experimental design parameters, instructions, and results.

TABLE 3

Bid-Quantity Outcome Experiments $A_1$, $A_2$, $A_3$[a]

| Subject | A1 sessions | | | | A2 sessions | | | | | | A3 sessions | | | | |
|---|---|---|---|---|---|---|---|---|---|---|---|---|---|---|---|
| | Lindahl prices $V'_i(5 \text{ or } 6)$ | Final bids | | | Lindahl prices $V'_i(6 \text{ or } 7)$ | Final bids | | | | | Lindahl prices $V'_i(6 \text{ or } 7)$ | Final bids | | | |
| | | A1.1 | A1.2[b] | A1.3 | | A2.1[b] | A2.2 | A2.3[b] | A2.4 | A2.5 | | A3.1 | A3.2[c] | A3.3 | A3.4 |
| 1 | 3 | 4 | 6 | 4 | -5 | -5 | -6 | -6 | -4 | -6 | -5 | -4 | (-4) | -4 | -3 |
| 2 | 3 | 6 | 2 | 4 | 13 | 13 | 12 | 14[d] | 13 | 14 | 13 | 14 | (6) | 13[d] | 14 |
| 3 | 8 | 10 | 9 | 3 | 8 | 7[d] | 8 | 7 | 7 | 6 | -5 | -6 | (-7) | -5 | -3 |
| 4 | 13 | 9 | 13 | 15 | 3 | 4 | 5 | 4 | 3 | 5 | 13 | 13 | (7) | 10 | 14 |
| 5 | 18 | 16 | 15[d] | 19 | | | | | | | 3 | 1 | (5) | 4 | 4 |
| 6 | | | | | | | | | | | 8 | 9 | (9) | 5 | 8 |
| 7 | | | | | | | | | | | 3 | 0 | (4) | 5 | 2 |
| 8 | | | | | | | | | | | 8 | 11 | (9) | 10 | 2 |
| Final quantity, X* | | 5 | 4 | 5 | | 6 | 6 | 6 | 6 | 7 | | 6 | 0 | 6 | 7 |
| Final trial, t* | | 30 | 30 | 29 | | 29 | 26 | 29 | 19 | 15 | | 28 | 30 | 29 | 16 |
| Trial bound, T | | 30 | 30 | 30 | | 30 | 30 | 30 | 20 | 15 | | 30 | 30 | 30 | 16 |

[a] Reprinted from V. L. Smith (Ed.), *Research in Experimental Economics*, Volume 1, JAI PRESS INC., 1979.
[b] These experiments either stopped very near agreement or failed to reach technical agreement because the collectives overbid the cost of the public good.
[c] Parentheses provide final trial bids for this "wide disagreement" session.
[d] Random subject chosen for simulated budget balancing bid.

the hypothesis that the theoretical Lindahl prices explain subject bids. The results (Smith, 1979) yield $R^2$ from 0.82 to 0.99 across the three sets of experiments, with $\hat{\beta}_0$ not significantly different from zero and $\hat{\beta}$ not significantly different from unity.

These experiments provide rather encouraging evidence to suggest that small collectives can voluntarily provide Lindahl public good equilibria. Of course one observes this whenever a fund drive by a private society ends successfully, but in such nonlaboratory environments one does not observe individual valuations. Hence there is no way of relating success or nonsuccess to valuations to examine the efficiency of the mechanism.

### 6.2. BOHM EXPERIMENT

In a Swedish experiment (Bohm, 1972) consumers (who had volunteered to come to a TV studio for a payment of Kr. 50) were randomly assigned to six different groups and asked to state how much they were willing to pay under six different cost sharing rules to watch a particular TV program that had not yet been shown to the public. The sixth group made hypothetical choices while for the remaining five the program would be shown if and only if the aggregate of the amount offered were sufficient to cover the cost. Each group was led to believe that there were parallel groups in other rooms whose responses were to be merged with theirs. In this way a group, for example of size 23 (treatment I), would find it credible that with offers of only several Kr. each the program cost (Kr. 500) was covered. Unknown to the subjects, the program was to be shown whatever the amount of the offer.

Among the various experimental groups the amounts each consumer paid, conditional on the aggregate amount offered exceeding cost, were as follows (the mean offer in Kr. appears in parentheses):

I. The amount stated (Kr. 7.61).

II. A percentage of the amount stated, normalized so that cost is just covered (Kr. 8.84).

III. Either the amount stated, a percentage of this amount, Kr. 5, or nothing, to be determined by a lottery (Kr. 7.29).

IV. Kr. 5 (Kr. 7.73).

V. Nothing. The costs would be paid by the broadcasting company, i.e., out of general taxes (Kr. 8.78).

VI. Nothing. The response was hypothetical (Kr. 10.19).

According to Bohm's analysis only treatment VI led to offers which differed to any (classically) significant degree from the others. Several interpretations and observations seem relevant to this experiment:

1. Treatment I corresponds to the Auction Mechanism applied to an indivisible public good. The theory discussed previously suggests that there are strong incentives for revealing demand under this mechanism and from our experiments we have evidence that in the context of an iterative process this mechanism produces incentive compatible outcomes. Consequently, notwithstanding the conventional wisdom on public goods, Bohm's treatment I should not be expected to yield strong free-rider tendencies unless this is a peculiarity of single trial responses. The theory that has maintained that free-riding will occur in this context has not taken account of the opportunity losses incurred by failure to cover cost.

2. Irrespective of these considerations, if treatment I is regarded as the "free-rider" control experiment against which comparisons are made, then the effect of each of the treatments II, IV, V, and VI is to raise the average offer in what might be considered the expected direction. That is, subjects might be expected to offer more in II than in I in the expectation that their share of cost in II is unlikely to exceed that in I. Similarly, IV provides a modest fixed imputation of the cost regardless of one's offer, and similarly for V and VI. If the preexperimental hypothesis had been that these were the directions in which the treatment outcomes would diverge, then regardless of the significance tests by classical standards, one would have to conclude that the experimental results increased to some degree the credibility of the hypothesis.

3. The lower offers elicited under treatment III are not in accordance with expectations based upon the above arguments. However, treatment III is by far the most complex or ambiguous, psychologically. The lower average offer in III is consistent with the "ambiguity hypothesis" which would assert that where outcomes are defined by psychologically "rich" (complicated, mysterious, uncertain) processes, subjects are more conservative, or cautious, in their responses. This phenomenon is suggested in a somewhat different context (Ellsberg, 1961; Sherman, 1974) but may have application in the Bohm experiment.

4. Each subject was asked for a single response. Although the subjects "accepted the question as . . . posed and (most) . . . gave their responses in a matter of a minute or less (Bohm, 1972, p. 126)," the result is not likely to be the same as would obtain if the subjects arrived at a final decision through a process involving many response-outcome iterations.

## 6.3. THE PBS STATION PROGRAM COOPERATIVE

In 1974 the Public Broadcasting Service began a three-year experiment to develop a decentralized process for the selection of programs to be broadcast over the noncommercial television network. Some results of the first two seasons of experience with this Station Program Cooperative (SPC) have been reported by Ferejohn & Noll (1976). Approximately 150 participating stations made actual selections from 93 programs in the first experiment and 136 in the second. The process consisted of 12 iterations (with each station manager communicating through his teletypewriter) and converged rapidly (in 7 iterations) to 25 produced programs the first year and (in 10 iterations) to 38 produced programs the second year. The cost of program $j$ for station $i$ on trial $t$ was

$$C_j \left[ \frac{0.8b_i}{B_j(t-1)} + \frac{0.2n_i}{N_j(t-1)} \right],$$

where $C_j$ was the producer's cost of program $j$, $b_i$ is the budget and $n_i$ the population served for any station $i$ selecting program $j$, and $B_j(t-1)$ is the aggregate budget and $N_j(t-1)$ the aggregate population served for all stations selecting program $j$ on trial $t-1$.

This cost sharing rule has the essential features of the Auction Mechanism, i.e., (1) each manager risks forfeiting his private net benefit if he fails to "vote for" a program, and (2) he has veto power over the cost allocated to him by the choices of all other stations. However, it has the undesirable characteristic that stations can only accept or reject a program at a bid determined mechanically by the above formula. A station willing to pay some amount for a particular program, but less than the formula allocation, must perforce decline to select the program, while a station willing to pay more than its formula allocation has no way of signaling this intensity by increasing its bid. But these are obvious armchair criticisms that may or may not be operationally significant. One must take seriously a mechanism that yields large scale allocations judged to be satisfactory by the participating agents.

## 7. Conclusion

This paper has been mute in its reference to the theme of this conference— the evaluation of econometric models. This is because the message of the paper calls for us to start over in resource allocation theory and in the econometric modeling of microeconomic phenomena. There is no conflict between the scientific objectives of econometric modeling and experimental methodology. Indeed, it is questionable whether or not econometrics can be given any scientific content whatsoever in the absence of experimental data and replication.

The problem with any attempt to provide econometric models of market behavior (laboratory or nonlaboratory) is that we simply do not have any adequate theory. Competitive price theory requires that there be such a large number of buyers and sellers that each effectively becomes a price taker. Yet experimental markets with as few as 3–4 buyers and as many sellers converge with astonishing rapidity to within a narrow range of the supply and demand equilibrium using the double auction institution in which every participant is a price maker *not* a price taker. Furthermore, these results can be modified in experiments that alter the rules governing the institution of contract; for example, by allowing only sellers to make quotations or by requiring sellers to post take-it-or-leave-it offers. But to date we have no theory of price formation under these alternative institutions that lends itself to econometric modeling. Economic theorists sometimes suggest that complete information on supply and demand is sufficient, if not necessary, to the attainment of a competitive equilibrium. Yet, as we have seen above, there are experimental supply and demand configurations in which convergence to the competitive equilibrium is weakened by the state of complete information. This suggests that economic theory seriously lacks an adequate treatment of the role of information in price adjustment processes.

In short, we have no theory of price adjustment processes or institutions that is operational enough to allow an econometric modeling of experimental markets. The traditional *ad hoc* difference-differential equation dynamics does not deal with process. The literature on price search theory appears to be dealing with the appropriate ingredients of a satisfactory theory, but as yet this work is still based on too simplistic a set of assumptions to capture the search-learning process that seems to characterize institutions such as the double auction.

Yet the challenge to theory unmistakable; there is a growing body of hard laboratory results based on numerous replications and a great diversity of price-making institutions. Furthermore, the studies by Bohm (1972) and Ferejohn & Noll (1976) for public goods, and by Tsao & Vignola (1977) for private goods suggest that models of laboratory behavior have direct relevance to the modeling of field behavior.[7] What is needed is a restructuring of theory to capture the institutional elements in the price formation process, whether the theory is to be tested with laboratory experiments or field data. In this paper we argue that we ought to begin with the laboratory results where value (cost) is induced, and hence an important extraneous source of variability is controlled.

---

[7] That is, these field studies report many results that are consistent with the results of laboratory experiments such as those reported by Smith (1967, 1979) and Belovicz (1979).

**376** VERNON L. SMITH

## ACKNOWLEDGMENTS

I am grateful to the National Science Foundation for research support and to Raymond Battalio, John Kagel, and Charles Plott for many valuable discussions and comments.

## REFERENCES

Arrow, K. Price–quantity adjustments in multiple markets with rising demands. In K. Arrow, S. Karlin, and P. Suppeo (Eds.), *Mathematical methods in the social sciences*. Stanford, Cal.: Stanford Univ. Press, 1960. Ch. 1, Pp. 3–15.

Arrow, K., & Capron, W. Dynamic shortages and price rises: The engineer–scientist case. *Quarterly Journal of Economics*, 1959, **75**(May), 292–308.

Baker, C. Auctioning coupon bearing securities: A review of Treasury experience. In Y. Amihud (Ed.), *Bidding and auctioning for procurement and allocation*. New York: New York University Press, 1976. Pp. 146–154.

Battalio, R., Kagel, J., Winkler, J., Fisher, R., Basmann, R., & Krasner, L. A test of consumer demand theory using observations of individual purchases. *Western Economic Journal*, 1973, **11**(December), 411–428.

Belovicz, M. Sealed-bid auctions: Experimental results and applications. In V. L. Smith (Ed.), *Research in experimental economics*. Vol. 1. Greenwich, Conn.: JAI Press, 1979, Pp. 279–338.

Bohm, P. Estimating demand for public goods: An experiment. *European Economic Review*, 1972, **3**, 111–130.

Carlson, J. The stability of an experimental market with a supply-response lag. *The Southern Economic Journal*, 1967, **33**(January), 299–321.

Ellsberg, D. Risk, ambiguity, and the Savage axioms. *Quarterly Journal of Economics*, 1961, **75**(November), 643–669.

Ferejohn, J., & Noll, R. An experimental market for public goods: The PBS Station Program Cooperative. *American Economic Review Papers and Proceedings*, 1976, **66**(May), 267–273.

Fiorina, M., & Plott, C. Committee decisions under majority rule: An experimental study. Social Science Working Paper #101, California Institute of Technology, December 1975.

Fouraker, L. E., & Siegel, S. *Bargaining behavior*. New York: McGraw-Hill, 1963.

Hess, A. C. Experimental evidence on price formation in competitive markets. *Journal of Political Economy*, 1972, **80**(March/April), 375–385.

Leibenstein, H. *Beyond economic man*. Cambridge, Mass.: Harvard Univ. Press, 1976.

Marschak, J. Statistical inference in economics: An introduction. In T. C. Koopmans (Ed.), *Statistical inference in dynamic economic models*. New York: Wiley, 1950. Pp. 1–50.

Marschak, J. Economics of inquiring, communicating, deciding. *American Economic Review, Papers and Proceedings*, 1968, **58**(May), 1–18.

McDonald, J., & Jacquillat, B. Pricing of initial equity issues: The French sealed-bid auction. *Journal of Business*, 1974, **47**(January), 37–52.

Miller, R., Plott C., & Smith, V. Intertemporal competitive equilibrium: An empirical study of speculation. *Quarterly Journal of Economics*, 1977, **91**(November), 599–624.

Plott, C. The application of laboratory experimental methods to public choice. Social Science Working Paper #223, California Institute of Technology, July 1978.

Plott, C., & Levine, M. A model of agenda influence on committee decisions: *American Economic Review*, 1978, **68**(March), 146–160.

Plott, C., & Smith, V. An experimental examination of two exchange institutions. *Review of Economic Studies*, 1978, **45**(February), 133–153.

Rickert, L. B. Tax-exempt prices skid as supply rises: Exxon issue part of $1 billion deluge. *Wall Street Journal*, May 4, 1977, p. 31.

Samuelson, P. Intertemporal price equilibrium: A prologue to the theory of speculation. *Weltwirtschaftliches Archiv*, 1957, **79**(2), 181–219.

Samuelson, P. *Economics*. (9th ed.) New York: McGraw-Hill, 1973.

Shapley, H. *Of stars and men*. Boston: Beacon Press, 1964.

Sherman, R. The psychological difference between ambiguity and risk. *Quarterly Journal of Economics*, 1974, **88**(February), 166–169.

Shubik, M. *Strategy and market structure*. New York: Wiley, 1959.

Smith, V. L. Effect of market organization on competitive equilibrium. *Quarterly Journal of Economics*, 1964, **78**(May), 181–201.

Smith, V. L. Experimental studies of discrimination versus competition in sealed-bid auction markets. *Journal of Business*, 1967, **40**(January), 56–84.

Smith, V. L. Experimental economics: Induced value theory. *American Economic Review Papers and Proceedings*, 1976, **66**(May), 274–279. (a)

Smith, V. L. Bidding and auctioning institutions: Experimental results. In Y. Amihud (Ed.), *Bidding and auctioning for procurement and allocation*. New York: NY Univ. Press, 1976. Pp. 43–64.(b)

Smith, V. L. Incentive compatible experimental processes for the provision of public goods. In V. L. Smith (Ed.), *Research in experimental economics*. Vol. 1. Greenwich, Conn.: JAI Press, 1979. Pp. 59–169.

Tsao, C., & Vignola, A. Price discrimination and the demand for Treasury's long term securities. Preliminary report circulated privately, 1977.

Vickrey, W. Counterspeculation, auctions, and competitive sealed tenders. *Journal of Finance*, 1961, **16**(March), 8–37.

*Wall Street Journal*. Exxon plans to use "Dutch" auction again to sell a $250 million tax-exempt issue. April 19, 1977, p. 31.

Williams, A. Intertemporal competitive equilibrium: Further experimental results. In V. L. Smith (Ed.), *Research in experimental economics*. Greenwich, Conn.: JAI Press, 1979. Pp. 255–278.

# [8]

# Price Controls and the Behavior of Auction Markets: An Experimental Examination

By R. Mark Isaac and Charles R. Plott*

Price ceilings and price floors are common in all market systems. The ancient Greeks and Hellenistic era Egyptians are known to have utilized price controls (see H. Michele, p. 272, and J. P. Levy, p. 41), and numerous public policy questions today involve them. Apparently for as long as price controls have existed, their effects have been debated. For example, Diocletion's favorable view of his price ceilings[1] was disputed by the religious philosopher, Lactantius, who charged that the policy led to "scarcity and...low grade articles" (p. 145).

The standard partial-equilibrium theory about the effects of price controls, the theory which is subjected to so much criticism, does not seem to have changed since Leon Walras. It is applied widely to a variety of market institutional arrangements including auction markets such as those studied below. If the demand schedule is downward sloping and if the supply schedule is increasing as shown in Figure 1, there should be an equilibrium price-quantity pair of ($.60, 20). Nonbinding price controls, such as a price ceiling at or above the equilibrium or a price floor below equilibrium, should have no effects on the market. If the controls are binding, such as a price ceiling at $.55 or a price floor at $.70, then the market achieves an inefficient price-quantity pair with the market price equaling the controlled price.

However, in spite of its prominent textbook status, the applicability of the model is questioned regularly.[2] Criticisms range from complete rejections of economics to elaborate theories of collusion. As an example of the latter, consider the "focal point" hypothesis as found in F. M. Scherer (p. 352). Perhaps the price ceiling will act as a focal point. Sellers, by focusing on a nonbinding ceiling, may be able to tacitly collude to keep prices above the equilibrium. Thus, the otherwise nonbinding price ceiling can have an effect on prices. A similar theory can be advanced about the effects of price floors. For us the existence of this general controversy and the focal point hypothesis regarding the dynamic effects of price controls seemed sufficient to justify a systematic examination of the subject.

The objectives of this study are to examine the applicability and/or accuracy of the textbook model as applied to laboratory auction markets. Our hope is that by studying the implications of price controls in simple controlled settings, we will be in a better position to analyze more complicated markets which have been the traditional subjects of academic and scientific concern. The choice to study auction markets, as opposed to other forms of market institutions, reflected an attempt to maintain continuity with other experimental studies. Our results are not exactly what we expected and they probably raise more questions than they answer.

*University of Arizona and California Institute of Technology, respectively. The financial support of the National Science Foundation and the Caltech Program for Enterprise and Public Policy is gratefully acknowledged. We thank Julie Laherty for her comments on an earlier draft.

[1] The following quotation is excerpted from *Roman Civilization* (pp. 464–66):

In response to the needs of mankind itself, which appears to be praying for release, we have decided that maximum prices of articles for sale must be established. We have not set down fixed prices, for we do not deem it just to do this, since many provinces occasionally enjoy the fortune of welcome low prices....

It is our pleasure, therefore, that the prices listed in the subjoined schedule be held in observance in the whole of our Empire. And every person shall take note that the liberty to exceed them at will has been ended, but that the blessing of low prices has in no way been impaired in those places where supplies actually abound....

Emperor Diocletian, *The Edict on Prices*, A.D. 301

[2] During the course of preparing this paper, we noted several heated local political discussions concerning "fair trading" of liquor products, rent ceilings, and wage floors for municipal employees.

TABLE 1

| | | Series I No Experience | | Series II Experience | | Mixed Experience | |
|---|---|---|---|---|---|---|---|
| | | Experiment | Period | Experiment | Period | Experiment | Period |
| No Controls | | I | all | III | 1–3, 7 | II | all |
| | | VII | 9 | VIII | 9 | | |
| | | IX | 9–10 | X | 9–10 | | |
| | | XII | 9–11 | VI | 7–11 | | |
| Controls at Equilibrium | Price ceiling at equilibrium | IV V | all all | | | | |
| | Price floor at equilibrium | | | VI | 1–6 | | |
| Nonbinding Controls | Price ceiling 5¢ above equilibrium | VII | 1–8 | III VIII | 4 1–8 | | |
| | Price floor 5¢ below equilibrium | IX | 1–8 | X | 1–8 | | |
| | Price ceiling 10¢ above equilibrium | XI | all | | | | |
| Binding Controls | Price ceiling 10¢ below equilibrium | XII | 1–8 | III VIII | 5–6 10 | | |

## I. Experimental Design

A total of twelve experimental sessions were conducted. These are listed in Table 1 according to the subject's laboratory market experience and according to the price-control institution imposed. The instructions were those of Plott and Vernon Smith (Appendix, pp. 147–52) and Ross Miller, Plott, and Smith (Appendices, pp. 610–21) with a price ceiling (floor) provision added as indicated below. Participants in Series I (recruited from Pasadena City College) had no previous experience in laboratory markets. All participants in Series II (recruited from Caltech) had participated in at least one other laboratory market with parameters differing from the experiments reported here.

The laboratory design of each experimental session consisted of an auction market with four buyers and four sellers. Preferences were induced following the theory of induced preference (see Smith; Plott). Buyers made money by buying from the sellers and reselling to the experimenter according to prespecified terms. Likewise, sellers made money by buying from the experimenter at prespecified costs and reselling to the buyers. In addition, each individual received a five-

cent trading commission. The value of the redemption values for each individual is indicated on Figure 1.

Each market involved a series of "trading periods" in which market participants were free to buy and sell. The individual parameters were identical each period. By application of the theory of induced preference (and/or derived demand) the individual parameters become limit prices which can be "summed" in accord with competitive market theory to produce the demand and supply curves represented in Figure 1. These curves remained constant over all periods and, except for small shifts upward by a constant, indicated below, were the same across all experiments.

Markets were organized as two-sided oral auction markets. All participants had free access to the market floor to make bids to buy (offers to sell) or to accept any outstanding offer (bid). Each bid canceled previous bids, and offers canceled previous offers. All ties were broken by random process.

The institutions being examined are a series of price ceilings and price floors. Specifically, the following paragraph is an example of a price ceiling: "During this experiment, no bids or offers may be made or accepted at a

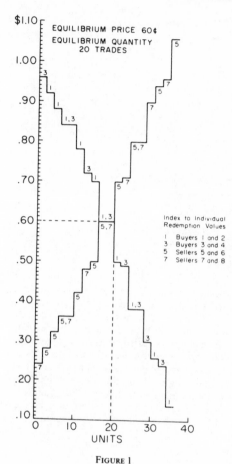

EQUILIBRIUM PRICE 60¢
EQUILIBRIUM QUANTITY
20 TRADES

Index to Individual
Redemption Values

| | Buyers 1 and 2 |
| 3 | Buyers 3 and 4 |
| 5 | Sellers 5 and 6 |
| 7 | Sellers 7 and 8 |

UNITS

FIGURE 1

the expense and the nature of the evidence obtained from the experiments we did run (see Table 1).

The results of the twelve experimental sessions are presented in the following section, with a particular emphasis upon the patterns which exhibit regularity, and upon the relationship between these results and the existing theoretical literature. Additionally, we will consider the significance of our results for future research.

We have focused the study on the following three aspects of market behavior:

1) Price Levels and Market Volume: Price level refers to the average price of a contract during a period. Sometimes the range of prices during a period is referenced. Volume refers to the number of contracts during a period.

2) Market Responses to Institutional Modifications: During the course of several experiments price controls were removed. Occasionally a control was added or changed (see Table 1).

3) Efficiency: The efficiency index developed by Plott and Smith is used here. Markets are 100 percent efficient if and only if the total of subjects' profits and commissions is maximized during a trading period. The efficiency is the actual sum of subjects' profits and commissions divided by the theoretical maximum of this sum. This measure is related to the maximum of consumer's plus producer's surplus.

## II. Experimental Results: Some Preliminary Conclusions

We can report two major results and a conjecture. The results are: First, that market behavior under price controls is more closely approximated by the competitive model than by the focal point model; and secondly, that markets under price controls exhibit behavioral regularities which are not included in standard analyses and some of which cannot be explained by the "traditional" competitive model. Specifically, four such regularities were noted: (i) controls at the competitive equilibrium cause market prices to diverge from the competitive equilibrium; (ii) the removal of nonbinding controls induces

price greater than___cents. Of course, you may still make or accept bids or offers at a price less than or equal to this amount."

In general, our experiments can be divided into seven categories as follows ($\bar{P} =$ maximum price, $\underline{P} =$ minimum price, $P_0 =$ competitive equilibrium):

(1) no price controls
(2) & (3) price controls precisely at predicted equilibrium ($\bar{P} = P_0$; $\underline{P} = P_0$)
(4) & (5) strictly nonbinding price controls ($\bar{P} > P_0$; $\underline{P} < P_0$)
(6) & (7) strictly binding price controls ($\bar{P} < P_0$; $\underline{P} > P_0$).

Not all categories were examined because of

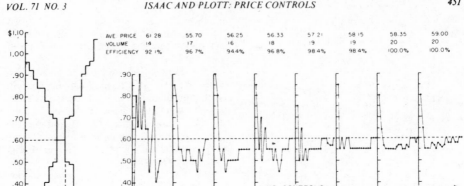

FIGURE 2

changes in market prices; (iii) inefficiencies induced by binding controls are greater than those predicted by the standard application of consumer's surplus analysis. The amount of additional loss depends upon the method of resolving the rationing problem; and finally, (iv) adjustment of prices when binding controls are removed appears to involve an initial discontinuity or "jump" rather than a continuous adjustment. The conjecture is that nonbinding controls act like a "buffer" which holds prices below (above) the "natural" market equilibrium in the case of price ceilings (floors).

Since the two results can be easily demonstrated, we have organized the following subsections, which contain a more detailed examination of the data, in a manner which highlights the nature of the conjecture. First, we discuss the behavior of markets with no controls at all. It is here that the concept of a natural equilibrium (as opposed to the equilibrium point of the competitive model) is explored. The second and third subsections, respectively, address the results of experiments with nonbinding controls and binding controls.

The experimental results are displayed in Figures 2 through 13. Shown in these figures are all contract prices arrayed according to the order (in time) in which the contract

occurred. The dotted line always indicates the competitive model equilibrium price (in the absence of controls). During some experiments institutional changes were made, for example, a price control may have been removed or imposed. A double line separates the periods where institutional changes are initially imposed and the nature of the change is indicated on the figure. The equilibrium price, average prices, volume, and efficiencies for each period are on the figures.

### A. *No Price Controls*

Three experiments were conducted with no price controls at all. These are Experiments I, II, and III (periods 1, 2, 3, and 7) on Figures 2, 3, and 4. In addition, price controls were removed for selected periods in other experiments (see Table 1).

Laboratory markets (including those examined here), when organized as a "double oral auction"[3] without price controls, invariably exhibit the following properties. These properties are important since they serve as standards against which the effects of price controls can be judged. (a) Efficiencies are high and approach 100 percent and stabilize

---

[3]We refer specifically to those in which, as here, small trading commissions are paid.

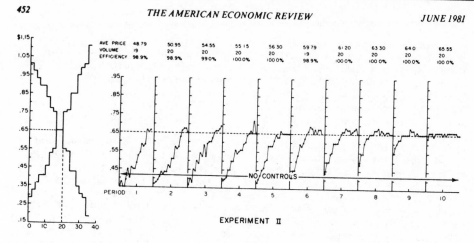

EXPERIMENT II

FIGURE 3

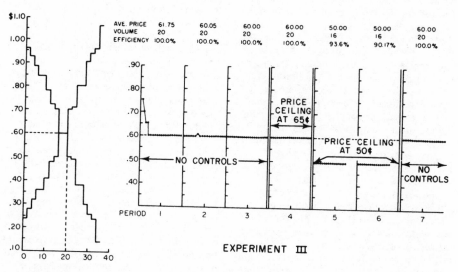

EXPERIMENT III

FIGURE 4

once high efficiencies are achieved (i.e., above 98 percent). (b) The variance of prices tends to diminish with replications of periods. (c) If there are many trades at prices other than the equilibrium, they tend to be on both sides of the equilibrium. (d) Average prices tend to stabilize near the competitive equilibrium price.

Experiment III (Figure 4) dramatically demonstrates the frequently observed power of the competitive model. Prices converge almost immediately to the competitive price

with zero variance and 100 percent efficiency. While subjects in this experiment did not know the market parameters, they had all had previous experience in laboratory markets. Subject experience is suspected to be a primary reason for the relatively rapid convergence and low variance of Experiment III relative to the other two no-control experiments (I and II).

Sometimes markets have sellers (buyers) who are willing to sell (buy) units at prices considerably below (above) the equilibrium price even though many trades occur at or above (below) equilibrium. These individuals, who do not seem inclined to "hold out" for one of the better deals are called "relatively soft" sellers (buyers). In Experiment I (Figure 2) notice that the first trade or two in every period is considerably above the other trades. All of these contracts involved the same "soft" buyer. In Experiment II (Figure 3) notice that many low-priced contracts occur at the beginning of each period. These all involved the same two soft sellers whose anxiousness to sell resulted in low contract prices. Exactly why this occurs is not known (in Experiment II, however, one of the soft sellers had no previous experience in laboratory markets) but whatever the reason the behavior is usually "corrected" by the last few periods. It is important to notice, however, that "softness" seems to affect neither the market efficiency (in all three experiments it is over 98 percent by the fifth period and increasing) nor the tendency for trades to occur on both sides of equilibrium. Properties (a), (b), and (c) are exhibited in all three experiments. However, to the extent that the average prices diverge from the equilibrium of the competitive model, we need a concept of a natural equilibrium. The effects of price controls then must be gauged relative to this natural tendency as opposed to the prediction of the competitive model.

The major difficulty with supporting our buffer conjecture above can now be made clear. Indeed the soft trader problem is the reason the result is listed as a conjecture instead of a conclusion. If soft buyers or sellers exist, the average price may remain removed from the competitive equilibrium price. Thus the influence of price controls must be measured against this natural tendency rather than the equilibrium of the model. But the natural tendency cannot be known until the market operates and since the softness of subjects may be modified by any market experience, the very act of observing the "natural equilibrium" which differs from that of the competitive model may cause it to change. Thus, there is currently no "fixed" measure against which the influence of price controls can be identified.

Our initial experimental design was not constructed to deal with this difficulty. At best we are able to establish within our design the plausibility of the buffer conjecture and identify certain properties of the buffer phenomenon if indeed it exists.

### B. *Nonbinding Controls*

Nonbinding price controls existed in all or parts of eight of the twelve experimental markets. The first experiments, reported here as Experiment IV (Figure 5) and Experiment V (Figure 6), involved a price ceiling at the competitive equilibrium price and Experiment VI (Figure 7) involved a floor at the competitive equilibrium. The results from these three experiments led to additional experiments with nonbinding controls "near" the equilibrium price (Experiments VII–XI on Figures 8–12, respectively). These will be covered in order below.

Two conclusions can be supported by a reference to all experiments with nonbinding controls. First, the market behavior under nonbinding price controls is more closely approximated by the competitive model than the focal point model advanced in the introduction. In *no* period of any experiment is the average market price closer to the price control than the competitive equilibrium price. When the ceiling is equal to the competitive equilibrium price, the average prices tend to diverge from the ceiling. When the nonbinding price control is not equal to the competitive equilibrium price, the average price (indeed the entire range of prices) of every period is closer to the competitive equilibrium. The rejection of the focal point model in favor of the competitive equilibrium model seems amply justified.

The second conclusion, on the other hand, highlights a possible incompleteness in the traditional model. Removal of a nonbinding price control affects the price level. The action seems to "disequilibrate" the market. Nonbinding price controls are removed in Experiments VI–X (Figures 7–11, respectively). In every case the removal of the nonbinding control is followed by a movement in the average price. The only case where the spirit of this conclusion is violated is Experiment III, period 4 (Figure 4) in which the nonbinding control was added after

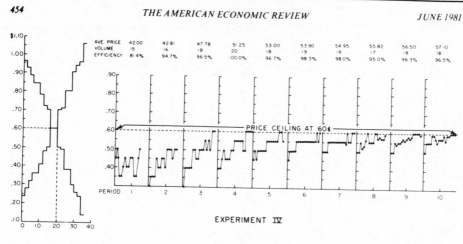

FIGURE 5

the market had already converged and induced no changes at all in the level of prices.

According to traditional models the equilibrating properties of markets depend only upon the magnitude of excess demand. Since the removal of nonbinding price controls does not affect the magnitude of excess demand, the traditional model cannot account for the resulting changes in the price level. Exactly how the traditional model must be supplemented is not clear. Perhaps the removal of controls makes available additional strategies to one side or the other, thereby giving differential advantages. Perhaps any "announcement" in experimental markets will cause "disequilibrations." Perhaps the change creates additional uncertainty, thereby encouraging additional search activity by some participants and conservative or soft trading on the part of the others. Clearly, both additional theory and experiments are needed before the reasons for the phenomenon can be identified.

We turn now to the conjecture, the "buffer hypothesis" by examining first the experiments with price controls placed at the competitive equilibrium (Experiments IV–VI on Figures 5–7). In the price ceiling experiments, IV and V, prices are almost stabilized at an average below the ceiling with few trades at the competitive equilibrium ceilings. Efficiencies remain below 98 percent with marginal units not being traded even

though in Experiment IV an efficiency of 100 percent was attained once during an early period. In the price floor experiment, VI (with experienced subjects), prices converged to the floor in a manner seemingly contradictory to the buffer hypothesis, but when the floor was removed (period 7), prices immediately dropped to a lower level. Thus, in the context of the buffer hypothesis the natural equilibrium was below the competitive equilibrium for this group of subjects. Efficiencies in this experiment approximate 100 percent.

Four experiments (VII–X) were conducted with nonbinding controls placed within five cents of the competitive equilibrium. The buffer hypothesis can be applied to all four sessions. The evidence is strongest for Experiments VII–IX where trades seldom if ever occur at prices between the price control and the competitive equilibrium. When the control is removed, prices immediately rise (fall) to above (below) the competitive equilibrium in the case of price ceilings (floor). In Experiments VII and IX the efficiency level did not behave in the stable manner characteristic of markets without controls. Instead, the efficiency sometimes attained the 98 percent level but did not remain. Experiment X differs because prices converged initially below the competitive equilibrium but even in this experiment prices fell when the nonbinding

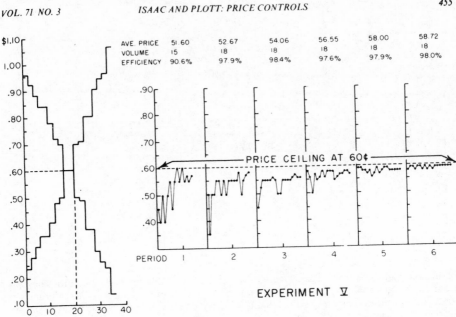

EXPERIMENT V

FIGURE 6

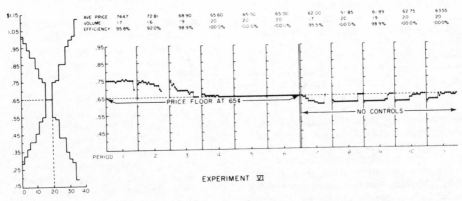

EXPERIMENT VI

FIGURE 7

floor was removed. Thus, for this experiment application of the buffer hypothesis must assume that the sellers were soft and the nonbinding floor acted to hold prices above the natural equilibrium.

In Experiment XI (Figure 12) a nonbinding ceiling was placed ten cents above the equilibrium. Since prices here converged very close to the competitive equilibrium and since

the control remained throughout the whole experiment, we have little to say about it. We suspect, however, that the buffer effect is weak at best here where the control is "far" from the equilibrium price.

As indicated above, we can at best speculate about the reasons for the buffer effect. It may have something to do with the information and "search." The results of Experiment

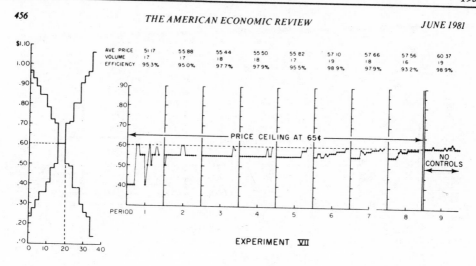

FIGURE 8

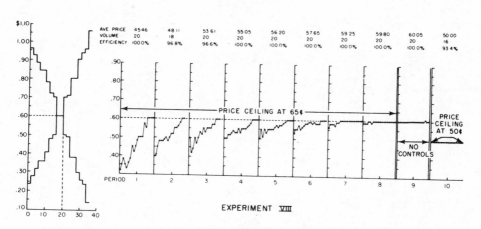

FIGURE 9

III, period 4, were revealing in this respect. Adding a nonbinding ceiling there made no difference at all.

### C. Binding Price Controls

For the first eight periods of Experiment XII (Figure 13) a price ceiling of fifty cents existed which was below the competitive equilibrium price of sixty cents. The ceiling was removed after the eighth period. In period 10 of Experiment VIII (Figure 9) and in periods 5 and 6 of Experiment III (Figure

4) a price ceiling below the equilibrium was imposed.

The experiments were motivated by the buffer hypothesis. Perhaps the buffer would work to keep prices below a *binding* control. In this respect the control could be viewed as the opposite of the focal point hypothesis as introduced above. Perhaps the ceiling (floor) acts as a signal to the buyers (sellers) and helps them coordinate to hold prices below (above) the ceiling (floor).

As can be seen from all the figures, this alternative hypothesis seems to be wrong.

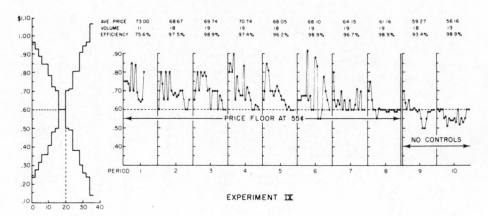

EXPERIMENT IX

FIGURE 10

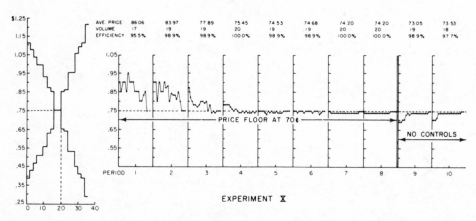

EXPERIMENT X

FIGURE 11

Prices converge rapidly to the binding ceilings. Price equals the ceiling and the volume equals the competitive supply function evaluated at the price ceiling. For the case of binding controls the market price behaves as predicted by the traditional model.

In the course of these experiments we discovered two modes of behavior we did not anticipate. The first "unexpected" results occurred when the controls were removed. The adjustment *path* of prices when the binding ceiling is removed differs somewhat from the standard dynamic hypothesis. In period 9 of Experiment XII the binding price ceiling

was removed. The mean price jumped immediately to more than thirteen cents *above* equilibrium and then converged down toward equilibrium rather than adjusting continuously upward as suggested by most dynamics models. A discontinuity in adjustment was also present when a binding price ceiling was added in Experiment III (periods 5 and 6) and then removed (period 7). In this market (in which subjects were experienced) prices simply adjusted back immediately to the previously attained equilibrium without "overshooting." This latter result suggests that information, in addition to possibly the

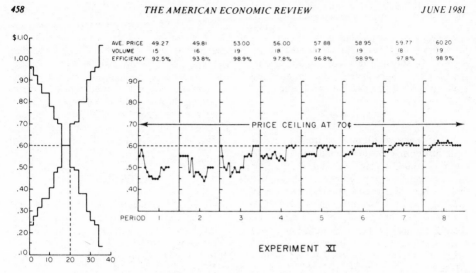

FIGURE 12

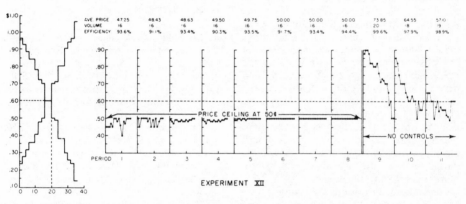

FIGURE 13

magnitude of excess market demand, plays a systematic role in the formation of adjustment paths. Of course more experimentation and theory are necessary.

Secondly, analysis of these experiments with binding controls reveals a source of inefficiency not often stressed in the economics literature. Efficiency losses can result from both the price ceiling as well as the choice of the rationing process used in conjunction with binding price controls. Because of the fifty-cent price ceiling in Experiment XII, at most sixteen units may legally be offered for

sale, yet effective demand at fifty cents is twenty-two units. The *minimum* possible loss of efficiency due to the price ceiling occurs when precisely the sixteen demand units with highest redemption value are traded. The maximum attainable efficiency under the price ceiling is 95.73 percent. Whether or not this maximum is attained depends upon the rationing process. In these experiments a first come, first served method was used in which ties were broken by a random process. As can be seen on Figure 13, this rationing process induces its own inefficiencies. In every period of Experiment XII efficiency is below the 95.73 percent. Naturally other methods of solving the allocation and queueing problem resulting from the price ceiling may have different efficiency properties.

## III. Summary

In summary, we found the familiar partial-equilibrium model works remarkably well to describe laboratory auction market behavior in the presence of price controls and, particularly, when the price controls are strictly binding. However, we also discovered some empirical regularities which the traditional theory cannot explain. Nonbinding price controls seem to affect the average level of prices. Furthermore, price levels and market efficiency can be influenced by removing nonbinding controls. Exactly how the standard model can be extended to explain these results is unclear. The crucial features of the institutions which induce the results have not been identified. Perhaps other institutions induce similar behavior. Perhaps many of our observations can be attributed to the single fact that institutions were *changed* and have nothing at all to do with the essential features of price controls. Nevertheless, the existence of empirical regularities seems undeniable and we offer them as a challenge to theorists who are extending the standard models to include expectations, strategic behavior, and/or the availability of market information to participants.

Subject to qualifications that must accompany any application of laboratory experimental methods, the results presented here are of potential interest to the public policy analyst. Diocletion claimed that his price ceilings would have no effect in regions where they were not binding. These results suggest that he might have been wrong. The observation that the price controls are not binding

(in the sense used in partial-equilibrium analysis) is not sufficient to conclude that the controls are neutral either as to the conduct of prices or to market efficiency. Conversely, the fact that market transactions are occurring below a price ceiling or above a price floor will not be sufficient to conclude that removing controls will leave prices and quantities unchanged.

## REFERENCES

Lactantius, "The Deaths of the Persecutors," in *Lactantius: The Minor Works*, translated by Sister Mary Francis McDonald, Washington 1964.

J. P. Levy, *The Economic Life of the Ancient World*, Chicago 1964.

Naphtali Lewis and Meyer Reinhold, *Roman Civilization*, Vol. II, New York 1951.

H. Michelle, *The Economics of Ancient Greece*, Cambridge 1957.

R. M. Miller, C. R. Plott, and V. L. Smith, "Intertemporal Competitive Equilibrium: An Empirical Study of Speculation," *Quart. J. Econ.*, Nov. 1977, *91*, 599–624.

C. R. Plott, "The Application of Laboratory Experimental Methods to Public Choice," in Clifford S. Russell, ed., *Collective Decision Making: Applications from Public Choice Theory*, Washington 1979.

_____ and V. L. Smith, "An Experimental Examination of Two Exchange Institutions," *Rev. Econ. Stud.*, Feb. 1978, *45*, 133–53.

F. M. Scherer, *Industrial Pricing*, Chicago 1970.

V. L. Smith, "Experimental Economics: Induced Value Theory," *Amer. Econ. Rev. Proc.*, May 1976, *66*, 274–79.

Leon Walras, *Elements d'Economie Politique Pure*, trans. W. Jaffe, *Elements of Pure Economics*, Homewood 1954.

# [9]

## Price Controls in a Posted Offer Market

*By* Don L. Coursey and Vernon L. Smith\*

The effects of price controls have been examined in markets organized under the double auction trading institution. R. Mark Isaac and Charles Plott (1981) and Smith and Arlington Williams (1981) report the following three principal conclusions from twenty-eight double auction experiments:

1) The hypothesis is rejected that non-binding price ceilings (floors) will serve as a focal point in the sense that buyers and sellers are attracted to prices at the ceiling (floor).[1]

2) Evidence is presented to support the hypothesis that nonbinding ceilings (floors) near the competitive equilibrium ($CE$) price will lower (raise) the convergence path of contract prices to the $CE$ price. Also, supported is the hypothesis that contract prices tend to converge to the level of a binding price ceiling (floor) from below (above) the control price.

3) Strong empirical evidence was presented which showed that upon the removal of either a binding or a nonbinding price ceiling (floor) prices tended to jump discontinuously above (below) the $CE$ level, only returning to that level after a period of adjustment.

This study seeks to determine whether these three conclusions are unique to the double auction institution of exchange by examining the effects of price ceilings in the posted offer institution of exchange. A posted offer market is characterized by sellers who publicly post nonnegotiable prices (that are selected privately) for a commodity at the beginning of each period of trading. Buyers then respond (in random order) by purchasing desired quantities of the commodity from the seller of their choice. Most retail markets use posted offer pricing, and we ordinarily associate price controls (as in the Nixon Administration) with such markets.

We report below the design and results of thirteen controlled laboratory posted offer experiments using an experimental design consisting of fixed supply and demand schedules. Across independent experiments the level of a price ceiling is varied in 5 cent steps from above to below the $CE$ level. In half of the experiments, the price control is removed midway through the trading periods of an experiment ("controlled/non-controlled" or $C/N$ experiments), and in other experiments, the price control is imposed upon the market only after the midpoint is reached ("noncontrolled/controlled" or $N/C$ experiments). By considering both the $C/N$ and $N/C$ treatments, more insight into the reported double auction price explosion effect is obtained.

### I. Experimental Design

All of the experiments use the PLATO computer version of the posted offer exchange mechanism as described in Jon Ketcham, Smith, and Williams (1980). Using this system, it is possible to induce value (see Smith, 1976) on the actions of buyers and sellers which define supply and demand schedules that are known to the experimenter, but not to the agents. Our design is characterized by four buyers capable of purchasing three units each and four sellers capable of selling three units each. The resale and cost values of these units are charted on the left in Figure 1.

All of the subjects who participated in the experiment were undergraduate students at the University of Arizona, and all had prior experience in at least one similar posted offer experiment *without* price controls and with different supply and demand parameters. The subjects received a special announcement that

\*University of Arkansas and University of Arizona, respectively. We are grateful to the National Science Foundation for Research support.

[1]A nonbinding price ceiling is a ceiling equal to or greater than the competitive equilibrium price. A binding ceiling is one which is below the competitive equilibrium price.

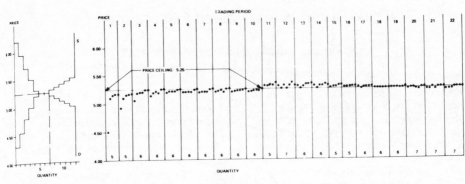

FIGURE 1

## II. Experimental Results

price controls would be in effect when appropriate, during each period of trading. Attempted violation of the price ceiling resulted in the rejection of a seller's offer until the price constraint condition was satisfied. Each trading period began with the sellers selecting (privately) the price at which they wished to sell units, and the number of units they wished to sell at this price. Once all of the sellers had finalized their offers, each seller was notified of the other sellers' offer prices, and the buyers were randomly queued to start the buying procedure. When there were no units available from a particular seller, an "out-of-stock" message was displayed. To provide incentive for the marginal units to trade each contract yielded a commission of 10 cents to both the trading buyer and seller. After each buyer had completed this purchase mode, the trading period was over.

All thirteen experiments consisted of twenty trading periods separated into two groups of ten periods each. For the $C/N$ type experiments, the price control was in effect for the first ten periods, and not in effect for the second ten periods. Conversely, the $N/C$ experiments began with ten periods of noncontrol and ended with ten periods of price control. The ceilings varied in 5 cent steps across independent experiments. Experiments were conducted with controls 5 cents above the competitive equilibrium (experiments P39, P56, P57, and P60), at the competitive equilibrium (P65, P74, and P101), 5 cents below (P85, P88, and P100), and 10 cents below (P81, P84, and P99).

Previous experimental studies of posted offer (bid) pricing (Fred Williams, 1973; Plott and Smith, 1978) have indicated that prices in this institution tend to converge from above (below) the *CE* price to a level somewhat higher (lower) than the *CE* price. The confirmed tendency of posted offer prices to converge from above strongly suggests that price ceilings at or 5 cents above the *CE* price, and certainly for binding ceilings below the *CE* price, will yield many if not all observed contracts at the ceiling price. In particular it seems quite likely, at least for the first few trading periods, that the focal point hypothesis will be confirmed as sellers, desiring to begin with "high" posted prices focus and "lock on" to the ceiling price even if it is nonbinding. These were our a priori expectations. Our most important finding is that these conjectures proved to be false.

The individual results for a typical experiment (P65) are displayed in Figure 1. In Figure 1, all contract prices are plotted in the order in which the contracts occurred. The *CE* price is indicated by the solid line at $5.25. The periods for which the price ceiling treatment condition was in effect are indicated on each figure.

Overall, we find qualitative continuity between the previous double auction results and our posted offer results. If we examine the convergence behavior of prices over time, the predictions of competitive price theory, with or without ceilings, is strongly sup-

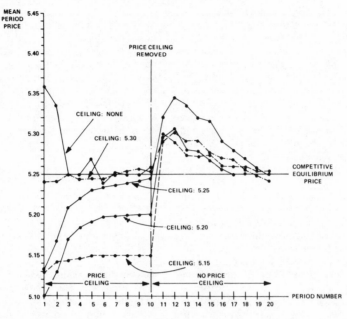

FIGURE 2

ported. This is shown in Figure 2 which plots the time-series of mean price across experiments for each trading period. The graph of the data for the first ten periods, in those experiments with no price ceiling, exhibits the familiar tendency to converge from above as reported in all previous posted offer experiments. This pattern is reversed when there is a price ceiling at any level from 5 cents above to 10 cents below the $CE$ price. Hence, the dynamic effect of price ceilings in posted offer markets is qualitatively the same as in double auction markets. In both markets the effect of a ceiling is to cause convergence from below to the constrained or unconstrained competitive price. However, this downward shift in the price convergence path is much more pronounced in double auction markets.

Since sellers in an unconstrained posted offer market tend to post initial prices that are high relative to the $CE$ price, why do they tend not to begin with posted prices at the ceiling price, when such ceilings are in effect? The answer appears to be as follows:

Sellers do not know what constitutes a "high" price, that is, they do not "know" the $CE$ price, nor do they know whether the ceiling price is binding or not, even if we assumed that the sellers would understand what is meant by a "$CE$ price" or a "binding" ceiling. However, from their experience with previous posted offer markets, each seller has learned that if he/she has a higher price than one or more other sellers, this increases the chance that no sales or profit will be made. Hence, an initial impulse to quote prices at the ceiling price is likely to be tempered by the thought that "others may charge less, so that I may fail to make a sale. Perhaps I should begin at a lower price." This type of behavior is certainly consistent with agent experience, and is also consistent with what we observe in markets with a price ceiling.

Price ceilings were removed in nine of the thirteen experiments. The effect on mean price by period is also shown in Figure 2. The removal of either a binding or a nonbinding price ceiling produces the jump discontinuity observed in the double auction experiments. However, unlike the double auction results, we cannot clearly identify a positive relationship between the size of the initial jump and the degree to which the original ceiling was binding. Also, the increase in prices is less explosive than in double auction markets. After the initial increase in prices, following the lifting of a ceiling price, the market tends to converge toward the free market *CE* price. A jump in prices following the removal of price control is often observed in the field, as, for example, with the removal of gasoline price controls in 1980. This behavior is often described as the result of "pent-up" or accumulated unsatisfied demand. But this explanation cannot describe our experimental market behavior since all purchases are for current period demand—there can be no accumulation of demand across trading periods. The phenomena would appear to be explainable only in terms of seller expectations that sales are feasible, and perhaps sustainable, at prices higher than the removed ceiling. If sellers differ in these expectations, posted offer prices are likely to exhibit an increased mean and variance for a few trading periods as sellers grope for a new sustainable level of prices and profits.

### III. Summary

In summary, we found that the standard competitive model is supported with respect to its performance in describing the *equilibrium* tendencies under price control in posted offer markets. Similar results had been reported previously for double auction markets. We also found that certain dynamic "irregularities" in double auction markets also occur in posted offer markets. The depression of initial prices in price ceiling markets has not been anticipated by traditional microeconomic theory. Binding as well as nonbinding price ceilings affect the negotiation process in both trading institutions, and tend to lower initial contract prices. Finally, an initial increase in contract prices follows the removal of either a binding or a nonbinding price ceiling, but ultimately prices approach the *CE* price.

### REFERENCES

Issac, R. Mark and Plott, Charles R., "Price Controls and the Behavior of Auction Markets: An Experimental Examination," *American Economic Review*, June 1981, *71*, 449–59.

Ketcham, Jon, Smith, Vernon L. and Williams, Arlington W., "The Behavior of Posted Offer Pricing Institutions," Southern Economic Association Meetings, November 5–7, 1980.

Plott, Charles R. and Smith, Vernon L., "An Experimental Examination of Two Exchange Institutions," *Review of Economic Studies*, February 1978, *45*, 133–53.

Smith, Vernon L., "Experimental Economics: Induced Value Theory," *American Economic Review Proceedings*, May 1976, *66*, 274–79.

_____ and Williams, Arlington W., "On Nonbinding Price Controls in a Competitive Market," *American Economic Review*, June 1981, *71*, 467–74.

Williams, Fred, "Effect of Market Organization on Competitive Equilibrium: The Multi-Unit Case," *Review of Economic Studies*, January 1973, *40*, 97–113.

# [10]

# ENTITLEMENTS, RIGHTS, AND FAIRNESS: AN EXPERIMENTAL EXAMINATION OF SUBJECTS' CONCEPTS OF DISTRIBUTIVE JUSTICE

*ELIZABETH HOFFMAN and MATTHEW L. SPITZER\**

## I. Introduction

THE research reported in this paper arose from a previous experimental study conducted by the authors.[1] That study involved bargains struck between two subjects who had opposing payoff functions and full information of one another's payoffs. By a flip of a coin one participant could choose a noncooperative outcome, unilaterally: the winner of the coin toss could simply choose an outcome which gave him $12 and left the other subject nothing, whether or not the loser agreed. However, if the two subjects cooperated, they could obtain from the experimenter $14, which could be split between the subjects in any mutually agreed-on manner. Cooperative game theory predicts that the subjects will cooperate and divide the rewards $13 to $1 (the Nash bargaining solution: an even division of the $2 gain from trade). Under no circumstances should the winner of the coin flip settle for less than $12, according to game

\* Associate Professor of Economics, Purdue University, and Associate Professor of Law, University of Southern California, Los Angeles, respectively. We wish to thank Brian Binger, Charles Plott, Margaret Jane Radin, and Jean Spitzer for their comments and suggestions on experimental design; Allan Axelrod, Erwin Chemerinsky, Richard Craswell, Dennis Curtis, Ronald Garet, Thomas Hammond, George Lefcoe, Martin Levine, Mordehai Mironi, Michael Moore, Stephen Morse, J. Keith Murnighan, Larry Simon, Alan Schwartz, Michael Shapiro, David Slawson, J. F. Strnad, Edward E. Zajac, and all of the participants at workshops before the USC Law Faculty and the Washington University Center for the Study of American Business for their helpful comments on drafts of this article; and Rao Kadiyala for his invaluable help with the statistical analysis. All errors are, of course, our own. Gary Adler, Faye Anderson, Lee Ann Duffy, Fellipe Prestamo, and Ellen Roth provided research assistance. Financial support was provided by National Science Foundation grant no. SES-8200266.

[1] Elizabeth Hoffman & Matthew L. Spitzer, The Coase Theorem: Some Experimental Tests, 25 J. Law & Econ. 73 (1982).

[*Journal of Legal Studies*, vol. XIV (June 1985)]

theory. In our experiments all of the subject pairs chose the joint profit-maximizing outcome, which the theory predicts, but they then divided the rewards $7 to $7. In effect, each winner of a coin flip agreed to take $5 *less* than the $12 that he could have obtained *without* the other subject's cooperation.

These results often startle economists (ourselves included), who usually assume that individuals will generally behave in a self-regarding manner. However, if one is willing to hypothesize that subjects behave "as if" they distribute the payoffs in accord with their perceptions of fairness. the results can be rationalized. In particular, we can construct a model based on the following set of related assumptions:

Model 1:
1. Each subject would concur with a particular concept of fairness in distribution (also known as a theory of distributive justice).
2. Each subject perceives the experimental institutions as triggering a particular aspect of his concept of justice, indicating which distribution or set of distributions is fair within that experiment.
3. The subject implements his perceptions of a fair distribution.[2]

In the results reported above, we hypothesize that subjects behave in accord with a theory of distributive justice that says that flipping a coin is not a just way of allocating unequal property entitlements.[3] Subjects perceived no morally justified difference between themselves, even though one "legally" owned a substantial property entitlement and the other did not. Because they were "morally equal," an equal split seemed to be the only fair allocation.

If this explanation of subject behavior is correct, then by systematically varying the experimental institutions and observing how subjects' payoff

---

[2] For a similar hypothesis, see Norman Frohlich & Joe Oppenheimer, with Pat Bond & Irvin Boschman, Beyond Economic Man: Altruism, Egalitarianism. and Difference Maximizing, 28 J. Conflict Resolution 3 (1984). See, however, the discussion of the "fundamental attribution error," the tendency to overattribute human behavior to human characteristics or traits, rather than situational determinants, discussed at the beginning of Section V. *infra*. In this paper, when we state that, for example, a subject "believes" a theory of fairness, we are to be read as meaning that a subject "behaves as if he believes" a theory. The shorter form is for convenience only.

[3] We make use of the following terminology in this paper: "Entitlements" are legally enforceable claims (in a real-politic sense) to economic resources. "Rights" are morally justified entitlements. See Robert Apsler & Henry Friedman, Chance Outcomes and the Just World: A Comparison of Observers and Recipients, 31 J. Personality & Soc. Psychology 887 (1975); and Philip Brickman, Adaptation Level Determinants of Satisfaction with Equal and Unequal Outcome Distributions of Skill and Chance Situations, 32 J. Personality & Soc. Psychology 191 (1975), for evidence that chance distributions of payments are not considered fair unless they are equal.

distributions change, we should be able to infer which theories of distributive justice subjects hold. We consider, in particular, three different candidates for subjects' concepts of fairness, drawn from three major families of theories of distributive justice: utilitarian, egalitarian, and natural law/desert. Specifically, we consider the self-regarding, economic man paradigm from utilitarian theory, an extreme egalitarian theory of equal sharing, and the Lockean theory of earned desert.

Each of the experiments reported in this paper allocated entitlements in a different manner and then allowed subjects to divide the value of those entitlements. The results suggest that subjects behaved in accord neither with the self-regarding utilitarian theory nor with the egalitarian theory of distributive justice, but rather in accord with the Lockean theory of earned desert. These experimental results show strongly that different methods of assigning property entitlements lead to significant differences in the frequency of self-regarding versus equal payoff divisions. Subjects appeared to treat their entitlements as rights to unequal payoff divisions when the experimental institutions led them to believe that they had "earned" those entitlements. Subjects continued to maximize joint profits (chose efficient outcomes) in all versions of the experiment.

Both behavioral scientists and lawyers should be interested in the results reported below. Experimental economists and psychologists should be particularly intrigued by the results, for they help to trace out the domain within which one may safely utilize the postulate of self-regarding behavior. Legal theorists may also be interested in property entitlements and moral rules for allocating payments. A large group of scholars believe that the law should (or does) reflect widely held moral norms.[4] Hence, it is important to learn of their content.[5] Application of the information pro-

---

[4] Justice Holmes was confident that our legal system represented society's morals. Separate consideration as to whether the outcomes of legal cases were *morally* acceptable was not necessary for Holmes. See, for example, Oliver Wendell Holmes, The Path of the Law, 10 Harv. L. Rev. 457 (1897). Similarly, Epstein's theory of strict liability is part of a corrective justice framework that expects the law to have a moral foundation. Richard A. Epstein, A Theory of Strict Liability, 2 J. Legal Stud. 151 (1973). Further, Radin has commented that Communitarians believe that the changing values of persons and communities should produce changing rules of property law. Margaret Jane Radin, Property and Personhood, 34 Stan. L. Rev. 957 (1982).

[5] Norms may be a product of nature or of socialization processes. Sociobiologists argue that a mechanism of natural selection provides survival advantages to those who hold certain moral beliefs. See generally, Edward O. Wilson, On Human Nature (1978) at 5. See also Paul H. Rubin, Evolved Ethics and Efficient Ethics, 3 J. Econ. Behav. & Organization 161 (1982), contending, inter alia, that modern man's disposition to share wealth with his less fortunate fellows (and his disposition to dislike wealthy individuals) can be explained as the product both of kin selection procedures, *id.* at 165, and primitive insurance ("reciprocal altruism") against "unlucky" events, such as poor animal hunts, in primitive hunter-

vided by the experiments reported herein may suggest important policies
for shaping the law.

We must note, however, that substantial difficulties may plague any
such applications of our results to the law. For example, an individual's
beliefs about morality may determine his behavior. But there is a substantial amount of experimental evidence tending to show that the correlation
between an individual's moral behavior (cheating, for example) in one
situation and moral behavior in similar (but not identical) situations tends
to be positive and significant, but small in size.[6] Therefore, one should be
very careful about predicting behavior generated by moral norms (for
example, cheating is bad) over different sorts of situations. To the extent
that one can make such predictions, however, they can help inform fundamental policy choices. In the final section of this paper we explore some
possible legal applications and discuss problems involved in using them to
inform policy.

## II.  THEORIES OF DISTRIBUTIVE JUSTICE

### A.  Utilitarian

Utilitarian theories assert that people ought to act so as to maximize
some function which is monotonically increasing in the utility of each of
the members of society (for example, sums or products of individual
utility functions).[7] We consider only one version of utilitarianism: each
person's utility is independent of any other person's utility and each

---

gatherer tribes. Rubin contends that both of these traits probably produced survival advantages in primitive tribes and that these traits survive today as "ethical intuitions" that are
counterproductive for our modern social organization. Others argue that beliefs about morality are produced by the socialization process. See, for example, Barry Holden, Liberal
Democracy and the Social Determination of Ideas, 25 Nomos: Liberal Democracy 289 (J.
Roland Pennock & John W. Chapman eds. 1983), discussing Marxist critiques of liberal
democratic theory.

[6] Walter Mischel, Personality and Assessment 23–26 (1968). This is the belief held by
most lay people and sociologists, and by many psychologists, including Freudians. For a
behavioral psychologist's view that humanity has not evolved a genetic moral sense, but
rather a "social environment in which individuals behave in ways determined in part by their
effects on others," see B. F. Skinner, About Behaviorism 191–95 (1974). In addition, we
should note that there is virtually no correlation between statements regarding morality and
subsequent behavior. However, our article deals with inference from behavior, not statements about it.

[7] Utilitarian accounts of property law abound in modern law and economics. See for
example, Harold Demsetz, Toward a Theory of Property Rights, 57 Am. Econ. Rev. 347
(1967); Guido Calabresi & A. Douglas Melamed, Property Rules, Liability Rules and In-
alienability: One View of the Cathedral, 85 Harv. L. Rev. 1089 (1972); and Frank I. Michelman, Property, Utility and Fairness: Comments on the Ethical Foundations of "Just Compensation" Law, 80 Harv. L. Rev. 1165 (1967).

CONCEPTS OF DISTRIBUTIVE JUSTICE 263

person weights his own utility more heavily than the utility of anyone else. This self-regarding version of utilitarianism suggests that subjects will regard any distribution in which they have more money as more desirable. This belief will lead subjects to act so as to maximize their own holdings, appearing to be "greedy."

This version of utilitarianism generates the paradigm of the "economic man," who under most economic and game-theoretic models makes self-regarding decisions about whatever entitlements he is endowed with.[8] Where property rights are well defined, the rational economic agent is assumed to enter only into bargains that he believes will leave him no worse off than if he had not traded at all. In particular, he does not give away claims to resources unless he gets some commensurate reward in return. Altruism may exist, but it is generally ignored in economic and game-theoretic modeling.[9]

## B. *Egalitarian*

Egalitarian theories all posit that a just distribution gives everyone an equal share of resources. The theories differ over *what* exactly should be equalized. For example, needs theories claim that people who are equal in terms of their needs for resources should get equal holdings. One such theory is the psychologist's attempt to create an inventory or hierarchy of basic needs.[10] A second is the analysis of human needs in recent Roman Catholic social encyclicals. Roman Catholicism builds theories of rights and justice on assessments of dignity, which is achieved by satisfying natural human needs.[11] Third, Marxian political theory offers to make

---

[8] But see Garrell Pottinger, Explanation, Rationality, and Microeconomic Theory, 28 Behavioral Sci. 109 (1983), arguing that the utility-maximizing model of choice in decision theory fails both as a description of the behavior of human beings making decisions in real-world settings, and as a description of the behavior of subjects in the modern experimental works that detect the preference-reversal phenomenon. Pottinger suggests developing a model in which individual agents, uncertain about their preferences, make satisficing choices. *Id.* at 122. His criticism, however, does not consider normative theories of entitlements and rights.

[9] Altruism is used only to mean interdependent utility functions. That is, one person is made happier by another person becoming happier, without any change in the first person's private holdings. The few economists who have developed models that allow for altruism include Gary S. Becker, A Treatise on the Family (1981); Mordecai Kurz, Altruistic Equilibria, in Economic Progress, Private Values, and Public Policy (Bela Belassa & Richard Nelson eds. 1977); Robert J. Aumann, Acceptable Points in Cooperative *n*-Person Games, in 4 Contributions to the Theory of Games, Annals of Mathematics Studies (no. 40) (A. W. Tucker & R. D. Luce eds. 1959); and David Collard, Altruism and Economy (1978).

[10] See, for example, Abraham Maslow, Motivation and Personality, ch. 5 (1970).

[11] See Yale Divinity School, Moral Claims, Human Rights and Population Policies, 35 Theological Stud. 83 (1974), at 100 and following pages.

need the measure of right, but insists that this is impossible, not only in capitalist society, but also in the first phases of communist society. Hence, "From each according to his ability, to each according to his needs," applies in the later phases of communist society only.[12] Fourth, liberal political theory has tried to link distributive justice to the satisfaction of minimum needs.[13] Rawls's *Theory of Justice,* for example, tolerates inequality between persons only where the inequality will redound to the benefit of the worst-off person in society.[14]

Our experiments explore the very simplest form of egalitarianism: equal sharing regardless of other characteristics. This version of egalitarianism is championed by many psychologists, who argue from theory and experimental evidence that a norm favoring equality or payment according to need is so strong that people will only deviate from it in limited circumstances.[15] Subjects who hold such beliefs should always split payoffs equally, regardless of how they obtained those payoffs. This is, of course, exactly what subjects did in our original set of experiments.[16]

## C. *Natural Law/Desert*

Natural law/desert theories assert that, as a matter of natural law, someone or other *deserves* resources. The only variant of this group of theories of distributive justice that we explore is Locke's.[17] The Lockean theory posits that an individual deserves, as a matter of natural law, a property entitlement in resources that have been accumulated or developed through the individual's expenditure of effort.[18] The individual de-

---

[12] See, for example, Karl Marx, Critique of the Gotha Program, in Karl Marx and Frederich Engels: Basic Writings on Politics and Philosophy 112, 119 (Lewis S. Feuer ed. 1959).

[13] See, for example, Frank Michelman, In Pursuit of Constitutional Welfare Rights: One View of Rawls's Theory of Justice, 121 U. Pa. L. Rev. 962 (1973). However, see also Dandridge v. Williams, 397 U.S. 471 (1970), finding that the state's maximum grant provision for recipients of benefits under the AFDC program did not violate the Equal Protection Clause and that benefits need not be correlated with actual needs.

[14] John Rawls, A Theory of Justice (1971).

[15] See Morton Deutsch, Equity, Equality, and Need: What Determines Which Value Will Be Used as the Basis of Distributive Justice, 31 J. Soc. Issues 137 (No. 3, 1975); Edward E. Sampson, On Justice as Equality, *id.* at 45; Shalom Schwartz, The Justice of Need and the Activation of Humanitarian Norms, *id.* at 111; and Elaine Walster & G. William Walster, Equity and Social Justice, *id.* at 21, for reviews of the psychological literature on distributive justice up to 1975.

[16] Hoffman & Spitzer, *supra* note 1.

[17] John Locke, Second Treatise of Civil Government, ch. 5 (1978).

[18] See generally, C. B. MacPherson, The Political Theory of Possessive Individualism: Hobbes to Locke 197–221 (1962) on this theory.

serves the entitlement because he has "mixed his labor" with the resource. A subject who holds a Lockean theory of distributive justice will behave in a self-regarding manner whenever he perceives that he has "mixed his labor" with a resource.

A literature in social psychology, termed equity theory, seems to fit with the Lockean theory. Equity theory argues, from first principle and experimental evidence, that people allocate payments so as to equalize individual ratios between payments and intrinsic inputs.[19] Unfortunately, equity theory provides, in general, no testable hypotheses. Equity theorists commonly define "intrinsic inputs" to include difficulty of the work, the time spent, the amount of work completed, and salient personal characteristics such as intelligence, family name, or social status. "Payments" include both benefits and harms produced by the experimental situation. However, because many of the inputs are not observable, and because of the difficulty of predicting, in general, which characteristics will be salient, one cannot construct the ratios between inputs and payments to test the behavioral predictions.[20]

Despite these formidable empirical obstacles, equity theory is not com-

---

[19] Note that this rule is equivalent to an economic rule which allocates rewards to keep the ratios of payments to the *average* product of labor equal: $w_1/AP_{L1} = \ldots = w_n/AP_{Ln}$. This is in contrast to the *efficient* payment rule which equates the ratios of wages and *marginal* products of labor: $w_1/MP_{L1} = \ldots = w_n/MP_{Ln}$. The ideal of equity theory was originally formalized by J. S. Adams, Inequity in Social Exchange, in Advances in Experimental Social Psychology (Leonard Berkowitz ed. 1965), and by George Caspar Homans, Social Behavior: Its Elementary Forms (1961). The idea is based on an Aristotelian notion of social justice. Subsequent researchers have refined the equal ratio formula, but the basic idea remains a cornerstone of equity theory. See, for example, John C. Allessio, Another Folly for Equity Theory, 43 Soc. Psychology Q. 336 (1980); Norman H. Anderson, Equity Judgments as Information Integration, 33 J. Personality & Soc. Psychology 291 (1976); Karen S. Cook & Toby L. Parcel, Equity Theory: Directions for Future Research, 47 Soc. Inquiry 75 (No. 2, 1977); Arthur J. Farkas & Norman H. Anderson, Multidimensional Input in Equity Theory, 37 J. Personality & Soc. Psychology 879 (1979); Elaine Walster, Ellen Berscheid, & G. William Walster, New Directions in Equity Research, 25 J. Personality & Soc. Psychology 151 (1973); and Karl E. Weick, The Concept of Equity in the Perception of Pay, 11 Ad. Sci. Q. 414 (1966).

[20] See for example, in Reinhard Selten, The Equity Principle in Economic Behavior, in Decision Theory and Social Ethics: Issues in Social Choice 289 (1978), the discussion of the *equity core*, and *n*-person game-theoretic generalization of equity theory, in which the solution depends on a set of weights, $w_1, \ldots, w_n$, which "are the weights of the players according to the standard of comparisons." *Id.* at 297. These weights, Selten notes, "are not always uniquely determined by the character of the situation." Nevertheless, he contends that "generally the nature of the problem suggests a finite number of alternative possibilities." *Id.* at 294. This does not entirely save equity theory, or the equity core, however, for as long as there are several possible sets of weights, and they predict different outcomes, the "theory" has very limited power. Further, unless there is some reliable way for the researcher to predict which finite number of sets of weights will be "suggested" to his subjects by the situation, equity theory loses *all* predictive power.

pletely useless. In certain experimental settings subjects behave as if the amount of effort is the only salient input and as if equal ratio payment should guide their behavior. Experimental subjects who are paid more than equal coworkers frequently give some of their payoffs to the lower-paid coworkers, thereby restoring an equitable ratio of payments to inputs.[21]

## D.   *Non-Value-oriented Explanations*

The three classes of theories of distributive justice discussed above—utilitarian, egalitarian, and natural law/desert—all represent value-oriented explanations. In contrast, we classify purely authoritarian and sociobiological[22] explanations of morally relevant behavior as non value oriented. The purely authoritarian explanation posits that people will behave as if they are morally justified in treating their entitlements as rights whenever an authority (herein termed a *moral authority*) tells them that their entitlements are rights.[23] The moral authority may, of course, refer to value-oriented theories when telling people to believe that a certain distribution is just. For example, an authority might tell people that they are justified in acting in a self-regarding fashion because each of them has special needs. Nonetheless, a moral authority need not resort to such an approach. It might, instead, merely tell people that a certain distribution is just, and make no reference whatsoever to any value-oriented theory. Similarly, the sociobiological theory posits that genetic material governs much morally relevant behavior and that genes producing behavior that

---

[21] Walster, Berscheid, & Walster, *supra* note 19, originally proposed this idea as a somewhat formal theory. Other experimental support includes the following: Ronald L. Cohen, Mastery and Justice in Laboratory Dyads: A Revision and Extension of Equity Theory, 29 J. Personality & Soc. Psychology 464 (1974); Gerald S. Leventhal, Thomas Weiss, & Gary Long, Equity, Reciprocity, and Reallocating Rewards in the Dyad, 13 J. Personality & Soc. Psychology 300 (1969); Stanley J. Morse, Joan Gruzen, & Harry T. Reis, Nature of Equity Restoration: Some Approval-seeking Considerations, 12 J. Experimental Soc. Psychology 1 (1976); and Rudy V. Nydegger & Guillermo Owen, The Norm of Equity in a Three-Person Majority Game, 22 Behavioral Sci. 32 (1977).

[22] See Wilson, *supra* note 5.

[23] The authoritarian theory is, in virtually all respects, empirically indistinguishable from the assertion, found in works of those skeptical of experimental work, that subjects merely do what they believe will please the experimenter. Any behavioral proposition that can be put as (*a*) "I want to please the experimenter and he wants X" can also be phrased as (*b*) "I will do whatever is just and the experimenter, who is a valid source of moral authority, has said X = justice." To the extent that our paper finds significant support for the authoritarian theory, it may also give support to the critics of experimental techniques. At the very least, these results suggest that the experimenter must pay closer attention to his instructions and the incentives instilled in his subjects.

enhances survivability of the line (maximizes inclusive fitness across generations) will eventually predominate.

The experimental design described below introduces a treatment variable that may be interpreted as a form of moral authority. The instructions in some of the experiments *tell* the subjects that they have "earned" their entitlements. If the authoritarian theory has an explanatory power, subjects thus instructed should be more willing to treat their entitlements as legitimate rights.[24] The design has no features which could be interpreted in the context of a sociobiological model.[25]

## III. Experimental Design

### A. General

All the experiments reported here involved two people who were fully informed about one another's payoffs.[26] Bargaining was face to face and public and involved more money than most students can earn for an hour's work in their next-best alternative employment. Side payments were allowed. Contracts were in writing and strictly enforced. All payments were made in public. Subjects were given no motivational instructions: that is, they were not told what their objectives should be in choosing numbers or in forming contracts.

### B. Experimental Instructions

1. *Game-Trigger, Moral Authority Experiments.* As the subjects arrived at a designated room they were randomly assigned the letters A or B. Each pair was placed in a separate room, with a monitor being the only other person present. The monitor provided the following set of instructions to the subjects, who first read them silently and then listened to the monitor read them aloud.[27]

---

[24] Note, however, that if subjects hold Lockean theories of distributive justice, the moral authority language of the instructions may simply trigger the belief that the Lockean concept is appropriate in the experimental setting. If that is the case, subjects' behavior cannot unambiguously be said to be authoritarian.

[25] Because nothing in our experiment even remotely involves life-or-death decisions or seems to suggest similarly momentous life decisions, our experiment does not seem to relate to the sociobiological explanation.

[26] Some of the discussion of experimental design is taken from Hoffman & Spitzer, *supra* note 1.

[27] These instructions were read aloud by one of the principal investigators or the research assistants on this project. Because the principal investigators knew of the theories being explored, and because the research assistants all immediately guessed the hypotheses being tested, it is *possible* that the instructions were read with intonations that implicitly directed

## Instructions

### General

You are about to participate in an experiment in decision-making. The purpose of the experiment is to gain insight into certain features of complex economic processes. If you follow the instructions carefully, you might earn a considerable amount of money. You will be paid in cash at the end of the experiment.

### Specific Instructions to Participants

You are person ———. The other participant is person ———.

This experiment requires that two decisions be made. Each decision will involve choosing a number. The number chosen will correspond to an actual dollar amount which will be paid to you at the end of this experiment. The number and corresponding payoffs for the first decision are on page five of these instructions; the number and payoffs for the second decision are on page six. Pages five and six list not only the value of each number to you (under column ———), but also the value of each number to the other participant (under column ———).

Before each decision, both participants $\underline{A}$ and $\underline{B}$ will play a game. Whoever wins this game earns the right to be designated "controller" for that decision. The rules of this preliminary game are as follows.

/ / / / / / / / / / / / / / / / /

Above here is a picture of 17 vertical hash marks. Each player must, on each turn, cross out 1, 2, 3, *or* 4 hash marks. After a player has crossed out as many hash marks as he or she wishes, it is the other player's turn to cross out 1, 2, 3, *or* 4 hash marks. The game continues until all hash marks have been crossed out. The person who crosses out the last hash mark *loses* the game. $\underline{A}$ will go first on the first decision, $\underline{B}$ will go first on the second decision.

*Example:* A goes first and crosses out 4 marks

++++/ / / / / / / / / / / / /

Then B crosses out 4 marks

++++++++/ / / / / / / / /

Then A crosses out 4 marks

++++++++++++/ / / / /

Then B crosses out 4 marks

++++++++++++++++/

$\underline{A}$ must cross out the last mark on his turn, so $\underline{A}$ loses the game and $\underline{B}$ has earned the position of the controller.

If you win the game and are designated controller, you may, if you wish, choose any number you like by filling out the form on page seven and giving it to the

---

the subjects to behave in certain ways. This seems unlikely, however, since the two principal investigators held different preferences regarding the outcomes of the experiments. Yet the results from the experiments conducted at Purdue, under Elizabeth Hoffman's direction. did not differ significantly from the results of those conducted at USC, under Matthew Spitzer's direction.

monitor. However, if you lose the preliminary game and are not designated con-troller, you may still attempt to influence the controller to form a *joint agreement* and choose some other number. In order to induce the controller to reach an acceptable *joint agreement,* you may offer to pay part of your earnings to the controller.

*Example:* Assume that A wins the preliminary game and earns the position of controller for the first decision. Assume also the following payoffs for A and B.

| Number | A's Payoff | B's Payoff |
|--------|-----------|-----------|
| 1 | $4 | $1 |
| 2 | 5 | 2 |
| 3 | 3 | 5 |

Once A has become controller, he or she may choose number 2 without consult-ing B. However, B may attempt to persuade A to join in a joint decision to choose another number and/or division of payoffs. If a joint agreement is reached, *both* parties must sign the agreement form on page seven, stating both what the chosen number will be and how much money will be transferred from one participant's earnings to the other's. For example, A and B might sign the agreement form on page seven choosing number 3 and directing that $2.00 be paid from B to A. Once the agreement form is signed the monitor will note that for this decision A is to be paid $5.00 at the end of the experiment, representing the $3.00 original payoff for the number 3 plus the $2.00 transferred from B, and that B is to be paid $3.00, representing the $5.00 original payoff less the $2.00 transferred to A.

The monitor can only enforce written decisions recorded on the form set out on page 7. You are, however, free to make any other sort of informal agreement that you wish.

*No physical threats are allowed.* If any party makes a physical threat, the threatened party will get his or her maximum payoff and the threatening party will get nothing.

Are there any questions? We ask you to answer the questions on the attached sheet to make sure you understand the instructions.

## Questions

(Refer to your payoffs on page 5 [listed immediately below])

1. Number —— makes me the most money. Number —— makes me the least money.

2. If I become controller, I can make $—— even if the other person doesn't agree.

3. If A and B reach a joint decision to choose number 4 and B pays A $2.00, I make $——.

4. If I am the controller, I may choose the number which corresponds to my maximum payoff without making a joint agreement with the other participant. TRUE or FALSE? ——

5. Which of the following do you prefer? ——
   *a)* $1.50 for sure.
   *b)* A fair coin toss which pays $0 for heads and $11 for tails.

PAYOFF SHEET

| | DECISION #1 | |
|---|---|---|
| Number | A's Payoff | B's Payoff |
| 1 | $0.00 | $12.00 |
| 2 | 4.00 | 10.00 |
| 3 | 6.00 | 6.00 |
| 4 | 7.50 | 4.00 |
| 5 | 9.00 | 2.50 |
| 6 | 10.50 | 1.00 |
| 7 | 12.00 | 0.00 |

| | DECISION #2 | |
|---|---|---|
| Number | A's Payoff | B's Payoff |
| 1 | $0.00 | $12.50 |
| 2 | 1.50 | 11.00 |
| 3 | 3.00 | 9.50 |
| 4 | 4.50 | 8.00 |
| 5 | 6.00 | 6.50 |
| 6 | 10.00 | 5.00 |
| 7 | 11.50 | 1.50 |
| 8 | 13.00 | 0.00 |

AGREEMENT FORM

Decision _____

Number Chosen _____

$ _____ to be paid from _____ to _____

Signed: _____
A

_____
B

In essence, these instructions told subjects that they had to choose a number between 1 and 7 (decision 1) or 1 and 8 (decision 2) and that they would be paid in cash according to the discrete payoff functions given on pages 5 and 6 of the instructions. In addition, one subject won, by playing the hash mark game, the right to choose the number unilaterally and was told that he had *earned* that right by winning the game.

After reading the instructions and examining their payoffs, subjects were tested on their understanding of the rules and the consequences of decisions they might make.[28] After both subjects had answered all of the

[28] Tests are included with the instructions.

questions correctly, and after the monitor had answered all the subjects' remaining uncertainties about the rules of the game, the subjects played the hash mark game. The winner of the game was told orally that he had earned the right to be controller. The subjects were then instructed to proceed with the experiment (by choosing a number).

2. *Coin-Flip, Moral Authority Experiments.* This set of instructions resembled the previous experiment in all respects save one. The controller was chosen by a flip of a coin instead of by winning the hash mark game. However, the winner of the coin flip was still told by the experimenter that he had earned the property entitlement. The instructions for this experiment were identical to the above instructions except for the section on the hash mark game. In place of the section beginning, "Before each decision, both participants A and B will play a game," and ending, ". . . choose any number you like by filling out the form on page seven and giving it to the monitor," the new instructions say,

Before each decision, the monitor will flip a coin. Whoever wins this coin toss earns the right to become "controller" for that decision. If you win the coin toss and are designated controller, you may, if you wish, choose any number you like by filling out the form on page seven and giving it to the monitor.

3. *Game-Trigger, No Moral Authority Experiments.* The next set of experiments also resembled the game-trigger, moral authority experiments in almost all respects. The difference is that whenever the moral authority instructions say "earns the right" or "earns the position," the no moral authority instructions simply say "is designated." In addition, the example and the questions suggest that less moral authority is given to the controller. The example and the questions are given below; other than the changes just discussed, the instructions are identical to those reproduced above.

*Example:* Assume that A wins the game and is designated controller for the first decision. Assume also the following payoffs for A and B.

| Number | A's Payoff | B's Payoff |
|--------|-----------|-----------|
| 1 | $4 | $1 |
| 2 | 5 | 2 |
| 3 | 3 | 5 |

Once A has become controller, he or she may choose any number without consulting B. However, B may attempt to persuade A to join in a joint decision to choose another number and/or division of payoffs. If a joint agreement is reached, *both* parties must sign the agreement form on page six, stating both what the chosen number will be and how much money will be transferred from one participant's earnings to the other's. For example, A and B might sign the agreement form on page six choosing number 1 and directing that $1.00 be paid from A to B. Once the agreement form is signed, the monitor will note that for this decision A is to be paid $3.00 at the end of the experiment, representing the $4.00 original payoff for number 1 less the $1.00 transferred to B, and that B is to be paid $2.00, representing the $1.00 original payoff plus the $1.00 transferred from A.

QUESTIONS

1. Number —— makes me the most money. Number —— makes me the least money.
2. If the other participant is the controller and he picks number 4, I make ——.
3. If I agree to pay $1 to the other participant, and we agree on number 2, I make ——.
4. If I am the controller, I can choose any number without consulting the other participant. TRUE or FALSE? ——

4. *Coin-Flip, No Moral Authority Experiments.*[29]  These experiments resemble the game-trigger, no moral authority experiments in the same way that the coin-flip moral authority experiments resemble the game-trigger moral authority experiments. The only difference between the coin-flip, no moral authority experiments and the game-trigger, no moral authority experiments is that subjects were told that one subject would be designated controller by a flip of a coin. There was no reference to a hash mark game.

## C. Subjects

The subjects were upper-level economics and management majors and management graduate students at Purdue University and law students, upper-level arts and sciences students, and university staff at the University of Southern California. They were recruited in classes and by telephone and told only that they would participate in an economic decision. They were promised $4 per hour *plus* their earnings. Extra subjects were recruited in case of no-shows and paid at least $2 just for showing up. All subjects were inexperienced in this particular kind of experiment and friends were not allowed to participate together. After each experiment, we explained the nature of the experiment and the scientific importance of not telling their friends about it. Later subjects appeared to be as naive about the experiment as earlier subjects had been, and there did not seem to be any time trend in the results.

---

[29] These experiments replicate the Hoffman and Spitzer experiments, *supra* note 1, using the precise wording used in the moral authority experiments. We also ran some game-trigger experiments using those original Hoffman and Spitzer instructions. The results are generally unaffected.

## D.  *Correspondence between Experimental Institutions and Theories of Distributive Justice*

Assumption 2 of our model requires that subjects perceive the features of the experiment to trigger their beliefs about distributive justice. Therefore, we must inquire about the reasonableness of our experimental treatments. We argue below that the game trigger would lead a Lockean to believe that the winner could treat his entitlements as rights, but that a coin flip would not. We also argue that our moral authority instructions might trigger, as a matter of blind (non-value-oriented) faith, the belief that one is justified in treating the entitlements as rights. However, we also recognize that the moral authority instructions could be reinforcing latent Lockean beliefs.

Considering the Lockean theory first, we would argue that a Lockean who wins the hash mark game would regard himself as deserving the property entitlement because he had expended labor to get it. A skeptic might reply, however, that both parties expended an equal amount of effort in the game. Consequently, the controller's power should belong to both parties equally. Nonetheless, we think that a Lockean theory of property has room within it for differences in *efficacy* of effort: even if two people spend the same amount of time or try as hard, the person who does a better job still deserves the resource. In our experiment, subjects were likely to interpret winning the game as evidence that the winner did a better job of playing the game and is therefore justified in treating the entitlement of the controller's position as a right.

At this juncture, the skeptic might reply that one cannot accept our response without paying closer attention to the subjects' perceptions of the nature of the game. The game is simple, in the sense that the person who goes first can always win (if he plays the right strategy).[30] If the subject sees this and figures out the right strategy, he may decide that control follows from going first, not from effort. And, if the subject fails to see this, he may decide that control is merely random. Either way, he has not mixed his labor with the resource.

We respond in the following way. If the subject figures out the winning strategy, he is likely to regard his knowledge as the product of superior effort expended in solving the game. It is true that the subject's ability to figure out the game will be a product of natural ability and training, both of which are partly a matter of chance. However, a Lockean would not

---

[30] The winning strategy is for the person who moves first to cross out one, thus ending on 16. Thereafter, he makes sure that he ends on 11 and then on 6. In each case he can ensure that outcome, regardless of how many his opponent crosses out. If the person who moves first crosses out more than one, his opponent can win by ending on 11 and then on 6.

regard this type of chance as arbitrary, because to do so is to destroy the internal logic of his theory. Without some fortuitous chance, there is no possibility of proper desert.

If the subject does not figure out the game, virtually nothing changes in the analysis above. After all, even if the subject fails to solve the hash mark game, he will almost certainly perceive that the game is one of skill and effort, such as chess or "go." As long as a Lockean subject continues to regard returns to his skill as naturally justified, he will view the entitlement of the controller's position as a right. Only if the subject perceives the outcome of the game as random will the Lockean fail to regard control as a right. Such a circumstance seems highly unlikely, however, for even the dullest subject will probably observe that if he had played differently on earlier moves he might not have lost the game. And, since he did not figure out the game, he is not likely to observe that the person who goes first can always win. He would thus conclude that skill at previous moves, and not chance, determined the outcome.[31]

Next, we doubt that a Lockean would regard winning the coin flip as mixing labor with a resource, justifying the controller's position as a right. If a subject convinced himself that his luck was a product of his effort (perhaps by living a particularly good life) then he might perceive his victory as a desert. However, this position seems quite incompatible with basic Lockean beliefs, since it boils down to a belief that any good fortune is a product of labor. Such a belief, if accepted by a Lockean, would justify *all* entitlements as rights. This would be, in essence, the utilitarian position, and not the Lockean.

Third, it is unclear whether our moral authority instructions would lead subjects to regard the position of controller as a morally justified right, without any reliance on a value-oriented theory of distributive justice. First, assume that subjects regard the experimenter as a valid, authoritative source of moral pronouncements.[32] Next, examine the direction given to the subjects in the moral authority instructions. All the moral authority instructions refer to *earning* a right. "Earning" may be seen as a reference to a Lockean desert. Hence, a subject who is told that the

---

[31] In the experiments, subjects were not told the game was deterministic, although some subjects seemed to know that. Interestingly, however, those who knew, and profited from that special knowledge, seemed to regard it as making them more worthy of winning. Their opponents, rather than seeing that knowledge as random, also seemed to view it in a Lockean manner. On the rare occasions that both subjects knew the winning strategy, there was some discussion of randomness.

[32] For a discussion of science as a source of moral authority, see S. Milgram, Obedience to Authority (1974).

controller *earns* the right may come to either of the following conclusions:
1. a moral authority has assured the subject, in a non-value-oriented manner, that he may regard the position of controller as a right; or
2. the experimenter has suggested that subjects should decide issues of distributive justice using Lockean theory.[33]

The implications of these two propositions differ markedly. Thus, if our moral authority treatment variable produces significant effects, we are uncertain whether we have produced a non-value-oriented belief in a morally justified right (authoritarian explanation) or instilled the Lockean theory of rights into the subjects. However, if the moral authority treatment variable produces significant effects even when the coin flip is used, it would provide strong evidence in favor of the non-value-oriented explanation. Only if the subject believed that his luck had been produced by his labor would the outcome be ambiguous, but we have already shown above that a Lockean would not be likely to hold such a belief.

## IV. EXPERIMENTAL RESULTS

Table 1 summarizes the results of all eighty-two experimental decisions. Notice first that 91 percent of the decisions are joint profit maximizing. Thus these results are generally consistent with those we have already reported.[34] Second, there appear to be significant differences in the payoff divisions among at least three of the four experimental treatments. Looking first at the extremes, in the no moral authority experiments, 61 percent of the decisions are nearly equal splits.[35] However, in the game-trigger, moral authority experiments more than half of the divisions give the controller more than his individual maximum and 68 percent give the controller at least his individual maximum. Only 32 percent are within $1

---

[33] Such a suggestion might trigger an existing, latent belief that one should behave as a Lockean; or it might implant a new idea.

[34] Hoffman & Spitzer, *supra* note 1. Thus, these experiments also provide significant tests of the Coase Theorem. Moreover, these results can be interpreted, in brief, to show that the Coase Theorem is extremely robust with respect to different methods of allocating the entitlements, even where the different methods of initial allocation produce widely differing attitudes toward the justice of treating the entitlements as rights. These insights are also explored in Elizabeth Hoffman & Matthew L. Spitzer, Experimental Tests of the Coase Theorem with Large Bargaining Groups, 15 J. Legal Stud. (forthcoming).

[35] The only effect of the change in instructions shows up in the coin flip/no moral authority experiments. The original set of experiments reported in Hoffman & Spitzer, *supra* note 1, resulted in 100 percent equal splits. These new coin flip/no moral authority experiments show only ten of twenty-two exactly equal and fourteen of twenty-two nearly equal, giving a significant instruction effect. However, the statistical results discussed below are largely unaffected by this instruction effect. The only difference is that the differences between the coin-flip and game-trigger payoff divisions are slightly weaker with the new instructions.

TABLE 1
SUMMARY OF EXPERIMENTAL RESULTS

| EXPERIMENT | NUMBER OF DECISIONS ($N$) | NUMBER OF JOINT MAXIMA ($N_1$) | EQUAL SPLIT ($N_2$) | EQUAL ± $1.00 ($N_3$) | DIVISION OF PAYMENTS | | | |
|---|---|---|---|---|---|---|---|---|
| | | | | | Controller Receives his Maximum ($N_4$) | Controller Receives more than Maximum ($N_5$) | Halfway between Equal and Controller Max ($N_6$) | Other ($N_7$) |
| A. Coin flip: | | | | | | | | |
| 1. No moral authority | 22 | 20 | 10 | 4 | 3 | 3 | 2 | 0 |
| 2. Moral authority | 20 | 19 | 9 | 1 | 5 | 1 | 2 | 2 |
| B. Game trigger: | | | | | | | | |
| 1. No moral authority | 22 | 18 | 9 | 4 | 2 | 4 | 3 | 0 |
| 2. Moral authority | 22 | 21 | 4 | 3 | 3 | 12 | 0 | 0 |
| Total | 86 | 78 | 32 | 12 | 13 | 20 | 7 | 2 |

CONCEPTS OF DISTRIBUTIVE JUSTICE 277

of an equal split. The other experimental treatment is intermediate: 50 percent of the coin-flip, moral authority decisions are within $1 of an equal split, while 30 percent give the controller at least his individual maximum.

Table 2 shows the average amount in excess of an equal split received by the controller in each experimental pair.[36] We call it a "greed index." The average greed index also appears different in each experiment, ranging from $1.00 for the coin-flip, no moral authority experiments to $4.52 for the game-trigger, moral authority experiments.

Table 3 summarizes a parametric and a nonparametric[37] one-way analysis of variance test for the null hypothesis that the mean greed indices are the same in the four experimental treatments. Both tests reject the null hypothesis: each particular combination of allocation mechanism and moral authority instructions leads subjects to treat the property entitlements differently in dividing the payoffs. In the no moral authority experiments they tend to ignore the differential property entitlements and split payoffs equally. In the game-trigger, moral authority experiments most subject pairs treat the differential property entitlements seriously. A mean greed index of $6.25 would mean the average is at least the controller's individual maximum; $4.52 puts the average at more than two-thirds what the economic model predicts the self-regarding controller would do. In contrast, the greed index in the coin-flip, moral authority experiments is one-half the index in the game-trigger, moral authority experiments.

Since the four treatment cells are not the same, the question arises whether the two-way treatments resulted in significant differences in greed indices. In other words, first, are the pooled coin-flip results different from the pooled game-trigger results? Second, are the pooled no moral authority results different from the pooled moral authority results? In addition, are there significant interaction effects among the treatment variables? Interaction effects occur if the treatment effects are not "parallel" to one another. For example, in the results described above, pooled

---

[36] We present it as an average for each experiment so the data will be independent and identically distributed. Each number is an average of two highly correlated numbers, since the two outcomes in each experiment are not independent of one another. Each experiment is, however, independent of every other experiment and within each experimental treatment all are identically distributed. The subjects were drawn from the same subject pool and given the same set of instructions.

[37] The nonparametric Kruskal-Wallis test is almost as powerful as the analysis of variance when all the assumptions are met; but it does not assume that the observations are normally distributed. Since many of the observations are zero and the distribution truncates at zero, the assumption of normality does not hold. Sources for the tests summarized in Table 3 are as follows: parametric one-way analysis of variance, Gerald L. Ericksen, Scientific Inquiry in the Social Sciences (1970), at 200; Kruskal-Wallis test, Sidney Siegel, Nonparametric Statistics for the Behavioral Sciences (1956), at 185.

TABLE 2

AVERAGE DOLLAR AMOUNT MORE THAN AN EQUAL SPLIT RECEIVED BY THE CONTROLLER IN EACH EXPERIMENTAL PAIR: "GREED INDEX"

| No Moral Authority | | | | Moral Authority | | | |
|---|---|---|---|---|---|---|---|
| Difference | Rank of Difference | Difference | Rank of Difference | Difference | Rank of Difference | Difference | Rank of Difference |
| | | | | Coin Flip | | | |
| 0 | 8 | .25 | 18.5 | 0 | 8 | 3.25 | 28 |
| 0 | 8 | .25 | 18.5 | 0 | 8 | 4.25 | 30 |
| 0 | 8 | 2.00 | 24 | 0 | 8 | 5.25 | 34.5 |
| 0 | 8 | 3.125 | 26.5 | 0 | 8 | 5.25 | 34.5 |
| 0 | 8 | 5.25 | 34.5 | .50 | 21 | 6.125 | 40.5 |
| .125 | 16 | | | | | | |
| Total | | 11 | 178 | | | 24.625 | 220.5 |
| Average | | 1.00 | 16.18 | | | 2.4625 | 22.5 |
| N | | 11 | 11 | | | | 10 |
| | | | | Game Trigger | | | |
| 0 | 8 | .90 | 23 | 0 | 8 | 6.00 | 39 |
| 0 | 8 | 2.50 | 25 | .75 | 22 | 6.125 | 40.5 |
| 0 | 8 | 3.75 | 29 | 3.125 | 26.5 | 6.25 | 42.5 |
| 0 | 8 | 5.0 | 31.5 | 5.00 | 31.5 | 6.25 | 42.5 |
| 0 | 8 | | | 5.25 | 34.5 | | |
| .25 | 18.5 | | | 5.50 | 37 | | |
| .25 | 18.5 | | | 5.505 | 38 | | |
| Total | | 12.65 | 185.5 | | | 49.753 | 362 |
| Average | | 1.15 | 16.86 | | | 4.523 | 32.91 |
| N | | 11 | 11 | | | | 11 |

278

## TABLE 3
### ONE-WAY ANALYSIS OF VARIANCE TESTS: PARAMATRIC AND NONPARAMETRIC

| Test | Calculation of Test Statistic | Degrees of Freedom (Df) | Appropriate Test Statistic | Value of Test Statistic | Test | Rejection Significance Level (%) |
|---|---|---|---|---|---|---|
| Parametric one-way analysis of variance (unequal numbers in each cell) | Sum of squares for treatments (SSTR) $= \sum_i \sum_j y_{ij}\bar{y}_{ij} - y..\bar{y}...$  Sum of squares for error (SSE) $= \sum_i \sum_j (y_{ij} - \bar{y}_{ij})^2$ | 3  40 | $F = \dfrac{SSTR/3}{SSE/40}$ | 6.80 | F(3,40) | 99+ |
| Kruskal-Wallis nonparametric one-way analysis of variance | $H = \dfrac{12}{N(N+1)} \sum_{j=1}^{k} \dfrac{R_j^2}{n_j} - 3(N+1)$ | 3 | $\chi^2 = H$ | 12.50 | $\chi^2(3)$ | 99+ |

NOTE.—Null Hypothesis: All four experimental treatments yield the same greed index. Alternative Hypothesis: The greed indices are different. Key: $y_{ij}$ = observation $i$ in cell $j$; $\bar{y}_{ij}$ = mean of cell $j$; $y..$ = sum over all $i$ and $j$ (grand total); $\bar{y}...$ = grand mean; $R_j$ = sum of rank in cell $j$; $n_j$ = number of observations in cell $j$; $N$ = total number of observations.

279

coin-flip greed indices are lower than pooled game-trigger greed indices, and no moral authority indices are lower than moral authority ones. There would be interaction effects if either the game-trigger, no moral authority greed index were higher than the game-trigger, moral authority greed index or if the coin-flip, moral authority index were higher than the game-trigger, moral authority index.

An inspection of Table 2 suggests that the treatments are parallel. Coin flip, no moral authority has the lowest greed index and game trigger, no moral authority is lower than game trigger, moral authority. Thus there does not appear to be any interaction effect.

Table 4 presents a two-way analysis of variance on the allocation mechanisms and the moral authority instructions.[38] This test suggests that the moral authority instructions make the most difference in how subjects divide payoffs. The difference in allocation mechanisms is weakly significant, but the interaction effect is insignificant, as expected.

Given the lack of interaction, it is admissible to compare the allocation mechanisms and moral authority instructions with independent, two-sample tests. This procedure reduces the mean squared error of the sample comparison and may, therefore, allow the allocation mechanisms to show up more clearly different from one another.

Table 5 compares the allocation mechanisms and the moral authority instructions separately.[39] As in Table 3, we conducted both a parametric and a nonparametric test.[40] These results indicate that, examined alone, the difference in allocation mechanisms is slightly more significant: that is, with a one-tailed test we can say with 94 percent probability that the game trigger yields a higher mean greed index than the coin flip. However, as the two-way analysis of variance has already shown, the moral authority instructions seem to be more powerful than the allocation mechanism in inducing differences in payoff divisions. The allocation mechanism is significant only at the 94 percent level; the moral authority instructions are significant at better than the 99 percent level.

## V.  DISCUSSION OF RESULTS

The results first suggest that subjects behaved as Lockeans instead of utilitarians or egalitarians, in that they tended to regard the position of

---

[38] Sources for the test in Table 4 are as follows: two-way analysis of variance with equal numbers in each cell, William L. Hayes, Statistics for the Social Sciences (1973), at 501–5; adjustment for different numbers in each cell, C. Radhakrishna Rao, Linear Statistical Inference and Its Applications (1965), at 211–14, and conversations with Rao Kadiyala, Purdue University, Spring 1983.

[39] Sources for the tests summarized in Table 5 are Ericksen, *supra* note 37, at 162, and Siegel *supra* note 37, at 121.

[40] The Mann-Whitney *U*-test is the two-population equivalent of the Kruskal-Wallis test.

TABLE 4

PARAMETRIC TWO-WAY ANALYSIS OF VARIANCE: UNEQUAL NUMBERS IN EACH CELL

| Null Hypothesis | Calculation of Sum of Squares | SS | df | Mean Square (MS) | $F = \dfrac{MS}{MSE}$ | Rejection Significance Level $F(1,39)$ (%) |
|---|---|---|---|---|---|---|
| 1. Coin flip and game trigger yield same greed index | $\sum_i y_{i.}\,\bar{y}_{i.} - y\cdot\cdot\,\bar{y}\cdot\cdot$ | 13.97 | 1 | 13.97 | 3.16 | 92 |
| 2. No moral authority and moral authority yield same greed index | $\sum_j y_{.j}\,\bar{y}_{.j} - y\cdot\cdot\,\bar{y}\cdot\cdot$ | 65.37 | 1 | 65.37 | 14.37 | 99+ |
| 3. No interaction between allocation mechanism and moral authority instructions | $\sum_i \sum_j \sum_k y_{ijk}\,\bar{y}_{ijk} + y\cdot\cdot\,\bar{y}\cdot\cdot - \sum_i y_{i.}\,\bar{y}_{i.} - \sum_j y_{.j}\,\bar{y}_{.j}$ | 8.50 | 1 | 8.50 | 1.92 | Less than 90 |
| Error | $\sum_i \sum_j \sum_k (y_{ijk} - \bar{y}_{ijk})^2$ | 172.26 | 39 | 4.417 (MSE) | | |
| Total | $\sum_i \sum_j \sum_k (y_{ijk} - \bar{y}\cdot\cdot\,)^2$ | 260.83 | 42 | | | |

NOTE.—Key to items not keyed in Table 3: $y_{ijk}$ = observation $k$, allocation mechanism $i$, moral authority instructions $j$; $\bar{y}_{ijk}$ = mean of cell $ij$; $y_{i.}$ = sum of observations for allocation mechanism $i$; $\bar{y}_{i.}$ = mean for allocation mechanism $i$; $y_{.j}$ = sum of observations for instructions $j$; $\bar{y}_{.j}$ = mean for instructions $j$.

**TABLE 5**

**PARAMETRIC AND NONPARAMETRIC COMPARISONS OF GREED INDICES FOR ALLOCATION MECHANISMS AND MORAL AUTHORITY INSTRUCTIONS**

| Null Hypothesis | Test | Calculation of Test Statistic | Value of Statistic | df | Test | One-tailed Rejection Significance Level (%) |
|---|---|---|---|---|---|---|
| Coin flip and game trigger yield same greed index | t-test | $t = \dfrac{(y_1. - y_2.)}{\sqrt{\frac{1}{n_1} + \frac{1}{n_2}}\sqrt{\frac{(n_1 - 1)\sigma_1^2 + (n_2 - 1)\sigma_2^2}{n_1 + n_2 - 2}}}$ | 1.53 | 41 | $t(41)$ | 94 |
| | Mann-Whitney $U$-test | $U = n_1 n_2 + \dfrac{n_1(n_1 + 1)}{2} - R_1.$ $Z = \dfrac{U - \frac{n_1 n_2}{2}}{\sqrt{\frac{n_1 n_2(n_1 + n_2 + 1)}{12}}}$ | 1.54 | 41 | $Z$ | 94 |
| No moral authority and moral authority yield same greed index | t-test | $t = \dfrac{(y_{.1} - y_{.2})}{\sqrt{\frac{1}{n_1} + \frac{1}{n_2}}\sqrt{\frac{(n_1 - 1)\sigma_1^2 + (n_2 - 1)\sigma_2^2}{n_1 + n_2 - 2}}}$ | 3.70 | 41 | $t(41)$ | 99+ |
| | Mann-Whitney $U$-test | $U = n_1 n_2 + \dfrac{n_1(n_1 + 1)}{2} - R_{.1}$ $Z = \dfrac{U - \frac{n_1 n_2}{2}}{\sqrt{\frac{n_1 n_2(n_1 + n_2 + 1)}{12}}}$ | 2.39 | 41 | $Z$ | 99+ |

NOTE.—Key to items not keyed in Tables 3 and 4:
$n_1$ = number of observations in smaller sample in each case,
$R_1.$ = sum of ranks in smaller sample (allocation mechanism),
$R_{.1}$ = sum of ranks in smaller sample (moral authority instructions).
$\sigma_1^2$, $\sigma_2^2$ = sample standard deviations in each case.
$\sigma^2 = \frac{\Sigma(y - \bar{y})^2}{n - 1}$ in general.

controller as a justified right to a greater extent after playing the hash mark game than after a coin flip. Utilitarian subjects should have behaved in a greedy fashion in both game-trigger and coin-flip experiments, whereas egalitarian subjects should have equal split in both. In sum, we would argue that the subjects behaved as Lockeans, except where there was no obvious morally relevant distinction between themselves, at which time they fell back to egalitarian norms.

At this point, a skeptic might argue that our results are actually more consistent with the utilitarian (though not with the egalitarian) theory of distributive justice. Because there are two decisions, with control determined by a coin flip, and because subjects are probably risk averse, splitting equally and forgoing the two coin flips maximizes expected utility.

We believe, as an empirical matter, that the "insurance" explanation for equal splits in the coin flip games is wrong. First, in all of the equal split coin-flip games, the coin was flipped and a controller was chosen *before* the negotiations that led to an equal split. This means that the controller, who agreed to an equal split, would have to prefer $14.50 with certainty to $12 with certainty and a 50 percent chance of either $12.50 (B's second-decision maximum) or $13 (A's second-decision maximum). The expected value of that lottery is either $18.25 (B) or $18.50 (A). To gauge the risk preference of our subjects, we sampled approximately half of them with the question:

Which of the following do you prefer?
a) $1.50 for sure.
b) A fair coin toss which pays $0 for heads and $11 for tails.

The overwhelming majority, over 90 percent, chose *b* over *a*, suggesting that our subjects were not extremely risk averse. And utilitarian subjects would have to be *extremely* risk averse to find an equal split attractive in our experiments. Hence we find the insurance rationale unlikely.[41]

Interpreting the moral authority results is less clear cut. They may, as suggested above, show that subjects can be prodded to regard entitlements as rights, without reference to a value-oriented theory of fairness (authoritarian explanation). Such an explanation gains plausibility from the significance of the moral authority instructions with the coin-flip experiments, since a Lockean would be hard-pressed to find morally justified rights.

---

[41] On this subject, generally, see Hoffman & Spitzer, *supra* note 1. Moreover, Alvin E. Roth & Michael W. K. Malouf, Game-Theoretic Models and the Role of Information in Bargaining, 86 Psychology Rev. 574 (1979) show experimental evidence that imperfect information may induce more nonegalitarian behavior.

However, the alternative interpretation, that the moral authority instructions legitimized a Lockean set of values in the subjects, cannot be ruled out. The combination of the moral authority and the game-trigger treatments produced the highest greed index. Perhaps subjects basically thought as Lockeans, but were uncomfortable with the Lockean result that some people end up with a larger slice of the pie. Therefore, it is possible that the moral authority instructions reinforced the Lockean tendency to regard "earned" entitlements as rights.

## VI. Applicability of Experimental Results

In this section we explore the applicability of our results to nonlaboratory settings. First, as we noted above,[42] there is a substantial body of evidence that suggests the "moral" quality of a person's behavior may vary widely from setting to setting. People will lie in one setting but tell the truth in another. They will cheat in one setting but abide by the rules in another. Therefore, a policy analyst should demand a large number of studies replicating our findings in various settings before relying on them with confidence.

Second, a large literature suggests that humans have a tendency to overattribute observed human behaviors to the subjects' personalities and to underattribute the behavior to situational or institutional constraints.[43] For example, in a famous experiment, subjects were told that another subject wrote an essay supporting a position on a major public issue (legalizing marijuana) in which the position was chosen by a political science instructor, debate coach, or experimenter. The subjects were asked about the true views of the essay's author, and responded by drastically overestimating the author's agreement with the essay. In sum, subjects overattributed the behavior to personality or traits, and underattributed the behavior to institutional constraints.[44]

There has been some criticism of the fundamental attribution error, however. For example, Kulik reports experiments suggesting that there is a strong tendency to attribute an individual's behavior to his traits if the

---

[42] Note 6 *supra*.

[43] See generally Richard Nisbett & Lee Ross, Human Inference: Strategies and Shortcomings of Social Judgment 120–27 (1980). On a somewhat related point, one should also be aware that Darwinian-style mechanisms may operate that "naturally select" individuals who are self-regarding, that is, who are never egalitarian, for certain positions in institutions. For example, corporations with self-regarding CEOs may always perform better than corporations with Lockean/egalitarian CEOs. Over time, one should expect to find virtually no egalitarian behavior from corporations.

[44] *Id* at 121.

behavior is expected and to the situation if the behavior is unexpected.[45] Further, Quattrone presents experimental results that suggest that previously reported data showing a strong tendency to overattribute a causal role to personal traits can best be explained as a special case of "anchoring" plus inadequate adjustment.[46] He contends that when circumstances are such as to direct a subject's attention to the causal role of the environment, instead of personal traits, subjects first "anchor" their estimates of causal responsibility to some easily observable item of data, especially explicit features of the environment, and then (inadequately) adjust their estimates toward some less extreme value.[47]

To the extent that the fundamental attribution error may be a serious problem, there are no assurances that we as principal investigators are free from this bias when formulating hypotheses about subject behavior. Situational constraints may have affected behavior in ways that we could

---

[45] James A. Kulik, Confirmatory Attribution and the Perpetuation of Social Beliefs, 44 J. Personality & Soc. Psychology 1171 (1983).

[46] George A. Quattrone, Overattribution and Unit Formation, 42 J. Personality & Soc. Psychology 593 (1982).

[47] See in accord, Arthur G. Miller, Edward E. Jones, & Steve Hinkle, A Robust Attribution Error in the Personality Domain, 17 J. Experimental Soc. Psychology 587 (1981). The usefulness of the "fundamental attribution error" as a conceptual tool has also been questioned by John H. Harvey, Jerri P. Town, & Kerry L. Yarkin, How Fundamental is "The Fundamental Attribution Error"? 40 J. Personality & Soc. Psychology 346 (1981). They argue that individual traits may determine behavior to a much greater extent than most modern psychologists assume when they do work on the "fundamental attribution error." And because there is no easily verifiable, philosophically defensible test for causation of human behavior, judgments about causation in this area must be, at least in part, interpretive and personal for the observer. Further, even if there is a bias in causal judgment, such a bias is not necessarily an error. A bias is "a subjectively based tendency to prefer a given cognition over its possible alternatives, whereas error may be defined as an inconsistency between a hypothesis and one or more propositions so strongly believed in as to be considered as facts." *Id.* at 348. See also V. Lee Hamilton, Intuitive Psychologist or Intuitive Lawyer? Alternative Models of the Attribution Process, 39 J. Personality & Soc. Psychology 767 (1980), where the author argues that the subjects in the experiments that have verified the "fundamental attribution error" may have been answering questions so as to ascribe moral blame, rather than merely to describe the frequency of occurrences of experimental events. If the subjects were, in fact, making moral judgments, then, Hamilton argues, it is incorrect to label the subjects' responses "erroneous," as if the subjects only had been trying to describe the frequency of events. Glenn D. Reeder, Let's Give the Fundamental Attribution Error Another Chance, 43 J. Personality & Soc. Psychology 341 (1984), responds to Harvey, Town, & Yarkin first by conceding that personality traits may affect behavior, but then by contending that the issue was never in question. On Harvey, Town, & Yarkin's point that causation is inherently personal and interpretive, Reeder replies that, at least for the purposes of measuring efficacy in *prediction*, all of the important conceptions can be operationalized well enough to detect bias. Last, although Reeder accepts the distinction between error and bias, he claims that the literature provides mounting evidence of both error and bias in human causal judgments.

not or did not model.[48] Therefore, a policy analyst must be doubly insistent about demanding replication of our experiments in varying settings.[49]

To design an appropriate set of attempts at replication, we would need to ask two questions. First, do individuals' beliefs about property extend from the laboratory setting to any naturally occurring settings? Second, to the extent that individuals' beliefs about property *do* extend from laboratory to nonlaboratory settings, which nonlaboratory phenomena resemble (to subjects) the laboratory treatment variables (coin flip vs. game trigger and moral authority vs. no moral authority)?[50]

## A. *Behavior Induced by the Experimental Setting*

The question whether observed behavior is induced by the laboratory experimental setting, in its most general form, concerns the dependence (or independence) of human choice on the specific institutions within which the behavior takes place. To put the point slightly differently, how *many* institutional features exert substantial influence on subjects' behavior? Experimental economists have endeavored to uncover general, systematic relationships among preferences and institutions as inputs, and subject choices or market outcomes as outputs, by relying on at least the following two axioms.

---

[48] If the same behavior is evidenced in replications, it does not really matter whether the subjects "really believe" Lockean theories of property. As long as they behave "as if" they do, a policy modeled on the assumption that people are Lockeans will have predictable effects. Ultimately, what matters for the predictability of behavior is that people behave as if they hold certain beliefs, regardless of what they may or may not believe. The problem with a purely situational explanation for subject behavior in morally relevant laboratory environments, however, is that applications to the naturally occurring world may be more sensitive to "small" differences between the laboratory and naturally occurring environments.

[49] E. Tory Higgins & Susan L. Bryant, Consensus Information and the Fundamental Attribution Error: The Role of Development and In-Group versus Out-Group Knowledge, 43 J. Personality & Soc. Psychology 889 (1982), suggest that people more often attribute causal responsibility for human actions to the personal traits (as opposed to the situational determinants) of nonpeers than of peers. Inasmuch as our subjects were almost entirely nonpeers of the principal investigators, we urge again that future investigators test our results and search for causal explanations that are alternatives to our hypotheses. Jerald M. Jellison & Jane Green, A Self-Presentation Approach to the Fundamental Attribution Error: The Norm of Internality, 40 J. Personality & Soc. Psychology 643 (1981), present experimental results supporting the theory that trait-oriented (internal) explanations are socially preferred (produce more social approval for the explainer) than do situational (external) explanations.

[50] Vernon L. Smith, Microeconomic Systems as an Experimental Science, 72 Am. Econ. Rev. 923 (1982), discusses the importance of making the experimental institutions "parallel" naturally occurring institutions. Psychologists refer to "external validity" when they speak of "parallelism" between the laboratory and the naturally occurring environment. See, for example, D. T. Campbell & J. C. Stanley, Experimental and Quasi-experimental Designs for Research (1966).

1. "Relationships between preferences, institutional parameters, and outcomes are independent of the sources of preferences."[51]

2. "The relationship between outcomes, preferences and institutions is (supposed to be) independent of the nature of the social alternatives."[52]

These two axioms basically mean that experimental economists assume that preferences induced by monetary payoffs will be treated as real preferences. In addition, they assume that subjects in experiments will make decisions on the basis of those preferences in the same way that they would make decisions based on similar preferences in a naturally occurring environment.

In the context of our experiments, an individual's response to a particular method of allocating property entitlements might fail to extend beyond the laboratory setting if he behaved as though he believed some theory of property *only* in the laboratory setting, and not in nonlaboratory settings. For example, a subject might believe that he should behave as a Lockean in an experiment, but as a utilitarian elsewhere. There are at least three obvious reasons for such behavior.

First, the authoritarian explanation's appeal depends, in part, on the subject's willingness to accept the validity of the authoritative source. If a subject believes in "science," but cares little for traditional social authority figures (such as governmental leaders), then the authoritarian explanation will be overconfirmed in the experimental setting. Similarly, if an authority's pronouncement regarding morality has little force in diffuse settings, such as modern political environments, the authoritarian explanation again will be overconfirmed in the laboratory. Conversely, if the subject believes that all valid authority is justified only by some traditional social institution, then the subject attaches reduced importance to the experimenter's authority. Here the authoritarian explanation will be underconfirmed. A priori, we suspect that the authoritarian explanation will be overconfirmed in the laboratory. Science is generally regarded as a potent source of social authority, which is reinforced by face-to-face contact in our experiments.[53]

[51] Louis L. Wilde, On the Use of Laboratory Experiments in Economics, in The Philosophy of Economics 137, 145 (J. Pitt ed. 1980).

[52] Charles R. Plott, The Application of Laboratory Experimental Methods to Public Choice, in Collective Decision Making: Applications from Public Choice Theory (1979). The textual discussion represents an exploration of the applicability of these two axioms to our experiments. For comprehensive treatments of these issues, see Charles R. Plott, Industrial Organization Theory and Experimental Economics, 20 J. Econ. Lit. 1485 (1982); and Vernon L. Smith, *supra* note 50.

[53] See S. Milgram, *supra* note 32 and *id.*, Some Conditions of Obedience and Disobedience to Authority, 6 Int'l J. Psychiatry, 259 (1968), in which he reports that subjects were led

Second, all the theories of property, including the authoritarian, may be confounded by some sort of observer effect. A subject might wish to behave in some manner, for example, in accord with the economist's belief that all entitlements are rights, but not wish to do so while being *watched* because the Lockean theory of property is more polite.[54] Two considerations suggest that observer effects should not be particularly troubling for our experimental results. First, we gave the subjects no motivational instructions. Hence, subjects' theories of politeness probably affect their dealings to no greater extent than they do outside the laboratory. Second, many nonlaboratory applications also involve *observed* behavior. Whether one is talking about nuisance disputes between neighbors,[55] compulsory copyright licensing of cable television,[56] or settling lawsuits,[57] the participants' behaviors are seen by all those with whom they bargain, and probably by some observers as well.

Of course, there also will be many areas where behavior is *not* observed. One example is taxpayers' compliance with the Internal Revenue Code. Each taxpayer makes his decision to evade in private and does not have to face those who may be hurt by his decision.[58] For such areas, our

---

to believe they were administering severe and harmful shocks to the experimenter's confederates. Even though the subjects were reluctant to inflict pain, they continued to administer "shocks" on the instructions of the experimenter, in the interest of benefiting scientific research. Unfortunately, however, this evidence tells nothing about the strength of authority inherent in "science" vis-à-vis other social institutions.

[54] Wilde, *supra* note 51, indicates that one may eliminate these effects with respect to fellow subjects by making the subject's payoffs private. However, these observer effects cannot be eliminated where the theory being tested, such as the Coase Theorem, requires full information for the subjects. In addition, the experimental monitor will always be observing the outcomes.

[55] See, for example, Robert Cooter, The Cost of Coase, 11 J. Legal Stud. 1 (1982); Robert Cooter & Stephen Marks, with Robert Mnookin, Bargaining in the Shadow of the Law: A Testable Model of Strategic Behavior, 11 J. Legal Stud. 225 (1982); Robert C. Ellickson, Alternatives to Zoning: Covenants, Nuisance Rules, and Fines as Land Use Controls, 40 U. Chi. L. Rev. 681 (1973); and *id.*, Suburban Growth Controls: An Economic and Legal Analysis, 86 Yale L. J. 385 (1977); Richard Posner, Economic Analysis of Law (2d ed. 1977).

[56] Stanley M. Besen, Willard G. Manning, Jr., & Bridger M. Mitchell, Copyright Liability for Cable Television: Compulsory Licensing and the Coase Theorem, 21 J. Law & Econ. 67 (1978).

[57] See for example, Cooter and Cooter & Marks, *supra* note 55; Alan Schwartz, The Case for Specific Performance, 89 Yale L. J. 271 (1979); and Steven Shavell, Suit Settlement and Trial: A Theoretical Analysis under Alternative Methods for the Allocation of Legal Costs, 11 J. Legal Stud. 55 (1982).

[58] Taxpayer noncompliance is estimated to cost the U.S. Treasury about $100 billion per year. See Joint Committee on Taxation Staff Pamphlet, in Hearings on Tax Compliance Before the Senate Finance Committee, 98th Cong., 1st Sess., June 23, 1983 (finding tax loss of $81 billion for legal sector and $9 billion for illegal sector); Administration's Fiscal Year 1984 Budget Proposal II, pt. 2, at 2–47.

results may not apply. However, for other areas, where people *are* observed, if people hold the same theories about politeness in laboratory and nonlaboratory settings, observer effects should not vary much.[59]

Last, it might be argued that some subjects act differently in laboratory settings because the stakes are not large enough to make subjects treat the experiment as "real life." Two factors suggest that this probably poses no great difficulty. First, we replicated our original experiments[60] with two changes in payoffs. In one series, we divided all payoffs by four.[61] In the next, we multiplied all payoffs by four.[62] Neither change produced any change in the results; all subjects split the payoffs equally. These results strongly suggest that the size of the payoffs should not be a source of

[59] If, on the other hand, subjects regard observation by the experimenter as different from observation by others, the results might be affected. For example, if the subject regarded the experimenter as a potential source of moral censure, similar to a clerical figure, but did not so regard nonlaboratory business, we would observe more "polite" behavior in the experiment.

[60] Hoffman & Spitzer, *supra* note 1.

[61] Payoffs for these experiments were (in dollars):

| | DECISION 1 | | | DECISION 2 | |
|---|---|---|---|---|---|
| NUMBER | A | B | NUMBER | A | B |
| 1 | 0 | 3.00 | 1 | 0 | 4.00 |
| 2 | 1.50 | 3.50 | 2 | .25 | 3.50 |
| 3 | 2.00 | 2.00 | 3 | .50 | 2.50 |
| 4 | 2.50 | 1.50 | 4 | 1.50 | 2.00 |
| 5 | 3.00 | .50 | 5 | 1.75 | 1.75 |
| 6 | 3.50 | .25 | 6 | 3.00 | 1.50 |
| 7 | 4.00 | 0 | 7 | 3.50 | .25 |
| | | | 8 | 3.00 | 0 |

[62] Payoffs for those experiments were (in dollars):

| | DECISION 1 | | | DECISION 2 | |
|---|---|---|---|---|---|
| NUMBER | A | B | NUMBER | A | B |
| 1 | 0 | 48.00 | 1 | 0 | 44.00 |
| 2 | 16.00 | 40.00 | 2 | 4.00 | 40.00 |
| 3 | 24.00 | 24.00 | 3 | 8.00 | 32.00 |
| 4 | 32.00 | 16.00 | 4 | 16.00 | 24.00 |
| 5 | 36.00 | 8.00 | 5 | 22.00 | 22.00 |
| 6 | 40.00 | 4.00 | 6 | 36.00 | 16.00 |
| 7 | 44.00 | 0 | 7 | 42.00 | 4.00 |
| | | | 8 | 36.00 | 0 |

concern. In the experiments where payoffs were four times as large, a controller had to give up at least $20 to be able to split equally. This much money should be enough to get student subjects' serious attention.[63]

Second, debriefing the subjects after the experiments tended to confirm that they were treating the experimental situation as "real." When we asked subjects who had equally split why they had done so, they responded that they were dealing with real money, and that fair outcomes are important in real situations. To the extent that subjects are capable of characterizing their own behavior accurately, their responses suggest they were not acting in a frivolous manner.

## B.  Matching Control Variables and Institutions

It is only a first step to show that the behaviors and beliefs of experimental subjects about theories of property accurately characterize human behaviors and beliefs found in some nonexperimental setting. A policy analyst still must carefully match experimental control variables and naturally occurring phenomena, particularly institutional features. "Matching" experimental conditions to control variables requires one of the following extensions of our original model.

Model 2:
  4. Subjects believe the Lockean theory of property in game-trigger experiments and revert to egalitarianism in the coin-flip experiments.
  5. Subjects perceive that the allocative features of some nonlaboratory institution strongly resemble, in a moral sense, the game-trigger or coin-flip control variable.
  6. Subjects will behave as Lockeans or egalitarians in the nonlaboratory setting.

Model 3:
  7. Subjects respond to the moral authority instructions by regarding entitlements as rights.
  8. Subjects regard a nonlaboratory pronouncement as morally similar to the experimenter's moral authority instruction.
  9. Subjects will react to the nonlaboratory pronouncement by regarding entitlements as rights.

The experimental results provide support for assumption 4 and strong, but somewhat ambiguous, support for 7. Assumptions 5 and 8 would be difficult to demonstrate empirically and will, therefore, probably remain

---

[63] The opportunity cost of time for most students is under $5 per hour.

as assumptions underlying applications of our results to nonlaboratory settings.[64] In particular, matching judicial decisions to either coin-flip/ game-trigger or moral authority/no moral authority controls could be very tricky.

Finding such parallels between the laboratory and the naturally occurring world could be very important, however. Consider court decisions, which often distribute property entitlements. First, demonstrating parallels between the laboratory and the naturally occurring world could help to predict the manner in which people would regard the outcomes of judicial decisions. Those scholars and reformers who believe that society's institutions, including the courts, should be molded on widely held moral notions, could possibly use this information to design judicial institutional change.[65] Even if institutional design is put aside, a scholar could use this information to predict litigants' behavior following a decision.

Second, such parallels could reveal something about the manner in which people regard their own holdings, for *all* their holdings are the indirect result of judicial decisions. Their revealed attitudes toward judicial decisions which allocate entitlements may be reflected in their attitudes toward and behavior in regard to their own holdings. For example, if people in general are Lockeans about "earned" resources but egalitarians about randomly assigned resources, they may behave differently if they earn wealth than if they simply inherit it.

Regardless of these temptations to match our experimental treatments to the judicial system, it probably cannot be done exactly. As the discussion below will show, there is such a wide variety of views of the legal system that an exact matching process becomes impracticable. To see in detail how the wide variety of views stymies the matching process, first consider assumption 5 above. Our coin-flip/game-trigger treatment variable was designed to suggest to Lockean subjects that randomly distributing entitlements (coin flip) was morally arbitrary, but that distributing entitlements in response to effort (game trigger) produced morally justified rights. This pair of correspondences, randomness leading to

---

[64] See Elizabeth Hoffman, James R. Marsden, & Andrew Whinston, Efficient Use of Economic Data (unpublished manuscript) (Purdue Univ. School of Management 1984), for a discussion of how one might go about testing whether laboratory results are "parallel" to experimental results.

[65] One would need to argue, of course, that there is some slippage between current institutional design and widely shared moral perceptions. See, for example, Roberto Mangabeira Unger, The Critical Legal Studies Movement, 96 Harv. L. Rev. 563 (1983), locating the catalyst for the "critical" enterprise in prevailing beliefs about democracy not realized in current institutional design. However, such a discussion is beyond the scope of this paper.

moral arbitrariness and effort leading to moral justification, might not carry over into the judicial arena.

First, consider randomness. One who thinks of the legal process as fundamentally determinist (nonrandom) may or may not regard judicial outcomes as morally arbitrary. For example, a person who believes that every legal decision has a moral premise within it, that courts can and do rely on ascertainable natural law to provide these moral premises, and that courts correctly apply these moral premises to produce good decisions, will believe that judicial decisions are both fundamentally nonrandom and morally justified.

Alternatively, a legal positivist is likely to believe that the only concepts that are intelligible are those that may be reduced to basic sense impressions (for example, sight and smell) and to include all moral terms as nonsense. At the same time, however, a logical positivist is likely to believe that legal decisions are predictable (for example, plaintiffs will win all tort claims in California). Thus, he will regard judicial decisions as nonrandom, but also morally arbitrary.

In contrast to both the natural lawyer and the legal positivist, an extreme legal realist would probably believe that judicial decisions are entirely a product of individual judges' preferences and deny any moral significance to those preferences.[66] Thus, he would regard judicial decisions as both random and morally arbitrary.[67]

Now consider the element of effort. First, someone might believe that judicial outcomes are determined, in the sense that cases are always won by the side that does the best job of litigating, regardless of the merits of

[66] See, for example, Felix S. Cohen, The Ethical Basis of Legal Criticism, 3–7, 33–36 (1959), where he contends that on the basis of logic (not ethics) alone, past results can be reconciled with any possible future resolution in a lawsuit. Modern law and economics scholars routinely model the trial process as a random variable. See, for example, Shavell, *supra* note 57; and Patricia Munch Danzon & Lee A. Lillard, Settlement out of Court: The Disposition of Medical Malpractice Claims, 12 J. Legal Stud. 345 (1983) (citing others in n.1). For positions approaching this extreme, see Jerome N. Frank, Law and the Modern Mind, 136–39, 141–43 (1930); and Felix S. Cohen, Transcendental Nonsense and the Functional Approach, 35 Colum. L. Rev. 809 (1935).

[67] There is at least one piece of anecdotal evidence that suggests that judges' decisions should not appear to be too blatantly random. One New York judge who chose between sentencing a convict to twenty days or thirty days in jail by flipping a coin was later removed, partly because of his coin-flip decision. See E. R. Shipp, Judge Friess, Censured for Lodging Suspect in '80, Said to Be Resigning, N.Y. Times, December 14, 1982 at B 4; William G. Blair, Flip of Coin Decides Jail Term in Manhattan Criminal Case, N.Y. Times, February 2, 1983 at A1; E. R. Shipp, 2 New York State Justices Defend Ex-Judge at a Misconduct Hearing, N.Y. Times, February 6, 1983 § 1, at 21; and E. R. Shipp, Ex-Jurist Who Made Coin-Toss Decision is Barred from Being New York Judge Again, N.Y. Times, April 7, 1983, at 17, col. 1.

the case. Such a person might spend substantial sums of money to hire the best lawyers in an effort to win the case. If such a person were the legal positivist, described above, it is unclear how he would regard such a judicial outcome. Because victory and the resulting entitlement go to the side that has expended greater (or better) effort, the entitlement might be viewed as justified, on Lockean grounds. However, because such a person regards the underlying legal rules as morally arbitrary, the entitlement might be seen as arbitrary.

In contrast, the natural lawyer described above might believe that judicial decisions produced good, morally justifiable results, but that judges were impervious to litigants' efforts to influence them. He would probably have no *Lockean* reason to regard judicially determined entitlements as morally justified, and yet might still regard these entitlements as morally justified because of natural law.

Putting together these observations, we can show that, in the context of the courts, a subject's regarding judicial decisions as random is neither necessary nor sufficient for the subject's regarding the outcomes as morally arbitrary. Similarly, a subject's regarding the outcome as a result of effort expended is neither necessary nor sufficient for regarding the outcome as morally justified. Hence, it is difficult, without gathering accurate empirical evidence about the distribution of jurisprudential beliefs in the population, to say anything about the moral implications of the coin-flip/ game-trigger control variables. Unfortunately, however, gathering such data could be very difficult, since many people have thought very little about such issues. Hypothetical questions about them would not be likely to generate reliable answers, even if the respondents made a serious effort to be honest in their responses.

Assessing 8, concerning the intermediate belief about the moral similarity of the experimental instructions and judicial pronouncements, will also depend on subjects' jurisprudential views. The legal positivist will regard such utterances as morally arbitrary, while the natural lawyer will regard the same pronouncements as morally justified. Thus, the same information on jurisprudential views needed to assess the coin-flip/game-trigger controls would be needed to assess the moral authority instructions.

In sum, applying either model in the judicial context in general seems quite difficult. The great variety of possible views of the judicial process renders impracticable any precise matching of our experimental institutions to the legal system as a whole.

In marked contrast, our results may say a great deal about shaping *particular* legal doctrines. If our results are ultimately replicated in a number of settings, we might try, using the model of those who believe that the law should conform to widely held notions of fairness, to outline changes in particular legal rules suggested by our results. Consider first the law of contract and the following assumptions:

**Model 4:**

10. Subjects are Lockeans in game-trigger experiments and egalitarians in coin flip experiments.
11. Subjects perceive a contractual situation to be morally similar to the game-trigger or coin-flip experiment.
12. Subjects will be Lockeans or egalitarians, respectively, in those situations.
13. The law should be made to serve the interests of Lockeans or egalitarians, respectively, in those situations.[68]

The analysis will focus on all, above. For our first example, assume that a buyer and a seller agree that the seller will build a unique good and deliver it to the buyer for some price. Each knows that some third party who values the unique good more than the buyer does may materialize. Under such circumstances, the rules regarding breach of contract will allocate the third party's surplus value between the buyer and seller.[69] If the buyer and the seller regard the third party's arrival as a pure matter of chance, and they regard the third party's arrival as morally similar to the coin flip, then our analysis suggests that they would regard as fair an equal division of the surplus value. To the extent that courts can accurately measure the amounts involved, this analysis suggests considering a rule which effects such an equal division.[70] On the other hand, if the seller or buyer expends *effort* to find the third party, and they regard the third party's arrival as morally similar to winning a hash mark game, then, as good Lockeans, they may regard the third party's surplus value as belonging to the person who located him. In such circumstances, the court should consider choosing a breach of contract rule that allocates all or most of the value to the "working" party.

For our second example, the contract doctrines of impossibility and

[68] This article does not explore the following important questions: (1) Should the law serve the moral preferences of the citizens? (2) Does it not already do so? Instead, this article assumes that the answers to these questions are yes and no, respectively, and then proceeds to show how our analysis might help to improve the ability of the law to serve society's moral preferences. In addition, it should be noted that in this section of the paper we assume people *do* hold moral beliefs.

[69] See generally A. Mitchell Polinsky, Risk Sharing through Breach of Contract Remedies, 12 J. Legal Stud. 427 (1983).

[70] Polinsky suggests divisions that approach equal divisions so as to maximize the transferable expected utility of the buyer and seller, together, especially when the buyer and seller have similar risk preferences. *Id.*

frustration might also be shaped by our inquiry.[71] These two doctrines operate so as to discharge contracting parties' obligations if certain random, unforeseen events occur. According to traditional learning, a contract will be discharged through impossibility if parties agree to do something which, quite literally, becomes impossible because of some intervening event. For example, if A and B agree that A will paint B's house, and then B's house burns down, A cannot paint the house. The doctrine of impossibility will discharge A's contractual obligation. Frustration will discharge contractual obligations when events destroy the "object" of the contract, although performance may be literally possible. For example, if A and B agree that A will rent B's room (which has a marvelous window overlooking some parade grounds) on the day of the big parade, and then the parade is suddenly canceled, the doctrine of frustration will discharge the contract.[72]

These two doctrines seem to apply to situations where some random event produces some loss (or perhaps even gain) for the contracting parties. If these events are regarded as similar to the coin-flip treatment in our experiments, people will tend to regard the (undischarged) contractual assignment of entitlements as unjustified whenever such an event occurs. Under such circumstances, the law can conform to widely held notions of fairness by discharging the contract and then splitting the losses equally between the parties. Administrative considerations may ultimately preclude this route, however, suggesting instead that the courts use rules which are proxies for splitting losses.

When it is possible or appropriate, discharging the contractual obligations would probably be administratively easy in comparison to splitting the losses. To decide whether or not the contractual obligations should be discharged, in turn, one would have to decide whether the subsequent event was random—like a flip of the coin. For example, one would not wish to discharge A's contractual obligations in the two examples above if A had burned down B's house or if A had canceled the parade himself.[73] Moreover, such an inquiry would not be unusually difficult.

---

[71] See generally E. Allan Farnsworth, Contracts 670–706 (1982); M. P. Furmston & G. Cheshire, Cheshire and Fifoot's Law of Contract 512–34 (10th ed. 1981). Actually, the law of impossibility has turned, in modern times, into a law of "impracticability," and the comments in the text may be taken to refer to both sets of doctrine.

[72] See Krell v. Henry (1903) 2 K.B. 740.

[73] Where the party claiming discharge by reason of impossibility or frustration is *at fault* in producing the event, the courts refuse to discharge the contract. See Furmston & Cheshire, *supra* note 71, at 521–22; and Farnsworth, *supra* note 71, at 678 n.8, 684. Under such circumstances, Lockean notions of desert may be appropriate, for the party at fault may have "earned" the loss. Further, where the parties have contracted regarding the event the court will not discharge the contractual obligations. See Furmston & Cheshire, *supra* note 71, at 521; and Farnsworth, *supra* note 71, at 684–86, 692.

In contrast, splitting the losses equally would require that the court *measure* the losses. But, measuring the losses might be so difficult and uncertain that the court might be driven to use some concrete, arbitrary rule of thumb to apportion those losses. To see this, consider again the example where A agreed to paint B's house. That contract created consumer surplus for B (the amount by which his personal valuation of the contract exceeded the contract price) and producer surplus—roughly described as profit—for A. When B's house burned down, B's consumer surplus and A's profit were destroyed, along with any materials and efforts expended by A before the fire in partial performance of the contract.

To split the losses equally, a court would have to evaluate not only the materials and efforts expended in partial performance, but also lost profits and consumer surplus. But valuing lost profits and consumer surplus might be so burdensome and uncertain that a court might, instead, let these two losses lie on A and B, respectively,[74] as a rough form of splitting losses and concentrate only upon splitting the loss of the materials and efforts expended in partial performance. On this question, the court could choose between (1) completely refusing to allow recovery by A, (2) allowing A to recover to the extent that partial performance actually bestowed some benefits on B, (3) allowing A to recover full costs, or (4) some other rule. Similarly, the court could choose analogous rules to govern B's claim for the return of any progress payments B might have paid to A. The final combination of rules[75] probably would be based both on the extent to which the rules effectuate equal splitting of losses and on administrative efficiency. But choosing such a final set of rules lies beyond the scope of this paper.

Last, our results may also help a court to choose between "cost of completion" damages and "diminution in market value" damages in construction contracts. For example, Muris worries that courts might produce inefficiencies by awarding cost of completion damages, instead of diminution in market value, for certain breaches of construction con-

---

[74] This has, in general, been the approach of the law in this area. Furmston & Cheshire, *supra* note 71, at 524–33.

[75] The English law in this area was changed rather dramatically by the Frustrated Contracts Act of 1943. At common law, reliance losses were not recoverable and neither were progress payments (which might also have been full payment) paid before the frustrating event. The 1943 Act changed the common-law rules in two important respects. First, the Act allows parties to recover progress payments made before the frustrating event, but offsets against this any sums actually expended toward complying with the frustrated contract. Second, it allows recovery for benefits actually conferred. *Id.* at 527–31. This change could be regarded as the selection of a different set of proxies for splitting losses. Note that there is no theoretical reason why, in general, the 1943 Act comes closer to equal splits than did 'ne common law.

tracts.[76] If the contractor breaches, but the cost of completion far exceeds the purchaser's subjective (above market) valuation of correct performance, it would be inefficient for the contractor actually to complete performance. As a consequence, if the court were to award either specific performance or cost of completion damages, the parties could create a surplus by agreeing to release the contractor from his obligation to perform. A pessimist—one who believes that disputes over dividing surplus are very costly and impede contract formation—would worry about creating such a surplus and would prefer instead to award only diminution in market value as damages. Our present results suggest that norms of distributive justice may help to solve disputes over surplus division, and that the court may choose to award either specific performance or cost of completion damages without worrying a great deal about inefficiencies from bargaining breakdown. Of course, the court may decide to award only diminution in market value for other reasons, but a consideration of these other reasons lies beyond the scope of this paper.

## VII. Conclusion

In general, this article's findings suggest that there is less need for governmental supervision of the bargaining process to ensure efficiency than one might otherwise suppose. Cooter,[77] for example, contrasts the Coase Theorem with the "Hobbes Theorem." The Coase Theorem represents, for Cooter, the optimistic outlook that disputes over dividing the surplus that is generated by cooperation can be solved so as to let cooperation proceed. The Hobbes Theorem represents the "polar opposite": the pessimistic outlook that such disputes can never be solved and that cooperation will never take place. Pessimists—those who believe in the Hobbes Theorem—see a role for the government in overseeing bargaining and arranging property rights so as to produce fewer situations where cooperation (contracting) is needed. Our results suggest that the Coase Theorem has relatively more appeal than the Hobbes Theorem, and that the courts need not choose rules because of worries about the inefficiency that might be generated by disputes over the division of surpluses.[78]

---

[76] Timothy J. Muris, Cost of Completion or Diminution in Market Value: The Relevance of Subjective Value, 12 J. Legal Stud. 379 (1983).

[77] *Supra* note 55.

[78] For other support for these results, see Hoffman & Spitzer, *supra* notes 1 and 35; Glenn W. Harrison & Michael McKee, Experimental Evaluation of the Coase Theorem, 28 J. Law & Econ. (forthcoming).

# [11]

## THE EFFECTS OF MARKET PRACTICES IN OLIGOPOLISTIC MARKETS: AN EXPERIMENTAL EXAMINATION OF THE ETHYL CASE

DAVID M. GRETHER* and CHARLES R. PLOTT*

*This study reports on the performance of experimental markets characterized by industrial structure and practices similar to those at issue in the Ethyl case. The central question is whether price competition is affected by the practices of advanced notification of price changes and "most-favored nation" contracts or is determined by industrial organization and concentration alone.*

### I. INTRODUCTION

In May of 1979 the United States Federal Trade Commission (FTC) filed a complaint[1] against the producers of lead-based antiknock compounds, the gasoline additives which raise the octane level. The FTC asked the four domestic producers in the industry to cease and desist from using market practices that, according to FTC theory, facilitated a reduction in price competition in violation of Section 5 of the Federal Trade Commission Act, 15 U.S.C. §45. As part of the general defense, experts claimed that the conduct of the industry could be explained as resulting from industrial structure alone, the practices had no discernible effect, and thus the relief sought by the FTC would be ineffective and should be denied. This study reports the behavior of laboratory markets characterized by the prominent structural features of the lead-based antiknock compound industry with and without practices similar to some of those at issue in the litigation.

The industry structure is one of the major parameters in all theories applied in the analysis of the case, and there is little or no controversy over its key features. The products, tetraethyl lead, tetramethyl lead, and mixes of these two compounds, are homogeneous across producers. Demand generally is believed to be inelastic in the vicinity of existing prices. Entry was highly unlikely during the period of the complaint (January 1, 1974 to May 31, 1979) because demand was expected to be reduced significantly due to Environmental Protection Agency regulations regarding the phaseout of the use of lead in gasoline. The products are used only as a gasoline additive. There are only four firms in the industry, Ethyl Corporation, E. I. du Pont de Nemours and Company, PPG Industries, Inc., and Nalco Chemical Corporation. The two largest firms apparently possess excess capacity, and the other two firms are relatively small, twelve percent and eighteen percent of the market respectively. Ten large buyers out of one hundred and fifty or more account for approximately sixty percent of the market.

*California Institute of Technology. Professor Plott has served as an FTC Bureau of Competition consultant on the Ethyl case. This research was stimulated by problems which surfaced in that context. Some initial experimental work was financed by the FTC. General funding by the National Science Foundation, the Guggenheim Foundation, and the Caltech Program for Enterprise and Public Policy is gratefully acknowledged. We also wish to thank James Angel who was the senior research assistant for the project.

1. Ethyl Corporation, E. I. du Pont de Nemours and Company, PPG Corporation and Nalco Chemical Corporation, Docket no. 9128. Federal Trade Commission.

Three practices are challenged by the FTC complaint:

A.  *Advanced Notice and Price Announcements.*   Suppliers agreed to give at least thirty-day notice of all price increases. These price announcements were transmitted to customers by telephone and telegram and, in addition, were announced to the press. Price announcements usually were made in advance (three to eight days) of the thirty-day deadline by firms initiating a price change.

B.  *Most Favored Nation.*   The two large producers consistently used "most favored nation" clauses in contracts, and the other two suppliers used them in various ways. The central feature of this practice is to guarantee to each customer that no other customer will obtain a like quantity and quality at a lower price.

C.  *Delivered Pricing.*   Delivered pricing is practiced by all four firms. Each firm quotes a list price for a given compound delivered to the purchaser regardless of the location of the producer.

The Commission's administrative law judge summarized the facts as follows:

> The facts relating to the use of the challenged practices by the respondents are not controverted. All respondents use thirty-day advance notice of price increases; until mid-1977, all respondents issued press notices of price changes; all respondents utilize *delivered* pricing, and *uniform* delivered pricing with respect to all list price transactions. Respondents Ethyl and DuPont utilize most favored nation clauses in their contracts with customers (these respondents did not have contracts with all customers); and Nalco had most favored nation clauses in all its contracts until 1978, and with a few contracts thereafter (this respondent also did not have contracts with all its customers). Use of the practices having been established, it remains to determine the effect of the practices on competition. [U.S. Initial Decision, 1981, p. 135]

The FTC claim is that the practices, combined with various features of the industrial structure, enabled suppliers to maintain prices above competitive levels (Complaint Counsel's Proposed Finding, 1981). The theory is based on the hypothesis that competition is aided by uncertainty about rival firms' actions and/or reactions to pricing decisions. First, the use of delivered pricing policies reduces the dimensions in which price concessions can be made thereby reducing the uncertainty about the terms which competitors have offered to individual customers and the magnitude of price changes. Secondly, the greater the use of the most favored nation clauses by a firm, the more the tendency of a firm to charge all customers the same price for a given product and give secret price discounts to no one. The delivered pricing policy buttresses this most favored nation practice by making the term, "price," reasonably unambiguous. That is, it helps prevent effective special price discounts which might exist under some other name. The two practices together thus reduce uncertainty about a competitor's actions and, by virtue of the market structure, facilitate the stability of higher prices through a process of conjectural variations.[2] The most favored nation clause can also add stability in another way. Buyers tend to believe that any price concession or discount obtained will automatically be

---

2. For a model of the influence of the speed of the detection of price changes see George J. Stigler, "A Theory of Oligopoly," *Journal of Political Economy,* 72 (February 1964): 44-61.

extended to other customers. A discount to a single customer would thus be more costly to the supplier than the production and delivery cost of the marginal product and would thus be less likely to be granted. Knowing this, buyers as individuals (and thus as a group) bargain less tenaciously and are a less important source of potential disruption of price stability. The conclusion is that the first two practices contribute to price stability at whatever price level happens to have been established.

The advance notice provision helps establish the price level. Price increases usually are announced several days before the deadline for an announcement. This announcement, made publicly through the newspapers, would be transmitted to competitors immediately. Other firms which have a similar thirty-day advance notice policy have several days in which to respond. If they match the higher price, then all firms have stable prices at the higher level. If any firm does not match the price, then the announced price increase will be rescinded,[3] and the non-matching firm will gain no volume from its nonconforming behavior. In this strategic environment, each firm has a dominant strategy to match the price increase as long as it anticipates higher profits from *joint* upward price movements. No firm has an incentive to "chisel" or "undercut" the prices of others. Thus the process of prior announcement provides a dynamic element through which price levels may be established and the practices taken as a group serve to coordinate actions and reduce price competition.[4] A natural theoretical extension of the argument leads to a prediction that prices should equilibrate at the lowest of the optimum industry prices from the individual firm's point of view.

Economic experts (Dennis M. Carlton, Michael L. Glassman, George A. Hay, H. Michael Mann, and Jesse W. Markham) who testified in the case have been in substantial agreement about the facts of the case regarding the economic structure of the industry. The plausibility of the government's theory as it relates to the basic principles of economics also was not a subject of debate. The controversy surfaced in the analysis of industrial conduct and the role of the challenged practices. This general agreement presented a special opportunity for the application of experimental methods. The questions posed in the litigation did not deal with market structure, but the appropriate behavioral principle and models that apply to markets with that structure.

Nonprice competition and discounts could be observed. Neither advance notice nor price publication was always followed. Market shares changed. Transportation costs were relatively low. Most favored nation clauses were not in all contracts. Information about competitors' list prices was readily available from customers and there was frequently little time delay between the time a price change was announced and the first time information of the change reached a competitor. Opinions about costs and profits differed. Such facts led to differing evaluations about how much competition actually exists in the industry and what would be expected to be seen in terms of such variables in an industry with a market structure like that of the lead-based antiknock compound industry.

---

3. The product is homogeneous so small price differences can precipitate large volume changes. Furthermore, some suppliers included "meet or release" clauses in contracts which guaranteed that the supplier would meet the lowest price in the market or release the buyer from contractual obligations.

4. For a summary of other conditions and practices which are thought to have this effect see Scherer (1970, chapters 6 and 7).

The Commission's administrative law judge summarized the controversy as follows:

> Respondents' economic experts were unanimous in their opinion that the structure of the industry was the determining factor on the competitive performance of the industry; and that the industry was performing as competitively as would be expected based on the structure. Dr. Hay, complaint counsel's expert, testified that the structural characteristics in conjunction with the challenged practices had reduced the vigor of competition, and that in the absence of the practices, competition would have been more vigorous. [U.S. Initial Decision, 1981, p. 136]

The issue to be explored in this study is the potential effect of practices similar to some of those in the Ethyl litigation over and above that of industrial structure. Can such a set of practices facilitate a reduction in price competition or do prices and profits above the competitive equilibrium levels necessarily constitute an equilibrium within an industry with this structure? The laboratory markets studied below were designed to answer that question. The practices examined are similar to practices challenged by the FTC complaint, and the industries studied are similar in structure (but much smaller in scale) to the lead-based antiknock compound industry.

## II. EXPERIMENTAL DESIGN

### A. Procedures

Subjects were recruited from Pasadena City College, the California Institute of Technology, and the Pasadena business community. All subjects had participated in at least one laboratory experimental market prior to participating in the experiments reported here.

All experiments were conducted at the California Institute of Technology and each lasted between three and four hours. Subjects were assigned randomly to an incentive structure as explained below and to an office. Instructions were read (see Appendix), questions were answered publicly, and subjects completed a "test" designed to check their understanding of the rules, incentive structure, etc. The suppliers were given a sheet not seen by buyers on which the market demand function was graphed and its meaning was explained to them.

Most of the experiments reported here were not conducted according to any plan known to the subjects. This reduced the possibility of overt collusion. The exceptions are experiments 8 through 11 which were held on consecutive nights with the same subjects, but on any given night they did not know the nature of the experiment for the next night. The possibility of collusion external to the experimental setting was reduced also by a policy of changing the demand and supply functions by a scalar so the price units were not readily comparable.

### B. Parameters

Lead-based antiknock compounds are added to fuel to increase the octane ratings. The two basic products, tetraethyl lead ("TEL") and tetramethyl lead ("TML") are homogeneous products in that no qualitative differences exist among the products sold by different manufacturers. Mixtures of these two basic products are also sold. Octane ratings can be increased by additional processing (catalytic reforming), or through the use of other chemical products, but these methods are more costly. Thus, the commodities are homogeneous with no substitutes in the price ranges under consideration.

The product homogeneity was incorporated in the laboratory markets but only a single commodity existed in the laboratory markets rather than the two basic commodities and the mixes. Individual demands for a single, homogeneous commodity were created, by application of induced preference theory,[5] in the following manner. Buyers made money by purchasing from sellers and reselling to the experimenter. Likewise, sellers made money by buying from the experimenters and reselling to the buyers. The cost schedule faced by individual sellers dictated their capacity, marginal costs, and other aspects of variable costs. It was unnecessary for sellers to carry inventory of the product because they could, up to capacity limits, produce instantly to satisfy demands, and they would only incur the variable cost associated with production.

The market demand and supply functions are displayed in figure 1. The actual shape of the demand function is approximately the right half of an inverted parabola with the equation

$$p = 1.81 - Q^2/256.$$

With this equation and the supply function as shown, the competitive equilibrium is $.54 per unit. Demand elasticity is .218 in the range of the competitive equilibrium. Substitutes are likely to become available in volume once they become economically feasible relative to lead-based compounds which accounts for the substantially reduced demand at the higher prices. Demand in the experimental market in the range of the competitive equilibrium probably is more inelastic than is the demand for lead-based antiknock compounds at current price levels. However, as price increases, elasticity increases; for example, elasticity is .69 at $1.05 and it is 1.10 at $1.25. By multiplying the units in the experiment by a factor of two million and considering the time period to be two weeks, each unit would represent two million pounds, and its value would be two million times the price. Naturally such scalar transforms preserve all of the relevant economic parameters.

There were nine buyers in the experiment. The market demand function shown is the aggregation of the individual demand functions, but the individual functions may be inferred as follows. Index the buyers as 1 through 9, and let the numbers under the demand function represent the buyer who had a unit with a limit price at that value. The demand function (or limit price function) of buyer 5, for example, had one unit at $1.43 and a second at $.61. As may be seen from the figure, buyers 1 through 8 are all about the same size and constitute about 70 percent of the market, depending upon the price level. Buyer 9 is a passive buyer representing a large number of small consumers and about 30 percent of the market. This buyer was instructed to call suppliers at random (unless one had a lower announced price; then, to call the lowest priced seller) and to purchase a single unit at the quoted price without negotiating.[6] These statistics are to be compared with those of the industry in which the eight largest buyers account for about 50 or 55 percent of all sales and the largest twelve account for from 60 percent to 70 percent.

---

5. See Smith (1976) and Plott (1979).

6. The individual would ask the price and then ask if it was the best price. If the price was twice or more what had been charged by other sellers, the passive buyer would not purchase. If the quoted price was anything less, a purchase would be made.

### FIGURE 1

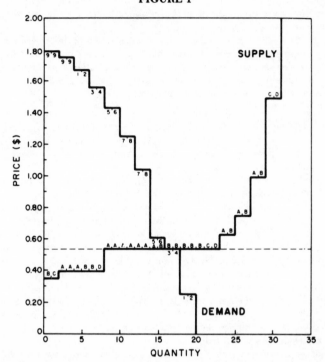

Market supply as shown in the figure as flat at approximately $.54 with substantial excess capacity at that price. At the competitive equilibrium of $.54, the laboratory market would be at 78 percent of capacity and at a slightly higher price (*e.g.*, $.65) the industry would be at only 56 percent of capacity. Marginal costs increase rapidly as the capacity limits are reached but, as shown in the figure, some capacity still becomes available at price levels of $1.50.

The sellers are indexed A, B, C, D.[7] Both A and B are large sellers with similar cost and capacity structures. The firm marginal cost curve can be deduced from the supply curve. The letter over the supply curve indicates that firm can supply a unit at that marginal cost. Thus firm A can supply three units at $.40, seven additional units at $.54, and an additional unit at each of $.63, $.75, and $1.00.

As may be seen from the individual costs, the two large sellers have about 82 percent of the total capacity. At industrial scale this would translate into a capacity of 988 million pounds per year for the two large suppliers at the low competitive price and about 208 million pounds capacity for the two small suppliers. If the price doubled, total capacity would be increased by 29 percent and all of this would be from the two big suppliers. At a price of $.65 the two large suppliers would have an excess capacity of 572 million pounds per year. These parameters are all within the

---

7. For some of the experiments sellers were named A, B, I, O because the letters B, C, and D sound similar and caused some time delays as a result.

ranges estimated by experts.[8] The industrial concentration on the supply side of the markets studied is slightly higher than that of the industry. Presumably, this biases the results against the FTC case.

The number of sellers was fixed at four for the duration of the experiment. Neither entry nor plant expansion was possible beyond that implicit in the supply curves. This aspect reflects the generally accepted proposition that the anticipated decline of demand for lead-based antiknock compounds would deter entry since long-run returns to marginal firms would be unfavorable.

### C. Practices

Communication took two forms: telephone and a digital display device. Buyers (sellers) had phone numbers for sellers (buyers) but not other buyers (sellers). During a period they were free to call each other for contracts but no phone conversations were allowed between periods.

The digital display device was designed for price announcements. The device as shown in figure 2 consisted of four modules. Each module of the device had a push-button keypad, much like that of a hand-held calculator, and thirteen digital receiver units, each capable of displaying a three-digit number and thirteen receiver panels. Thus, if a seller entered a number on the keypad, this number would be displayed simultaneously on all thirteen receiver units connected with the keypad. It was possible for a seller to have a receiver panel and see the price (s)he displayed but not, for example, the prices of other sellers. Each buyer had four receivers, each carrying the number entered from one of the keypads. If, for example, every seller had a keypad, each could enter a price that would be seen by those with receivers attached to that keypad. By altering who had access to the sending and receiving units and the rules of communicating, practices similar to those of the Ethyl case could be implemented and studied.

The market practices in each experiment may be characterized by four different variables, so the practices are indexed by a four-tuple. The first component denotes the agents who were allowed to make the price announcements previously explained. The letters N, A, L, which constitute the range of the first variable, represent: N = no price announcements; A = all sellers make price announcements; L = large sellers make price announcements. The second component, which denotes those who were able to receive the price announcements, takes the two values as follows: A = all participants receive the price announcements; B = only the buyers and not the sellers receive the announcements. The third variable takes the value Y if a most favored nation practice was imposed uniformly on sellers making price announcements, and it takes the value N if not. If N is in the third place, then firms may discount from announced prices. The fourth and final variable takes the value Y if prior notification is required for price increases, and it takes the value N if not. Thus, to give an example, the notation (ABYY) means that all firms had policy price announcements which were received only by buyers; all firms used most favored nation clauses and prior notification of price increases.

Delivered price or press release policies were not examined which reflects limitations placed on the experiments by previous experimental work in the field and

---

8. One firm in the industry, Nalco, may have had a larger capacity, relative to other firms, than the figure used here. Complaint counsel's "Proposed Finding of Facts, Supporting Memorandum, Conclusions of Law and Order," 1981, pp. 36-38.

**FIGURE 2**

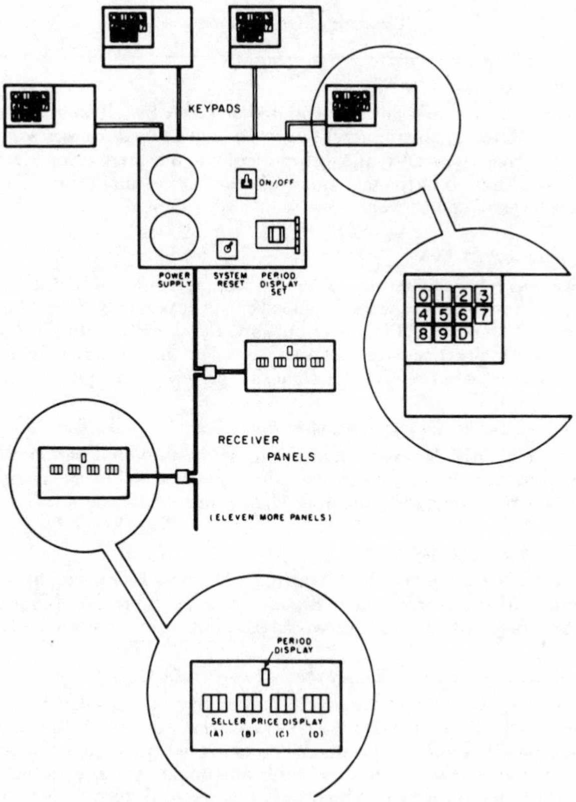

current experimental technology. The inclusion of transportation costs, mixing, and other complications which would expand the single homogeneous commodity to one with several dimensions (*e.g.*, the commodity plus transportation services) would have also placed a substantial burden on the study. Literally speaking, since transportation costs were always zero in these experiments, the delivered pricing policy is always in effect.

The primary focus of the study is on only two treatment conditions, the case where there are no practices and the case where all practices are used by the two largest sellers. In the course of the experiments, however, the opportunity to obtain a preliminary examination of some of the variations in the practices presented itself. The seven treatment conditions on which some data were gathered are listed in table 1 and are ordered according to the degree to which all of the practices were present.

Of primary interest are the cases (N-NN) and (LAYY). The treatment (N-NN) seems to be the most analogous to the situation that is expected to exist if the remedy sought by the FTC is implemented successfully. The treatment (LAYY) is most analogous to the situation that now exists.

## TABLE 1

### Treatment Conditions

*Privately negotiated prices (N-NN)*

In this market, contract prices were negotiated privately by telephone. Each supplier was free within the constraints set by costs to follow whatever pricing policies desired, but the device was not available for price announcements. Suppliers necessarily relied on customers as the sole source of information about the pricing policies and price levels of competitors.

*Nonpublic price lists (ABNN)*

This practice was implemented by use of the display device. Each supplier was given a keypad, but the prices were displayed to the buyers only. Sellers could not see the prices of other sellers. Discounts from announced prices were allowed so the most favored nation practices were not operative. The "bait and switch tactics" of advertising a low price but refusing to sell at that price were not permitted.

*Nonpublic price announcements with most favored nation (ABYN)*

This is the same as (ABNN) except that given the most favored nation clause no discounting from the announced price was allowed. Thus, all buyers paid the same price during a period when the same price was being announced.

*Public price announcements (LANN)*

Both large sellers had keypads, and all participants, both sellers and buyers, had receiver units. Discounts from these announced prices were possible and were negotiated privately. All prices of the two small sellers were negotiated privately.

*Public price announcements and most favored nations (AAYN)*

All sellers had keypads and all participants had receiver units, so price announcements were seen by all participants. All contracts were executed at the announced prices. These practices have elements of the delivered price policy since prices could be communicated and understood easily and unambiguously. In this context the most favored nation clause, which prohibits secret discounts, acts in many respects identically to that used in the lead-based antiknock compound industry.

*All practices (LAYY) and (AAYY)*

Price increases were allowed only after one full period of advance notification. This was accomplished with the aid of a second keypad in (LAYY)* and by a special signal in (AAYY). For example, if a large seller desired to increase price in period 8, it was announced to all participants prior to the beginning of period 7. Price decreases could be made at any time, but once price was reduced, it could not be raised without the proper notification. In this treatment, volume data for all suppliers was also made available at the end of each period, thereby reflecting a situation in which information is reasonably accurate.

---

*A seller who wished to make a price announcement did so by entering a period number in the display. A public signal would then be made by the experimenter which alerted all participants that a price announcement was to be made for the period entered on the display. All participants would then check the receiver units. After a brief wait, the new price for the announced period would be entered.

On *a priori* grounds it would be expected that market behavior under treatment (ABNN) would be approximately the same as (N-NN). If competitors cannot monitor price announcements directly and if the announced prices themselves are subject to discount, it would be expected that there would be very little difference from no announcements at all. Advertising might have an effect on buyer behavior to the extent that search costs are important and to the extent that advertised prices reflected actual prices. Aside from this effect, which is expected to be small in these markets, (ABNN) and (N-NN) are reckoned to be the same. Similarly, (AAYY) should be the same as (LAYY). The volume of the two small sellers is so low that they should adjust to the pricing policies of the larger sellers.

The other three treatments are of independent interest. The treatments (ABYN) and (AAYN) are similar to circumstances which could evolve from Robinson-Patman provisions. All buyers pay the same list prices, costlessly known to them. Under (AAYN) sellers have access to the same pricing information as buyers, whereas under (ABYN) sellers do not. The treatment (LANN) provides some insight into the pure effect of public price announcements.

## III. COMPETING MODELS

Two different questions are examined. (1) Do the practices make a difference? (2) What models most accurately capture experiences with the behavior of markets with the structure described above? The first question is a purely statistical question once the experimental design has been set. The second question is more complicated because of the existence of a rich and varied set of models which differ according to the role of time, product differentiation, the nature of the information, etc. The models explored here are all static and are based on the hypothesis that the product is perfectly homogeneous across sellers.

The models can most easily be explained by reference to cases in which all functions are differentiable. The numbers listed as predictions, however, are derived from the discrete analogs. The individual large seller, $i$, has an incentive to satisfy the equation

$$P(x_1 + x_2 + 2k) + x_i \frac{\partial P(x_1 + x_2 + 2k)}{\partial x_i} \left( 1 + \frac{\partial x_j}{\partial x_i} \right) - \frac{\partial C(x_i)}{\partial x_i} = 0,$$

where $x_i$ is the volume of seller $i$; $P(x_1 + x_2 + 2k)$ is the inverse market demand function; $k$ is the constant volume of a smaller seller constrained by capacity; $C(x_i)$ is the cost function of seller $i$. The equation simply reflects optimizing behavior and the assumption that small sellers behave in a price follower role and are aggressive only to the extent necessary to sell a volume of $k$.

The term $\partial x_j/\partial x_i$ is the reaction by firm $j$ as anticipated by firm $i$ to a change in the volume of firm $i$. A continuum of models may be derived from this formulation by letting $\partial x_j/\partial x_i$ range from $-1$ to 1 (Telser 1972, 152-53). The term is in a sense a measure of perceived interrelatedness and indicates that competition goes down as such awareness goes up. For purposes of analysis the class of admissible models was restricted arbitrarily to only four.

*Competitive Equilibrium and the Bertrand Model.* If $\partial x_j/\partial x_i = -1$, the behavioral equation above becomes $P = MC$. The competitive interpretation is that sellers view their actions as having no perceptible influence on price because any volume increases will be offset by volume decreases elsewhere. The Bertrand oligopoly interpretation is that the firm believes customers may be stolen from a competitor by slight price reductions and such reductions will be met only passively if at all.

If the market shares between the two large sellers are equal or near equal, this equation is satisfied at $.54. The volume prediction is eighteen units per period.

*Cournot Equilibrium.*   If $\partial x_i / \partial x_i = 0$, each seller is assuming that price reductions will be met with sufficient speed to protect sales volume measured in physical units. If quantities rather than prices are viewed as the control variables, then according to this model each seller plays a best reply strategy against the quantities offered by the other seller. The equilibrium is thus of the Nash variety. If volumes are nearly equal, the price which supports the Cournot equilibrium is $1.04. The volume prediction is fourteen units.

*Price Leadership Joint Maximum.*   Each of the two large firms may believe that price cuts will stimulate further price cuts. If it is believed the competitive reaction will be sufficiently vigorous to protect existing volume and also share in new market volume created by lowered prices, then $\partial x_i / \partial x_i > 0$. A joint maximum occurs if $\partial x_i / \partial x_i = 1$. With this assumption a quick derivation will demonstrate that the price result is the same as if the two large firms combined to form a price-leading dominant firm. The price prediction of the model is $1.25, and the total volume prediction is twelve units per period.

*Global Joint Maximum.*   If all sellers maximized total joint profits, the price would be $1.42, and volume would be ten units per period.

Models of this sort while commonly used are obviously incomplete. No hint is provided about which model might apply for any given treatment variable. The controversy generated by the Ethyl case adds a new dimension and justifies the formation of three hypotheses. One is that the treatments have no effect at all and thus the same model should apply across all treatments. An alternative taken from the FTC arguments is that the treatments have an effect on prices and that prices under treatment (LAYY) will equilibrate near the price leadership joint maximum and (N-NN) yield prices below that. A third is that prices under treatments which incorporate only some of the practices should lie in between those of (LAYY) and (N-NN).

## IV. EXPERIMENTS

Eleven experiments were conducted under several different configurations of the practices as shown in table 2.[9] In all cases the economic parameters are identical and

---

9. A total of twenty-four experiments were conducted. The first eight were considered as pilots in which many of the system bugs were eliminated. Several of the twenty-four were conducted prior to the construction of the price signaling device discussed above and all were discarded because of various problems relating to procedures, records, mistakes, *etc.* Two more experiments were eliminated, one because of a rule infraction involving a binding commitment to a future contract, and a second because it was conducted in a different facility where telephone conversations could be overheard by other buyers and sellers. The latter problem was discovered only after a subject called it to the authors' attention near the end of the experiment.

## TABLE 2

### Periods of Experiments in which Various Practices Were Operative

| Group | Price Publication {N, A, L}* | Receiver Units Holders {A, B}** | Most Favored Nation {Y, N}*** | Advance Notification {Y, N}*** | 1 | 2 | 3 | 4 | 5 | 6 | 7 | 8 | 9 | 10 | 11 |
|---|---|---|---|---|---|---|---|---|---|---|---|---|---|---|---|
| I | N | — | N | N | 1-20 | 1-20 | 1-11 | 1-4 | | | | | | | |
| I | A | B | N | N | | | 16-17 | 16-18 | | 1-11 | 20-25 | | 1-8 | | |
| II | A | B | Y | N | | | | | 1-10 | | | 1-15 | | | |
| III | L | A | N | N | | | | 5-15 | | | | | | | |
| IV | A | A | Y | N | | | | | 11-16 | | | | 18-20 | 22-25 / 1-9 | 10-16 |
| V | L | A | Y | Y | | | 12-15 | | | 12-18 | 1-19 | 16-23 | 9-17 | 10-21 | 1-9 / 17-18 |
| V | A | A | Y | Y | | | | | | | | | | | |
| V | L | A | N | Y | | | | | | | | 24 | | | |

*N = no seller published; A = all sellers published; L = only large sellers published.

**A = all participants see price publication; B = only buyers see price publication.

***Y = yes, the provision is operative; N = no, it is not operative.

constant for the duration of the experiment. In most cases a change in practices occurred during the course of the experiment so that the effect of a change in practices could be studied.

## V. RESULTS

The average transaction prices for all periods of all experiments are graphed in figure 3. The graphs also contain a reference to the practices which were in force when the transactions occurred. For example, in the first eleven periods of experiment 3 which operated without the practices, average price can be seen converging toward the competitive equilibrium. Imposition of the practices during period 12 is accompanied by an immediate average price jump. When the practices are removed in period 15, the average price immediately falls.

It is apparent from figure 3 that there is a substantial correlation between prices in consecutive periods. Thus, in assessing statistically the effects on transaction prices of the different market institutions, all observations cannot simply be combined into a single data set and use ordinary least squares. Estimation of a variety of dynamic models with autocorrelated error structures was considered, but rejected for two reasons. First, it is clear that generally accepted theoretical models of the dynamic adjustment of these types of markets do not exist. Second, and more important, this paper did not wish to deflect attention away from the basic issue, *viz.*, did the different institutional arrangements affect prices in a systematic and economically (as well as statistically) significant fashion? The statistical analysis performed was quite simple: rather than pooling observations sequentially within a given experimental setting, observations were combined at corresponding points across treatments and experiments. For example, one data set consists of all first periods of each treatment; another of all second periods; etc. This procedure should remove any serial dependence but, of course, does so at the cost of a substantial reduction in sample size. Note also that treating the first, second, *etc.* observations after each treatment change as a "first period" observation is to some degree arbitrary.

The seven treatment variables listed in table 1 were incorporated as binary variables in an analysis of variance, and the results are reported in table 3.[10] Each coefficient shown is the average price over all experiments for the indicated period of the treatment. For example, the average of first periods prices for treatment (ABYN) is $.70, and the average of first periods prices for treatment (AAYY) is $.85. The average of last periods prices (for treatments longer than four periods) is lowest for (ABYN) at $.52 and is highest for (AAYY) at $.90.

The analysis of price data is contained in three different subsections below, and an analysis of volume and efficiency follows those. Unless otherwise stated, all results will refer to the final period average prices of treatments lasting at least five consecutive periods. The tables summarizing the results provide data for other periods also but for the sake of brevity we shall not discuss them in detail.

---

10. The average prices for each period are taken as the dependent variable for the analysis of variance and they were not weighted to reflect differences in sample size (which for most treatments were small) as the volume or number of transactions is endogeneous to the system.

## FIGURE 3a

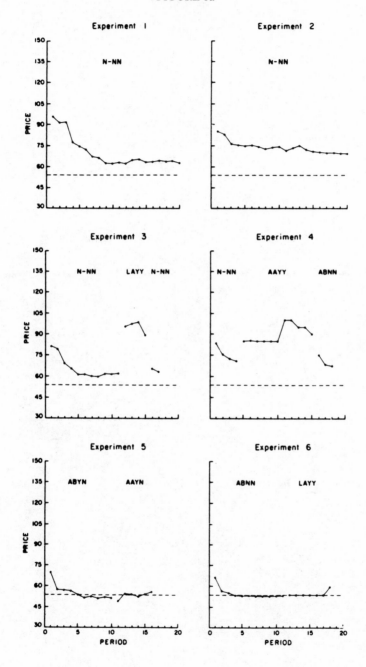

## FIGURE 3b

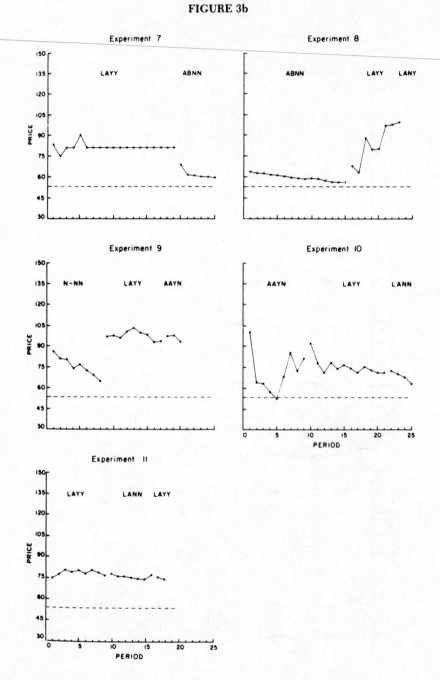

## TABLE 3

| | | First Period (n=25) | | Second Period (n=25) | | Third Period (n=23) | | Fourth Period (n=21) | | Fifth Period (n=18) | | Sixth Period (n=18) | | Seventh Period (n=17) | | Eighth Period (n=15) | | Last Periods* (n=18) | |
|---|---|---|---|---|---|---|---|---|---|---|---|---|---|---|---|---|---|---|---|
| | | Estimated Coefficient | Standard Error | Estimated Coefficient | Standard Error | Estimated Coefficient | Standard Error | Estimated Coefficient | Standard Error | Estimated Coefficient | Standard Error | Estimated Coefficient | Standard Error | Estimated Coefficient | Standard Error | Estimated Coefficient | Standard Error | Estimated Coefficient | Standard Error |
| I | N-NN | 83 | 5.8 | 79 | 5.4 | 78 | 5.8 | 73 | 4.5 | 72 | 6.0 | 71 | 6.0 | 68 | 5.6 | 66 | 4.4 | 66 | 5.7 |
| | ABNN | 69 | 7.1 | 62 | 6.6 | 62 | 6.5 | 59 | 5.8 | 58 | 6.9 | 58 | 6.9 | 60 | 6.5 | 56 | 5.0 | 57 | 6.6 |
| II | ABYN | 70 | 14.3 | 57 | 13.2 | 57 | 13.0 | 56 | 10.0 | 54 | 12.0 | 52 | 12.0 | 53 | 11.2 | 51 | 8.7 | 52 | 11.4 |
| III | LANN | 79 | 8.2 | 73 | 9.3 | 72 | 9.2 | 69 | 7.1 | 75 | 12.0 | 75 | 12.0 | 77 | 11.2 | — | — | 77 | 11.4 |
| IV | AAYN | 82 | 8.2 | 72 | 7.6 | 70 | 7.5 | 55 | 7.1 | 53 | 8.5 | 62 | 8.5 | 86 | 11.2 | 68 | 8.7 | 69 | 8.1 |
| V | LAYY | 80 | 5.0 | 77 | 4.7 | 81 | 4.9 | 80 | 3.8 | 79 | 4.9 | 81 | 4.9 | 82 | 4.6 | 85 | 3.9 | 80 | 4.7 |
| | AAYY | 85 | 14.3 | 86 | 13.2 | 85 | 13.0 | 85 | 10.0 | 85 | 12.0 | 85 | 12.0 | 100 | 11.2 | 100 | 8.7 | 90 | 11.4 |
| Standard Error Regression | | 14.3 | | 13.2 | | 13.0 | | 10.0 | | 12.0 | | 12.0 | | 11.2 | | 8.7 | | 11.4 | |
| R² | | .15 | | .27 | | .36 | | .59 | | .56 | | .54 | | .66 | | .83 | | .59 | |
| I | | 77 | 4.6 | 72 | 4.4 | 71 | 4.5 | 68 | 3.8 | 66 | 4.6 | 65 | 4.5 | 64 | 4.4 | 62 | 3.7 | 62 | 4.3 |
| II | | 70 | 14.4 | 57 | 13.9 | 57 | 13.5 | 56 | 10.6 | 54 | 12.2 | 52 | 12.0 | 53 | 11.7 | 51 | 9.8 | 52 | 11.3 |
| III | | 79 | 8.3 | 73 | 9.8 | 72 | 9.6 | 69 | 7.5 | 75 | 12.2 | 75 | 12.0 | 77 | 11.7 | — | — | 77 | 11.3 |
| IV | | 82 | 8.3 | 72 | 8.0 | 70 | 7.8 | 55 | 7.5 | 53 | 8.6 | 62 | 8.5 | 86 | 11.7 | 68 | 9.8 | 69 | 8.0 |
| V | | 81 | 4.8 | 78 | 4.6 | 82 | 4.8 | 81 | 3.8 | 80 | 4.6 | 82 | 4.5 | 85 | 4.4 | 87 | 4.0 | 82 | 4.3 |
| Standard Error Regression | | 14.4 | | 13.9 | | 13.5 | | 10.6 | | 12.2 | | 12.0 | | 11.7 | | 9.8 | | 11.3 | |
| R² | | .04 | | .11 | | .67 | | .47 | | .46 | | .46 | | .55 | | .73 | | .52 | |

*Of treatments at least five periods long.

A. *Practices as a Group*

A central issue raised by the Ethyl case is whether the practices taken as a set have an effect independent of the market structure. One answer is found in the data for the last periods.

*Conclusion 1.* Average price under treatment (LAYY) is higher than average price under treatment (N-NN).

In the markets examined by this study a one-sided t-test of the hypothesis that prices under (LAYY) are equal to those under (N-NN) is rejected at the .05 level of significance ($t = 1.9$). The alternative hypothesis is that prices under (LAYY) are higher.

As argued earlier, little difference between (AAYY) and (LAYY) was expected. Furthermore, since prices under (LAYY) and (AAYY) are not significantly different from each other ($t = 0.8$) it seems reasonable to ask if prices in (N-NN) are less than prices under (LAYY) and (AAYY), and the answer is yes ($t = 2.3$) at the .025 level. This paper also argued *a priori* that (ABNN) was similar to (N-NN). If one groups (ABNN) with (N-NN), the resulting prices are significantly lower than they are in (AAYY) and (LAYY) ($t = 3.0$) at significance levels of .005. None of the pooling would be objectionable on statistical grounds, *i.e.*, the F-statistics are not close to being significant.

The average prices under (LAYY) vary a good deal from experiment to experiment, while those obtained with (N-NN) appear to be less variable. Using F-statistics to test the equality of the variances (for single periods) leads to rejection of the null hypothesis (level of significance .01) in some periods but not for others. In order to ensure that the reported results were not sensitive to the assumptions underlying the F- and t-statistics, the Wilcoxin rank sum statistic (Lehmann 1975, ch. 1) was computed for the fourth, eighth, tenth, and final periods (of regimes at least five periods long). Generally the results are the same as those reported in the preceding paragraph. Prices under (LAYY) are significantly higher than those used under (N-NN), and grouping the various treatments simply increases the significance levels.

It is concluded that the practices together operate to decrease price competition beyond that which can be attributed to structure alone. This conclusion holds when comparing (N-NN) against (LAYY), and continues to hold where one groups the treatment *a priori* close to (N-NN) and compares the prices with those in (AAYY) and (LAYY). In fact the only effect of the grouping is to increase the level of significance, but the qualitative conclusion is the same throughout, *viz.*, as a group practices matter.

B. *Results: Model Accuracy*

Which of the competing models most accurately capture the behavior of prices? Prices with none of the practices (average of last periods was $.66) tend to be above the competitive equilibrium ($.54) with the difference significant at the .05 level (one-tailed test; see table 4) and are far below the Cournot or joint maximum equilibria.

*Conclusion 2.* Prices under treatment (N-NN) are above the competitive equilibrium.

From the sum of squared residuals in table 4 it can be seen that the likelihood ratio (which depend only on the ratios of the resultant sums of squares) favors the competitive equilibrium model over the Cournot or any of the other models. On this

### TABLE 4

t-Ratios and Sum of Squared Residuals
For Alternative Models

| Treatment | | Competitive (54) | Cournot (104) | Leader's Joint Maximum (125) |
|---|---|---|---|---|
| ´N-NN | t | 2.1* | 6.7ᵇ | 10.4ᵇ |
| | SSR | 2,012.2 | 7,202.2 | 15,360.2 |
| LAYY | t | 5.5ᵇ | 5.1ᵇ | 9.6ᵇ |
| | SSR | 5,492.2 | 4,892.2 | 13,586.2 |
| AAAY | t | 3.2ᵇ | 1.2 | 3.1* |
| | SSR | 2,732.2 | 1,632.2 | 2,661.2 |

a.    significant at .05 level.
b.    significant at .01 level.

criterion, conclusion 3 is accepted. This conclusion is not sensitive to pooling (ABNN) with (N-NN).

*Conclusion 3.* Prices under treatment (N-NN) are closer to the predictions of the competitive equilibrium than to the predictions of the other models.

Average price under (LAYY) is $.80 almost midway between the competitive equilibrium and the Cournot prediction and approximately five standard deviations away from each. Statistical tests lead to the rejection of a hypothesis that the data were generated from either model at conventional significance levels. Of course, the likelihood ratio favors the Cournot equilibrium over the competitive equilibrium (slightly) or the predictions of any other of the listed models. Thus, by that criterion, strictly applied, the Cournot model wins. Prices from treatment (AAYY) are higher ($.90) and are not significantly different from Cournot at conventional levels ($t = 1.2$). As well, they are significantly different from the predictions of other models, providing a bit more support for the Cournot model. However, when (LAYY) and (AAYY) are pooled, the mean price is closer to the Cournot than under (LAYY) alone but the reduction in variance does not appreciably influence significance levels obtained with (LAYY) alone. Thus, conclusion 4 is obtained from the data.

*Conclusion 4.* Prices generated in markets with all the practices are almost equidistant from the competitive equilibrium and the Cournot equilibrium.

With respect to the questions initially posed the following answers can be supplied. First the prices in markets without any of the practices are above the competitive equilibrium. Thus some support is generated for the idea that market structure alone will foster noncompetitive results.[11] Secondly, the practices as a set cause significantly higher prices. Of the models considered, the most appropriate model in

---

11. A more extensive examination of this proposition should include as a hypothesis that the shape of the supply curve may be important.

markets without practices is the competitive model. In markets with practices the competitive model and the Cournot model apply with equal force with a slight advantage to Cournot.

The fact that the joint maximum models can be rejected is important. A reasonable extension of the FTC theory of the Ethyl case leads to a type of leadership joint maximum prediction and so the natural extension of the FTC model may thereby be rejected as well. This result leaves the authors without a complete theory of the influence of the practices. It could be argued that prices near the Cournot equilibrium constitute a "local equilibrium" in a process that would terminate ultimately at the joint maximum had it not gotten "stuck." The "lumpiness" of the units induces a type of discontinuity near the Cournot equilibrium which might be difficult to pass through.[12] It might be conjectured that "smoother" demand functions would yield the leadership joint maximum. Certainly this conjecture may be checked with additional experimentation.

## C. *Analysis of Individual Practices*

This study was not designed to explore the possible effects of each practice independently. Only seven of the twenty possible treatment variables were implemented. However, early in the study it became clear that it might be possible to gather some data on the issue of the effects of individual practices without compromising the major goal of studying the practices as a group. The discussion in this section should be regarded as conjectures as to what additional experiments would yield, and points out that most of the findings are not statistically significant at conventional levels.

The following ANOVA model summarizes what the data was thought to contain. Paired comparisons were conducted but that analysis led to the same general conclusions. See table 5.

$$\bar{p} \;=\; 66X_0 \;+\; 62X_1 \;+\; 13X_2 \;+\; (-7)X_3 \;+\; 25X_4$$

| SE | (5.85) | (5.85) | (9.48) | (10.95) | (9.48) |
| t | (11.25) | (10.54) | (1.37) | (-.67) | (2.68) |

$\bar{p}$ = average price in cents of last period's regimes

$X_0$ = 1 if regime is N-NN; 0 otherwise

$X_1$ = 1 if price publication takes values $A$ or $L$; 0 otherwise

$X_2$ = 1 if all participants receive price publication; 0 otherwise

$X_3$ = 1 if most favored nations is required; 0 otherwise

$X_4$ = 1 if advanced notice is required; 0 otherwise

Sum of squared residuals = 1780.67

Standard error or regression = 11.70

Number of observations = 18

---

12. See Scherer (1970, pp. 206-208) for a discussion of how lumpy demand makes price coordination difficult.

### TABLE 5

Pairwise t-Ratios

| Treatment | N-NN | ABNN | ABYN | LANN | AAYN | LAYY | AAYY |
|-----------|------|------|------|------|------|------|------|
| N-NN | 0 | 0.803 | 1.098 | 0.863 | 0.303 | 1.895ᵃ | 1.883ᵃ |
| ABNN | 0.803 | 0 | 0 380 | 1.518 | 1.148 | 2.839 | 2.505 |
| ABYN | 1.098 | 0.380 | 0 | 1.551 | 1.216 | 2.271 | 2.357 |
| LANN | 0.863 | 1.518 | 1.551 | 0 | 0.572 | 0.243 | 0.806 |
| AAYN | 0.303 | 1.148 | 1.216 | 0.572 | 0 | 1.175 | 1.502 |
| LAYY | 1.895 | 2.839ᶜ | 2.271ᵇ | 2.271ᶜ | 1.175 | 0 | 0.811 |
| AAYY | 1.883 | 2.505ᵇ | 2.357ᵇ | 0.806 | 1.502 | 0.811 | 0 |

a.   $t_{05}$ = 1.796

b.   $t_{025}$ = 2.201

c.   $t_{01}$ = 2.718

This model was tested against a model with all of the $X$ variables interaction terms. The hypothesis of zero interaction cannot be rejected. However, the design as implemented had only seven (of 20) nonempty cells so the test is not very powerful which means further experimental results may only be conjectured.

*Conjecture:* The effects of the variables are additive.

This conjecture, if supported, will be very important. Additivity has been assumed in econometric efforts to ascertain, from the effects of changes in individual practices, information about how practices function as a group. If additivity can be rejected, the principles of measurement used in the court proceedings could be questioned. Failure to reject additivity means the procedures used by expert witnesses passed an important test.

The positive coefficient of $X_2$ supports the idea that *public* price announcements decrease competition though the difference in price levels 66 and 75 is not statistically significant. The relatively low coefficient on $X_1$ suggests that the effect is muted if advertisements are unmonitored by competitors. The negative (not significant) coefficient on $X_3$ suggests that further experiments will demonstrate that the most favored nations clause, when taken alone, will have a negative effect on price. Such a conjecture is contrary to the information theory advanced by the FTC. The final (significant) coefficient can be interpreted as a positive effect on prices of the advance-notice-of-price-changes practice.

The results regarding most favored nation and/or Robinson Patman type institutions are particularly interesting. It is conjectured that one key to understanding the influence of this practice is the structure of the demand side of the market. Small buyers pay higher prices. It may be that if small buyers constitute a large fraction of the market volume, prices with a most favored nation clause will be higher. Conversely, if the bulk of the market volume is from large buyers. the effect of the practice will be to lower prices.

## D. *Results: Volume and Efficiency*

Volume for the more competitive regimes (N-NN, ABNN, ABYN) tends to be greater than when the market practices are in effect (AAYY and LAYY). In fact, of the eight cases in the former group, five exceed all seven observations in the latter, two are tied with the maximal volume under (LAYY) and only one is less than the maximum (by one unit). As the differences are by and large not great, this paper shall not attempt a quantitative analysis. Volume tends to be higher in the *a priori* more competitive regimes and the probability of such an extreme occurrence by chance (in terms of ranks) is less than five percent.

The efficiencies tend to be near 100 percent. Thus, possibly contrary to expectations, at least in these markets the practices do not appear to lower efficiency systematically. Prices under the practices did not get sufficiently higher than the competitive equilibrium to substantially affect efficiency. This result is possibly related to the "lumpy" demand.

Finally, comments are made on the within period price variances. Two results appear noteworthy. First, there is a general tendency for variances to decline over time. Second, and of greater interest, there is substantially more price variability without the market practices. In fact there are a number of periods of (AAYY) and (LAYY) when all transactions take place at the same price which never occurs under (N-NN), (ABNN), or (ABYN).

## VI. CONCLUSIONS

The central issue for this study is whether or not market practices of the sort used in the lead-based antiknock compound industry can have an influence over and above industrial structure. The behavior of the simple markets studied here, with economic parameters as stipulated for the lead-based antiknock compound industry, depends significantly upon the existence of such practices. Market structure alone will not necessarily account for all prices and profits above the competitive equilibrium level. Without these practices prices are near, but still above, the competitive equilibrium and with all the practices present prices are significantly higher, about midway between the Cournot equilibrium and the competitive equilibrium. This result supports a presumption that facilitating practices in addition to industrial concentration is required to explain industrial performance. Of course the existence of the practices themselves may be due to structure.

The results of these experiments are consistent with other experimental findings. The behavior of the no-practice (telephone) markets are consistent with the original work of Hong and Plott (1982) who discovered a tendency for telephone markets to converge near the competitive equilibrium. Aspects of the practices resemble posted prices which are known to have an upward influence on prices (Plott and Smith 1978; Hong and Plott 1982; Smith 1981). The results are also consistent with those of Stoecker (1980) who demonstrates that conspiracy is not necessary for markets to diverge from competitive equilibrium. Thus, the conclusions advanced here can be seen as part of a more general pattern of results.

These results also suggest a more extensive investigation of the interrelationships among practices and the detail of the individual strategies they evoke. The FTC advanced such an extension of theory utilizing a hypothesis that information about a competitor's actions is the key variable. The data, however, indicate an incompleteness of that particular theory as follows: (i) a type of joint maximization model that may be deduced from the theory received little or no support from the data, and

(ii) one practice that appears to increase information about a competitor's actions resulted in lower prices. This is not to say that the FTC theory is without merit, since many of the other qualitative results are in accord with its theory.

The most difficult and important questions are related to the relevance of this study to the Ethyl case. Have similar practices led to higher prices in the lead-based, antiknock compound industry? Experiments alone cannot answer that question. In fact, experiments with the industry itself would not answer the question with certainty because the industry is so complicated that events would undoubtedly intervene to cloud any results. The experimental analysis makes clear, however, that efforts to measure the effects of the practices by the examination of industrial data necessarily encounter difficulties. Care must be exercised in the choice of the background set of practices against which the measurements are to be made. The analyst cannot simply assume, for example, that the prices will be near the Cournot equilibrium in the "absence" of practices because some types of practices induce near competitive equilibrium behavior. Furthermore, in assessing the effects of all practices the analyst might be able to rely on generating an overall assessment by examining the influence of one practice at a time, but an appropriate test of overall additivity could not be performed. The general conclusion drawn from the experiments is that practices analogous to those of the industry resulted in the highest prices of all the treatments studied. Naturally questions regarding the bases of the analogy with the industry will arise. Such questions may be answered by additional experimentation with other practices and parameters.

The Ethyl case itself has two closely related and important dimensions which these experimental markets do not address. Practices are endogenous to the operations of naturally occurring markets, while practices in the experimental markets were fixed and imposed. If the results of the experimental markets are indeed suggestive of the influence of the practices in the antiknock compounds markets, then sellers have an incentive to invent, design, and promulgate functionally equivalent practices. Interestingly enough, acceptance of such practices may be a Nash response by buyers even though collective acceptance is to their collective disadvantage. The structure of the industry may provide a set of conditions sufficient for institutional evolution and, regardless of the decision of the Commission, if enforced by the court, the respondents may develop alternative practices that are functionally equivalent. The experiments presented here do not address this important question. The second question not addressed by the research is the possibility that the practices perform functions in addition to those explored in the experiments related to cost reduction, risk reduction, etc. The absence of these latter considerations reflects the purpose for which the experiments were designed. That purpose was to test the claim, which has now been rejected, that the practices would in principle have no effect at all.

## APPENDIX:
## INSTRUCTIONS

### General

This is an experiment in the economics of market decisionmaking. Various governmental agencies have provided funds for this research. The instructions are simple and if you follow them carefully and make good decisions you might earn a considerable amount of money, which will be paid to you after the experiment.

In this experiment we are going to simulate a market in which some of you will be buyers and some of you will be sellers in a sequence of market trading periods. Each period you will be given an envelope labeled Buyer or Seller, containing an incentive sheet which describes the value to you of any decisions you might make during that period. An envelope for a given period is to be opened just before the beginning of that period. *You are not to reveal this information to anyone.* It is your own private information. A blank sample is attached here. [Note: While these are the instructions as read to the subjects, the actual procedures differed slightly. The incentive sheets were stapled together. When the sheet from one period was filled out and removed at the end of the period the next period's incentive sheet was then exposed.]

*Specific Instructions to Buyers*

During each market period you are free to purchase from any seller or sellers as many units as you might want. Study the incentive sheet. For the first unit that you buy *during a trading period* you will receive the amount listed in row (1) marked *1st redemption value*; if you buy a second unit you will receive the additional amount listed in row (5) marked *2nd unit redemption value*; etc. The profits from each purchase (which are yours to keep) are computed by taking the difference between the redemption value and purchase price of the unit bought. *Under no conditions may you buy a unit for a price which exceeds the redemption value.* In addition to this profit you will receive a 5 cent commission for each purchase. That is,

[your earnings = (redemption value) – (purchase price) + (.05 commission)].

Suppose for example that you buy two units and that your redemption value for the first unit is $200 and for the second unit is $180. If you pay $150 for your first unit and $160 for the second unit, your earnings are:

$$\$ \text{ earnings from 1st} \ = \ 200 - 150 + .05 = 50.05$$

$$\$ \text{ earnings from 2nd} \ = \ 180 - 160 + .05 = 20.05$$

$$\text{Total } \$ \text{ earnings} \ \ \ \ \ = \ 50.05 + 20.05 = 70.10$$

The blanks on the table will help you record your profits. The time of purchase, seller number, and the purchase price of the first unit you buy during the first period should be recorded on row (2). You should then record the profits on this purchase as directed on rows (3) and (4). At the end of the period record the total of profits and commissions on the last row on the page. Subsequent periods should be recorded similarly.

*Specific Instructions to Sellers*

During each market period you are free to sell to any buyer or buyers as many units as you might want. Study the sample form. The first unit that you sell during a *trading period* you obtain at a cost of the amount listed in row (2) marked *cost of 1st unit*; if you sell a second unit, you incur the cost listed in row (6) marked *cost of 2nd unit*; etc. The profits from each sale (which are yours to keep) are computed by taking the difference between the price at which you sold the unit and the cost of the unit. *Under no conditions may you sell a unit at a price below the cost of the unit.* In addition to this profit you will receive a 5 cent commission for each sale. That is,

[your earnings = (sale price of unit) – (cost of unit) + (.05 commission)].

Your total profits and commissions for a trading period, which are yours to keep, are computed by adding up the profit and commissions on sales made during the trading period.

Suppose for example your cost of the first unit is $140 and your cost of the second unit is $160. For illustrative purposes we will consider only a two-unit case. If you sell the first unit at $200 and the second unit at $190, your earnings are:

$$\$\text{ earnings from 1st} \;=\; 200 - 140 + .05 = 60.05$$

$$\$\text{ earnings from 2nd} \;=\; 190 - 160 + .05 = 30.05$$

$$\text{Total }\$\text{ earnings} \qquad =\; 60.05 + 30.05 = 90.10$$

The blanks on the table will help you record your profits. The time of sale, buyer number, and the sale price of the first unit you sell during the first period should be recorded on row (1). You should then record the profits on this sale as directed on rows (3) and (4). At the end of the period record the total of profits and commissions on the last row on the page. Subsequent periods should be recorded similarly.

### Market Organization

The market in this commodity is organized as follows. We open the market for a trading period (a trading "day"). The period lasts for _____ minutes. Any buyer (seller) is free to telephone any seller (buyer) at any time during the period and place an order for one unit to be delivered at the end of the period. The price will be at the published price of the seller. (Note that contracts are only between buyers and sellers.) Each party is to say to the other the following: *(price), (the other trader), (time)*. An order is place *only* after both parties have made the above statement. All orders are for single units.

After an order is placed, the buyer and seller will record the time of the order and the published price on their record sheets. These should be recorded as demonstrated.

### Final Observations

1. Each individual has a large folder. All papers, instructions, records, etc. should be put into this folder. Leave the folder with us before leaving tonight. *Take nothing home with you.*

2. We are able to advise you a little on making money. First you should remember that pennies add up. Over many trades and a long period of time very small amounts earned on individual trades can add up to a great deal of money. Secondly, you should not expect your earnings to be steady. You will have some good periods and some bad periods. During bad times try not to become frustrated. Just stay in there and keep trying and earn what you can. It all adds up in the end.

Some people rush to trade. Others find it advantageous to "shop" or spread their trading over the period. We are unaware of any particular "best" strategies and suggest that you adapt accordingly.

The record forms sometimes lead people to think in terms of "markup" and "markdown" strategies. While we see not general problems here, they can lead to occasional mistakes in computing the returns from decisions.

3. Under no circumstances may you mention anything about activities which might involve you and other participants after the experiment (*i.e.*, no physical threats, deals to split up afterwards or leading questions).

4. Each individual will be paid in private. Your earnings are strictly your own business.

### Description of Market and Behavior

There are four sellers (A, B, I, O). From previous market behavior it appears that demand is inelastic (price changes do not substantially affect overall market volume) and prices have varied over a wide range. Sellers A and B have relatively large capacity, while I and O are smaller. There is also likely to be substantial excess capacity.

### Prices

Sellers A and B advertise prices by entering the price on the keyboard in the seller's office. These will be announced immediately through the public display. Sellers I and O operate telephone contracts with individually agreed upon prices. For A and B:

1. Price increases must be announced one *full* period prior to the period in which the price increase is to be effective.
2. Price decreases are effective immediately.
3. No discounts from advertised prices are permissible.

Display:

| Period | | | Price | | |
|---|---|---|---|---|---|
| | | | | | |

For A and B

```
        Computation                      Computation
          Period                            Period
├────────────┼──────────────┼────────────────┼────────────┤
t₀                        t₀ + 1                        t₀ + 2
```

Price increases in $t_0 + 2$ must be made before this point (last minute changes will result in an extension of the $t_0 + 1$ open). If price is *reduced* in $t_0 + 1$ this reduced price is the *highest* (s)he can charge in $t_0 + 2$.

### Approximate Price/Volume Relationships

The attached chart (Market Demand) provides a model of the relationship between price and total market sales volume. Choose any price on the vertical axis and move your finger horizontally to the curve (stepladdered). The distance moved horizontally to the curve indicates the approximate volume at that price. As can be seen, price decreases beyond a certain point result in very small increases in total market volume.

The numbers distributed along the curve reflect the total dollar volume of sales for all sellers together at each price.

Costs of sellers have a similar structure but they are not identical. Considerable capacity is available at costs in the mid fifty-cent range, especially for A and B. In these ranges sellers could easily supply more units than the buyers would want (as indicated by the volume on the attached chart).

# EXAMPLES

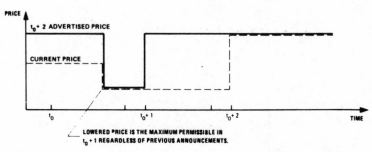

LOWERED PRICE IS THE MAXIMUM PERMISSIBLE IN $t_0 + 1$ REGARDLESS OF PREVIOUS ANNOUNCEMENTS.

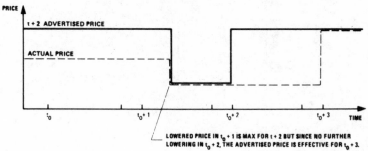

LOWERED PRICE IN $t_0 + 1$ IS MAX FOR $t + 2$ BUT SINCE NO FURTHER LOWERING IN $t_0 + 2$, THE ADVERTISED PRICE IS EFFECTIVE FOR $t_0 + 3$.

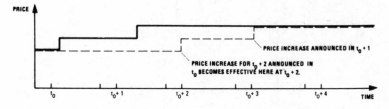

PRICE INCREASE ANNOUNCED IN $t_0 + 1$

PRICE INCREASE FOR $t_0 + 2$ ANNOUNCED IN $t_0$ BECOMES EFFECTIVE HERE AT $t_0 + 2$.

## MARKET DEMAND

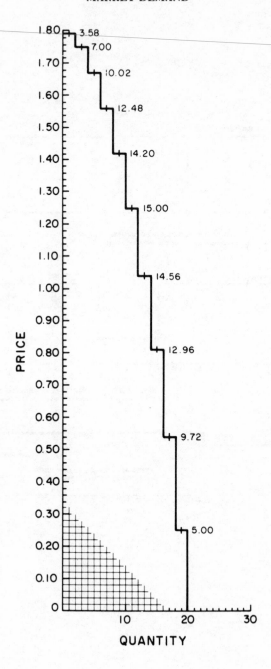

## SAMPLE — INCENTIVE SHEETS

RECORD OF EARNINGS

Trader No._____

| Period No. | Earnings |
|---|---|
| 1. | _____ |
| 2. | _____ |
| ⋮ | |
| 24. | _____ |
| 25. | _____ |

TOTAL EARNINGS _____

Name _____

Social Security No. _____

Buyer No._____ Period No._____

### RECORD OF PURCHASES AND EARNINGS -- BUYER

| Time | Seller # | Tentative Price | Unit Bought | Trading Period Number | | Unit Bought | Trading Period Number | | Time | Seller # | Tentative Price |
|---|---|---|---|---|---|---|---|---|---|---|---|
| | | | 1 | 1 | 1st unit redemption value | 11 | 41 | 1st unit redemption value | | | |
| | | | | 2 | Purchase price | | 42 | Purchase price | | | |
| | | | | 3 | Profit (row 1 - row 2) | | 43 | Profit (row 41 - row 42) | | | |
| | | | | 4 | Profit + commission | | 44 | Profit + commission | | | |

| Time | Seller # | Tentative Price | Unit Bought | Trading Period Number | | Unit Bought | Trading Period Number | | Time | Seller # | Tentative Price |
|---|---|---|---|---|---|---|---|---|---|---|---|
| | | | 10 | 37 | 10th unit redemption value | 20 | 77 | 20th unit redemption value | | | |
| | | | | 38 | Purchase price | | 78 | Purchase price | | | |
| | | | | 39 | Profit (row 37 - row 38) | | 79 | Profit (row 77 - row 78) | | | |
| | | | | 40 | Profit + commission | | 80 | Profit + commission | | | |
| | | | | | | | 81 | Total per period | | | |

Seller No._____ Period No._____

### RECORD OF SALES AND EARNINGS -- SELLER

| Time | Buyer # | Tentative Price | Unit Sold | Trading Period Number | | Unit Sold | Trading Period Number | | Time | Buyer # | Tentative Price |
|---|---|---|---|---|---|---|---|---|---|---|---|
| | | | 1 | 1 | Selling price | 11 | 41 | Selling price | | | |
| | | | | 2 | Cost of 1st unit | | 42 | Cost of 11th unit | | | |
| | | | | 3 | Profit (row 1 - row 2) | | 43 | Profit (row 41 - row 42) | | | |
| | | | | 4 | Profit + commission | | 44 | Profit + commission | | | |

| Time | Buyer # | Tentative Price | Unit Sold | Trading Period Number | | Unit Sold | Trading Period Number | | Time | Buyer # | Tentative |
|---|---|---|---|---|---|---|---|---|---|---|---|
| | | | 10 | 37 | Selling price | 20 | 77 | Selling price | | | |
| | | | | 38 | Cost of 10th unit | | 78 | Cost of 20th unit | | | |
| | | | | 39 | Profit (row 37 - row 38) | | 79 | Profit (row 77 - row 78) | | | |
| | | | | 40 | Profit + Commission | | 80 | Profit + Commission | | | |
| | | | | | | | 81 | Total per period | | | |

GRETHER AND PLOTT: MARKET PRACTICES: AN EXPERIMENTAL EXAMINATION    507

## REFERENCES

Complaint Counsel's Proposed Findings of Fact, Supporting Memorandum, Conclusions of Law and Order, vol. 1, April 30, 1981 [Public Version], pp. 108-112.

Fouraker, Lawrence E. and Siegel, Sidney, *Bargaining Behavior*. New York: McGraw-Hill, 1963.

Hay, George A., "The Oligopoly Problem: Theory and Policy," Mimeographed. Undated.

Hong, James and Plott, Charles R., "Rate Filing Policies for Inland Water Transportation: An Experimental Approach," *Bell Journal of Economics*, 13, Spring, 1982, 1-19.

Lehmann, E. L., *Nonparametrics: Statistical Methods Based on Ranks*. San Francisco: Holden-Day, 1975.

Lepage, Yves, "A Combination of Wilcoxin's and Ansari-Bradley Statistics," *Biometrika*, 58, 1971, 213-217.

_____, "A Table for a Combined Wilcoxin Ansari-Bradley Statistic," *Biometrika*, 60, 1973, 113-116.

Official Transcript of Proceedings before the Federal Trade Commission in the Matter of Ethyl Corporation, *et al.*, Docket no. 9128, 1980.

    Testimony of Dr. Dennis Carlton, pp. 7043-7066.

    Testimony of George Hay, pp. 3749-4404.

    Testimony of Dr. Jesse W. Markham, pp. 6808-09, 6861.

Plott, Charles R., "The Application of Laboratory Experimental Methods to Public Choice," in *Collective Decision Making: Applications from Public Choice Theory*, edited by Clifford S. Russell. Baltimore, Md.: Johns Hopkins University Press for Resources for the Future, 1979.

_____, and Smith, Vernon L., "An Experimental Examination of Two Exchange Institutions," *Review of Economics Studies*, 45, February 1978, 133-153.

Scherer, Frederic M., *Industrial Market Structure and Economic Performance*, Chicago: Rand McNally, 1970.

Smith, Vernon L., "Experimental Economics: Induced Value Theory," *American Economic Review*, 66, May 1976, 273-279.

_____, "An Empirical Study of Decentralized Institutions of Monopoly Restraint," in *Essays in Contemporary Fields of Economics in Honor of E. T. Weiler (1914-1979)*, edited by George Horwich and James P. Quirk. West Lafayette, Indiana: Purdue University Press, 1981.

Stigler, George J., "A Theory of Oligopoly," *Journal of Political Economy*, February 1964, 72, 44-61.

Stoecker, Rolf, *Experimentalle Untersuchung des Entscheidungsverhaltens im Bertrand-Oligopol*. Vol. 4 of *Wirtschaftstheoretische Entscheidungsforschung*. Institut für Mathematische Wirtschaftsforschung, Universität Bielefeld. Bielefeld, West Germany: Pfeffersche Buchhandlung, 1980.

Telser, Lester, *Competition, Collusion, and Game Theory*. Chicago: Aldine/Atherton, 1972.

United States of America before Federal Trade Commission. Public Record. Initial Decision, Docket no. 9128. "In the matter of *Ethyl Corporation, et al.*" August 5, 1981.

# [12]

Journal of Economic Behavior and Organization 5 (1984) 191–222. North-Holland

## THE EFFECTS OF MARKET ORGANIZATION ON CONSPIRACIES IN RESTRAINT OF TRADE

R. Mark ISAAC*

*University of Arizona, Tucson, AZ 85721, USA*

Valerie RAMEY*

*Stanford University, Stanford, CA 94305, USA*

Arlington W. WILLIAMS*

*Indiana University, Bloomington, IN 47405, USA*

Received August 1983, final version received December 1983

Mindful of the market structure–conduct–performance paradigm fundamental to industrial organization research, this paper uses laboratory experimental techniques to study the impact of conspiratorial opportunities on market performance. We compare 'posted-offer' markets where sellers (but not buyers) are allowed conspiratorial opportunities with observations from three control groups: (1) posted-offer markets without conspiratorial opportunities, (2) 'double-auction' markets with conspiratorial opportunities and (3) posted-offer markets with true single-seller monopolists. The basic conclusions generated by our experimental design are: (1) seller conspiracies in posted-offer markets tend to raise prices (but not profits) relative to similarly organized markets without conspiracies, (2) posted-offer conspiracies tend to generate higher prices (but not profits) than double-auction conspiracies, and (3) posted-offer monopolies tend to generate higher profits (but not prices) then posted-offer conspiracies.

## 1. Introduction

One of the fundamental paradigms of industrial organization research is the distinction between market structure, conduct and performance [see, for example, Scherer (1980)]. While this trichotomy might be used merely as a system of analytical organization, it can also take on the role of a theory of causality in which market structure determines conduct which determines performance. This latter structure–conduct determinism is evident in parts of the U.S. antitrust laws in which particular market structures or types of participant conduct are illegal *per se* regardless of any examination of the resulting market performance. A striking example of a *per se* prohibition is that which proscribes virtually any attempt to fix prices and/or quantities. As

*The authors gratefully acknowledge financial support from the National Science Foundation (through grants to Williams and to Professor Vernon L. Smith) and the University of Arizona College of Business and Public Administration (through its faculty summer research grant program).

the Supreme Court ruled in the Socony–Vacuum Case,[1] 'this Court has consistently and without deviation adhered to the principle that price fixing agreements are unlawful *per se* under the Sherman Act...'.

In a recent paper, Isaac and Plott (1981) report on the results of laboratory market experiments designed to test the linkages between the structural opportunities for market conspiracy, the conduct of participants, and ultimate market performance. They report that some of the links implicit in *per se* prohibition of price fixing were indeed strong. The opportunity for conspiracy was typically followed by the discussion of that possibility among the market participants. These discussions were, in turn, typically followed by agreements to implement conspiracies which were, in turn, followed by at least some market conduct indicative of attempts to enact the conspiratorial designs.

The weakest link found by Isaac and Plott was between the initial attempts to implement the conspiracies and the ultimate market performance. The conspirators (who could not discuss side payments nor look to any 'government' to enforce the agreements) were often unable to translate their designs into cartel-like outcomes (price, quantity or profitability). The authors state that, while the markets appear to have behaved differently than in the control (non-conspiracy) experiments, there was no clear evidence of a successful conspiracy equilibrium away from the competitive price and quantity. Contributing factors were (1) the conspirators did not know (except through actual trading) the nature of the market parameters, and (2) the high frequency of apparent cheating on the conspiratorial agreements.

Isaac and Plott conclude their paper with a conjecture that the market exchange mechanism could be an important determinant of market conduct and performance when conspiracies exist. Specifically, they suggest that their use of oral double-auction trading rules might have magnified the tendency for individuals to cheat on the conspiracies and that their results might have been different if the markets had been organized using posted-offer trading rules.[2] Posted-offer trading, by eliminating the possibility of price reductions within a given trading period, might serve to increase the ability of the conspirators to obtain consistently favorable market prices. On the other hand, posted-offer trading eliminates the possibility of successful first-degree price discrimination, which could render conspiracies less effective in extracting exchange surplus. This occurs because in posted-offer markets sellers have no mechanism for insuring that buyers with the highest marginal

---

[1] *United States v. Socony–Vacuum Oil Co., Inc.*, 310 U.S. 150 (1940).

[2] In posted-offer markets (see section 2), each seller posts an offer price and quantity, then buyers, in a random sequence, make purchases given the 'take it or leave it' prices entered by sellers. In double-auction markets, the trading procedures parallel those used on the floors of major stock and commodity exchanges; both buyers and sellers have the right to enter and accept price quotes (see footnote 6).

values (highest demand steps) will be forced to buy at the highest posted prices. Since each buyer rationally chooses the lowest offer price, it is the shopping sequence of buyers (rather than the ranking of marginal valuations) that determines the matching of purchase prices and marginal valuations. In this paper we report the results of a series of experiments designed to address the conjecture that market organization can make a difference in the performance of markets with opportunities for conspiracy in restraint of trade.

The posted-offer market is not simply a contrived alternative to the double auction. Because sellers post offer prices and quantities and then watch as buyers 'shop' among the postings, it characterizes the price formation mechanics found in certain retail markets. The critical distinction, however, is not merely one of retail versus wholesale markets. The essence of the posted-offer market is that it arises when it is relatively costly (perhaps prohibitively so) for sellers to negotiate a separate price for each trade. The posting of a multiple-unit 'take-it-or-leave-it' offer price replaces unit by unit bargaining. Certainly, the relatively large transactions costs of individual haggling are evident in many (but not all) retail markets as well as in some wholesale markets.[3] There are other types of transactions costs which could generate a posted-offer type market. One example, explored by Hong and Plott (1981), is government regulation. In some circumstances, a firm which is otherwise free to set price may be required to post that price with a government (or quasi-government) agency. These posted prices might be regulated in that they can be changed only at statutory intervals or with prescribed notice.[4] Thus, a posted-offer market captures the flavor not only of many retail markets but also of certain types of intermediate or professional markets for goods and services.

This research reports the results of six experiments in which conspiratorial opportunities are allowed among the sellers in a posted-offer market. Observations from these experiments are compared with experimental observations from three 'control' conditions: (1) posted-offer markets using identical market parameters but lacking conspiratorial opportunities, (2) true

[3]For example, in some U.S. oilfields, large purchasers of crude oil will post bids to buy crude oil from the producers.

[4]On June 18, 1982, the U.S. Supreme Court ruled illegal as a form of price fixing a coordinated price-posting system of Arizona doctors. According to the Tucson *Citizen*, the case involved two medical 'foundations' in Arizona representing over 70% of the physicians in the Phoenix and Tucson areas. The foundations announced a fee schedule after consulting with the member physicians. There was no indication of profit sharing arrangements in this plan. Since the fee schedules were technically maximum prices, individual physicians apparently still had some freedom to deviate from the posted scheduled, although private insurers, according to the *Citizen*, 'had to agree to pay member physicians up to the maximum fees for treating insured patients' if they desired foundation approval for their plans. The lower courts and the Supreme Court dissenters argued for a 'rule of reason' approach to the question, while the Supreme Court majority embraced the *per se* prohibition against price fixing.

single-seller monopolies using the same posted-offer market parameters and
(3) double-auction conspiracies using these same parameters (as a check of
the robustness of the Isaac–Plott conclusions using our design).

Since our primary conjecture is that using the posted-offer institution will
increase the frequency of cartel-like outcomes compared to the findings of
Isaac and Plott, a failure to observe them would raise further serious
questions about the validity of the antitrust structures based on structure–
conduct–performance criteria. Suppose, however, that non-competitive
outcomes are clearly observed. This would tend to support the traditional
arguments that, since certain market structures or patterns of conduct
foreshadow undesirable market performance, their occurrence can be a cause
for action even without checking their 'reasonableness'. Yet, given the results
of Isaac and Plott, this linkage would be much more subtle than previously
thought.

The paper is organized as follows: section 2 briefly describes the computer
operated posted-offer market, section 3 describes the experimental design and
market parameters, section 4 reports the experimental results, section 5
summarizes our conclusions and suggests areas for further research.

## 2. PLATO posted-offer trading procedures

The posted-offer experiments reported below use the PLATO
computerized trading mechanism described in detail by Ketcham, Smith and
Williams (1984). This program allows buyers and sellers sitting at individual
PLATO computer terminals to exchange an undefined homogeneous
commodity for a maximum of 25 market 'days' or trading periods. The
display screen for each buyer (seller) shows his/her private record sheet
listing marginal valuations (costs) for a maximum of five units potentially
purchased (sold) in each period. Sales are 'to order' in the sense that there
are no penalties, or carry-over inventories, associated with untraded units.
Consequently the assigned marginal valuations and costs induce the well-
defined flow supply and demand conditions described in section 3 [see Smith
(1982b) for a detailed discussion of induced valuation theory].

Each trading period begins with buyers being placed in a 'waiting loop'
and sellers being requested to select an offer price by typing a price into the
computer keyset. This offer is displayed privately on the seller's screen. The
seller is then asked to select a corresponding quantity to be made available
at that offer price. The maximum number of units a seller can offer
corresponds to the number of the last unit whose cost is not greater than the
offer price. The minimum number of units a seller can offer corresponds to
the number of the first unit whose cost is not greater than the offer price.
This procedure permits individual induced marginal costs to be declining,
constant or increasing. Since it is time and effort costly for a seller to
calculate the profit that any given offer may provide, PLATO always informs

the seller of the potential profit (loss) if all offered units are sold. When a seller is satisfied with the selected price and quantity, he/she taps a touch sensitive 'offer box' displayed on the screen. This action places, irrevocably, that seller's offer into the market. Before touching the 'offer box' the seller may change the price and/or quantity as many times as desired.

The viewing screen of each buyer displays one touch sensitive 'price box' for each seller in the market. After all sellers have entered their offers, each seller's offer price is posted in one of these boxes. PLATO then places the sellers in a 'waiting loop', randomly orders the buyers in a 'shopping' sequence, and then informs the first buyer that he/she may now begin purchasing the good. To purchase a unit from a particular seller, the buyer touches the box displaying that seller's offer price and then depresses a 'confirm' key on the keyset. Repeating this sequence causes a second unit to be purchased, and so on. Upon confirming the acceptance of a seller's offer, the seller is informed of this fact by PLATO and the contract information is automatically logged in both the buyer's and seller's record sheet. A buyer is allowed to purchase up to his/her buying capacity from any seller or sellers. A buyer cannot, however, purchase a unit whose price is greater than the unit's marginal valuation, and cannot buy from a seller who has sold all of the units offered. When a seller's last available unit is sold the price appearing in the buyer's box for that seller is replaced with the message 'out of stock' on the buyer's screen. After the first buyer has finished making purchases, the next buyer in random order may begin purchasing, and so on. The period ends when the last buyer completes this buying procedure.

It is important to emphasize that buyers and sellers have only limited information. All unit values (costs) assigned to individual buyers (sellers) are strictly private, known only to the subject (and the experimenter). Each buyer sees all of the seller's offer prices but not the quantities available at these prices. In the experiments reported below sellers saw the prices posted by other sellers, but the PLATO computer program allows this information to be suppressed.

The opportunities for conspiracy were organized as follows. In all of the multiple seller experiments, the sellers were told that, because of the multisite nature of the experiment, it was complicated to use the computer program to move from one trading period to another, and that this process would be facilitated if the sellers would leave their terminals for a few moments and wait in chairs adjacent to the terminals.[5] While seated in these chairs,

---

[5]This was not necessarily a ruse. We had a very specific reason for wanting to control the transition from one period to another. In the PLATO posted-offer program, the participants choose to move to the next trading period by pressing the NEXT key. Having pressed NEXT, subjects see a message that the market is 'waiting for *N* traders to get ready' before moving to the next period where *N* decrements as more press NEXT. The next period begins when all have pressed NEXT. If we had not controlled the transition, two undesirable events could have occurred. First, in the experiments with no conspiracy followed by conspiracy, buyers might very well have perceived that the period-to-period transition took only a few seconds in periods 1–10,

participants were given a printed summary of the previously posted offer prices of each seller and the quantity actually sold by each seller. (Providing this information was an attempt to keep participant information parallel with the Isaac–Plott experiments in which all trades were recorded on a blackboard.)

During non-conspiracy experiments, participants waited silently for about two minutes and then returned to their terminals. During conspiracy experiments, the participants were informed of the opportunity for discussion in language virtually identical to that of Isaac and Plott. Specifically, the participants were told that, while waiting in the chairs, they were free to discuss all aspects of the market except that (1) they could not discuss side-payments or physical threats, and (2) they could not discuss quantitative information about their payoff tables. The conspirators had a maximum of four minutes for discussion. Buyers (located in Indiana) were given no information about sellers' collusive opportunities.

## 3. Experimental design and market parameters

Market participants were volunteers recruited from the undergraduate student populations at Indiana University and the University of Arizona. All subjects were 'experienced' in the sense that they had participated in a previous posted-offer experiment (using entirely different market parameters). The experiments were run 'multisite' with buyers (in Indiana) and sellers (in Arizona) interacting through the PLATO computer system based at the University of Illinois.[6] Upon arriving at the PLATO lab subjects were paid $3 for keeping their appointment and then assigned to an individual computer terminal. At the experiment's conclusion subjects were paid, in cash, their accumulated earnings from the experimental market.

Table 1 classifies trading periods in each of the 14 experiments that we report on as being characterized by one of the following experimental conditions:

(1) Posted-offer, no conspiracy — all subjects (4 buyers, 4 sellers) were isolated at their terminals both during and between trading periods. No verbal communication was allowed; market information was transmitted solely via the posted-offer mechanism.

---

but up to four minutes thereafter. Second, in the conspiracy periods, buyers might have had an additional reason to assume the existence of a conspiracy if the repeated pattern was that the message 'waiting for 4' appeared on the screens in just a few seconds and then remained for up to four minutes. Therefore, we used a random number device to move some, but not all, of the seller terminals into the 'ready' mode across the waiting interval. Our concern was to standardize information flowing to the buyers. Coursey, Isaac, Smith (1984) offer evidence that buyers might strategically alter behavior based upon their perceptions of sellers' market power.

[6]The only exception to this rule was in the case of the monopoly experiments. Two of the experiments had the single seller in Indiana and the four buyers in Arizona.

Table 1

Experiment classification.

| | Experiment | Number of buyers, sellers | Final period | C.E. price |
|---|---|---|---|---|
| Posted-offer no seller conspiracy, periods 1–10; | po66 | 4,4 | 19 | 2.20 |
| conspiracy, periods 11–20 | po67 | 4,4 | 20 | 7.05 |
| Posted-offer seller conspiracy, all periods | po55 | 4,4 | 23 | 6.80 |
| | po59 | 4,4 | 15 | 6.80 |
| | po77 | 4,4 | 16 | 3.85 |
| | po83 | 4,4 | 15 | 5.75 |
| Double-auction seller conspiracy all periods | da64 | 4,4 | 10 | 6.80 |
| | da65 | 4,4 | 10 | 3.20 |
| | da69 | 4,4 | 10 | 5.10 |
| | da71 | 4,4 | 11 | 4.90 |
| Posted-offer monopoly, all periods | po92 | 4,1 | 25 | 5.75 |
| | po94 | 4,1 | 25 | 4.15 |
| | po102 | 4,1 | 20 | 5.75 |
| | po107 | 4,1 | 25 | 5.75 |

(2) Posted-offer, seller conspiracy — as discussed at the end of section 2, four sellers (in Arizona) were allowed to gather at a table away from their terminals for a four-minute verbal communication session between each trading period. Four buyers (in Indiana) were isolated and not informed that sellers were permitted to communicate. Sellers were not permitted to discuss side-payments or to make explicit mention of their individual unit costs during the communication sessions.

(3) Double-auction, seller conspiracy — conspiracy rules were the same as in posted-offer conspiracies, but using the PLATO double-auction mechanism.[7]

(4) Posted-offer, monopoly — a single seller was given a marginal cost array corresponding to the lowest 10 units in the supply array used in the non-monopolistic markets. Four buyers were isolated but were aware that there was a single seller.

From table 1 we note that four experiments were run using each of the double-auction and posted-offer seller conspiracy conditions, four experiments were run under the posted-offer monopoly condition, and two posted-offer experiments were run in which ten 'no conspiracy' trading

[7]The PLATO double-auction mechanism is described in detail by Williams (1980), and Smith and Williams (1983). In the interest of brevity, the specifics of computerized double-auction trading are not described in this paper.

periods were followed by a sequence of trading periods where sellers were allowed to conspire between periods.

Individual cost and valuation assignments and the resulting induced aggregate market supply and demand arrays are shown on the left of fig. 1. The competitive equilibrium (C.E.) quantity ($Q_0$) is seven units per period with C.E. prices defined over the ten cent interval centered on $P_0$ and bounded above (below) by the seventh step on the demand (supply) array. The market supply and demand arrays differed by an additive constant across experimental replications. The monopolist's profit maximizing price is sixty cents above $P_0$ ($P_m = P_0 + 0.60$) with three units exchanged ($Q_m = 3$). Buyers (sellers) earn the difference between unit valuation and price (price and unit cost) for each unit traded plus a five cent 'commission' to cover subjective transaction costs. Thus, buyers have a small inducement to trade a third unit at $P = P_m$. To equalize individual buyer earnings over the course of a posted-offer experiment, the four valuation sets (shown in fig. 1) were randomly reassigned or rotated among the buyers each trading period. Note that this design feature, (1) has no effect on the induced market demand across periods, (2) practically eliminates the possibility that, at ($P_m, Q_m$), two buyers would earn zero total profit (net of commissions), and (3) would presumably have little or no effect on contract prices since the only strategic action available to buyers is under-revelation of demand.

At a C.E. allocation ($P_0, Q_0$), total exchange surplus (exclusive of commissions) is \$6.00 per period split equally between buyers and sellers. At the sellers' joint profit maximizing allocation ($P_m, Q_m$) producer surplus is \$4.35 and consumer surplus is \$0.75. Defining an index of allocative efficiency ($E$) as actual buyer plus seller earnings (exclusive of commissions) expressed as a percentage of the maximum possible group earnings (at a C.E.), we note that $E = 85$ at ($P_m, Q_m$) if the three lowest marginal cost units trade.

Another criterion for evaluating market performance and, more specifically, the ability of monopolists and cartels to extract supracompetitive profit from the market is given by an 'index of monopoly effectiveness' defined as follows:

$$M = (\pi - \pi_c)/(\pi_m - \pi_c), \quad \text{where}$$

$\pi$ = sellers' realized total profits,
$\pi_c$ = theoretical total seller profits at C.E.,
$\pi_m$ = theoretical total seller profits at $P_m$.

Note that $M > 0$ holds if the seller(s) effectively raises profit above the C.E. level, with $M = 1$ corresponding to the theoretical single-price monopoly profits. If successful first-degree price discrimination is achieved, $M$ would be greater than 1. The use of this index of monopoly effectiveness to analyze the

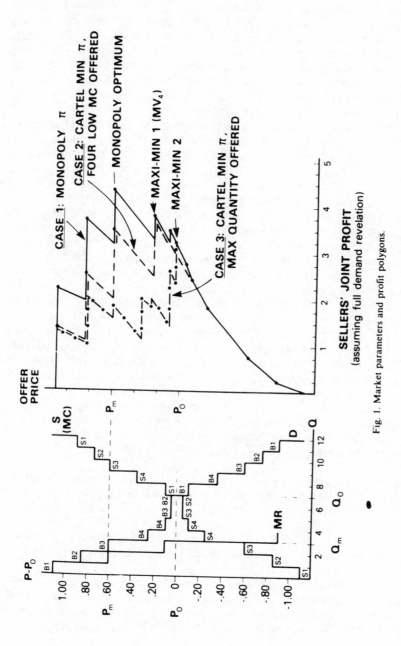

Fig. 1. Market parameters and profit polygons.

effects of seller conspiracies can paint a somewhat different picture than aggregate price and quantity data. A monopolist or cartel that sets price above $P_m$ will have a great impact on the market yet earn a smaller profit than at the C.E. This occurred in period 1 in po55, where sellers posted prices so high that no buyer could profitably purchase. A double-auction conspiracy with end-of-period price movements toward the C.E. may generate mean prices near the C.E. but large $M$ statistics if that price series resulted in successful price discrimination.

Before turning to the next section and the presentation of our experimental results, it is important to make note of some market design features that may be relevant to predicting outcomes in the posted-offer seller-conspiracy and monopoly experiments. First, since $Q_m = 3$, a four-seller cartel fixing prices at $P_m$ would have at least one member being completely rationed out. It seems reasonable to conjecture that the highest offer price allowing all four sellers to trade one unit could have some drawing power especially since specific discussions of earnings redistribution schemes were prohibited. Second, for a given offer price above $P_0$, it is quite possible that a cartel's (group) profit will be less than a monopolist's (assuming full demand revelation by buyers in both cases). This is true by virtue of the fact that our monopolists must trade 'up' the marginal cost array (lowest cost units first) while our cartels (not being fully 'rationalized') might not trade up the market supply array (although each seller must trade up his/her individual marginal cost array). A simple example of this is if each seller offers one unit for sale at $P_m$ and buyers choose (unknowingly) not to purchase the lowest-cost unit supplied. Thus at a fixed price and assuming full demand revelation, cartel profits can be considered a random variable rather than being strictly determined as in the monopoly case. The random nature of cartel profits is illustrated in the right-hand portion of fig. 1 which displays three possible group profit polygons for sellers. These profit polygons are constructed assuming that all sellers quote a single offer price, buyers fully reveal demand at this price, and one of the following conditions holds:

*Case 1.* Each seller offers for sale all units for which price exceeds marginal cost and the *lowest-cost* units supplied to the market always trade first (as in the case of pure monopoly).

*Case 2.* Each seller offers for sale only his/her first (lowest-cost) unit and the *highest-cost* of these units supplied to the market always trade first.

*Case 3.* Each seller offers for sale all units for which price exceeds marginal cost and the *highest-cost* units supplied to the market always trade first (the highest-cost unit available to buyers at a given point in time is constrained by the fact that each seller must trade his/her units in sequence from low-cost to high-cost).

Note that cases 1 and 3 place upper and lower bounds, respectively, on cartel profits for a given offer price assuming full demand revelation.

Two important points can be made based on the profit information displayed in fig. 1. First, the discrete (integer quantity) supply and demand arrays generate discontinuous seller profit polygons; the 'saw-toothed' nature of these polygons could cause a simple sequential price-search process (by a group-profit maximizing cartel or monopolist) to converge to any of the top four steps on the demand array, depending on the choice of the starting price and the size of the price increment/decrement. Second, the profit polygon labelled case 2 has a maximum value at a price corresponding to the *fourth* step on the demand curve ($P_m - 0.35$). For a cartel strategy based on each seller offering a single unit for sale at a fixed price, ($P_m - 0.35$) can be thought of as a maxi-min theoretic equilibrium; it maximizes the minimum possible cartel profit for a given offer price. If sellers offer for sale all units for which the offer price exceeds marginal cost, then the maximum value of the (case 3) profit polygon ($P_0 + 0.05$, the upper bound of the C.E. range) becomes the maxi-min price.

Taking all of these considerations into account, one might conjecture that a monopolist, and quite certainly a cartel, would have a difficult time finding and then maintaining prices at $P_m$. In particular, the fourth demand step appears to have potential drawing power for cartels quoting a single offer price.

# 4. Experimental results[8]

## 4.1. Double-auction, seller-conspiracy experiments

Figs. 2–5 display sequential contract prices and descriptive statistics for da64, da65, da69 and da71. These four double-auction control experiments were conducted to see if the basic seller-conspiracy results of Isaac–Plott could be replicated using our market parameters, experimental procedures and the PLATO computerized double-auction mechanism with multisite trading.

The data appear to be generally consistent with the Isaac–Plott results. In three of the four markets (da64, da65, da71) most prices were above the C.E. range but well below $P_m$. The opportunity for seller conspiracies and attempts to implement conspiracies appear to have caused these markets to deviate from the well-documented, robust tendency for C.E. convergence in

---

[8]As in Isaac–Plott, the 'early' links between the opportunity for conspiracy, discussions of conspiracy, plans for conspiracy and attempts to implement the conspiracy were robust. Therefore, we will focus our discussion on the 'final' link, that to market performance.

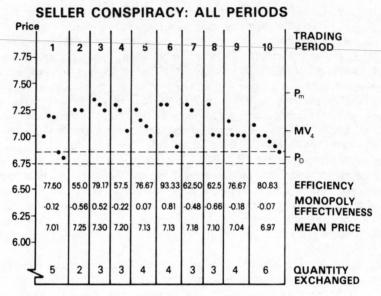

Fig. 2. Experiment da64.

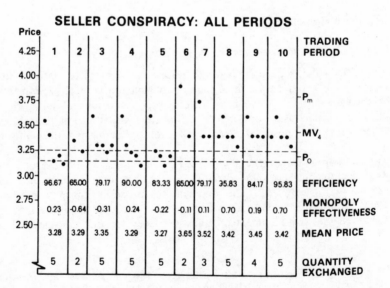

Fig. 3. Experiment da65.

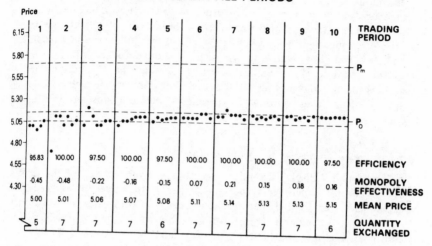

Fig. 4. Experiment da69.

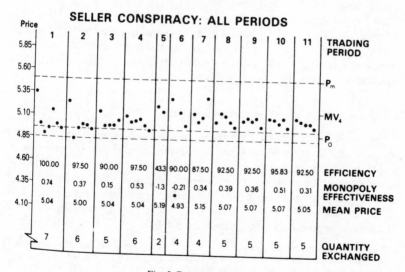

Fig. 5. Experiment da71.

double-auction markets.[9] Note, however, that none of the trading periods
had a zero variance price series. The conspiracies were not successful in
'fixing prices' in the sense of agreeing on a constant price from which no
deviations were to occur. Price series frequently started above the mean and
then decayed toward the C.E. in order to induce low-valuation buyers to
trade. Note, however, that the price series are not consistent with first-degree
price discrimination. Market efficiency and exchange volume in da64, da65,
and da71 were low relative to typical double-auction standards. In contrast
to this result, da69 converged rather quickly to the C.E. displaying an
average market efficiency near 100%. Isaac and Plott did not observe this in
any of their seller-conspiracy experiments but did observe this under
conditions of buyer conspiracy.

### 4.2. Posted-offer, no-conspiracy experiments

Figs. 6 and 7 display descriptive statistics and offer prices for the second
set of control experiments (po66 and po67). In these two posted-offer
experiments an initial ten period interval with no conspiratorial
opportunities served as a competitive control series for the posted-offer seller-
conspiracy and monopoly experiments presented below. Unaccepted offers to
sell are plotted as open circles and accepted offers (contract prices) are
plotted as solid dots. The mean contract price in both experiments converged
to the range of C.E. prices (from above) by the eighth trading period. This
result is consistent with the extensive documentation of the behavioral
properties of the PLATO posted-offer mechanism presented by Ketcham,
Smith and Williams (1984). We are thus confident that, in the absence of
conspiratorial opportunities, our market design will yield a behavioral
equilibrium which corresponds closely to the C.E.

### 4.3. Posted-offer, seller-conspiracy experiments

We next report the data from six posted-offer experiments with seller
conspiracies. Two (po66 and po67) provide intra-group comparisons by
introducing the opportunity to conspire after 10 periods without
conspiratorial opportunities. Four others (po55, po59, po77 and po83) allow
for intergroup comparisons by allowing seller conspiracies from period 1. In
all six experiments, the links from the opportunity to conspire to actual
attempts to implement a conspiracy were robust.

---

[9]See Smith (1982b), propositions 4 and 5, for additional discussion and documentation of
double-auction convergence properties. One ('inexperienced subject') double-auction experiment
without conspiratorial opportunities was conducted using the market design shown in fig. 1. The
results were consistent with previous double-auction experiments; the mean price was within 10
cents of $P_0$ after one trading period (averaging $P_0 + 0.05$ over all periods), volume was 6 or 7
units in all periods, and efficiency averaged 91 percent over all periods (somewhat low by
double-auction standards).

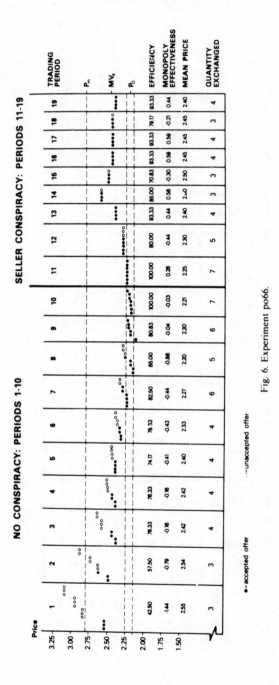

Fig. 6. Experiment po66.

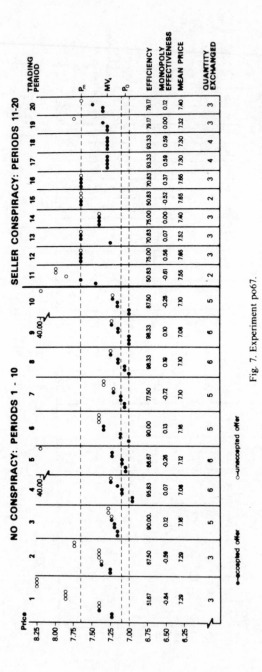

Fig. 7. Experiment po67.

In the experiments where seller conspiracies were allowed only after period 10 (figs. 6 and 7), notice that market performance became less competitive after the opportunities for conspiracy were allowed. However, neither group of sellers chose to consistently fix contract prices at $P_m$. Sellers in po66 coordinate the offer price posted, and contracts appear to have stabilized at a price very near the fourth step on the demand curve where, with full demand revelation by buyers, each seller trades one unit. Note that full revelation occurred in periods 16 and 17 but that under-revelation in period 18 was followed by a five cent price decline (and full revelation) in period 19. Experiment po67 displayed less price stability than po66 during periods 1–10 as well as periods 11–20. In periods 17 and 18, four contracts occurred at the fourth step on the demand array but this was followed by two periods of dispersed offers and an upward movement of the mean contract price.

Figs. 8 through 11 display sequential offer prices and descriptive statistics for experiments po55, po59, po77 and po83 where sellers were allowed to communicate prior to each trading period. Experiment po55 is striking in that sellers conspire to fix the market price at the C.E. price. In contrast with this, sellers in experiment po77 formed a fairly effective cartel, posting offers at $P_m$ in six of the final seven trading periods. Showing more sophistication than other seller groups, the cartel rotated the assignment of which individual would post a price above $P_m$ and thus not trade a unit. Experiments po59 and po83 both appear to have stabilized at a price near the fourth demand step. Prices in po59 were five cents below the fourth step in periods 10–15 with buyers fully revealing demand in five of these six periods. In po83, offer prices were slightly above the fourth demand step in periods 12–15 thus prohibiting a fourth unit from trading and lowering cartel profits. However, the gradual lowering of offer prices in the last few periods is a pattern consistent with eventually stabilizing at the highest price where buyers are willing to trade four units.

For the six posted-offer seller-conspiracy sessions we thus observe one market converging to the monopoly optimum price, one converging to the C.E. price, and four generating final contract prices in a range near the fourth demand step.

## 4.4. Posted-offer, monopoly experiments

Finally, we turn to the four experiments (po92, po94, po102 and po107) designed to observe the behavior of the same posted-offer market operating under a true monopoly. Figs. 12 through 15 display descriptive statistics and sequential offers for these experiments.

The seller in po102 was the least successful monopolist. He chose to offer units at the C.E. price in the last twelve periods of the experiment. This occurred in spite of the fact that in periods 1, 5, 6 and 8 charging a price above the C.E. resulted in larger profits. Based on informal comments at the

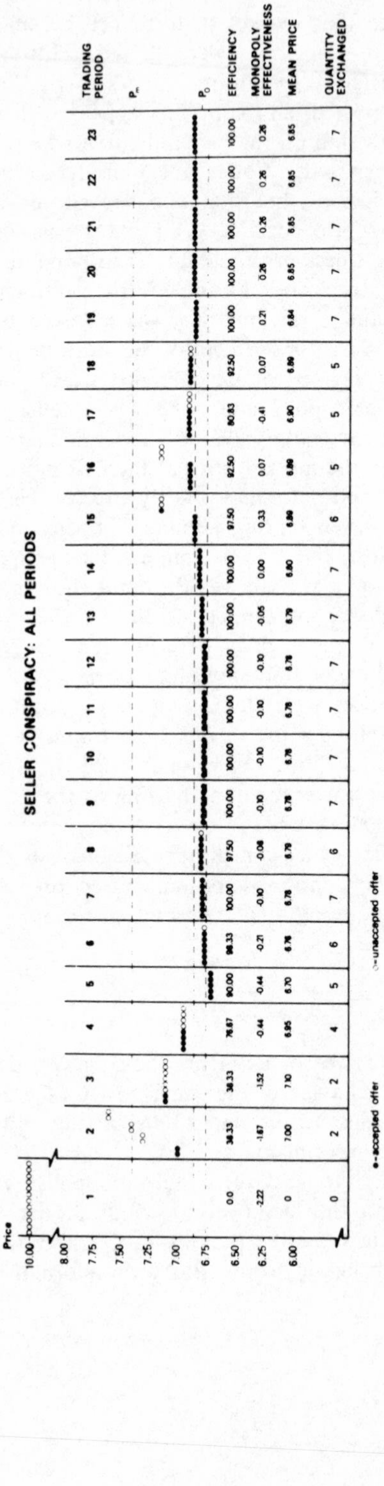

**SELLER CONSPIRACY: ALL PERIODS**

Price axis: 10.00, 8.00, 7.75, 7.50, 7.25, 7.00, 6.75, 6.50, 6.25, 6.00

● = accepted offer     ○ = unaccepted offer

| TRADING PERIOD | $P_c$ | $P_0$ | EFFICIENCY | MONOPOLY EFFECTIVENESS | MEAN PRICE | QUANTITY EXCHANGED |
|---|---|---|---|---|---|---|
| 23 | | | 100.00 | 0.26 | 6.85 | 7 |
| 22 | | | 100.00 | 0.26 | 6.85 | 7 |
| 21 | | | 100.00 | 0.26 | 6.85 | 7 |
| 20 | | | 100.00 | 0.26 | 6.85 | 7 |
| 19 | | | 100.00 | 0.21 | 6.84 | 7 |
| 18 | | | 92.50 | 0.07 | 6.80 | 5 |
| 17 | | | 80.83 | 0.41 | 6.90 | 5 |
| 16 | | | 92.50 | 0.07 | 6.88 | 5 |
| 15 | | | 97.50 | 0.33 | 6.88 | 6 |
| 14 | | | 100.00 | 0.00 | 6.80 | 7 |
| 13 | | | 100.00 | -0.05 | 6.79 | 7 |
| 12 | | | 100.00 | -0.10 | 6.79 | 7 |
| 11 | | | 100.00 | -0.10 | 6.79 | 7 |
| 10 | | | 100.00 | -0.10 | 6.79 | 7 |
| 9 | | | 100.00 | -0.10 | 6.79 | 7 |
| 8 | | | 97.50 | -0.08 | 6.79 | 6 |
| 7 | | | 100.00 | -0.10 | 6.79 | 7 |
| 6 | | | 98.33 | -0.21 | 6.79 | 6 |
| 5 | | | 100.00 | -0.44 | 6.70 | 5 |
| 4 | | | 76.67 | -0.44 | 6.95 | 4 |
| 3 | | | 38.33 | -1.52 | 7.10 | 2 |
| 2 | | | 38.33 | -1.67 | 7.00 | 2 |
| 1 | | | 0.0 | -2.22 | 0 | 0 |

Fig. 8. Experiment po55.

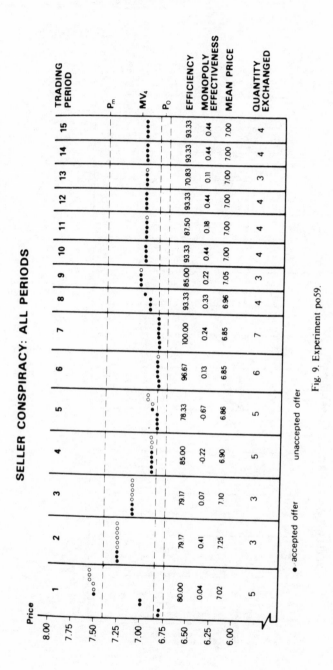

Fig. 9. Experiment po59.

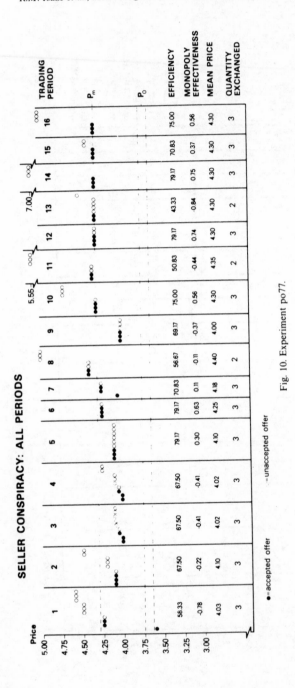

Fig. 10. Experiment po77.

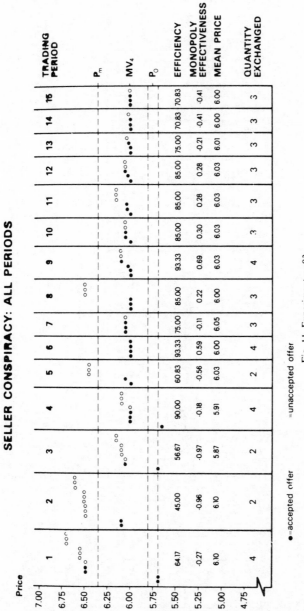

Fig. 11. Experiment po83.

212                    *R.M. Isaac et al., Market organization and conspiracies in trade*

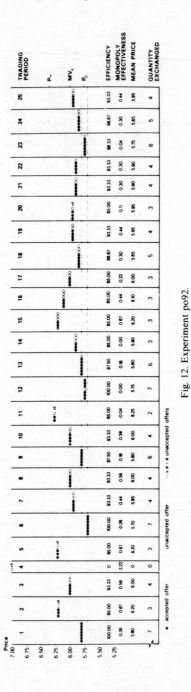

Fig. 12. Experiment po92.

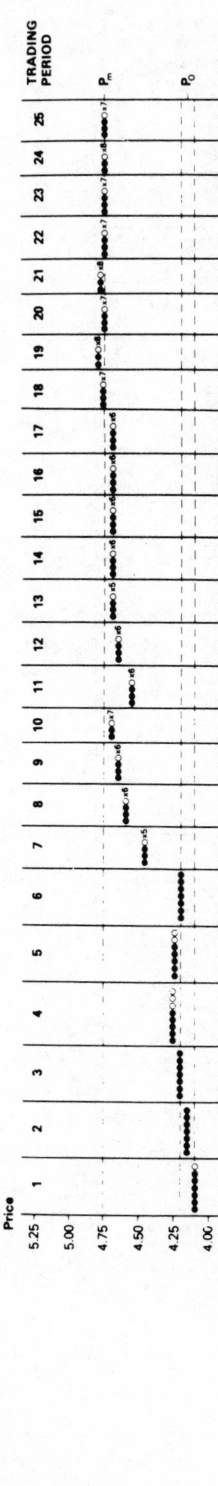

| TRADING PERIOD | 1 | 2 | 3 | 4 | 5 | 6 | 7 | 8 | 9 | 10 | 11 | 12 | 13 | 14 | 15 | 16 | 17 | 18 | 19 | 20 | 21 | 22 | 23 | 24 | 25 |
|---|---|---|---|---|---|---|---|---|---|---|---|---|---|---|---|---|---|---|---|---|---|---|---|---|---|
| EFFICIENCY | 98.33 | 100.00 | 100.00 | 96.67 | 96.67 | 100.00 | 85.00 | 85.00 | 85.00 | 56.67 | 85.00 | 85.00 | 85.00 | 85.00 | 85.00 | 85.00 | 85.00 | 85.00 | 85.00 | 85.00 | 65.00 | 85.00 | 85.00 | 65.00 | 85.00 |
| MONOPOLY EFFECTIVENESS | -0.26 | 0.00 | 0.26 | 0.30 | 0.26 | 0.21 | 0.33 | 0.67 | 0.78 | 0.04 | 0.56 | 0.78 | 0.87 | 0.87 | 0.87 | 0.87 | 0.87 | 1.00 | 0.18 | 1.00 | 0.17 | 1.00 | 1.00 | 0.13 | 1.00 |
| MEAN PRICE | 4.10 | 4.15 | 4.20 | 4.25 | 4.24 | 4.19 | 4.45 | 4.60 | 4.65 | 4.70 | 4.55 | 4.65 | 4.69 | 4.69 | 4.69 | 4.69 | 4.69 | 4.75 | 4.80 | 4.75 | 4.79 | 4.75 | 4.75 | 4.76 | 4.75 |
| QUANTITY EXCHANGED | 6 | 7 | 7 | 5 | 5 | 7 | 3 | 3 | 3 | 2 | 3 | 3 | 3 | 3 | 3 | 3 | 3 | 3 | 2 | 3 | 2 | 3 | 3 | 2 | 3 |

• = accepted offer  O = unaccepted offer  x# = # unaccepted offers

Fig. 13. Experiment po94.

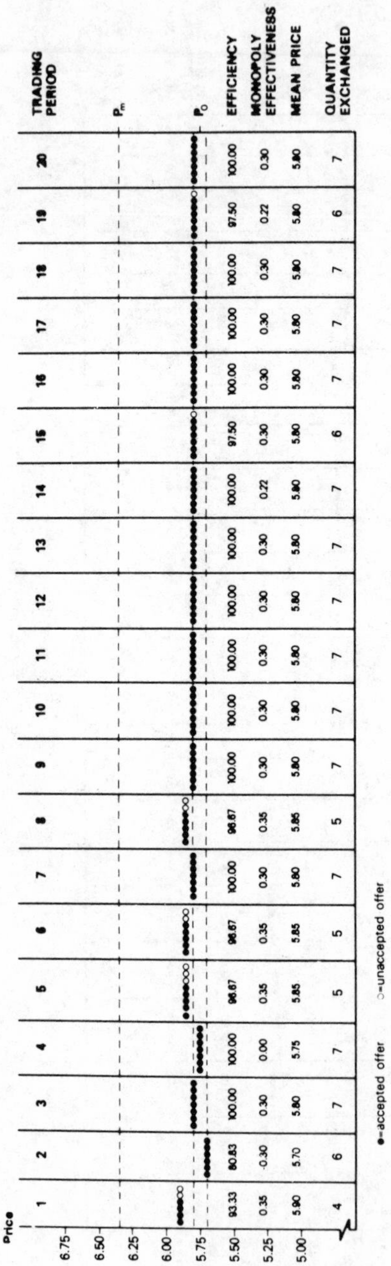

Fig. 14. Experiment po102.

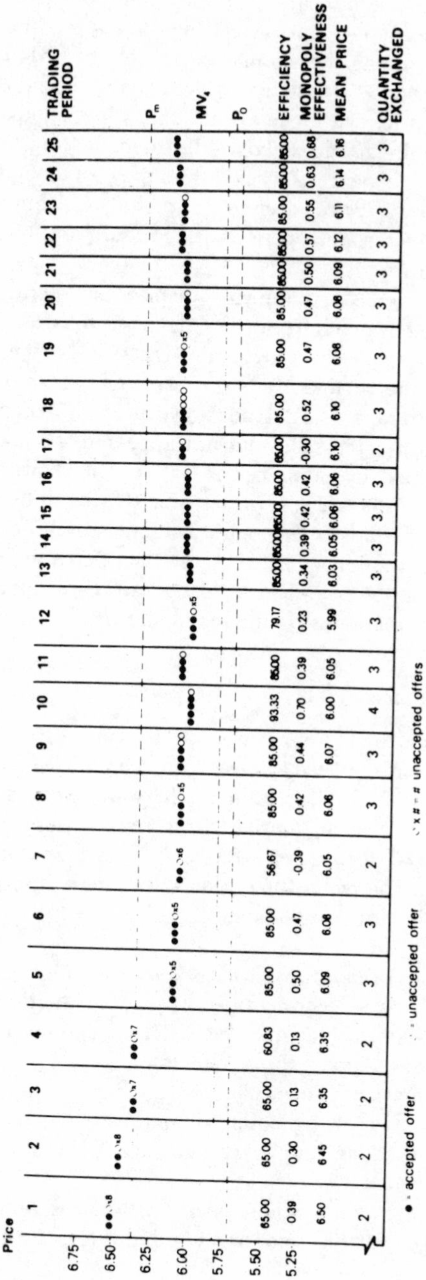

Fig. 15. Experiment po107.

experiment's conclusion, it appears that the monopolist was quite satisfied with his per period earnings and, given the effort-cost and preceived risk embodied in price searching, he simply chose not to deviate from the 5.85 offer price beyond period 9. In sharp contrast with this, the monopolist in po94 posted an offer price within ten cents of $P_m$ in periods 12 through 25. The seller's price searching was aided by full demand revelation after price increases in periods 7, 8 and 9. The withholding of one demand unit in period 10 resulted in a price decline in period 11, but there was full revelation after price increases in periods 12, 13 and 18 allowing the seller to successfully zero in on $P_m$.

The other two monopoly experiments display less extreme results. The contract prices in po92 wander from the C.E. price to a level slightly below $P_m$, eventually stabilizing in the range from the C.E. to the fourth demand step during the last nine periods. It is unclear what (if any) price-searching strategy the monopolist was using. Under-revelation of demand did occur in periods 11, 14 and 20 but the seller did not appear to be making full use of the information provided by other periods. In po107 the monopolist's offer price drifts in a range from the fourth demand step to midway between this price and $P_m$ during periods 5 through 25. Under-revelation of demand in periods 3 and 4, when the seller posted $P_m$ as the offer price, resuited in a 26 cent price decline in period 5 and most likely had a restraining influence on the monopolist's offer prices during the remainder of the experiment.

### 4.5. Analysis of pooled data

Fig. 16 presents a visual comparison of the time series of four market performance criteria (normalized mean price, volume, efficiency index and monopoly effectiveness index) for each of the four experimental groupings. The chartings are sample means derived from observations pooled across all intragroup experimental replications. Based on this empirical evidence (and figs. 2–15) we offer the following three general summary statements regarding *intragroup* market behavior:

(1) Opportunities for seller conspiracies tend to inhibit the empirically documented C.E. convergence properties of both the double-auction and posted-offer mechanisms. Of the ten seller-conspiracy experiments, two (da69, po55) do not support this statement.
(2) Double-auction markets with seller conspiracies do not converge to the monopoly profit-maximizing equilibrium (given the market parameters and procedure used in our experiments). All four double auctions support this statement.
(3) Posted-offer markets with either seller conspiracies or monopolies tend not to converge to the monopoly equilibrium (using our market

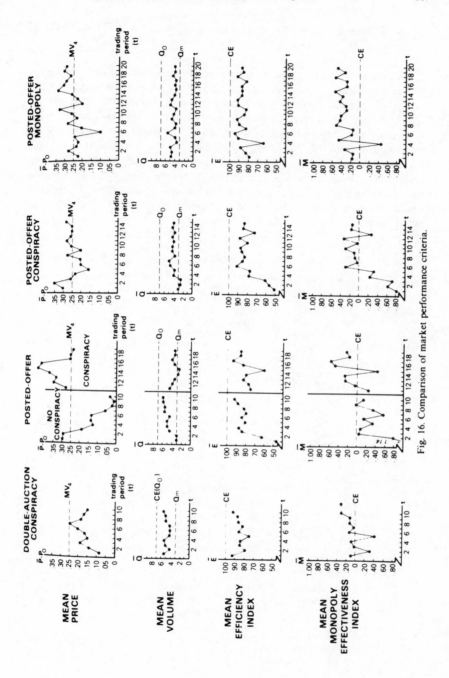

Fig. 16. Comparison of market performance criteria.

parameters and procedures). Two of ten experiments (po77, po94) do not support this statement.

We now present the results of a series of *inter*group statistical comparisons of relative market performance based on *intra*group data poolings. Tables 2 through 5 present various null hypotheses and corresponding actual and critical values of the Wilcoxon matched-pairs rank-sum statistic, $T$. In this non-parametric statistical procedure mean observations are matched period by period across the two samples implied by the statement of the null hypothesis. The absolute value of paired differences are then ranked from lowest (1) to highest ($n$). The test statistic, $T$, is the sum of the rankings for which the sign of the difference in means is consistent with the prediction based on the null hypothesis. Small values for $T$ are required to reject the null hypothesis.

Table 2

Price comparison: Wilcoxon test on paired normalized period means.

| $H_0$ | Actual Wilcoxon $T^a$ | Critical Wilcoxon $T^b$ | Reject $H_0$? |
|---|---|---|---|
| p.o. conspiracy $\leq$ d.a. conspiracy | 8 | 11 ($n = 10$) | Yes |
| p.o. conspiracy $\geq$ p.o. monopoly | 29 55,57 | 11 ($n = 10$) 30 ($n = 15$) | No |
| p.o. conspiracy $\leq$ p.o. no-conspiracy | 0 | 11 ($n = 10$) | Yes |

[a]Range of $T$ is given if ties occurred.
[b]One tailed test, $\alpha = 0.05$.

Table 3

Quantity comparison: Wilcoxon test on paired period means.

| $H_0$ | Actual Wilcoxon $T^a$ | Critical Wilcoxon $T^b$ | Reject $H_0$? |
|---|---|---|---|
| p.o. conspiracy $\geq$ d.a. conspiracy | 4,6 | 11 ($n = 10$) | Yes |
| p.o. conspiracy $\leq$ p.o. monopoly | 38,40 85,88 | 11 ($n = 10$) 30 ($n = 15$) | No |
| p.o. conspiracy $\geq$ p.o. no-conspiracy | 3 | 11 ($n = 10$) | Yes |

[a]Range of $T$ is given if ties occurred.
[b]One tailed test, $\alpha = 0.05$.

Table 4

Monopoly effectiveness index comparison: Wilcoxon test on paired period means.

| $H_0$ | Actual Wilcoxon $T$ | Critical Wilcoxon $T^a$ | Reject $H_0$? |
|---|---|---|---|
| p.o. conspiracy $\leqq$ d.a. conspiracy | 44 | 11 $(n=10)$ | No |
| p.o. conspiracy $\geqq$ p.o. monopoly | 9  10 | 11 $(n=10)$  30 $(n=15)$ | Yes |
| p.o. conspiracy $\leqq$ p.o. no-conspiracy | 15 | 11 $(n=10)$ | No |

<sup></sup>[a]One tailed test, $\alpha = 0.05$.

Table 5

Efficiency index comparison: Wilcoxon test on paired period means.

| $H_0$ | Actual Wilcoxon $T^a$ | Critical Wilcoxon $T^b$ | Reject $H_0$? |
|---|---|---|---|
| p.o. conspiracy $\geqq$ d.a. conspiracy | 12,13 | 11 $(n=10)$ | No |
| p.o. conspiracy $\leqq$ p.o. monopoly | 45  104 | 11 $(n=10)$  30 $(n=15)$ | No |
| p.o. conspiracy $\geqq$ p.o. no-conspiracy | 21 | 11 $(n=10)$ | No |

[a]Range of $T$ is given if ties occurred.
[b]One tailed test, $\alpha = 0.05$.

The information presented in table 2 indicates that period mean prices in the posted-offer conspiracy experiments stochastically dominate those generated in both the posted-offer competitive and the double-auction conspiracy control groups. We may not conclude that period mean prices generated by posted-offer monopolies dominate those generated by posted-offer conspiracies. The same set of qualitative conclusions is conveyed by table 3; period mean exchange volume in both the posted-offer competitive and double-auction conspiracy control groups exceeds volume generated in posted-offer conspiracies. No significant difference is found between mean volume in posted-offer conspiracy and posted-offer monopoly.

Turning to the two measures of market performance based on actual vs. theoretical profit ($M$ and $E$) we obtain somewhat different results. From table 4 we see that the only significant difference indicated for the three treatment-control group comparisons is that $M$ is significantly larger in the true monopoly experiments relative to the posted-offer conspiracy experiments. Given our inability to reject the equality of mean price and volume in this comparison, we might have predicted this result based on our discussion (section 3) of the nature of the profit function faced by a cartel versus the one faced by the true monopolist. Recall that the monopolist's profit function represents the upper bound of the cartel's stochastic profit function (assuming full demand revelation and a single price quote coming from all cartel members). Our inability to reject the null hypothesis in the other two comparisons stresses the fact that an elevated mean price does not necessarily translate into an elevated profit level for sellers. The results presented in table 5 indicate that we may not reject any of the stated *a priori* null hypotheses regarding efficiency. It should be noted, however, that for the fifteen-period comparison of posted-offer conspiracy vs. posted-offer monopoly ($T = 104$), a reversal of the inequality in the statement of the null hypothesis would lead us to conclude that efficiency in monopolistic markets is significantly greater than in markets with seller conspiracies ($T = 16$). This suggests that the increase in monopoly profit over cartel profits revealed in table 4 was not accompanied by a significant decrease in buyer profits.

## 5. Parting comments

The results presented here demonstrate that opportunities for seller conspiracy in a posted-offer market can foster market prices consistently above the competitive equilibrium. This phenomenon is above and beyond the previously observed tendency of such markets to converge to the competitive equilibrium from above. There is not, however, a clear tendency for prices to rise to levels at or near the theoretical monopoly predictions given the market parameters used in this study. Even though prices did not tend to coincide with the theoretical monopoly prediction, posted-offer conspiracies generated prices not significantly different from those of the true monopolies (see table 2). We cannot interpret this as meaning that the posted-offer conspirators were as successful as the true monopolists given the conspirator's significantly lower performance on our index of monopoly effectiveness (see table 4).

When viewed in light of the previous experimental results of Isaac and Plott, our data suggest at least two points about the relationships between market structure and market performance: (1) market structures allowing conspiracy can affect market performance, and (2) the nature of the links between market structures allowing seller conspiracy and the ultimate market outcomes are complex in that the nature of the trading institution can make a difference. Essentially identical conspiratorial opportunities seem to be more effective in raising prices (but not profits) in posted-offer markets than in markets organized as double auctions. We conjecture that one primary cause of the apparently different effects on pricing decisions of the opportunities for conspiracy in posted-offer markets (as opposed to double auctions) is the temporary rigidity of prices in the former. This inflexibility seems to substantially reduce the temptation to cheat on the conspiracy agreements.

Several interesting questions remain for future study. Within the realm of the posted-offer trading institution, there are several features of structure and/or conduct that could influence the success of opportunities for conspiracy: (1) non-passive buyer responses, (2) the type of information available to market participants, (3) the market supply and demand parameters, and (4) the possibility of side-payments within a cartel. The difference in pricing behavior among our four monopoly experiments demonstrates the power of strategic buyer withholding of demand. One question for further study is to examine the conditions under which such withholding is more or less likely to occur. The nature and amount of information about market parameters is a variable which has already drawn the attention of U.S. antitrust authorities.[10] In our design, each conspirator knew all exchange prices and quantities traded, but not the cost conditions of other sellers nor the true demand parameters of the buyers. The effect of changing this information mix is an open question.

Another area for further research involves looking at other market trading institutions. For example, part of the electrical conspiracy of the 1950s involved a different kind of trading mechanism, the sealed-bid auction. In addition, neither of the two exchange mechanisms studied so far has looked at sellers who produce for inventory instead of 'to order'. We speculate that the trading institution will continue to be shown to be an important component of the relationship between market structure and economic performance.

The use of laboratory experimental techniques in industrial organization and general microeconomic research is a relatively new and rapidly evolving methodology with inherent advantages and limitations [see, for example, Plott (1981, 1982), Smith (1982a, b) and Isaac (1983)]. From a positive perspective, variations in the trading institution and opportunities for communication among market participants were conducted using an experimentor-controlled underlying set of market parameters. Critical measures of market performance were directly observable relative to theoretical predictions and hypothesis testing based on experimental replications of a particular market environment was relatively straight-forward. However, it is important to stress that the direct relevance of our laboratory data to policymaking or predicting outcomes in 'naturally occurring' markets (external validity) should not be assumed. Smith (1981)

[10]For example, see *Tag Manufacturer's Institute v. Federal Trade Commission* 174 F 2d 462 (1st Cir. 1979).

has cautioned that bilateral comparisons of experimental treatment groups should not be used as a basis for universal extrapolation. Such results should not be construed as suggesting a generalized condemnation or recommendation of any component of market structure or policy without reference to the entire set of potential alternatives.

# References

Coursey, Don, R. Mark Isaac and Vernon L. Smith, 1984, Natural monopoly and contested markets: Some experimental results, Journal of Law and Economics 27, April, 91–114.

Hong, James T. and Charles R. Plott, 1982, Implications of rate filing for domestic dry bulk transportation on inland waters: An experimental approach, Bell Journal of Economics 13, Spring, 1–19.

Isaac, R. Mark, 1983, Laboratory experimental economics as a tool in public policy analysis, Social Science Journal 20, July, 45–58.

Isaac, R. Mark and Charles R. Plott, 1981, The opportunity for conspiracy in restraint of trade, Journal of Economic Behavior and Organization 2, 1–30.

Ketcham, Jon, Vernon L. Smith and Arlington W. Williams, 1984, A comparison of posted-offer and double-auction pricing institutions, Review of Economic Studies, forthcoming.

Plott, Charles R., 1981, Experimental methods in political economy: A tool for regulatory research, in: A. Furguson, ed., Attacking regulatory problems: An agenda for research in the 1980's (Ballinger, Cambridge, MA).

Plott, Charles R., 1982, Industrial organization theory and experimental economics, Journal of Economic Literature 20, Dec., 1485–1527.

Scherer, F.M., 1980, Industrial market structure and economic performance (Rand McNally, Chicago, IL).

Smith, Vernon L., 1981, Experimental microeconomy and microeconomic policy: Does experimental economics have any regulatory policy implications?, Southern Economic Association meetings, Nov.

Smith, Vernon L., 1982a, Reflections on some experimental market mechanisms for classical environments, in: L. McAlister, ed., Research in marketing: Choice models for buyer behavior (JAI Press, Greenwich, CT).

Smith, Vernon L., 1982b, Microeconomic systems as an experimental science, American Economic Review 72, Dec., 923–955.

Smith, Vernon L. and Arlington W. Williams, 1983, An experimental comparison of alternative rules for competitive market exchange, in: R. Engelbrecht-Wiggans, M. Shubik and R. Stark, eds., Auctions, bidding and contracting: Uses and theory (New York University Press, New York).

Williams, Arlington W., 1980, Computerized double-auction markets: Some initial experimental results, Journal of Business 53, July, 235–258.

# [13]

# Market contestability in the presence of sunk (entry) costs

Don Coursey*

R. Mark Isaac**

Margaret Luke**

and

Vernon L. Smith**

*This article extends previous laboratory experimental research to examine the competitive discipline of contested markets with a "natural monopoly"-type cost structure where sunk costs are neither zero nor infinite. Several alternative conjectures as to how or whether sunk costs can weaken the discipline of contested markets are presented and interpreted in the context of the experimental design. Sunk costs are found to weaken the support for "strong" interpretations of the contestable markets hypothesis and thus yield a wide diversity of dynamic patterns of market performance. Yet the disciplining power of contestability remains impressive, with no indications of sustained monopoly pricing.*

## 1. Introduction

■ The core of the contestable markets theory is the hypothesis that, with completely free entry and exit, a market that exhibits economies of scale—the traditional "natural monopoly" cost structure—will not exhibit monopoly behavior, even if only a single producing firm is observed in the market (Demsetz, 1968; Bailey, 1980; Bailey and Panzar, 1980; Baumol and Willig, 1981; Baumol, 1982; Baumol, Panzar, and Willig, 1982). That is, in the absence of any other restrictions on entry and exit, scale economies alone do not constitute an effective barrier to entry. Coursey, Isaac, and Smith (1983), hereafter CIS, have reported the results of a series of experiments in which each of two firms has identical decreasing marginal cost and the same capacity, but demand is insufficient to accommodate (profitably) any output in excess of the capacity of either firm. The conditions of these experimental markets further provide the "hit-and-run," zero sunk costs (Baumol, 1982; Baumol, Panzar, and Willig, 1982) of the contestable markets hypothesis. In CIS these results are compared with that of an uncontested market with one monopoly firm; i.e., a market in which sunk costs are effectively infinite for a potential entrant. The CIS experiments strongly support the contestable markets hypothesis, namely that to observe approximately competitive behavior by a single producing firm with substantially decreasing costs, it is sufficient that (a) sunk costs are zero and (b) there are two contesting firms acting noncooperatively in the sense that there is no explicit nonprice communication between them that leads to collusive restriction in supply. Furthermore, it is necessary that (c) the producing firm's

---

* University of Wyoming.

** University of Arizona.

We are indebted to the National Science Foundation and the Federal Trade Commission for research support under grants to the University of Arizona. We particularly want to acknowledge the helpful comments of Dan Alger and the editors and referees of this Journal.

market is contested by at least one other firm with the same cost structure. This follows from the observation that competitive outcomes tend to prevail when there are two contesting firms, but monopoly outcomes tend to prevail when there is one uncontested seller.

The purpose of the research reported here is to broaden the CIS study to examine the competitive discipline of contested markets where sunk cost is neither zero nor infinite. Several authors have conjectured that sunk costs might weaken the discipline of contested markets, and CIS have established that, behaviorally, the competitive discipline does fail in the polar case in which the sunk cost of a potential entrant is infinite.

In Section 2 we explore further the notion of sunk costs as a barrier to entry. In Section 3 our experimental design and its relation to the theory are presented along with some hypotheses. Section 4 is a brief description of the posted-offer trading institution employed. Section 5 discusses the use of programmed buyer responses versus subject buyers as a treatment variable. Section 6 contains the experimental results and interpretation. Section 7 summarizes the findings and proposes some general conclusions.

## 2. Sunk costs, conjectural variations, and entry barriers

■  In enumerating the assumptions of a theory of market performance, there is a distinction to be made between structural and behavioral assumptions. The former include characteristics of the production or cost technologies available, market or other limitations on the potential number of producing firms, and the formal or informal rules under which exchange contracts are negotiated (the trading institution). The latter include such attributes as the risk attitudes of sellers and interfirm expectations (conjectural variations). In testing a theory using experimental methods, it is appropriate to begin with an experimental design in which the structural conditions are reproduced as faithfully as possible in the laboratory. If the theory is then "falsified," relative to any competing theories, by the experimental evidence, this suggests that one or more of the behavioral assumptions of the theory are in question. If the theory is not "falsified" by the experimental evidence, then it is natural to explore the robustness of this result with respect to changes in the structural variables of the theory.

In the previously reported tests of the contestable markets hypothesis, the structural conditions specified by the theory (costless entry and exit) were met precisely for a market with a "natural monopoly" cost structure and two contesting firms. The behavioral assumptions about sellers' expectations have two functions: they complete the contestable markets hypothesis and they allow for the construction of alternative hypotheses. The contestable markets hypothesis argues that the structural conditions allow for what Baumol calls "hit-and-run" entry. That is, any situation in which an incumbent firm attempts to price at a level generating positive profits will induce entry, even if there is a conjecture that the profit opportunities are transient. The CIS article presented alternative scenarios (based on different conjectural variations) which predicted other outcomes (tacitly supported cartel-like pricing and unimpeded monopoly behavior by a surviving firm). The data from the experiments falsified the alternative hypotheses and supported the contestable markets hypothesis.

Since CIS found support for the contestable markets hypothesis under the conditions specified in the theory, the present research turns to the search for potential boundaries of falsifiability. Specifically, we explore the effect of sunk costs on the previous design with two contesting firms.

We shall use the term "sunk costs" in a manner consistent with the definition used by Baumol and Willig (1981).[1] The significance of a sunk cost is that it is a fixed opportunity

---

[1] Definition: Let $C(q, s)$ represent the short-run cost function applicable to an output rate of $q$ units per period sold in some market for $s$ time periods in the future. The $K(s)$ is the sunk cost of access to this market for $s$ periods if

$$C(q, s) = K(s) + G(q, s),$$

where $G(0, s) = 0$.

cost of the *entry* decision; i.e., sunk costs can be avoided by a decision not to enter a particular market. The concept is to be distinguished from fixed costs that are independent of any operating decision. Fixed costs which are not sunk (e.g., the fixed cost of aircraft usable on any route) are independent of the decision to supply any particular market. Hence, sunk costs may be a deterrent to entry in any particular market, but once incurred, they do not affect profits over the life of the sunk investment.

Consider a market with a natural monopoly cost structure but with zero cost of either entry or exit. The contestable markets hypothesis states that even where only one firm is observed serving the market, that firm is void of monopoly power. What happens under exactly the same conditions if firms must incur positive sunk entry costs? Several authors have asked this or a similar question in the contestable markets literature. Bailey and Panzar say that "the difficulty [potential barriers to entry] arises from the presence of sunk costs, *not* economies of scale" (1981, p. 128). Baumol and Willig provide two conjectures. First, they argue that the need to incur sunk costs can create barriers to entry: "The risk of losing unrecoverable entry costs, as perceived by the potential entrant, can be increased by the threat (or the imagined threat) of retaliatory strategic or tactical response of the incumbent" (1981, p. 418). Second, in a footnote, they suggest that, with different expectations on the part of the potential entrant, the need to sink costs could enable a potential entrant to overcome other barriers to entry: "The entrant who deliberately incurs substantial sunk costs . . . may thereby make it far more difficult for the incumbent to dislodge him" (Baumol and Willig, 1981, p. 419). Schwartz and Reynolds suggest that "once we deviate even slightly from the strict assumptions of perfect contestability, pricing and entry decisions depend upon the nature of firm interactions" (1983, p. 489). These and similar conjectures regarding the way in which sunk costs might affect the performance of an otherwise contestable market motivate the new series of experiments reported below.

## 3. Experimental design, hypotheses, and research strategy

■ The aggregate demand and marginal cost schedules (identical to those used in CIS) are shown in Figure 1. Marginal unit costs and values are measured in deviations from the average variable cost of unit 10, $AVC(10)$. Table 1 provides a parameter summary for the experimental design.

The sunk costs were imposed by requiring that a firm purchase an entry permit as a condition for being allowed to post a price. The permits cost $2 each and, once purchased, were valid for five consecutive periods. In terms of the Baumol and Willig (1981) definitions, each of the firms considering buying a permit faced a short-run planning horizon ($s$) equal to five periods and a level of sunk entry costs ($K$) equal to $2. These values of $K$ and $s$ were chosen for the following reasons: Experience had shown that one could expect to obtain a maximum of about 25 experimental market periods of posted offer exchange within a two-hour time interval.[2] Previous studies (Smith (1962) and Isaac, McCue, and Plott (1980) are only two of numerous examples) have shown that economic agents can exhibit "convergent" behavior with repeated decisions. Therefore, $s$ should be small enough to allow the participants several opportunities to evaluate entry-exit responses in the presence of the sunk costs. Furthermore, $s$ must not be so small that the entry decision precludes a multiperiod *commitment* to contest the market, which may carry an implied threat to the security of the incumbent (see the second quotation above from Baumol and Willig (1981, p. 419)).

Likewise, there was a wide range of possible choice for $K$. In fact, CIS tested two polar values for $K$, zero and positive infinity. Zero sunk costs correspond to the costless right to post a price in any period as specified by the contestable markets hypothesis. The other

---

[2] Subjects knew an approximate maximum amount of time they would participate in the experiment, but there was no common knowledge of the end period.

FIGURE 1

MARKET PARAMETERS

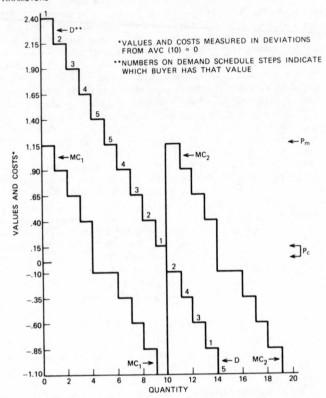

pole is represented by markets in which there is (by experimenter fiat) precisely one actual or potential seller. We sought to choose a level of $K$ which would provide an informative test in the sense that many competing hypotheses would be both plausible and observationally distinct. At very low levels of $K$ (one or two cents) or at very high levels (at amounts which, for the entrant, are greater than the total monopoly profit over five periods) these experiments would be testing hypotheses little different from CIS. An entry cost of $2 yields the following properties:

(1) If a firm achieves the theoretical monopoly price and quantity, it covers sunk costs in one period.

(2) There exists no competitive price $P_c \in [.04, .15]$ at which a seller could recoup the sunk costs in one period.

(3) There are prices supporting the competitive quantity at which the sunk costs could be recouped in 2, 3, 4, or 5 periods. The minimum of this set is $AVC(10) + .04$.

(4) There are prices which cover $AVC$ and support the competitive quantity but which do not allow the seller to cover sunk costs even if he sells all ten competitive units for five periods.

TABLE 1     **Parameter Summary**

| Parameter Description | Value |
|---|---|
| Number of Buyers | 5 |
| Number of Sellers | 2 |
| Price of Sellers' Permit, $K$ | $2.00 |
| Length of Sellers' Permit Validity, $s$ | 5 periods |
| Monopoly Price (Normalized)[1] = $P_m$ | $1.15 |
| Monopoly Quantity = $Q_m$ | 6 |
| Competitive Prices (Normalized)[2] | [.04, .15] |
| Competitive Quantity | 10 |
| Seller Quasi Rent per Period at $P_m$, $Q_m$ | 4.00 |
| Seller Quasi Rent per Period at $P_m$, $Q_m$, Less $\frac{1}{5}$ Permit Cost | 3.60 |
| Seller Working Capital Endowment[3] | 15.00 |
| Buyers' Surplus per Period at $P_m$, $Q_m$ | 3.75 |
| Seller Quasi Rent per Period at $P = .04$, $Q = 10$ | .40 |
| Seller Quasi Rent per Period at $P = .04$, $Q = 10$, Less $\frac{1}{5}$ Permit Cost | 0 |
| Buyers' Surplus at $P = .04$, $Q = 10$ | 12.35 |

[1] This is actually the lower of two equal-profit monopoly prices. The other is $1.40.

[2] The lower bound on competitive price is taken to be the smallest price supporting $Q = 10$ and covering variable costs plus $\frac{1}{5}$ permit costs. If the requirement of covering permit cost were excluded $P_c \in [0, .15]$.

[3] This cash endowment was awarded unconditionally to each seller. It provided capital for the purchase of permits, and to cover losses on sales, but it could be retained if a seller elected not to purchase permits.

Because of the prominence in this literature of the idea of an "incumbent" seller as differentiated from an "entrant," such a distinction among sellers was operationalized in this design. By a toss of a coin before each experiment, one seller was allowed the choice of being a seller of type A or type B. (The loser of the coin toss became the type not chosen by the winner.) Seller A was incumbent in that he was required to begin the experiment by purchasing seller permits for periods 1 to 5 and 6 to 10. The incumbent was a protected monopolist in periods 1–5. Seller B could observe the market prices and his own cost technology in periods 1–5, and was allowed the option of contesting the market (by purchasing permits) in any period beginning with period 6. Seller A could choose to continue to contest the market by purchasing a new permit in period 11 or any period thereafter.

To guard against differences in behavior in this design (compared with CIS) due to the wealth effects of requiring participants to pay for entry permits, the up-front "working capital" endowment of sellers was increased by $10 (the maximum possible permit expenditure in a 25-period experiment) from $5 to $15.

In this design, we identify six types of behavior which we hypothesized might be observed after period 5 (when the market becomes contestable):

(1) *Natural monopoly.* The market outcomes are at or near monopoly levels, with a single surviving firm satisfying all demand. This could occur through either of two routes: (a) The incumbent firm successfully threatens the entrant, by blocking entry or by driving the entrant out; or (b) the entrant commits sunk costs, and then proceeds to drive out the incumbent by undercutting his prices.

(2) *Tacit collusion.* Both firms enter the market and price consistently at noncompetitive levels.

(3) *Contestable markets hypothesis.* Both firms enter the market and price within (or near) the competitive range.

(4) *Limit pricing* (contestable markets hypothesis). Either the incumbent or the entrant exits the market, but the producing firm continues to price at the competitive level, thereby discouraging entry. We interpret this hypothesis as a subcase of the contestable markets hypothesis, since the emergence of a limit price is a direct consequence of the fact that the market is contested. It is, however, distinguishable from the contestable markets hypothesis as stated in (3) in that it requires one of the firms to make an exit decision. Contrary to the traditional limit pricing literature, this behavioral mode need not be associated with a price policy consciously intended to limit entry, but is a consequence of the market contesting process.

(5) *Unstable prices* (monopoly or contestable markets hypothesis). Either the incumbent or the entrant exits the market. The producing firm gains short-term positive profits by raising prices toward the monopoly level. The increased prices present a profit opportunity which eventually attracts the other firm to enter. If prices subsequently decline, one firm may again exit, followed by an increase in price, thus leading to unstable or cyclical behavior. In a finite experimental market, the experiment might end near the monopoly or competitive outcome, and in this sense the unstable price hypothesis may contain either the monopoly or competitive outcomes as subcases.

(6) *Market collapse.* Both firms exit the market and stay out. They are able, thereby, to retain the capital that would be expended to incur entry costs.

It may be helpful in understanding our methodological approach to the study of contestable markets to discuss (a) the state of our experimental knowledge before undertaking the sunk-cost experiments, and (b) our research strategy contingent on the outcomes of the initial series of six sunk-cost experiments. From the experiments reported by CIS we knew that the contestable markets hypothesis was strongly supported with zero sunk cost ($K = 0$), and that the monopoly outcome was supported when there was only one firm whose market was protected from any possibility of being contested by a second firm ($K = \infty$). Consequently, we supposed that there must be (at least one) finite value for $K$ in the interval $[0, \infty]$ at which we observe a switchover from competitive to noncompetitive outcomes. In designing any program of experimental research it is important to consider alternative possible outcomes, to evaluate their implications, and to develop a contingent research strategy. In the present context this means that attention focuses on the value of $K$, which theory tells us is of qualitative importance, but does not tell us how to choose. Our research plan was to begin with $K = \$2$, a "reasonable" value having the properties enumerated above. We conjectured that the contestable market result *might be* relatively *fragile,* so that sunk costs of $K = \$2$ might yield a predominance of noncompetitive outcomes supporting the alternative hypotheses (1) and/or (2). In that event our research plan would have called for additional experiments with $K < \$2$ to determine the value of $K$ below which the contestable markets hypothesis was supported. Alternatively, we conjectured that the contestable market result *might be* relatively *robust* so that at $K = \$2$ we might continue to observe strongly convergent competitive outcomes supporting hypothesis (3). In that case our research plan would have called for additional experiments with $K > \$2$ to search for the boundary of contestability. A third alternative was that with $K = \$2$ we might observe mixed results, either with outcomes supporting hypothesis (5) or outcomes distributed across several other hypotheses. This last category of results would suggest that for sunk costs $K = \$2$ the discipline of contestability is diminished, but that its weakening is relatively "continuous" rather than being manifest as a discrete jump at some $K$ in the interval $[0, \infty)$. In particular, if outcomes are distributed across several of the hypotheses, it suggests that when contestability is weakened, this increases the scope for nonstructural variables to influence outcomes (as suggested by the earlier quotation from Schwartz and Reynolds, 1983). Thus, individual variations in expectations may no longer be swamped by the power of costless entry. Since our results turned out to be best described by this third alternative (see Section 6), we decided not to expend additional resources to examine further the effect of $K$ on this multifarious result (subject payoffs alone average in excess of $150 per experiment). Instead, we addressed the internal question of whether our results for $K = \$2$ might be a result of strategic buyer behavior or the expectation of such by sellers (see Section 5). That is, given that $K = \$2$ has a treatment effect distinct from $K = 0$ and $K = \infty$, we ask whether this result might interact with a potentially important aspect of buyer market behavior.

## 4. The PLATO posted offer procedure

■ Most retail markets are organized under what has been called the "posted offer" institution (Plott and Smith, 1978). As we define it, in this institution each seller independently posts a take-it-or-leave-it price at which deliveries will be made in quantities elected by each individual buyer subject to seller capacity limits. These posted prices may be changed or reviewed frequently, infrequently, regularly, or irregularly, but in any case a central characteristic of this mechanism is that the posted price is not subject to negotiation.

The experiments reported here use the posted offer mechanism programmed for the PLATO computer system by Jonathan Ketcham (for a more detailed description see Ketcham, Smith, and Williams (1982)). This program allows subject buyers and sellers, sitting separately at PLATO terminals, to trade for a maximum of 25 market "days" or pricing periods. The display screen for each subject shows his record sheet, which lists a maximum of five units which can be purchased (sold) in each period. For each unit, the buyer (seller) has a marginal valuation (cost) which represents the value (cost) to him of purchasing (selling) that unit. These controlled, strictly private, unit valuations (costs) induce individual, and aggregate market, theoretical supply and demand schedules (Smith, 1976, 1982). That is, in an experiment, buyers (sellers) earn cash rewards equal to the difference between the marginal value (selling price) of a unit and its purchase price (marginal cost). Sales are "to order" in the sense that there are no penalties, or carry-over of inventories, associated with units not sold (or units not purchased). Consequently, the assigned marginal valuations and costs induce well-defined flow supply and demand conditions.

Each period begins with a request that sellers select a price offer by typing a price into the computer keyset. This offer is displayed privately on the seller's screen. The seller is then asked to select a corresponding quantity to be made available at that offer price. The maximum number of units a seller can offer corresponds to the number of the last unit whose cost is not greater than the offer price. The minimum number of units a seller can offer corresponds to the number of the first unit whose cost is not greater than the offer price. (The seller, however, is required to offer at least one unit, i.e., a seller cannot post a price for zero units.) This procedure permits individual induced marginal costs to be declining, constant, or increasing. If the seller faces declining marginal costs, as in the experiments reported below, these minimum and maximum quantity constraints prevent his choices from being such that a loss is guaranteed, but if price is below the first unit's marginal cost, a loss will be made on the first units sold which must be more than offset by profits on later units if an overall profit is to be earned in the period.[3] Since it is costly in terms of time and effort for a seller to calculate the profit that any given offer may provide, especially with declining costs, PLATO always informs the seller of the potential profit (loss) if all offered units are sold. When a seller is satisfied with the selected price

---

[3] Thus, in Figure 1 if a seller posts a price $P = \$.45$, the minimum quantity that can be offered is three units and the maximum is ten units. At this price the seller earns a positive profit only if sales are at least seven units.

and quantity, he presses a touch sensitive "offer box" displayed on the screen. This action irrevocably places that seller's offer into the market. Before touching the "offer box" the seller may change the price or quantity as many times as desired. Each seller sees the prices posted by the other seller only after both have entered their offers.

The screen viewed by the buyer displays one "price box" for accepting units offered by each seller. After all sellers have entered their offers, each seller's price is posted in these buyer's acceptance boxes. PLATO then randomly orders the buyers in a buying sequence, and the first is informed that he may now purchase the good. A buyer, once selected, can purchase from any seller. To purchase a unit from a selected seller, the buyer presses the box corresponding to that seller, then depresses a "confirm" key on the keyset. Repeating this sequence causes a second unit to be purchased, and so on. A buyer is allowed to purchase up to his buying capacity from any seller or sellers. However, a buyer cannot purchase a unit whose price is greate. 'han the unit's marginal valuation, and cannot buy from a seller who has sold all of the units offered. When a seller's last available unit is sold, the price appearing in the buyer's box for that seller is replaced with the message "out of stock" on the buyer's screen. After the first buyer has finished making purchases, the next buyer in random order may begin purchasing, and so on. The period ends when the last buyer completes this buying mode.

All participants in these experiments were "experienced" in the sense that all had previously participated in other experiments using the PLATO posted offer trading institution, although in different groups and with a different market design. Both with and without computer organization of markets, an occasional subject will display a gross misunderstanding of the rules or of the mechanics of the process (CIS, 1983; Isaac, McCue, and Plott, 1983). We saw absolutely no evidence of any such problems in the experiments reported here.

There is no difference in physical surroundings or computer interaction depending upon whether a seller has purchased an entry permit. This was done to minimize any extraneous incentives to purchase or not to purchase a permit. A seller who chooses not to purchase an entry permit remains at his terminal and watches the progress of the market. Since this is a posted offer market, sellers with and without permits are equally passive in computer terminal responsibilities once the market has opened to the buyers.

It is important to emphasize that buyers and sellers have only limited information. All unit values (costs) assigned to individual buyers (sellers) are strictly private, known only to the subject (and the experimenter). Each buyer sees all of the sellers' price offers but not the quantities available at these prices. In the experiments reported below sellers see the prices posted by each other (after both prices have been "locked in" and the trading period opens), but the PLATO computer program allows this information to be suppressed. Finally, buyers (sellers) know only their own purchases (sales) and profits.

## 5. The role of buyers

■  We report the results of twelve experiments. In the first six experiments (70, 79, 82, 87, 96, 97)[4] the role of the buyers is exactly as reported in CIS (using the computer procedures reported in the previous experiments). These six experiments serve as the most direct test of the effect of sunk costs in comparison with the CIS experiments.

After completing these six experiments, we still had observed no experiments yielding

---

[4] The contestable markets experiments reported in this article were not conducted sequentially, but were interspersed with a variety of other posted offer experiments conducted for other studies. In this report we retain the original sequential numbering that we use for all posted offer experiments. Thus, experiment 70 was our seventieth PLATO posted offer experiment, but it was our first contestable market experiment. With this numbering we can readily access the data for any experiment in response to questions or requests from readers (see the last sentence in footnote 7).

the standard natural monopoly outcome. We asked ourselves, "Was it possible that this could be owing to strategic (non-fully-demand-revealing) behavior on the part of buyers?" An implicit assumption of contestable market theory is that buyers reveal demand. An examination of the data shows that buyer withholding of demand occurred at a very low rate (1.24% of full revelation quantity). This is almost identical to the low level of the CIS contestable duopolies (1.16%) and much less than the CIS monopoly experiments (9.14%). It seems unlikely that such low rates of demand underrevelation could have any effect on seller behavior. However, two possibilities could mitigate this conjecture: (1) Low rates of demand underrevelation, if strategically timed (e.g., when prices are increased), might affect behavior disproportionately to their occurrence. (2) Seller behavior may be influenced by the *expectation* that buyers will withhold demand at the higher prices. Consequently, we conducted six additional experiments in which demand was fully revealed and this was *known* to the sellers. In these six experiments (113–116, 118–119) the decisions of the buyers were programmed into the PLATO system, with the program automatically providing full demand revelation. That this computerized response would take place, and that the "buyers" would purchase "all that was profitable to them at the given prices" was explained to the sellers, so that it was not credible for sellers to harbor even the expectation that demand might be underrevealed.

## 6. Results and interpretation

■ Tabl  2 provides a classification of experimental price outcomes for the four monopoly and six contestable market experiments reported in CIS, and the twelve sunk-cost experiments conducted for this article. The price behavior for each experiment is classified according to which of the six hypotheses (discussed in Section 3) the observed behavior supports. Each experiment is also classified according to a price observation which is measured by the ruling (low) seller price in the reference period. This reference period is period 18 in the CIS experiments and period 23 in the sunk-cost experiments. Since the incumbent firm's market is uncontested in the first five periods of the sunk-cost experiments, period 23 is the eighteenth contestable market period, and is therefore comparable to period 18 of the CIS experiments. Where appropriate, we distinguish strong and weak forms for the reference period price prediction of each alternative hypothesis. Thus, according to the natural monopoly hypothesis, only one firm survives; the strong form of the hypothesis predicts a price closer to the monopoly than to the competitive price set, $\hat{P} \geq (P_c^* + P_m)/2$.[5] The tacit collusion hypothesis is also interpreted in terms of these strong and weak forms, except that both firms remain active in the market. Similarly, the strong form of the contestable markets hypothesis predicts prices in the competitive equilibrium set, $\hat{P} \in [0, P_c^*]$, while the weak form predicts prices closer to the competitive than to the monopoly price set, $\hat{P} \leq (P_c^* + P_m)/2$. Note that these different interpretations of the theoretical hypotheses are not mutually exclusive; outcomes satisfying the strong form of the contestable markets hypothesis must also satisfy the weak form, but not *vice versa*. The unstable price hypothesis refers to the pattern of price behavior over the entire experiment, although the reference period outcomes yield observations that are either weakly or strongly competitive, and therefore support the contestable markets hypothesis. In effect, the only difference between the outcomes we observed under hypotheses (3) and (5) is that the former reflected a strong (essentially monotone) convergence to the competitive level.

Table 3 summarizes the results of binomial tests of the contestable markets hypothesis from all 22 experiments. In these tests the null hypothesis corresponds to a naive random

---

[5] $P_c^*$ is the highest price in the range of competitive equilibrium prices. $P_m$ is the lower of the two monopoly prices.

*Experimental Economics*

TABLE 2    **Classification of Outcomes by Hypothesis and Treatment Condition (Experiment Numbers in Parentheses)**

| Hypothesis Supported (Entry Cost ($K$) and Buyer Condition) | Subject Buyers Make Purchase Decisions | | | Programmed Buyers Reveal Demand |
|---|---|---|---|---|
| | $K = +\infty$*  (CIS) | $K = 0$*  (CIS) | $K = \$2.00$** | $K = \$2.00$** |
| **(1) Natural Monopoly** | | | | |
| Strong $\hat{P} \geq P_m$ | 2  (36, 46) | 0 | 0 | 0 |
| Weak: $\hat{P} \geq \dfrac{P_c^* + P_m}{2}$ | 4  (34, 35, 36, 46) | 0 | 0 | 0 |
| **(2) Tacit Collusion** | | | | |
| Monopoly: $\hat{P} \geq \dfrac{\hat{P}_c^* + P_m}{2}$ | N.A. | 0 | 0 | 0 |
| Strong Competitive (Contestable Markets Hypothesis: $\hat{P} \leq P_c^*$ | N.A. | 0 | 0 | 1  (116) |
| Weak Competitive (Contestable Markets Hypothesis): $\hat{P} \leq \dfrac{P_c^* + P_m}{2}$ | N.A. | 0 | 0 | 2  (116, 119) |
| **(3) Contestable Markets Hypothesis** | | | | |
| Strong: $\hat{P} \leq P_c^*$ | 0 | 4  (45, 47, 51, 42) | 2  (96, 97) | 2  (113, 115) |
| Weak: $\hat{P} \leq \dfrac{P_c^* + P_m}{2}$ | 0 | 6  (37, 45, 47, 48, 51, 52) | 3  (70, 96, 97) | 2  (113, 115) |
| **(4) Limit Pricing (Contestable Markets Hypothesis)** | N.A. | 0 | 1  (82) | 0 |
| **(5) Unstable Prices** | | | | |
| Monopoly: $\hat{P} \geq \dfrac{P_c^* + P_m}{2}$ | N.A. | 0 | 0 | 0 |
| Strong Competitive (Contestable Markets Hypothesis): $\hat{P} \leq P_c^*$ | N.A. | 0 | 2  (79, 87) | 1  (118) |
| Weak Competitive (Contestable Markets Hypothesis): $\hat{P} \leq \dfrac{P_c^* + P_m}{2}$ | N.A. | 0 | 2  (79, 87) | 2  (114, 118) |
| **(6) Market Collapse** | N.A. | 0 | 0 | 0 |

* $\hat{P}$ = ruling price in period 18.
** $\hat{P}$ = ruling price in period 23 (the 18th period in which the market is contestable).

model of behavior in which prices have a uniform distribution over the range from the lowest competitive price to the highest monopoly price (0 to $1.40). Thus, the strong version of the contestable markets hypothesis postulates that $0 \leq \hat{P} \leq P_c^* = \$.15$, which occurs with probability $\theta_0 = .15/1.40 = .107$; i.e., the "hit" region of the contestable markets hypothesis is the subinterval $[0, .15]$ contained in the feasible price range $[0, 1.40]$. The weak version of the contestable markets hypothesis predicts that $0 \leq \bar{P} \leq (P_c^* + P_m)/2 = \$.65$, which occurs with probability $\theta_0 = .65/1.40 = .464$ under the null hypothesis. Under each version of the contestable markets hypothesis Table 3 reports tests of the null hypothesis that $\theta = \theta_0$ (all feasible prices up to the monopoly price are equally likely), against the contestable markets hypothesis that $\theta > \theta_0$ (prices in the contestable markets hypothesis range are more likely than predicted by the naive model), where $\theta$ is the binomial probability that any one observation will support the contestable markets hypothesis.

From Table 3 it is seen that neither version of the contestable markets hypothesis is supported when a single firm is protected from any possibility that a competitor will enter. Hence, if experiments with zero or finite positive entry costs provide support for the contestable markets hypothesis, this result will be attributable to the disciplinary function of free entry. Table 3 also shows that there is significant support for rejecting the null hypothesis when the market is contested by two firms. The "weak" version of the contestable markets hypothesis is supported by all 18 contested market experiments whether entry costs are zero or \$2. The fact that the weak version of the contestable markets hypothesis receives somewhat stronger support than the strong version in the eighteen contested experiments shows that structure alone (economies of scale, entry cost level, and two potential suppliers) is not sufficient to yield precisely the competitive outcomes. Dynamic or expectational elements have measurable effects in raising prices. The resulting increase in prices is small, however, and the contestable markets hypothesis is essentially correct in comparison with the "natural monopoly" theory for the entry conditions that have been studied.[6]

**TABLE 3**     **Binomial Tests of the Contestable Markets Hypothesis by Structural Treatment Condition**

| Form of Hypothesis | Uncontested Market; Infinite Entry Cost | | | Contested Market; Entry Cost = 0 | | | Contested Market; Entry Cost = \$2 | | |
|---|---|---|---|---|---|---|---|---|---|
| | $x$ | $n$ | $\alpha$ | $x$ | $n$ | $\alpha$ | $x$ | $n$ | $\alpha$ |
| Strong Contestable Markets Hypothesis | | | | | | | | | |
| $\bar{P} \leq P_c^*$ <br> $\theta_0 = .107$ | 0 | 4 | 1.00 | 4 | 6 | .0016 | 6 | 12 | .0008 |
| Weak Contestable Markets Hypothesis | | | | | | | | | |
| $\bar{P} < \dfrac{P_c^* + P_m}{2}$ <br> $\theta_0 = .464$ | 0 | 4 | 1.00 | 6 | 6 | .01 | 12 | 12 | .0001 |

$\theta_0$ = null binomial probability from assumption that (normalized) prices are uniformly distributed between 0 and \$1.40. The null hypothesis is that $\theta = \theta_0$ against the contestable markets hypothesis alternative that $\theta > \theta_0$.
$\bar{P}$ = ruling price in period 23.
$P_c^*$ = highest competitive price (\$.15).
$P_m$ = lowest monopoly price (\$1.15).
$x$ = number of experiments supporting given version of the contestable markets hypothesis.
$n$ = total number of experiments.
$\alpha$ = binomial probability of $x$ or more experiments supporting the contestable markets hypothesis if true probability = $\theta$.

---

[6] Dan Alger of the Federal Trade Commission reviewed an earlier draft of this article and suggested a Bayesian report based on the data of Table 3. Let $\theta$ have a uniform prior distribution (a member of the class of beta

Based upon the classification of experimental outcomes in Table 2, we offer the following qualitative observations:

*Observation 1.* The presence of sunk cost, in an amount which permits a positive net profit in the top of the competitive equilibrium price range, does not prevent entry. In all twelve new experiments, the B seller entered the market in period 6. In the thirteen cases in which a seller exited, and had an opportunity to reenter, the seller did reenter in every case.

*Observation 2.* There is evidence that sunk costs cause some weakening of the competitive discipline of contestability. In most cases this weakening appears to be temporary. Thus, in six of our twelve experiments there were price "run-ups," corresponding to temporary episodes of tacit collusion or the exiting of a firm, which were *not* observed in the CIS experiments with zero entry cost. This is illustrated in Figure 2(b) and 2(d) by the price charts for experiments 79 and 119.[7]

*Observation 3.* There is a tendency for observed quantities to be closer to the competitive prediction than is the case for measures of market efficiency. This is shown in the tabulations in Table 4. This difference is due to the efficiency loss from duplication of the sunk costs when two firms purchase permits. This duplication is part of the cost of achieving a competitive discipline when there are positive entry costs.

*Observation 4.* No one of the six hypotheses listed in Table 2 is uniformly supported by the twelve new sunk-cost experiments. A brief synopsis of these experiments is as follows:

*Experiments 70, 96, 97, 113, and 115 (contestable markets hypothesis).* In these experiments both sellers contest the market in the vast majority of the trading periods. The price and quantity convergence patterns are virtually indistinguishable from the six CIS experiments with zero entry cost. This is illustrated in the chart for experiment 96 in Figure 2(a).

*Experiments 79, 87, 114, and 118 (unstable pricing).* In each of these experiments a seller exited the market after several periods of low prices and the remaining seller raised the price close to or above the monopoly level. In each case the seller who left the market then reentered and the price declined. This pattern is illustrated by experiment 79 in Figure 2(b).

*Experiment 82 (limit pricing).* As in 79, 87, and 114, there was a sequence of contested periods with prices at or near the competitive range. Seller A exited for five periods, yet the incumbent *never* raised price outside of the competitive range (although prices rose to

---

distributions). Since the beta and binomial likelihood distributions are natural conjugates, the posterior distribution of $\theta$ is beta. Using our data, Alger calculates the posterior probability $\Pr(\theta > 0.5)$ for each treatment and each version of the contestable markets hypothesis as follows:

| Hypothesis | Treatment | | |
|---|---|---|---|
| | $k = +\infty$ | $k = 0$ | $k = \$2$ |
| Strong CMH | .031 | .77 | .50 |
| Weak CMH | .031 | .992 | .999. |

This report is more conservative than our tests in Table 3 for the strong version of the contestable markets hypothesis, since we (implicitly) assume that support for the contestable markets hypothesis is *a priori* unlikely (all feasible prices equally likely), which corresponds to using a nondiffuse beta prior in a Bayesian report.

   [7] Each of the charts in Figure 2 graphs prices and total quantity exchanged over the trading periods of the experiment. Trading period quantities sold are identified by seller category: "A" (for the original incumbent) or "B" (for the original potential entrant). Dark circles on the vertical price scale indicate offer price of the nontrading seller during each period. Recall that the potential for contesting begins only in period 6 and that the market is not necessarily contested in later periods. We have indicated by shading under the price bar those periods in which both firms were owners of active entry permits. Data similar to those in Figure 2 are available for all 18 reported experiments upon direct request to the authors.

FIGURE 2

DATA FROM FOUR EXPERIMENTS

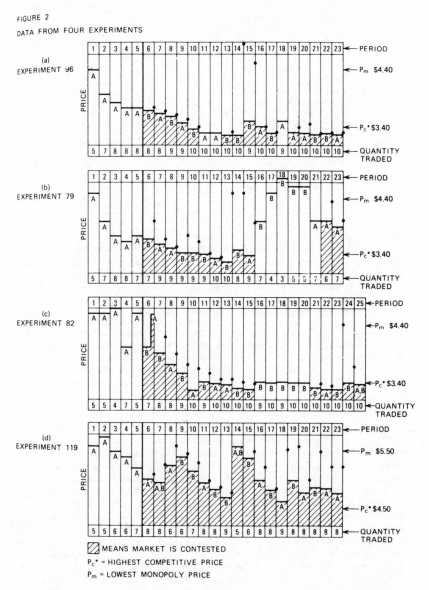

(a) EXPERIMENT 96

(b) EXPERIMENT 79

(c) EXPERIMENT 82

(d) EXPERIMENT 119

▨ MEANS MARKET IS CONTESTED

$P_c^*$ = HIGHEST COMPETITIVE PRICE

$P_m$ = LOWEST MONOPOLY PRICE

the top position of this range and seller B was earning positive profits). This appears to be "limit pricing," and is illustrated in Figure 2(c).

*Experiment 116 and 119 (tacit collusion).* In these experiments both sellers contested the market in all periods after the fifth. Yet the prices do not show the tendency to decline monotonically toward the competitive range as exhibited in the CIS experiments. In each

TABLE 4    Quantity and Efficiency Outcomes for 222
                Contestable Periods

| | Performance Criteria | |
| Outcome | Quantity | Efficiency |
|---|---|---|
| Closer to monopoly prediction than to competitive prediction | 69 (31.1%) | 124 (55.9%) |
| Equal distance between the monopoly and competitive predictions | 52 (23.4%) | 4 (1.8%) |
| Closer to the competitive prediction than to the monopoly prediction | 101 (45.5%) | 94 (42.3%) |
| TOTAL | 222 (100%) | 222 (100%) |
| At or below monopoly prediction | 27 (12.2%) | 43 (19.4%) |
| Greater than monopoly prediction | 195 (87.8%) | 179 (80.6%) |
| TOTAL | 222 (100%) | 222 (100%) |

case the sellers are able to coordinate one or more increases in prices, but the effort is temporary and the price coordination is unstable. In the end prices are closer to the competitive than to the monopoly price. (See Figure 2(d).) This behavior is consistent with an attempt to obtain "tacit collusion," although these cases do not confirm the hypothesis that such collusion will be a success. Since this behavior was not observed by CIS with zero entry cost, it is plausible to conjecture that entry costs may have some "commitment" effect which supports temporary episodes of tacit cooperation.

*Observation 5.* Certain hypotheses found no observational support. There was never any collapse of the market. Nor was there any indication that the combination of scale economies and intermediate-level sunk costs ever facilitated a permanently effective, monopoly-sustaining barrier to entry. Of 222 potentially contested periods, the observed market price was closer to the competitive range than to the theoretical monopoly price in 144 (64.86%) periods (see Table 4).

*Observation 6.* The failure to observe a sustained natural monopoly outcome appears not to be a result of strategic behavior by the five buyers. This outcome continued to be absent when we switched to the second series of (six) experiments in which sellers knew that buyer responses were programmed to yield passive, simple maximizing behavior. We did, however, observe an increase in the number of partially successful attempts to achieve a "tacit cartel" (two in the second series, none in the first). This suggests a qualitative effect in the form of reduced competition when human buyer subjects are replaced by programmed simple maximizing responses. A comparison of mean price difference in periods 18 to 23 in the two series of experiments reveals that the mean price was nine cents lower for the experiments with human buyer subjects. But this price difference was not significant ($t = 1.072$ based on the assumption that the period-by-period prices are independent, and $t = .506$ treating each experiment as an independent observation). Consequently, in Table 3 the two series of experiments are pooled for the binomial test. This small, statistically insignificant difference might be the result of one or more of the following: (i) random (subject) sampling error; (ii) the effect of the 1.24% underrevelation of demand; (iii) seller anticipation of the possibility of buyer withholding of demand, even if it only rarely occurs.

# 7. Conclusions

■  On the basis of the ruling price in the 18th period in which the market is contested, the effect of an entry cost is to weaken support for the strong form of the contestable markets hypothesis. Thus, with entry cost $K(0) = 0$, CIS report that 4 of 6 experiments support the strong contestable markets hypothesis. With $K(5) = \$2$, we find that 6 of 12 experiments support the strong contestable markets hypothesis. Further, according to this measure, entry cost has no effect on support for the weak form of the contestable markets hypothesis: CIS find that 6 of 6 experiments support the weak contestable markets hypothesis with zero entry cost, and we find that 12 of 12 experiments support the weak contestable markets hypothesis when $K(5) = \$2$. A comparison based on ruling prices in any single reference period, however, fails to capture the dynamics of the contesting process which is perhaps the most striking aspect of the observations generated in the new series of experiments. In the CIS experiments with zero entry cost, the price convergence paths were essentially monotone in all six cases, although individual experiments differed with respect to their speeds of convergence to the competitive range. In the twelve experiments reported in this article, we find that entry cost has a pronounced effect on market performance over time, with only five experiments replicating the strong convergence property of the CIS experiments. The remaining seven experiments, although in the end supporting the weak form of the contestable markets hypothesis, exhibited modes of behavior supporting the unstable price hypothesis, the limit price hypothesis, and transient episodes of the tacit collusion hypothesis. We think it is significant that in twelve "trials" not a single outcome supported the natural monopoly, tacit collusion (except in transient form), or market collapse hypotheses. Thus, the disciplining power of market contestability remains impressive, even where entry cost weakens that power enough to produce a wide diversity of dynamic patterns of interaction over time.

The results of these experiments may also have something to say about the way we think of the development and testing of hypotheses in industrial organization behavior. To those who expected that we would necessarily end up with a single correct I.O. "story," these results might be somewhat surprising. Yet, all of the various predictions of seller behavior are based upon different behavioral assumptions which are specific to the characteristics of the economic decisionmakers. Sometimes (as in the case of zero entry cost) the results are rather robust with respect to the risk preferences, conjectural variations, expectations, and other characteristics of the individuals. But there is no reason to believe that this must be the case in different market structures.

Readers familiar with traditional industrial organization research may notice a similarity in this discussion to the distinction between "structure" and "conduct" in determining market performance. If market "structure" means the observable, environmental variables such as numbers of buyers and sellers, presence or absence of entry costs, and scale economies, then these results suggest an interesting interpretation. Some aspects of market structure "matter," as is demonstrated by the change in market dynamics with the addition of entry costs. Also, some forms of structure may not matter, e.g., economies of scale. But structure, even where it matters, is not necessarily deterministic, thereby suggesting problems for those who would wish industrial organization research to restrict consideration to the reduced-form links between structure and performance which bypass issues such as expectations formation. While we cannot directly observe such concepts as expectations or conjectural variations, we can see variation in experimental outcomes among different contesting duopolists within a fixed structure (positive entry costs, increasing returns) and conclude that there are residual effects owing to agent characteristics. The intellectual challenge for industrial organization is to articulate falsifiable interpretations of such behavioral concepts as "expectations" which allow direct tests of the hypothesis that such concepts account for the variability of outcomes within a given structure.

## References

BAILEY, E.E. "Contestability and the Design of Regulatory and Antitrust Policy." Mimeo. September 11, 1980.
——— AND PANZAR, J.C. "The Contestability of Airline Markets during the Transition to Deregulation." Mimeo. May 6. 1980.

84 / THE RAND JOURNAL OF ECONOMICS

BAUMOL, W.J. "Contestable Markets: An Uprising in the Theory of Industry Structure." *American Economic Review*, Vol. 72 (March 1982), pp. 1–15.

———— AND WILLIG, R.D. "Fixed Costs, Sunk Costs, Entry Barriers, and Sustainability of Monopoly." *Quarterly Journal of Economics*, Vol. 96 (August 1981), pp. 405–431.

————, PANZAR, J.C., AND WILLIG, R.D. *Contestable Markets and the Theory of Industry Structure*. New York: Harcourt-Brace-Jovanovich, 1982.

COURSEY, D., ISAAC, R.M., AND SMITH, V.L. "Natural Monopoly and Contested Markets: Some Experimental Results." May 1983. *Journal of Law and Economics*, forthcoming.

DEMSETZ, H. "Why Regulate Utilities?" *Journal of Law and Economics*, Vol. 11 (April 1968), pp. 55–65.

ISAAC, R.M., McCUE, K., AND PLOTT, C.R. "Public Goods Provision in an Experimental Environment." Mimeo. June 1982.

KETCHAM, J., SMITH, V.L., AND WILLIAMS, A. "A Comparison of Posted Offer and Double Auction Pricing Institutions." 1982. *Review of Economic Studies*, forthcoming.

PLOTT, C.R. AND SMITH, V.L. "An Experimental Examination of Two Exchange Institutions." *Review of Economic Studies*, Vol. 45 (February 1978), pp. 133–153.

SCHWARTZ, M. AND REYNOLDS, R. "Contestable Markets, an Uprising in the Theory of Industry Structure: Comment." *American Economic Review*, Vol. 73 (June 1983), pp. 488–490.

SMITH, V.L. "An Experimental Study of Competitive Market Behavior." *Journal of Political Economy*, Vol. 70 (April 1962), pp. 111–137.

————. "Experimental Economics: Induced Value Theory." *American Economic Review*, Vol. 66 (May 1976), pp. 274–279.

————. "Microeconomic Systems as an Experimental Science." *American Economic Review*, Vol. 72 (December 1982), pp. 923–955.

# [14]

**Arlington W. Williams**
*Indiana University*

**Vernon L. Smith**
*University of Arizona*

# Cyclical Double-Auction Markets with and without Speculators*

## I. Introduction

This paper reports on laboratory experimental research designed to study the behavioral properties of two different market environments governed by cycling excess demand: (1) a market in which successive market periods are temporally isolated (autarky), and (2) a market in which agents (speculators) are allowed to carry commodity units from one period to another, thus temporally linking the cyclical phases of the market. We analyze observations from a total of 18 markets, all organized under double auction trading rules. The markets employ the PLATO computer network as the medium of public information transfer and private information display.

Our research builds on the previous experimental findings of Miller, Plott, and Smith (1977) (hereinafter MPS) and Williams (1979). These studies employed a common design where a sequence of "trading years" governed by stable supply are divided into a blue (low-demand) season and a yellow (high-demand) season. The supply and demand arrays were cyclically stable and resulted in a unique intertemporal competitive equilibrium. The experiments employed six

This study reports the results of 18 computerized "double-auction" market experiments characterized by cycling excess demand. Two such market designs are studied: one with stationary supply and cycling demand, the other with cycling supply and demand. Data from a series of control experiments under conditions of intertemporal isolation (autarky) are compared with data from experiments where the two cyclical market phases are linked by a subset of agents (speculators). Allowing intertemporal speculation is found to be a significant treatment variable in both market designs; however, price convergence patterns are not robust with respect to the design change.

* We gratefully acknowledge financial assistance from the National Science Foundation and research assistance from Don Coursey, who aided us in conducting many of the experiments reported in this study.

(*Journal of Business*, 1984, vol. 57, no. 1, pt. 1)

buyers, six sellers, and two agents called "traders" who, in equilibrium, carry four commodity units over from the blue to the yellow season in each trading year. Traders are restricted to buying in the blue season and selling in the yellow season and are not allowed to carry units over beyond a yellow season.

The MPS (1977) study initially demonstrated that, after several trading years, such markets generated contract prices near the intertemporal competitive equilibrium and significantly different from the seasonal competitive prices predicted under conditions from intertemporal autarky. Williams (1979) extended these results by replicating MPS's speculation experiment and comparing the results with actual contract prices from an autarky experiment using the same market design but without traders. The results of this potentially much more rigorous test of the ability of a class of speculators to reduce seasonal price fluctuations indicated that the existence of such agents was indeed a highly significant experimental treatment variable.[1]

After we describe the trading mechanism in Section II and our experimental subjects in Section III, Section IV reports the results of two speculation experiments and two autarky experiments that replicate the basic design used by Williams (1979) in his autarky-speculation comparison. We then report, in Section V, the results of 10 speculation experiments and four autarky experiments using an entirely new cyclical market design. This new design has a socially optimal intertemporal carry-over of nine units and is characterized by cycling demand and supply. In our PLATO computerized double-auction mechanism traders operate in a less restricted environment than in the previously cited laboratory markets. Most important, we are able to drop the explicit blue/yellow seasonal distinction entirely and allow traders to switch between buying mode and selling mode at will within or between trading periods. In addition, we explicitly introduce commodity perishability and scrap-value parameters.

While the previous experimental work with intertemporally linked double auctions clearly demonstrates that knowledge of the underlying market structure is unnecessary for the attainment of an observed behavioral equilibrium that is near the theoretical intertemporal com-

---

1. Hoffman and Plott (1981) have extended the MPS and Williams studies by comparing speculation experiments conducted under double-auction trading rules with similar experiments conducted under posted-offer trading rules. They conclude that contract prices tend to be higher under posted-offer rules and convergence toward the intertemporal competitive price slower than in double auctions. The result that, compared with the double auction, posted-offer pricing works to the disadvantage of the "silent side" of the market (buyers) is consistent with experimental evidence using stable supply and demand configurations without speculators reported by Ketcham, Smith, and Williams (1983). Plott and Uhl (1981) have also studied the behavior of a class of middlemen in a competitive market where direct exchange between buyers and sellers was not permitted.

petitive equilibrium, these studies provide important imformation to the participants concerning the cyclical nature of the market. In addition to dividing the market years explicitly into blue and yellow seasons, the buyers' (sellers') record sheets revealed their individual induced valuation (cost) structure for the entire experiment. In the experiments reported below, participants do not have "perfect foresight" into the future value or cost of their commodity units. Individual valuation and cost parameters are revealed privately by PLATO before the beginning of each period for that period only. Furthermore, participants do not know how many buyers, sellers, and traders are in the experiment, although they do know the total number of market participants. A priori, we were uncertain how these reductions in the subjects' information sets would affect market performance. Will speculators fail to perceive the profit opportunities inherent in the cyclical market? Even if speculators recognize the existence of potential opportunities for profit, will they choose to act on this in the presence of substantial perceived risk associated with inventory accumulation? Will intertemporal carry-over fall short of the socially optimal level? Given these possibilities, will markets with speculators behave differently from markets without speculators?

## II. The PLATO Double-Auction Exchange Mechanism with Traders

### Basic Trading Mechanics

The trading procedure employed in this study is a revised version of the PLATO computerized transformation of the oral double auction described in detail by Williams (1980). Buyers (sellers) are free at any time to enter a bid to buy (offer to sell) one unit of an undefined homogeneous commodity by typing their entry and then touching a rectangular area on their display screen (see fig. 1) labeled "ENTER BID" ("ENTER OFFER") at which time the entry is made public unless it violates some institutional rule. Any buyer (seller) is free to accept any seller's offer (buyer's bid) by touching a display screen area labeled "ACCEPT OFFER" ("ACCEPT BID"). The acceptor must then touch an area labeled "CONFIRM CONTRACT," at which time a binding contract is formed and the information is logged in both the maker's and taker's private record sheets. Bids, offers, and subsequent contracts are the only public information. The incorporation of PLATO's touch sensitive display screen into the double-auction software is not just an exercise in computer showmanship. The utilization of touch input serves to reduce the complexity of the task market participants confront. They are able to prepare a price quote for entry into the market and then to focus all their attention on the market information continually being presented on their display screen.

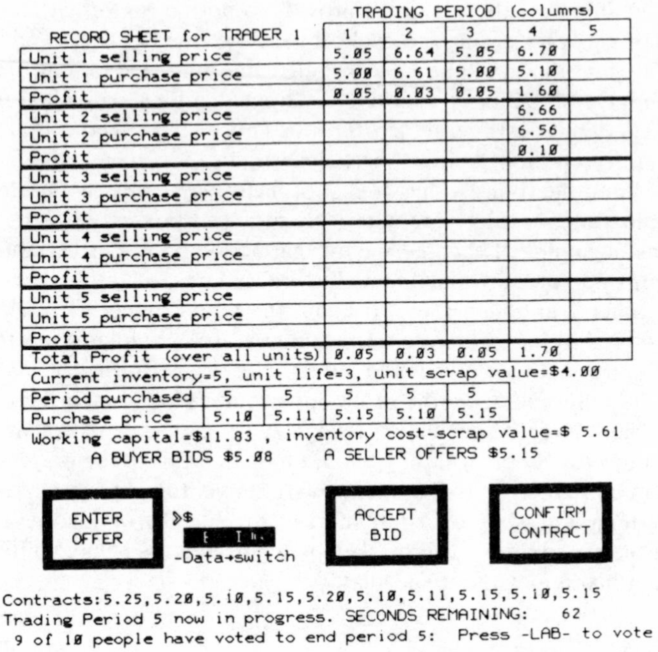

| RECORD SHEET for TRADER 1 | TRADING PERIOD (columns) | | | | |
| --- | --- | --- | --- | --- | --- |
| | 1 | 2 | 3 | 4 | 5 |
| Unit 1 selling price | 5.05 | 6.64 | 5.05 | 6.70 | |
| Unit 1 purchase price | 5.00 | 6.61 | 5.00 | 5.10 | |
| Profit | 0.05 | 0.03 | 0.05 | 1.60 | |
| Unit 2 selling price | | | | 6.66 | |
| Unit 2 purchase price | | | | 6.56 | |
| Profit | | | | 0.10 | |
| Unit 3 selling price | | | | | |
| Unit 3 purchase price | | | | | |
| Profit | | | | | |
| Unit 4 selling price | | | | | |
| Unit 4 purchase price | | | | | |
| Profit | | | | | |
| Unit 5 selling price | | | | | |
| Unit 5 purchase price | | | | | |
| Profit | | | | | |
| Total Profit (over all units) | 0.05 | 0.03 | 0.05 | 1.70 | |

Current inventory=5, unit life=3, unit scrap value=$4.00

| Period purchased | 5 | 5 | 5 | 5 | 5 |
| --- | --- | --- | --- | --- | --- |
| Purchase price | 5.10 | 5.11 | 5.15 | 5.10 | 5.15 |

Working capital=$11.83 , inventory cost-scrap value=$ 5.61
     A BUYER BIDS $5.08       A SELLER OFFERS $5.15

```
 ┌─────────┐              ┌─────────┐   ┌─────────┐
 │  ENTER  │  >$          │ ACCEPT  │   │ CONFIRM │
 │  OFFER  │  ▌  I ▐      │   BID   │   │ CONTRACT│
 └─────────┘  -Data→switch└─────────┘   └─────────┘
```

Contracts:5.25,5.20,5.10,5.15,5.20,5.10,5.11,5.15,5.10,5.15
Trading Period 5 now in progress. SECONDS REMAINING:   62
9 of 10 people have voted to end period 5:   Press -LAB- to vote

FIG. 1.—Basic screen display for a trader

Price quotes must progress so as to reduce the bid-ask spread. Only the highest bid to buy and the lowest offer to sell are displayed to the entire market and are open to acceptance. Any quotation that does not provide better terms to the other side of the market is placed in a queue that ranks bids from highest to lowest (offers from lowest to highest). After a contract occurs the highest queued bid and the lowest queued offer are automatically entered as the new bid-ask spread. The maker of a queued price quote is given continuously updated information on the quote's position in the queue. Queued entries may be withdrawn at any time by pressing a key labeled -EDIT-.[2]

Trading occurs over a maximum of 15 market periods each lasting a prespecified number of seconds (either 300 or 330 in the experiments reported below.) The market participants can bypass this stopping rule by unanimously voting to end a period. Registering a vote to end a trading period does not affect the individual's ability to participate

2. Smith and Williams (1983b) found that this variation of the basic PLATO double-auction mechanism, which incorporates an electronic limit order file or "specialist's book" (the bid and offer queues) with the bid-ask spread reduction rule, tends to outperform several other computerized double auctions in price stability and the rapidity of convergence to the competitive equilibrium.

actively in the market. The number of seconds remaining and the current vote to end the period are presented as shown at the bottom of figure 1 and are updated about every 1 or 2 seconds.

### Speculation Mechanics[3]

Market participants designated as traders have the unique ability to switch from buying mode to selling mode at any time by pressing a key labeled -DATA-. Traders are given a capital endowment to cover their initial inventory investment and can add to (subtract from) this amount over the course of the experiment by accumulating profits (incurring losses) from buying and then reselling commodity units for their own accounts.[4] Traders are paid in cash the amount of their final working capital defined as the capital endowment plus any accumulated profits or losses. The perishability of the commodity units is given by a pre-initialized "unit life," which determines the maximum number of periods that an inventory unit can be carried before it "expires." For example, if the unit life is set to three, as in the design II experiments reported below, a unit purchased during trading period 1 would expire at the end of trading period 4. Any inventory unit that expires is automatically sold at a pre-initialized scrap value and the resulting loss is subtracted from the trader's working capital. The scrap-value parameter allows us to normalize for the risk associated with inventory accumulation, when replicating specific supply and demand configurations that have been shifted by an arbitrary constant in order to disguise a design previously used within a given subject population. If at the end of any period a trader's working capital falls to zero he or she is automatically eliminated from the market and receives zero profit. Traders are informed of the final market period at the end of period $X$ where $X$ = (final period − unit life). At the end of the experiment all remaining inventory units are reimbursed at scrap value regardless of the period in which they were purchased.

When a trader buys a commodity unit the price and the period of purchase are logged in the trader's inventory table, as shown in figure 1. Inventory accumulation is governed by a financial inventory constraint and a physical inventory constraint. The financial constraint states that traders can continue accumulating inventory units as long as their working capital exceeds their total inventory cost net of scrap value (displayed on the trader's screen at all times). In other words, for the trader to continue buying, the working capital must cover the loss that would be incurred if all currently held inventory units were to

---

3. A set of screen prints displaying the instructions that PLATO presents to traders in preparation for the experiment is available from the authors.
4. Short sales are currently prohibited. If a trader attempts to enter an offer to sell a unit when his or her current inventory is zero, the following message appears on the viewing screen: "No units available for sale. Press -DATA- to become a buyer."

expire and be sold for their scrap value. We thus limit the amount of credit available to the traders. A physical inventory constraint exists because a maximum of seven units will fit in the inventory table given the horizontal space limitations of the display screen.

Traders' inventories are automatically maintained on a first in–first out basis. When an inventory unit is sold the unit is removed from the inventory table and the sale price, purchase price, and resulting profit are recorded in the trader's record sheet under the period in which the sale was made. Traders are limited to a maximum of five sales in any single period, again because the screen display area is limited.

## III.   Experimental Subjects

All of the experiments reported in the following sections use subjects drawn from the undergraduate and graduate student populations at the University of Arizona in Tucson and Indiana University in Blooming-ton. Most subjects were drawn from undergraduate economic theory classes. Many of the experiments were run "multisite" with subjects participating simultaneously at both locations. Except where explicitly noted, all subjects were experienced in the sense that they had partici-pated in at least one previous double-auction experiment (with com-pletely different market parameters) and had shown no significant problem grasping the institutional rules or trading mechanics of the computerized marketplace.[5] Experienced subjects are usually re-cruited by telephone, since they indicated a desire to participate again in such experiments by leaving their phone number with the experi-menter at the conclusion of the first experiment. Our revolunteer rate is nearly 100%.

After arriving at the experiment site, participants are each paid $3 for keeping their appointment and are then randomly assigned to individ-ual PLATO computer terminals. The double-auction program then (1) assigns each terminal to the condition of buyer, seller, or trader, (2) presents the instructions at an individually controlled pace, and (3) executes the experiment and stores the resulting data on disk for later recall and analysis. The role of buyer and seller were assigned ran-domly by PLATO. In the speculation experiments, however, the assign-ment of the trader's role was not random. Because of the complexity of the task confronted by traders, we chose for this role persons who were either very experienced with the basic mechanism or were other-wise considered unlikely to have difficulty understanding the mechan-ics of being a trader.

---

5. See Williams (1980), Ketcham et al. (1983), and Smith and Williams (1983*b*) for discussions of subject experience as an explicit experimental treatment variable in PLATO market experiments.

## IV.  Four Markets with Cycling Demand and Stationary Supply

### Experimental Design I

So that our initial results may readily be compared with the previous experimental work, our first experiments employ the same induced supply and demand configurations as the studies by MPS (1977, experiment 2) and Williams (1979). These supply and demand arrays are displayed on the left portion of figure 2. The 12 units in each array are distributed among four buyers and four sellers such that each has three units potentially traded.[6] Demand cycles between $D_o$ in the odd-numbered periods and $D^o$ in the even-numbered periods while supply remains stationary. This results in theoretical price-quantity autarkic equilibria of ($P_o = \$3.40$, $Q_o = 5$) in the odd-numbered periods and ($P^o = \$4.20$, $Q^o = 9$) in even-numbered periods. The intertemporal competitive equilibrium price, $P^*$, is \$3.80 with seven units exchanged in the odd-numbered periods ($Q_* = 7$), 11 units exchanged in even-numbered periods ($Q^* = 11$), and four units carried over from each odd- to the next even-numbered period. In each 300-second trading period buyers (sellers) earn the difference between their induced marginal valuation (sale price) and purchase price (marginal cost) for each unit purchased (sold) plus a 5-cent commission to cover subjective transaction costs and minimally to induce the trading of marginal units.

In experiments 1t-1 and 1t-2 reported below, two traders participated in the market in addition to the four buyers and sellers. The traders were given a \$5 capital endowment to cover their initial purchases. The commodity perishability parameter (unit life) was set to allow commodity units to be carried over a maximum of two trading periods beyond the period purchased. The scrap value was set at \$1.[7] Experiments 1a-1 and 1a-2 are autarkic markets replicating experiments 1t-1 and 1t-2, but with no traders.

### Experimental Results

The upper part of figure 2 displays sequential contract prices and descriptive statistics for experiment 1t-1. The rapidity with which prices converge to a range very close to $P^*$ is striking. The seasonal price fluctuations predicted under autarky are almost nonexistent from the very beginning of the experiment. There are 132 contracts over the seven market cycles in periods 1–14, compared with 126 contracts predicted by the intertemporal competitive model. Traders are involved in 53% (70) of the contracts, somewhat more than the 44.4%

6. The earlier studies cited used six buyers and six sellers, each having two units potentially traded.

7. The MPS and Williams studies used a \$3 capital endowment and had no scrap-value parameter. Our design I supply and demand arrays have been shifted up by a constant of \$1 (our scrap value) relative to those used in these earlier studies.

8       **Journal of Business**

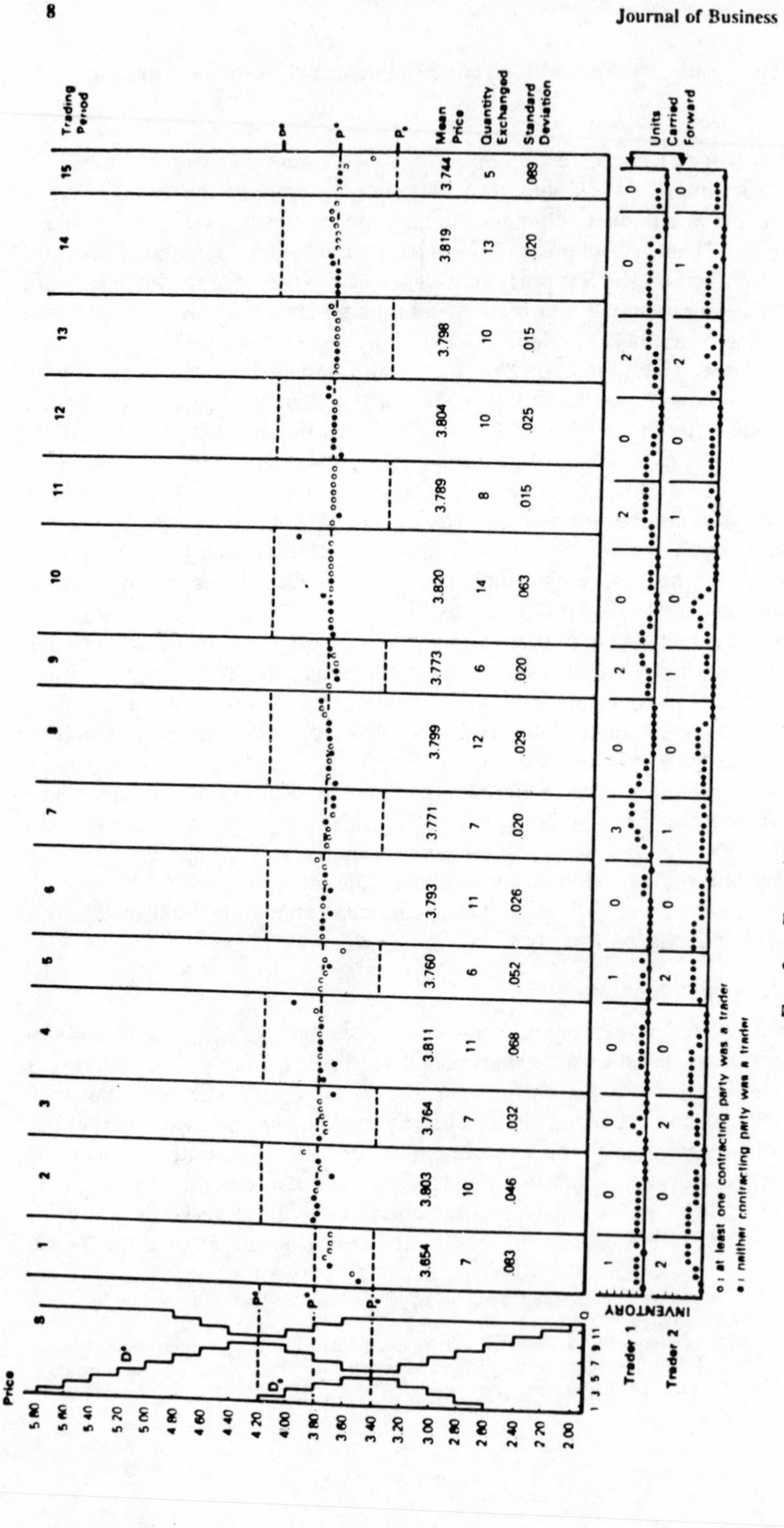

FIG. 2. — Experiment II-1 (design I, speculation)

(eight of every 18) predicted at the theoretical intertemporal equilibrium price.

The lower part of figure 2 displays the level of traders' inventories after each contract occurs. It follows that if a contract is plotted as an open circle (a trader was involved in the exchange) there must be a corresponding increase or decrease in a trader's inventory. We see that the traders were immediately active in the market, being involved in five of the first seven contracts. Note that a unit purchased by trader 1 during the first period was sold the same period. The practice of intraperiod trading became quite common throughout the entire experiment, since the traders were able to gain the 5-cent commission for sales of inventory units regardless of the capital gain.[8] There are even instances where traders are on both ends of an exchange (e.g., the sixth contract in period 8.) The "doomsday" effect built into the market by having all inventory units expire after the final trading period is evident in the period 15 price series. When the traders reduce their usual odd-period purchasing, prices immediately drop toward the autarkic equilibrium.

Figure 3 displays sequential contract prices, traders' inventory levels, and descriptive statistics for experiment 1t-2. The price variance is much greater and convergence toward $P^*$ much slower than in experiment 1t-1. With the exception of periods 2 and 4, prices tend to lag away from $P^*$ in the direction of the autarkic equilibrium. By the seventh complete market cycle (periods 13 and 14) prices appear to have stabilized near $P^*$. As in experiment 1t-1, the built-in doomsday effect is evident in period 15 where prices clearly diverge from $P^*$ toward $P_o$. Over periods 1–14 traders are involved in 43% (52) of the 121 total contracts. Both total exchange volume and the percentage of contracts involving traders are less than the theoretical prediction as well as what was observed in experiment 1t-1.

Figures 4 and 5 display sequential contract prices and descriptive statistics for experiment 1a-1 and experiment 1a-2 (design I, autarky), respectively. Prices in both markets display a clear tendency to lag behind the cyclical demand shifts, converging toward $P_o$ from above in the odd periods and toward $P^o$ from below in the even periods. This "hysteresis" effect was also present in the autarky experiment conducted by Williams (1979) and in two experiments with growing demand reported by Smith (1980) and to some extent in experiments with

8. Elsewhere (Smith and Williams 1983*a*), we report experimental results in which participants can be interpreted as revealing the subjective cost associated with double-auction trading. This measure indicates that such costs average between 5 and 10 cents per trade. However, many trades occur that yield a gain of less than 5 cents, indicating that for some individuals a 5-cent commission is more than sufficient compensation for transactions costs.

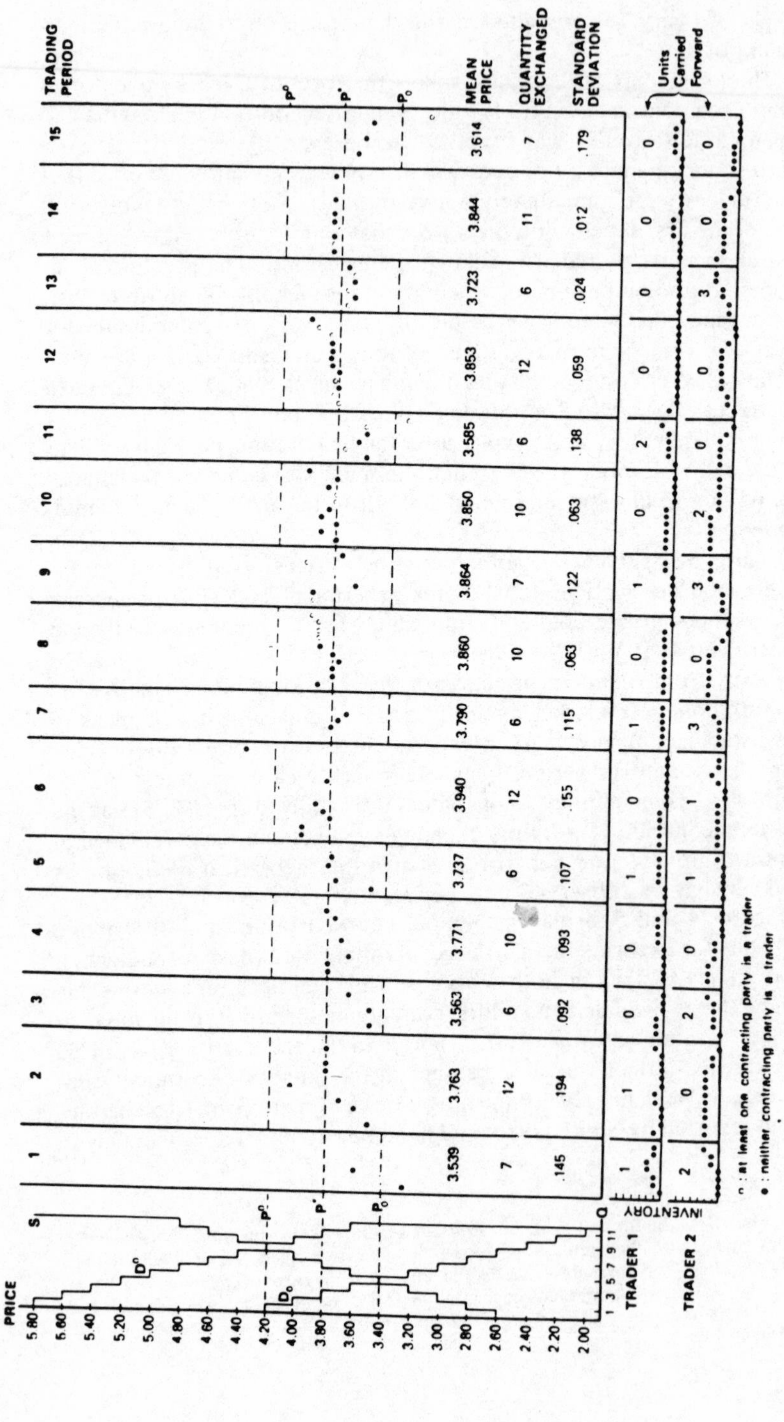

FIG. 3.—Experiment II-2 (design I, speculation)

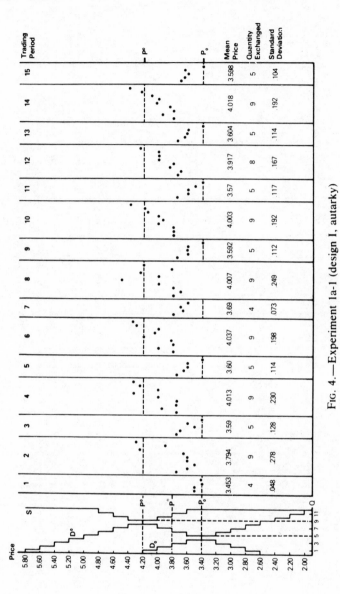

FIG. 4.—Experiment 1a-1 (design I, autarky)

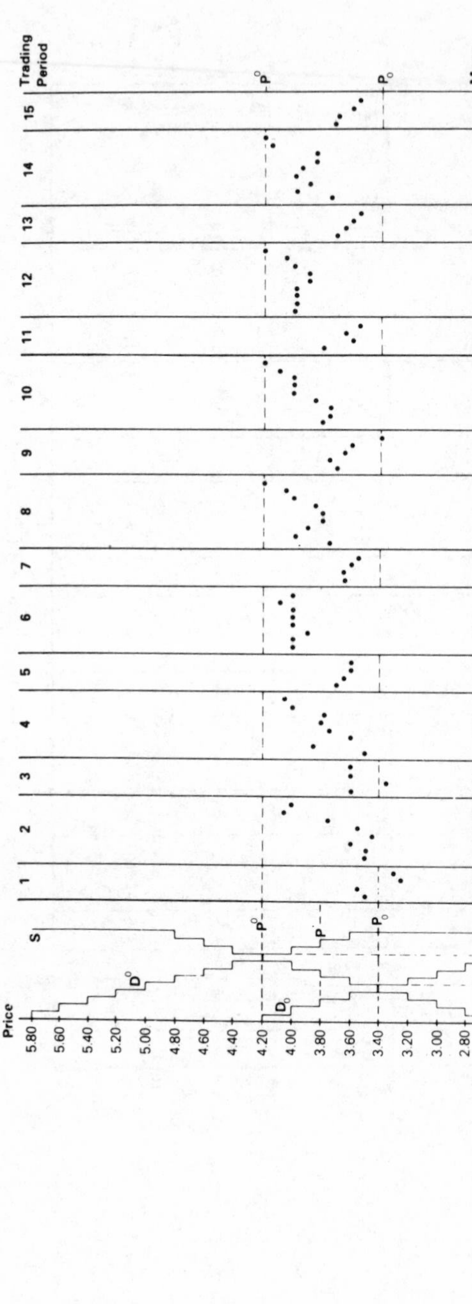


| Trading Period | 1 | 2 | 3 | 4 | 5 | 6 | 7 | 8 | 9 | 10 | 11 | 12 | 13 | 14 | 15 |
|---|---|---|---|---|---|---|---|---|---|---|---|---|---|---|---|
| Mean Price | 3.400 | 3.674 | 3.535 | 3.791 | 3.637 | 3.998 | 3.612 | 3.927 | 3.622 | 3.939 | 3.650 | 4.002 | 3.627 | 3.959 | 3.642 |
| Quantity Exchanged | 4 | 8 | 4 | 8 | 4 | 8 | 4 | 9 | 5 | 9 | 4 | 9 | 4 | 9 | 4 |
| Standard Deviation | .127 | .220 | .107 | .172 | .041 | .048 | .041 | .137 | .121 | .151 | .094 | .084 | .059 | .136 | .070 |

FIG. 5.—Experiment Ia-2 (design I, autarky)

TABLE 1      Contract Price Comparison: Speculation Experiments 1t-1, 1t-2 versus Autarky Experiments 1a-1, 1a-2

| Trading Period | Mean ($\bar{P} - P^*$) | | SD | | |
|---|---|---|---|---|---|
| | 1t-1,2 | 1a-1,2 | 1t-1,2 | 1a-1,2 | $Z_u$ |
| 1 | -.204 | -.374 | .136 | .106 | 2.74*** |
| 2 | -.019 | -.062 | .151 | .268 | 1.48* |
| 3 | -.128 | -.234 | .125 | .130 | 1.81** |
| 4 | -.008 | .109 | .085 | .240 | 1.30* |
| 5 | -.052 | -.183 | .089 | .097 | 2.99*** |
| 6 | .070 | .218 | .138 | .153 | 3.36*** |
| 7 | -.020 | -.149 | .083 | .076 | 2.76*** |
| 8 | .027 | .167 | .058 | .211 | 2.45*** |
| 9 | .022 | -.193 | .105 | .124 | 3.67*** |
| 10 | .033 | .174 | .066 | .181 | 2.40*** |
| 11 | -.099 | -.194 | .141 | .121 | 1.91** |
| 12 | .031 | .162 | .054 | .141 | 3.23*** |
| 13 | -.027 | -.186 | .044 | .100 | 3.63*** |
| 14 | .030 | .188 | .021 | .174 | 3.44*** |
| 15 | -.132 | -.182 | .168 | .099 | 1.50* |
| All odd | -.080 | -.210 | .132 | .120 | 6.92*** |
| All even | .024 | .137 | .095 | .213 | 5.27*** |

\* Reject $H_0$, $P = .10$ (direction predicted).
\*\* Reject $H_0$, $P = .05$ (direction predicted).
\*\*\* Reject $H_0$, $P = .01$ (direction predicted).

growing and then declining demand reported by Harrison, Smith, and Williams (1983).

Note that the first contract in periods 2–15 of experiment 1a-1 occurs in the 10-cent interval centered on $3.75. From this starting point slightly below $P^*$ prices tend to move toward the relevant autarkic equilibrium. The first price in each period is less stable in experiment 1a-2 but the general tendency for the price series to be negatively (positively) sloped during odd (even) periods is evident. In both experiments, monotonicity of price changes is somewhat more evident in odd periods than in even periods. The sustained lagging of price series throughout both autarky experiments suggest that a behavioral equilibrium may be characterized by a nonzero variance price pattern rather than the fixed price equilibrium of traditional competitive price theory.

Table 1 displays a period-by-period comparison of price observations pooled across the two experimental replications in each of the two treatment groups. The $Z_U$ statistic presented is the unit normal deviate of the nonparametric Mann-Whitney $U$ statistic. The test statistic indicates that we must reject central tendency equality (at the .05 level, direction predicted) in 12 of the 15 trading periods. In the other three periods the null hypothesis is rejected at the .1 level, direction predicted. Pooling experimental observations across all odd periods or all even periods results in strong rejection of the null hypothesis at the .01 level.

TABLE 2    Efficiency Comparison: Speculation Experiments 1t-1, 1t-2 versus Autarky Experiments 1a-1, 1a-2

| Trading Period | $E^o$ | | | | $E^*$ | | | |
|---|---|---|---|---|---|---|---|---|
| | 1a-1 | 1a-2 | 1t-1 | 1t-2 | 1a-1 | 1a-2 | 1t-1 | 1t-2 |
| 1 | 100.00 | 100.00 | 113.25 | 108.00 | 83.33 | 83.33 | 94.38 | 90.00 |
| 2 | 98.61 | 100.00 | 107.43 | 106.81 | 93.42 | 94.74 | 101.78 | 101.19 |
| 3 | 95.00 | 100.00 | 108.50 | 97.75 | 79.17 | 83.33 | 90.42 | 81.46 |
| 4 | 98.61 | 100.00 | 104.58 | 108.26 | 93.42 | 94.74 | 99.08 | 102.56 |
| 5 | 95.00 | 90.00 | 96.25 | 117.75 | 79.17 | 75.00 | 80.21 | 95.63 |
| 6 | 98.61 | 97.22 | 106.60 | 102.85 | 93.42 | 92.10 | 100.99 | 97.44 |
| 7 | 75.00 | 100.00 | 117.50 | 122.50 | 62.50 | 83.33 | 97.92 | 102.08 |
| 8 | 94.44 | 100.00 | 106.25 | 95.14 | 89.47 | 94.74 | 100.66 | 90.13 |
| 9 | 75.00 | 95.00 | 118.25 | 127.50 | 62.50 | 79.17 | 98.54 | 106.25 |
| 10 | 100.00 | 100.00 | 104.65 | 101.74 | 94.74 | 94.74 | 99.14 | 96.39 |
| 11 | 95.00 | 100.00 | 119.50 | 62.50 | 79.17 | 83.33 | 99.58 | 52.08 |
| 12 | 100.00 | 100.00 | 105.69 | 107.99 | 94.74 | 94.74 | 100.13 | 102.31 |
| 13 | 95.00 | 100.00 | 121.00 | 115.00 | 79.17 | 83.33 | 100.83 | 95.83 |
| 14 | 98.61 | 100.00 | 105.42 | 106.94 | 93.42 | 94.74 | 99.87 | 101.31 |
| 15 | 75.00 | 80.00 | 49.50 | 95.00 | 62.50 | 66.67 | 41.25 | 79.17 |
| 1–15 | 92.93 | 97.48 | 105.62 | 104.85 | 82.67 | 86.53 | 93.65 | 92.92 |

In spite of the informational and procedural differences introduced by the computerized trading environment, these results strongly support the basic conclusion that the existence of speculative agents tends to reduce price fluctuations in a market governed by cyclical demand and stationary supply. This result holds for a comparison either with autarky-theoretic prices or with actual observed autarky prices even in the presence of a very pronounced hysteresis effect.

A second and perhaps more important criterion for the comparison of market performance in the two treatment groups is allocative efficiency. Table 2 presents two efficiency measures ($E^o$ and $E^*$) for each period of the four design I experiments. The first measure, $E^o$, is defined as the actual profit (exclusive of commissions) earned by all market participants expressed as a percentage of the maximum potential profit available under intertemporal autarky; $E^*$ expresses actual profit (exclusive of commissions) as a percentage of the total profit earned at the intertemporal competitive equilibrium.

Under autarky the total surplus available to the participants (excluding commissions) is $4.00 in odd periods and $14.40 in even periods and is split equally between buyers and sellers. At an intertemporal competitive equilibrium the total surplus available is $4.80 in the odd periods ($.60 to buyers, $4.20 to sellers) and $15.20 in even periods ($11.00 to buyers, $4.20 to sellers). Thus, the maximum value of $E^*$ possible under autarky is 83.33 in odd periods and 94.74 in even periods or 92 over one market cycle. At an intertemporal equilibrium the value of $E^o$ would be 120 in odd periods and 105.56 in even periods or 108.96 over a market cycle.

Table 2 clearly reveals that the efficiency of the speculative markets tends to exceed that observed in the autarkic markets. Twenty-four out of 30 observations on speculative market efficiency exceed the maximum possible value under autarky. In a period-by-period comparison of mean efficiency the speculative mean exceeds the autarkic mean in all except period 11. A matched pairs $t$-test on the period 1–14 means yields $t_{(13)} = 3.53$. Using raw unpaired data yields $t_{(54)} = 4.34$ and $Z_U = 5.05$. The introduction of intertemporal speculators results in a highly significant increase in allocative efficiency.

## V. Fourteen Markets with Cycling Demand and Supply

Having demonstrated an ability to replicate the basic results of the previous double-auction speculation and autarky experiments using our subject pool and computerized trading mechanism, we now turn to an investigation of the behavioral characteristics of speculative and autarkic markets governed by an entirely new cyclical market design.

### Experimental Design II

Figure 6 displays the market supply and demand configurations induced on four buyers and four sellers in design II. This design is characterized by a stable cycling of both the supply and demand arrays where $(D'', S'') = (D_o + 1.80, S_o + 1.80)$. Note that the autarkic and intertemporal equilibrium prices are not unique but are defined over a 10-cent interval centered on $P_o$, $P''$, and $P^*$, where $P^* = (P_o + .80) = (P'' - .80)$. The autarkic and intertemporal competitive quantities are $Q'' = Q_o = 7$ and $Q^* = 11$ with nine units carried over from each odd to the next even period by traders. The autarkic price spread is thus double that of design I and the optimal carry-over is one unit more than double that in design I. In all of the design II experiments traders were given a capital endowment of $10. The unit life was set for three periods and the scrap value was set at $(P^* - 1.80)$. Each trading period lasted 330 seconds and, unlike the design I experiments, no commission was paid on traded units.

Table 3 displays additional information for each of the fourteen design II experiments.[9] The first four experiments, 2a-1, 2a-2, 2a-3, and 2a-4 are autarkic markets. The other 10 markets included speculators: two in experiment 2t-1 and three in the other nine experiments. All but one of the experiments used participants who were experienced with

9. The expression in parenthesis in col. 1 of table 4 is the name we have given the particular experiment for disk storage and recall. For example, 2a-1 (3pda13) means that experiment 2a-1 in this report was the thirteenth run on version 3 of the PLATO Double Auction TUTOR software. The correspondence for the design I experiments is as follows: 1t-1 (3pda05), 1t-2 (3pda82), 1a-1 (3pda07), 1a-2 (3pda81). The experiments were conducted over a span of more than 3¼ years beginning in June 1979.

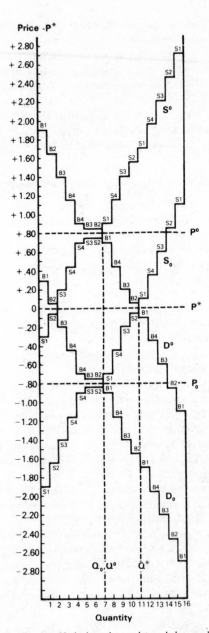

Fig. 6.—Design II–induced supply and demand arrays

TABLE 3          **Experiment Classification: Design II**

| Experiment | Number of Speculators | Experienced Buyers and Sellers? | Summary Price Information? | Final Period | P* |
|---|---|---|---|---|---|
| 2a-1 (3pda13) | 0 | yes | no | 14 | 3.80 |
| 2a-2 (3pda14) | 0 | yes | no | 13 | 3.80 |
| 2a-3 (3pda56) | 0 | yes | no | 14 | 6.60 |
| 2a-4 (3pda57) | 0 | yes | no | 14 | 5.30 |
| 2t-1 (3pda17) | 2 | yes | no | 12 | 5.80 |
| 2t-2 (3pda22) | 3 | yes | no | 14 | 4.50 |
| 2t-3 (3pda23) | 3 | no | no | 14 | 5.80 |
| 2t-4 (3pda29) | 3 | yes | no | 12 | 4.50 |
| 2t-5 (3pda34) | 3 | yes | no | 8* | 5.80 |
| 2t-6 (3pda37) | 3 | yes | no | 14 | 6.80 |
| 2tp-1 (3pda42) | 3 | yes | yes | 14 | 6.80 |
| 2tp-2 (3pda43) | 3 | yes | yes | 9† | 4.50 |
| 2tp-3 (3pda48) | 3 | yes | yes | 15 | 6.80 |
| 2tp-4 (3pda50) | 3 | yes | yes | 15 | 4.50 |

\* Terminated after period 8 because of computer problems.
† Terminated after period 9 because of computer problems.

PLATO double-auction trading mechanics; the exception was experiment 2t-3, which employed inexperienced buyers and sellers but experienced speculators. In experiments 2tp-1 through 2tp-4 all subjects were given access between trading periods to a table containing the quantity exchanged and the average, highest, and lowest contract price in all previous periods. The reasoning behind the introduction of this additional information will become clear in the next section. With the exception of experiments 2t-5 and 2tp-2 (which were terminated because of computer problems) the final period of trading was governed by a 2-hour time limit on our exclusive use of the PLATO facilities at our respective institutions.

*Experimental Results*

Figures 7*a*, 7*b*, and 7*c* plot the sequence of mean contract prices and the quantity exchanged for all 14 of the design II experiments. One observation that is immediately clear from figures 7*a* and 7*b* is that the rapid convergence of speculative market prices to the intertemporal competitive equilibrium, so apparent in experiment 1t, is not generally observed using the design II parameters. Experiment 2t-2 is the only market that appears to have stabilized at a price near (actually slightly below) $P^*$. The other nine speculation experiments exhibit various degrees of partial convergence to $P^*$; however, mean prices are clearly closer to $P^*$ than in the four autarky experiments (fig. 7*a*). This conclusion is supported by figure 8, which displays 99% confidence bands for the mean contract price in each trading period for both the pooled speculation and pooled autarky samples. Note that the bands do not

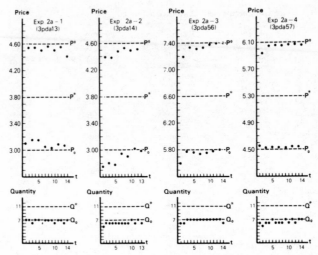

FIG. 7*a*.—Sequential mean contract prices: autarky experiments

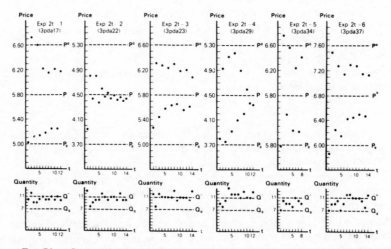

FIG. 7*b*.—Sequential mean contract prices: speculation experiments without summary information.

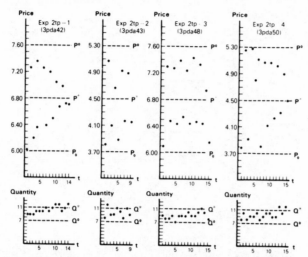

FIG. 7c.—Sequential mean contract prices: speculation experiments with summary information

intersect after period 2, which marks the end of the first market cycle. This is because of a gradual movement of the mean price in the speculative markets away from the autarkic equilibrium toward $P^*$ as traders become active in the market.

The autarkic market price data presented in figures 7a and 8 is further summarized by the pooled contract price frequency polygons presented in figure 9. Note that these sample distributions are derived from market cycles 3 through 7 and thus exclude contracts that occurred during the initial periods of trading. The distribution of odd-

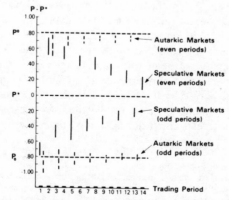

FIG. 8.—Confidence bands (99%) for mean contract price

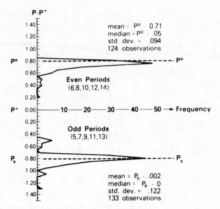

FIG. 9.—Contract price frequency polygons: autarky experiments

period contract prices can be characterized as symmetric with mean, median, and mode at the midpoint of the range of autarkic competitive equilibrium prices. In sharp contrast with this, the distribution of even-period prices can be characterized as asymmetric (downward skewed) with a mean 2.1 cents below the minimum of the range of competitive equilibrium prices and a median and mode at the minimum competitive equilibrium price. A comparison of the two sample distributions, expressed as deviations from the appropriate autarkic equilibrium price, yields $Z_U = 6.473$ (reject the null hypothesis, $p < .01$). The data clearly indicate that the hysteresis effect, noted in experiment 1a, is present in the even-period data but not in the odd-period data. We find this rather surprising and offer no formal behavioral-theoretic explanation for this empirical result.[10] We can, however, point out that this phenomenon can be interpreted as consistent with recent experimental evidence offered by us (Smith and Williams 1982) in support of what we might call a "weak-sellers" hypothesis. This simply states that, over a large number of experimental replications, there appears to be a tendency for contract prices to converge to a static, symmetric-rent, competitive equilibrium from below and that this effect can combine with certain design parameters (e.g., the distribution of exchange surplus) to determine the observed price convergence path. One explanation of the dissimilarities displayed by the figure 9 frequency polygons is that the weak-seller effect tends to offset the lagging of prices above $P_o$, predicted by the hysteresis effect during odd periods. But the weak-seller

10. A comparison of pooled price data from market cycles 5–7 of the two design 1 autarky experiments shows that there is no significant difference in the mean absolute price deviation from $P^*$ across market phases ($Z_U = .41$). Significantly higher price variance is, however, observed in even periods ($F_{78,44} = 2.8$) relative to odd periods.

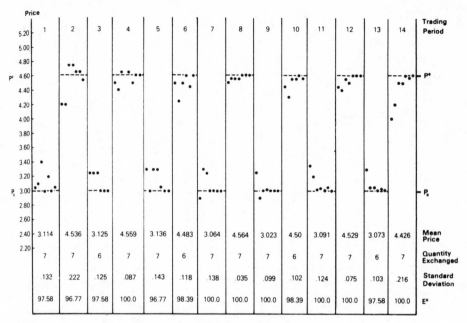

FIG. 10.—Experiment 2a-1 (design II, autarky)

and hysteresis effects combine during even periods to produce the distinct lagging of prices below $P''$. An alternative explanation is that the first phase of the market cycle is somehow weighted more heavily than the second in the price expectation formation process. This could easily be tested by conducting a set of experiments with the cyclical phases reversed.

Figures 10, 11, 12, and 13 display the actual sequence of contract prices and descriptive statistics for autarky experiments 2a-1, 2a-2, 2a-3, and 2a-4, respectively. Note that the markets are extremely efficient regardless of the cyclical phase. Prices in 2a-1 exhibit a hysteresis effect in both the odd-period and even-period phases. However, price convergence in 2a-2 and 2a-3 is generally from below in both cyclical phases. Market prices in 2a-4 converge very rapidly to the upper (lower) bound of the odd (even) period range of competitive equilibrium prices.

From figure 7*b* we note that experiments 2t-1 through 2t-6 display varying degrees of partial convergence to $P^*$. After we conducted these first six speculation experiments it seemed apparent that traders were quite frequently not fully aware of the market's cyclical nature or the opportunities for profit available to them through interperiod carryover of inventories. In an attempt to help focus the subjects' attention on the low-high (odd-even) price cycle we decided to provide them

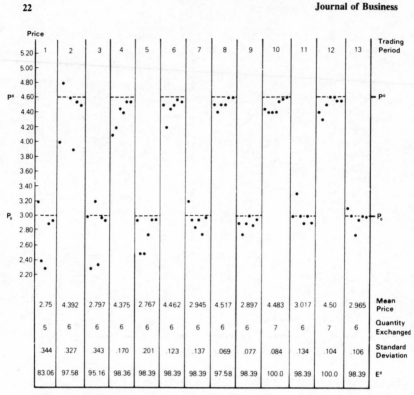

FIG. 11.—Experiment 2a-2 (design II, autarky)

(after each trading period) with a table containing the average, high, and low contract price from all past periods. It is evident from figures *7b* and *7c* that this additional information did not have a dramatic impact on the price convergence behavior in experiments 2tp-1 through 2tp-4 compared with experiments 2t-1 through 2t-6. We interpret the continued tendency for speculative markets to fail to converge to $P^*$ as evidence that speculators are unwilling to bear the risk required to eliminate the autarkic price spread completely. Not surprisingly, we have found that perceptive risk takers are the most successful speculators!

A statistical test of the effect on convergence speed of providing summary price information can be generated via estimation of the coefficients given in the following exponential decay function used to characterize the price convergence process:[11]

$$\ln \alpha(t) = a + bt + cI + d(t \times I),$$

11. Observations from the final trading period in an experiment were not included in the following estimates in order to eliminate price observations generated by end effects.

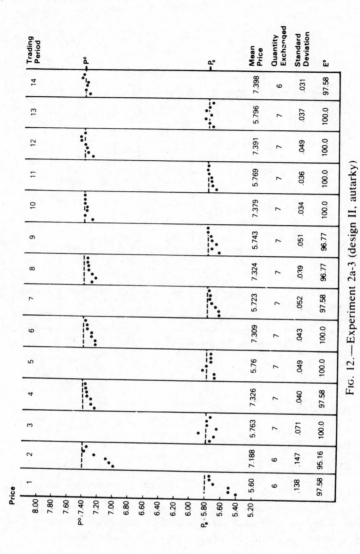

Fig. 12.—Experiment 2a-3 (design II, autarky)

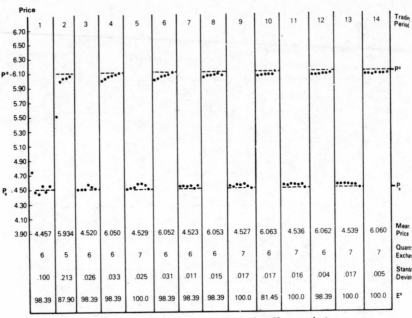

Fig. 13.—Experiment 2a-4 (design II, autarky)

where

$$\alpha^2(t) = \frac{1}{Q} \sum_{i=1}^{Q} [P_i(t) - P^*]^2;$$

$P_i(t) \equiv$ the $i$th contract price in trading period $t$;

$Q \equiv$ the total quantity exchanged during period $t$;

$P^* \equiv$ intertemporal competitive equilibrium price; and

$I = 1$ if summary price information was provided, 0 otherwise.

Thus, the price series in a particular period of trading is "close" to $P^*$ only if the price variance is low and the mean price is near $P^*$. Least-squares estimation of the equation specified above yields:

$$\ln \alpha = -.161 - .118t - .090I + .044(t \times I)$$
$$(p = 0) \quad (p = .652) \quad (p = .0921)$$

$$R^2 = .348, \ F_{(3,115)} = 20.5.$$

The rather surprising result is that the presentation of summary price information tends to retard slightly, rather than to speed up, the rate of price convergence to $P^*$. Both sets of experiments start the convergence process from an $\alpha$ value very close to .75 (note that the minimum autarkic equilibrium price spread is $-.75$ to $+.75$ in fig. 4). Choosing a

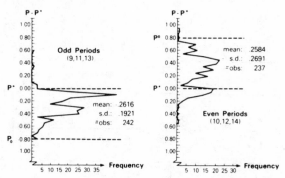

Fɪɢ. 14.—Contract price frequency polygons: speculation experiments

target value of $\alpha = .05$ (the range of intertemporal equilibrium prices is from $-.05$ to $+.05$) we find that $\alpha$ would decay to the target value after 25 periods of trading under the "no summary information" treatment and after 38 periods of trading when summary information is provided.

The substantial variation in prices generated during the final market cycles of the speculation experiments is illustrated by the separate odd- and even-period frequency polygons and descriptive summary statistics for pooled period 9–14 data, shown in figure 14.

Figures 15–18 plot the sequence of contract prices, each trader's inventory level, and descriptive statistics for speculation experiments 2t-1, 2t-2, 2t-3, and 2tp-3, respectively. In experiment 2t-1 we observe a partial elimination of the autarkic price spread with prices being fairly stable during the sixth market cycle (periods 11 and 12) at $(P_o + .27)$ and $(P^o - .41)$. It is tempting to conjecture that the traders were sophisticated enough to realize that it was in their combined best interest to maintain such a price spread.[12] However, the reason for its existence is clear after examining the sequence of traders' inventory levels presented in the lower part of figure 15. We note that trader 1 was responsible for most of the successful speculative activity in this market and that trader 2 was, after repeated losses, almost completely inactive over the last two market cycles. The net aggregate change in traders' inventories, starting with period 1, is $+2, +2, +1, -1, +4, -6, +5, -6, +4, -5, +5, -5$. This is insufficient to eliminate the cyclical price swings.

Trader 1 is very conservative over the first two market cycles, buying and then selling one unit in both periods 1 and 2. He then carries one unit over from period 3 to period 4, earns a sizable profit ($1.60) on this unit, and then falls into a pattern of buying in the odd periods and

12. The price spread that would maximize traders' joint profits is $(P_o + .35) - (P^o - .35)$ with a total of six units carried over from each odd- to each even-numbered period.

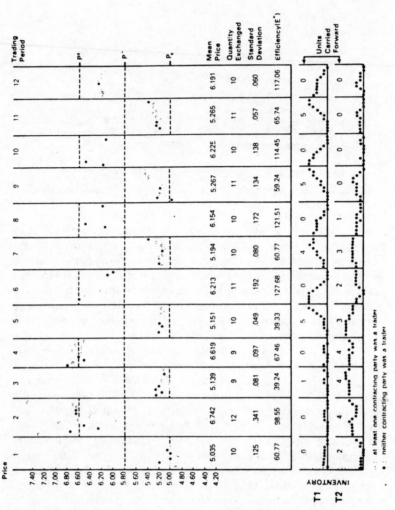

FIG. 15.—Experiment 21-1 (design II, speculation)

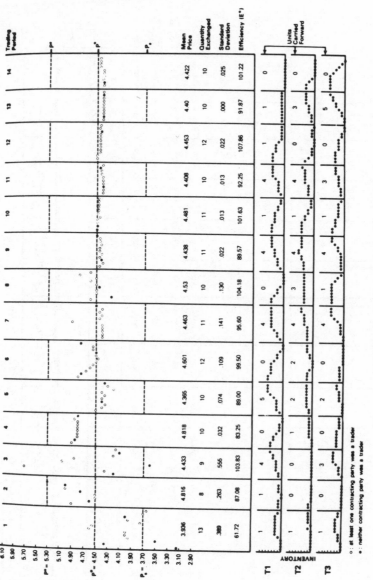

FIG. 16.—Experiment 2t-2 (design II, speculation)

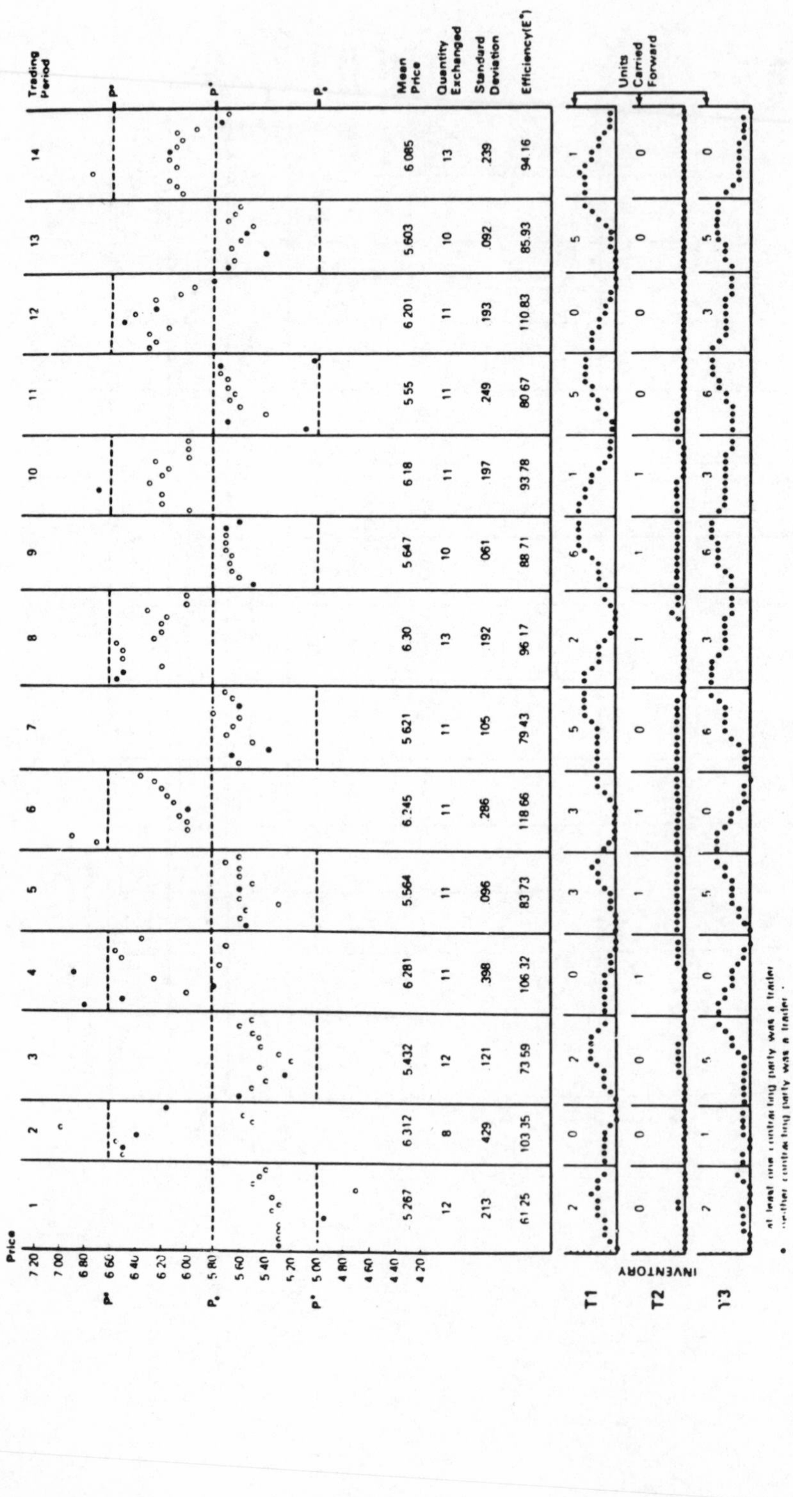

Fig. 17.—Experiment 2t-3 (design II, speculation)

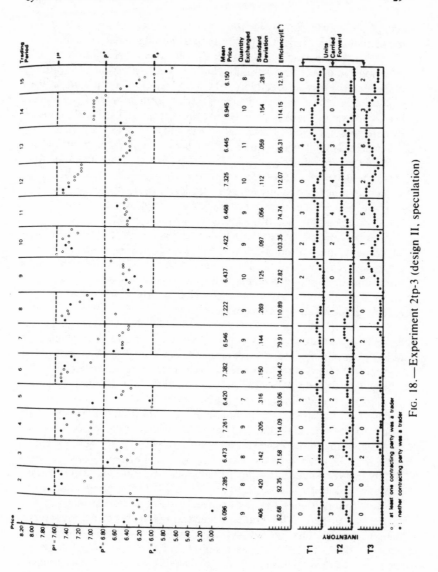

FIG. 18.—Experiment 2tp-3 (design II, speculation)

selling in the even periods for the remainder of the market. In contrast to this behavior, trader 2 quickly enters the market and carries two units over from period 1 to period 2; she then buys two additional units in period 2 and sells the two units purchased during period 1 for profits of $1.61 and $1.10, respectively. She then buys two more units in the high-price period for a total of four period 2 units carried over into period 3. One of these units is sold in the next period for a $2.20 loss, two are sold in period 4 for losses of $.39 and $.15, and the final unit is sold at a loss of $2.40 in period 5 (after which it would have been sold at its $4.00 scrap value for a loss of $3.50). For the remainder of the experiment trader 2 does not seem to recognize the proper buy-sell sequence, much to the advantage of trader 1, who amasses a working capital of $30.63 over the course of the experiment. By contrast, trader 2's working capital falls from $10.00 to $6.92.

After running experiment 2t-1 we decided to use three traders in the subsequent speculation experiments. The socially optimal intertemporal carry-over would thus be obtained if each trader bought and sold three units in each odd-even market cycle. Figure 16 displays price and inventory data from experiment 2t-2. Prices approach $P^*$ fairly rapidly, reflecting net inventory changes of $+3, -2, +6, -6, +8, -7, +10, -8, +8, -9, +8, -10, +8, -9$ for periods 1–14, respectively. Traders 1 and 3 are quite consistent in following a profitable buy-sell sequence but accumulate a working capital of only $12.19 and $11.99, respectively, for their efforts because the autarkic price spread is eliminated. Trader 2 does not follow the odd-even buy-sell pattern until period 11 and ends with a working capital of $9.64.

Figure 17 displays the price and inventory data from experiment 2t-3 which exhibits partial convergence to $P^*$ even though three traders were operating in the market. Net inventory changes for periods 1–14 are $+4, -3, +6, -6, +8, -5, +7, -5, +7, -8, +6, -8, +7, -9$. In this market trader 2 is almost totally inactive throughout the entire experiment but does manage to lose $2 of his $10 starting capital. In contrast to this, trader 1 is a very successful speculator earning $21.71 by the end of period 14. Trader 1 failed to unload all of his inventory units during the final period of trading and consequently is forced to absorb a $2.75 loss for selling a unit at scrap value. Trader 1 commented after the experiment that he had mistakenly purchased a unit at the beginning of period 14 when he meant to sell. This raised his inventory level to six units and since the maximum number of sales in any one period is limited to five, he was forced ultimately to pay for his error. Trader 3 is also quite successful in his speculative activities, earning $24.60 during the experiment.

Figure 18 plots price and inventory data from experiment 2tp-3 where all subjects were provided summary price information between

TABLE 4        Autarky–Speculation Efficiency Comparison: Design II

| Trading Period | $E^o$ | | $E^*$ | |
|---|---|---|---|---|
| | Autarky | Speculation | Autarky | Speculation |
| 1 | 94.15 | 103.15 | 55.86 | 61.20 |
| 2 | 94.35 | 148.90 | 55.98 | 88.34 |
| 3 | 97.78 | 113.61 | 58.01 | 67.40 |
| 4 | 98.59 | 154.24 | 58.49 | 91.51 |
| 5 | 98.79 | 97.14 | 58.61 | 57.63 |
| 6 | 98.79 | 177.29 | 58.61 | 105.19 |
| 7 | 98.59 | 108.18 | 58.49 | 64.18 |
| 8 | 98.18 | 189.02 | 58.25 | 112.15 |
| 9 | 98.79 | 122.73 | 58.61 | 72.82 |
| 10 | 94.96 | 187.28 | 56.34 | 111.11 |
| 11 | 99.60 | 128.63 | 59.09 | 76.32 |
| 12 | 99.60 | 179.37 | 59.09 | 106.42 |
| 13 | 98.99 | 128.39 | 58.73 | 76.17 |
| 14 | 99.19 | 164.05 | 58.85 | 97.33 |
| 1–14 | 97.88 | 142.99 | 58.07 | 89.84 |

periods. Net aggregate inventory changes for periods 1–15 are $+3$, $-3$, $+6$, $-5$, $+4$, $-5$, $+7$, $-6$, $+6$, $-2$, $+7$, $-6$, $+7$, $-8$, $-3$. Traders 1–3 ended with working capital of \$17.66, \$14.24, and \$19.06, respectively. Note that trader 3 has two inventory units remaining when time expires in the final trading period and must cover a \$2.93 loss on these units. A clear end effect is present in period 15 as traders 1 and 3 try to unload five inventory units in an odd period, causing prices to drop sharply back to and below the autarkic equilibrium.

Table 4 presents a pooled autarkic-speculative market efficiency comparison. The speculative markets generate a higher mean efficiency in all trading periods except period 5 (when they are almost identical). A matched pairs $t$-test using the mean value of $E^o$ given in table 4 yields $t_{(13)} = 5.183$. The design II parameters are such that at the autarkic competitive equilibria buyers and sellers split \$6.20 in surplus equally each period. At the intertemporal competitive equilibrium, total surplus available is \$10.45, with buyers (sellers) receiving \$.35 and sellers (buyers) receiving \$10.10 during each odd (even) trading period. Thus, an $E^o$ value of 100 implies a corresponding $E^*$ value of 59.33 and an $E^*$ value of 100 implies an $E^o$ value of 168.55. Except for period 5, the mean efficiency in the speculative markets exceeds the maximum possible efficiency in an autarkic market ($E^o = 100$, $E^* = 59.33$). Also, it is instructive to note the low-high (odd-even) efficiency cycle in the speculation experiments. This is due to the fact that purchases by traders were generally made in odd (low price) periods and resulted in an immediate profit only for the seller. Traders generally made profits on the sale of inventory units in even (high-price) periods.

## VI.  Summary

Using observations from two cyclical market designs, we have shown that the inclusion of a class of speculative agents tends to reduce significantly the observed magnitude of cyclical price swings relative to those observed in markets without intertemporal speculation. Including speculators also results in a significant increase in market efficiency.

In a market with shifting demand and stable supply (design I) we observe convergence toward the zero excess demand intertemporal equilibrium price when speculative agents are active in the market. Without speculators, prices display a marked lagging in the adjustment from one cyclical phase to the other. When a considerably different market design with shifting supply and demand is used (design II), prices do not generally converge to the intertemporal competitive equilibrium within the seven-cycle duration of most experiments. This slow rate of price convergence is attributed to risk-averse behavior by speculators, resulting in intertemporal carry-over below the socially optimal level. Without speculators, prices tend to cycle between the two (autarkic) equilibria. An investigation of the price series and resulting frequency distributions generated in odd (low-price) and even (high-price) periods shows a tendency for prices to lag somewhat below the competitive equilibrium during even periods but not during odd periods. An informal explanation is offered to account for this empirical phenomenon.

## References

Harrison, Glenn W.; Smith, Vernon L.; and Williams, Arlington W. 1983. Learning behavior in experimental auction markets. Unpublished manuscript. London: University of Western Ontario, May.

Hoffman, Elizabeth, and Plott, Charles R. 1981. The effect of intertemporal speculation on the outcomes in seller posted offer auction markets. *Quarterly Journal of Economics* 96 (May): 223–41.

Ketcham, Jon; Smith, Vernon L.; and Williams, Arlington W. 1983. The behavior of posted offer pricing institutions. Unpublished manuscript. Tucson: University of Arizona, January.

Miller, Ross M.; Plott, Charles R.; and Smith, Vernon L. 1977. Intertemporal competitive equilibrium: An empirical study of speculation. *Quarterly Journal of Economics* 91 (November): 599–624.

Plott, Charles R., and Uhl, Jonathan. 1981. Competitive equilibrium with middlemen: An empirical study. *Southern Economic Journal* 47 (April): 1063–71.

Smith, Vernon L. 1980. The relevance of laboratory experiments to testing resource allocation theory. In J. Kmenta and J. Ramsey (eds.). *Evaluation of Econometric Models.* New York: Academic Press.

Smith, Vernon L., and Williams, Arlington W. 1982. The effects of rent asymmetries in experimental auction markets. *Journal of Economic Behavior and Organization* 3 (March): 99–116.

Smith, Vernon L., and Williams, Arlington W. 1983*a*. The boundaries of competitive price theory: Convergence, expectation and transaction cost. Paper prepared for the Public Choice Society meetings, New Orleans, March 1981 (rev. February).

Smith, Vernon L. and Williams, Arlington W. 1983*b*. An experimental comparison of alternative rules for competitive market exchange. In R. Engelbrecht-Wiggans, M. Shubik, and R. Stark (eds.), *Auctions, Bidding and Contracting: Uses and Theory.* New York University Press.

Williams, Arlington W. 1979. Intertemporal competitive equilibrium: On further experimental results. In Vernon L. Smith (ed.), *Research in Experimental Economics.* Vol. 1. Greenwich, Conn.: JAI.

Williams, Arlington W. 1980. Computerized double-auction markets: Some initial experimental results. *Journal of Business* 53 (July): 235–58.

# [15]

# ECONOMETRICA

VOLUME 50          MAY, 1982          NUMBER 3

## ASSET VALUATION IN AN EXPERIMENTAL MARKET

BY ROBERT FORSYTHE, THOMAS R. PALFREY, AND CHARLES R. PLOTT[1]

The time path of asset prices is studied within a stationary experimental environment. After several replications prices converge to a perfect foresight equilibrium. A sequential market having an "informational trap" and a futures market are also studied.

## 1. INTRODUCTION

THEORIES OF ASSET PRICES have occupied a very special place in the history of economic doctrine as being both important and diverse. Importance is established with the key role of time in the analysis. Almost every economic commodity exists over time thereby manifesting one of the essential features of an asset. Diversity also follows from the incorporation of time because of the potential applicability of a host of subtheories which differ according to "motivational spirit" and rigor of development. Competing subtheories about the nature of choice over time, choice under uncertainty, learning and the informational content of prices can all lead to different theories of asset prices. In addition any theory of asset prices necessarily involves many parameters (information states, a priori expectations, preferences over time, etc.). As a result the discipline frequently has difficulty identifying a solid empirical base upon which to justify the acceptance or rejection of competing theories. This paper represents a first attempt to explore the potential of laboratory markets for adding to such base that exists.

The behavior of five different asset markets is reported. The markets were created in a laboratory environment and were very simple relative to the asset markets found in natural environments. The purpose of studying the simple markets is to find unambiguous answers to the following questions. (a) Do these asset markets exhibit any regularities relative to their organization and underlying parameters? (b) If regularities exist do they conform to the predictions of any of the standard mathematical models when the latter are applied in a natural way?

If the answer to either of these questions is "no" then one would be very suspicious of applications of the same models to more complicated markets. Models which are supposed to work in general should be expected to work in simple special cases. Obviously success of a model in simple special cases does not imply that the model will work in general and we make no such claim. Rather, we view the results reported here as simply a base upon which the study of more complicated situations can be conducted.

[1] The financial support of the National Science Foundation is gratefully acknowledged. The comments of William Brock, David Cass, Katherine Echol, Charles Holt, and James Jordan have been helpful. We also thank George Fox for his help in conducting the experiments.

In addition to the questions above some purely methodological questions are posed. The experiments themselves involved some experimental techniques that had not been used before. It was necessary to determine whether or not these techniques exerted an independent influence on market behavior before further studies could be conducted.

The theories we call upon can be divided into two broad classes. However, before discussing theories we should note the existence of *non*theories asserted in newspapers and social commentaries. These are in effect claims that asset prices are arbitrary. Such prices depend upon the idiosyncratic nature of individual behavior and convey little or no information at all about the states of the world or the magnitude of economic parameters. Some implications of this belief are that there are no reasons to study asset markets because there is nothing to learn and those who claim there is are confusing religion with science. Needless to say, most economists would disagree with this view and tend to dismiss it as "table talk" or "uninformed chatter" which is of no concern. It never appears in academic journals (at least we could find no good quotes). The fact is, however, that the profession has no simple way to disconfirm seemingly outlandish beliefs when held by skeptical students, colleagues in other disciplines, and decision-making politicians.

The first class of theories holds that asset prices are not arbitrary. Indeed the prices may exhibit a great deal of regularity. Those who accept theories of this first type would claim that the regularities may have very little, if anything, to do with underlying economics or the economy. Instead asset prices follow laws of random motion such as martingales. The only information that $P_t$ conveys might be something about the probability of various prices in the past. The implication of this line of theory is that one might study charts, charting techniques, and various other models of stochastic processes.

Included in this class of theories, would be purely expectational equilibria similar to one put forth by Keynes. The essential idea is captured in the following selection from his *General Theory*:

> Or, to change the metaphor slightly, professional investment may be likened to those newspaper competitions in which the competitors have to pick out the six prettiest faces from a hundred photographs, the prize being awarded to the competitor whose choice most nearly corresponds to the average preferences of the competitors as a whole; so that each competitor has to pick, not those faces which he himself finds the prettiest, but those which he thinks likeliest to catch the fancy of the other competitors, all of whom are looking at the problem from the same point of view. It is not a case of choosing those which, to the best of one's judgement, are really the prettiest, nor even those which average opinion genuinely thinks the prettiest. We have reached the third degree where we devote our intelligences to anticipating what average opinion expects the average opinion to be. And there are some, I believe, who practice the fourth, fifth and higher degrees (Keynes [10, p. 156]).

While one may argue about what Keynes "really means" one natural conclusion from such a behavioral hypothesis is that for any set of vectors of returns to individuals virtually any price vector can be an equilibrium given the proper set of beliefs. This is possible because each individual bases his valuations, and hence his choices, *entirely* on the expected valuations of other individuals without stipulating any connection with an underlying stream of returns from holding the asset. In essence, all investors are viewed as short-run speculators who are not concerned with the stream of returns generated directly from holding the asset. Here the informational content of prices is, loosely speaking, a reflection of the "average" trader's expectations of future prices of the asset.

The second set of theories all hold that asset prices exhibit regularities that are systematically related to the underlying returns generated by the asset. All such models stipulate a consistency among expected individual returns, possible capital gains and individual choice behavior, but they differ on how these are related. Individual learning models, for example, have individuals forming expectations about price changes and the asset price being determined by choices based on both those expectations and the individual's expected stream of dividend returns from holding the asset (Easley [2], Jordan [9], and Townsend [17]). The rational expectations hypothesis and the related perfect foresight equilibrium concept stipulate a further direct consistency between expectations and the actual price behavior (see, for example, Harrison and Kreps [8]). The efficient market hypothesis extends the relationship to the speed with which economic events are translated into market prices by claiming that "prices at any time fully reflect all available information" (Fama [3, p. 383]).

These three categories (one class of nontheories and two classes of theories) are intended only as a means of organizing our thoughts and discussions. Clearly they do not capture the details of the wide variety and complexity of existing models. The formal development of specific models is contained in Section 4.

## 2. THE LABORATORY MARKETS

The economic properties of each of the five markets we studied are listed below. It is hoped that the study of such special cases will lead to clearly interpretable results despite the complexities of individual and market behavior that is observed in laboratory environments.

(a) Each market year had two periods, $A$ and $B$. All period $A$'s (in a market) were identical in terms of the underlying distribution of returns and all period $B$'s in a market were identical. Thus each year was in a sense a replication of previous years.

(b) Each experiment consisted of a fixed group of subjects who participated in a sequence of six to eight market years. Each period $A$ and each period $B$ was seven minutes long.

(c) Assets had a one-year life. The supply of assets was constant for all periods of all years.

(d) Individual monetary returns from assets in any given period of a year were linear in the number of units of the asset held. That is, individual $i$ received returns (dividends) $d_A^i$ for each unit of the asset held at the end of any period $A$ and $d_B^i$ for each unit of the asset held at the end of any period $B$.

(e) Individuals were partitioned into trader "types." Individuals of a given trader type had identical returns but the returns differed across types.

(f) The markets were organized as oral double auctions.[2] All individuals were present for all periods. All bids, offers, and contracts were public and recorded publicly so the cost of gathering such information was minimal. Possibilities for explicit collusion did not exist.

(g) No short sales were permitted. This means that there was a fixed supply of the asset.

(h) Markets occurred sequentially except in Experiment 5.

(i) No futures markets existed with the exception of Experiment 5. In this market a period *B* futures market replaced the period *B* spot market.

Five markets were studied using subjects who were undergraduate male and female students at the California Institute of Technology. In three of the markets (Experiments 3, 4, and 5), only subjects who had been in one of the first two experiments were used and thus could be considered experienced.

In Experiments 1, 2, 3, and 5 there were nine traders; in Experiment 4 there were eight. At the beginning of a trading year each trader was endowed with two[3] "certificates" which had no face value but paid a "dividend" at the end of each of the two periods, *A* and *B*, during the year. The value of the dividend depended upon the individual and the period. That is, each certificate held by individual *i* at the end of a period could yield $X to individual *i* while each certificate held by individual *j* could yield $Y to individual *j*. Furthermore, a certificate could yield a different amount to a given individual in period *A* than it yielded to the same individual during period *B*. Because of these differences, there are gains from exchange with one individual selling the certificate to another.

The difference in individual returns was used only after considerable thought. The importance of the feature for the laboratory market is clear enough—it fosters the existence of gains from exchange. In addition, there are a number of reasons why streams of returns in naturally occurring markets might generally be different for different investors or for the same investor at different times. First of all, the evaluation of services of actual physical assets such as durable consumption goods might be greatest during early periods for some owners, while other owners might place a greater value in later periods. Secondly, for financial assets such as stocks for which the returns are dividends, different owners might be in different tax brackets or different risk classes. With the latter interpretation, $(d_A^i, d_B^i)$ might be considered as a set of "certainty equivalent" dividends, different for each risk class. Third, the investors may all be risk neutral and simply have different expectations over the streams of returns, which in fact are random variables.

The parameters for the five markets are given in Table I. The currency used in the experiments was called *francs*. Value for francs was established by application of the theory of induced value (Smith [15], Plott [12]). In Experiments 1, 2, and 5 each franc was worth $.002, in Experiment 3 each franc was worth $.001

---

[2] See the Appendix for instructions with the exact trading rules.
[3] In Experiment 4 each trader was endowed with three certificates.

TABLE I

EXPERIMENTAL PARAMETERS

| Experiment Number | Investor Type | Initial Francs on Hand | Initial Certificate Holdings | Dollar Value of Francs | Fixed Cost | Period A Dividend Value | Period B Dividend Value | Number of Investors |
|---|---|---|---|---|---|---|---|---|
| 1 & 2 | I | 10,000 | 2 | .002 | 10,000 | 300 | 50 | 3 |
|  | II | 10,000 | 2 | .002 | 10,000 | 50 | 300 | 3 |
|  | III | 10,000 | 2 | .002 | 10,000 | 150 | 250 | 3 |
| 3 | I | 20,000 | 2 | .001 | 20,000 | 600 | 350 | 3 |
|  | II | 20,000 | 2 | .001 | 20,000 | 350 | 600 | 3 |
|  | III | 20,000 | 2 | .001 | 20,000 | 450 | 550 | 3 |
| 4 | I | 12,100 | 3 | .01 | 13,000 | 150 | 50 | 4 |
|  | II | 12,100 | 3 | .01 | 13,000 | 100 | 250 | 4 |
| 5 | I | 15,000 | 2 | .002 | 15,500 | 403 | 146 | 3 |
|  | II | 15,000 | 2 | .002 | 15,500 | 284 | 372 | 3 |
|  | III | 15,000 | 2 | .002 | 15,500 | 110 | 442 | 3 |

and in Experiment 4 each franc was worth $.01. These conversion values may seem small at first but in fact the transaction prices in terms of francs were sufficiently high to make the dollar payoffs and values of decisions comparable to other experiments which have been successfully completed with subjects drawn from these subject pools. The average amount earned by a trader was about $16 for two and one-half hours participation.

Table I is read as follows. Consider Experiment 1 where there were three different types of investors with three individuals of each type. Each of the three was given 10,000 francs and two certificates at the beginning of each year. They were then allowed to trade freely according to their wishes subject to well-established rules during the year. Each certificate held at the end of period *A* yielded 300 francs and each held at the end of period *B* yielded 50 francs. They could also add to their franc holdings by selling certificates either from their endowments or from the ones they had purchased for potentially profitable resale. All francs held in excess of 10,000 francs were translated into dollars at the rate of $.002 per franc and this was the amount of money the individual was allowed to keep. The payoff for all other groups and all other experiments should be interpreted similarly.

As will be discussed below several models can be applied to predict what will evolve from these simple markets. Looking ahead, however, will enable the reader to understand the structure and interrelations among the experiments. The first three experiments can be explained rather well by a perfect foresight equilibrium model (to be described below). The remaining two experiments were then designed to explore some slightly different markets using the insights gained from the first three. Once a positive result has been established it is only natural to initiate an inquiry which seeks deeper reasons about why the model works and if it will continue to work under other parameters, institutions, and complications. Experiment 4 represents an attempt to create a market by simple parameter adjustments which would equilibrate to an inefficient allocation. Experiment 5 involves an institutional perturbation—a futures market.

## 3. EXPERIMENTAL PROCEDURES

The instructions contained in the Appendix are an extension of those used in other studies. Two major exceptions to traditional procedures were used, however, and should be emphasized because of their importance in assessing the methodological contribution of the experiments.

The first involves the use of francs. With the exception of Friedman's [4] study of cooperative duopoly, other experiments have used dollars directly as a medium of exchange. For these experiments, in which initial endowments of certificates were distributed costlessly, and in which separation of theoretical predictions required the use of relatively high nominal prices, the cost of using dollars directly would have been prohibitive. Thus payoffs here for a given year are of the form $\$ = a + bx$ where $b > 0$, $a < 0$, and $x$ is the quantity of francs held at the end of a trading year. While this theoretically should have no influence on behavior, it does involve a change in procedures relative to other experiments and is thus a candidate explanation for any problems which might occur.

The second break with tradition involves the nonpayment of commissions. It is known that the absence of trading commissions can cause slight divergences from demand and supply predictions (Plott and Smith [13]). Current theory holds that trading involves a slight cost which is overcome by a commission. Thus the lack of a trading commission can induce some small inaccuracies in models. On the other hand, the existence of a commission, since individuals can be on both sides of the market simultaneously, can lead to an infinite number of trades. The latter possibility was considered to be a greater problem than the former so commissions were omitted.

## 4. HYPOTHESES AND SPECIFIC MODELS

Our formal analysis will be concentrated upon models motivated by the second class of theories. If the models fail to work, then we would look to opinions in the first two classes of ideas (the "nontheory" class and the first theory class) for structuring future research priorities. On the other hand, if the models work, then we know the market behavior predicted by the first two views is not pervasive. The next steps would then involve attempts to understand why such models work and isolate the range of circumstances in which they can be relied upon. Perhaps ideas in the first classes are relevant when the situation becomes sufficiently rich but that can only be established by building up results from the simple cases which can (potentially) be thoroughly understood.

A two-period model for a discrete homogeneous asset seems to be the natural one to apply. There are $n$ types of investors, each of whom "knows" his/her stream of returns, $(d_A^i, d_B^i)$ for $i = 1, 2, \ldots$, from owning a unit of the asset in periods $A$ and $B$. The investors have no effective wealth limitations, but they possess a finite amount of the asset and there are no short sales. Furthermore, except for Experiment 5, the markets are sequential. The market for period $B$ holdings occurs after the market for period $A$ holdings has closed.

Price predictions for period $B$ are the same for almost all models. Direct application of a demand and supply model yields

$$P_B = \max_i d_B^i.$$

This follows from the constant per unit yields and the fixed supply. For experiments 1, 2, 3, and 4 the predicted period $B$ prices in francs are (300, 300, 600, 250) respectively. As shown in Figure 1 the demand function is perfectly elastic up to the wealth limitation of those who have the highest period $B$ yields. The wealth limitation was sufficiently large in the experiment that it was never binding. Presumably the limit prices for such individuals are the per unit yield and the maximum quantity demanded is constrained only by the initial allocation of francs. The supply of certificates is fixed.

This model yields our first hypothesis. It is known that experimental markets do not attain equilibrium immediately. Instead they tend to converge. Assuming traders impute zero costs to making transactions, there is a natural prediction about the average price during period $B$ of the final year, $\overline{P}_B^T$.

HYPOTHESIS 1: For experiments 1, 2, 3, and 4

$$\overline{P}_B^T = \max_i d_B^i.$$

In light of the results obtained by Plott and Smith [13] and Smith [15] about transaction costs and the role of commissions in experimental double-auction markets, the assumption that traders impute zero costs to making transactions is not realistic. Therefore, we also state a more general version of the above hypothesis which takes account of these costs. Denoting the transaction cost by $c$, we have:

HYPOTHESIS 1': For experiments 1, 2, 3, and 4

$$\overline{P}_B^T = \max_i (d_B^i - c).$$

Prediction of period $A$ prices is more involved. In the sequential market

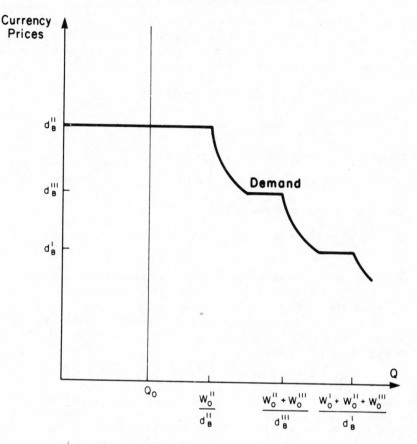

$d_B^i$: dividend of type i investor. Refer to Table I.

$Q_0$: total supply of certificates in period B.

$W_0^i$: holding of currency at the beginning of period B by investor i.

FIGURE 1—Period *B* theoretical demand and supply schedules.

structure informational assumptions are crucial for determining the nature of competing models of period *A* prices. Three different models will be considered.

First, it might be assumed that investors bring only their private information to bear on their market decisions and invest accordingly. Under this hypothesis, they take no account of potential speculative gains to be made in period *B*. The period *A* equilibrium price which results from the appropriate demand and supply model is

$$P_A^N = \max_i \left( d_A^i + d_B^i \right).$$

This will be referred to as the naive price equilibrium.[4] For experiments 1, 2, 3, and 4 these period $A$ prices in francs are 400, 400, 1000, and 250 respectively. Assuming zero transaction costs, this leads to our alternative prediction about the average period $A$ contract price in the final year.

HYPOTHESIS 2: For experiments 1, 2, 3, and 4

$$\bar{P}_A^T = \max_i \left( d_A^i + d_B^i \right).$$

We have called this the "naive expectations hypothesis."

Taking account of transaction costs, we have:

HYPOTHESIS 2': For experiments 1, 2, 3, and 4

$$\bar{P}_A^T = \max_i \left( d_A^i + d_B^i - c \right).$$

A second view of period $A$ price formation is motivated by the insight that market behavior may be influenced by individuals who attempt to earn short-term capital gains in addition to dividend returns. This view would be consistent with observing a period $A$ equilibrium price which exceeds the naive price. More specifically $P_A^N$ is a reasonable lower bound for the period $A$ price for the following reason. Let $i^*$ satisfy

$$P_A^N = d_A^{i^*} + d_B^{i^*} \geq d_A^j + d_B^j \qquad \forall j \neq i^*.$$

Then any investor of type $i^*$ is guaranteed $P_A^N$ in dividend earnings from every certificate owned or purchased in period $A$. Another way of saying this is that $i^*$ does not need to depend on capital gains in order to earn $P_A^N$. Thus such an investor is willing to purchase an infinite amount at prices below $P_A^N$ even without information about $P_B$. Thus $P_A^N$ provides one theoretical bound for $P_A$.

This line of reasoning yields a third prediction which is stated in a testable form in Hypothesis 3.

HYPOTHESIS 3: For experiments 1, 2, 3, and 4

$$\bar{P}_A^t \geq \max_i \left( d_A^i + d_B^i \right) \qquad\qquad (t = 1, 2, \ldots, T).$$

The next model is the rational expectations, or in this case, the perfect foresight equilibrium model. The demand in period $A$ is augmented by the

---

[4]Katherine Echol suggests that this should be called the maximin equilibrium and that a true "naive" equilibrium would have traders determining values on the basis of one-period dividends alone. This type of myopic behavior was probably circumvented by question one of the practice calculations section of the instructions.

perfectly forecasted theoretical equilibrium price of period $B$. That is,

$$P_A^F = \max_i d_A^i + P_B = \max_i d_A^i + \max_j d_B^j.$$

For experiments 1, 2, 3, and 4 the numbers, $P_A^F$, in franc prices are 600, 600, 1200, and 400 respectively. Again assuming the traders in these experimental markets impute zero costs in making transactions, this model yields the next prediction.

HYPOTHESIS 4: For experiments 1, 2, 3, and 4

$$\bar{P}_A^T = P_A^F = \max_i d_A^i + \max_j d_B^j.$$

We call this the "perfect foresight hypothesis."

Taking transaction costs into account we have:

HYPOTHESIS 4′: For experiments 1, 2, 3, and 4

$$\bar{P}_A^T = P_A^F - 2c = \max_i (d_A^i - c) + \max_j (d_B^j - c).$$

Some controversy exists about the mechanism through which a rational expectations equilibrium might be achieved. Grossman [6] suggests that the key is *replication* and that with replication investors will acquire information about the joint distribution of prices which determines the equilibrium price function. With replication investors have the opportunity to observe period $B$ prices and incorporate this information into their decisions in the period $A$ market. Not only does this argument suggest something about the *necessity* of replication for the existence of a rational expectations equilibrium, it also suggests something about the time path of prices through which the equilibrium will be attained. The next hypothesis captures the idea about the nature of convergence motivated by the Grossman model.

HYPOTHESIS 5: For experiments 1, 2, 3, and 4

$$|\bar{P}_A^t - P_A^F| > |\bar{P}_B^t - P_B| \qquad \text{for all } t.$$

In other words, convergence in period $A$ "follows" convergence in period $B$. We call this the "swing-back hypothesis."

In these markets investors enter in year one with no idea (or perhaps only a vague idea in the case of "experienced" investors) of the market price and they learn more about it in each subsequent year. Specifically in year one investors bring only their own private information to the market place. However, the perfect foresight equilibrium implicitly requires agents to possess information which they will normally receive by observing prices. Once prices are observed the lack of information which previously impeded attainment of a perfect foresight equilibrium no longer exists. Due to this, one would expect the trading to begin at the naive equilibrium price and monotonically converge to the perfect foresight equilibrium price as trading publicizes information that originally was private. In the absence of a period $B$ futures market, investors will be unable to incorporate period $B$ price information in their period $A$ decisions until after the first year of trading. Implicit in this observation is Grossman's notion that in such markets replication is a necessary condition for convergence to a perfect foresight equilibrium when only sequential spot trading is allowed. This is the sixth hypothesis and only applies to a sequential market organization in which futures markets are absent.

HYPOTHESIS 6: For experiments 1, 2, 3, and 4

(a)    $\bar{P}_A^1 = P_A^N$,

(b)    $\bar{P}_A^t - \bar{P}_A^{t-1} > 0$,    for $t > 1$.


Hypotheses 5 and 6 suggest that a very careful look at Experiment 4 is in order. This experiment represented an attempt to "trap" the market at an equilibrium other than that embodied in Hypothesis 4 by using the convergence path suggested by Hypotheses 5 and 6. The parameters of Experiment 4 are such that in the naive equilibrium no trade takes place in period $B$. As a result there would be no transacted price signals in period $B$ and so $P_B$ would not be known to the agents in subsequent years. Notice that for $j \in I$, $d_A^j + d_B^j = 200$ and for $i \in II$, $d_A^i + d_B^i = 350$ (see Table I). Thus under the naive hypothesis type II investors would purchase the entire supply in period $A$. Type II also has the higher return in period $B$ so they are demanders in period $B$ as well as in period $A$. Since the demanders in period $B$ hold the entire supply, no trades would occur in $B$. However notice that for $i \in II$, $d_A^i + P_B = 100 + 250 = 350$ but for $j \in I$, $d_A^j + P_B = 150 + 250 = 400$. Thus according to the perfect foresight equilibrium model group I should hold all certificates in period $A$ and sell to group II in period $B$. Experiment 4 was designed after the first three experiments and was intended as a check on the nature of the mechanisms which might motivate the perfect foresight equilibrium.

Experiment 5 involves a change in the market structure. A futures market is opened for period $B$ holdings which is held concurrently (in time) with the period $A$ spot market. From a static theoretical view this institutional perturbation makes no difference in the ultimate equilibrium values. The perfect foresight equilibrium values in francs are (845, 442) in periods $A$ and $B$ respectively. The natural conjecture is:

HYPOTHESIS 7: Hypotheses 1 through 6 apply to Experiment 5.

The more interesting aspects, however, are the implications about the necessity of replication for convergence to the perfect foresight equilibrium. Those who subscribe to the replication justification for the perfect foresight equilibrium, would argue that period $A$ prices should converge more rapidly in the presence of a futures market. This is because simultaneous markets allow information about capital gains to be incorporated immediately into investor decisions. This hypothesis is formalized as (where $S$ stands for any of the experiments involving sequential markets; $P_{AS}^F$ is the period $A$ perfect foresight price in sequential market experiment $S$, $S = 1, 2, 3, 4$):

HYPOTHESIS 8:

$$\frac{|P_{A5}^F - \bar{P}_{A5}^t|}{|P_{A5}^F - P_{A5}^N|} < \frac{|P_{AS}^F - \bar{P}_{AS}^t|}{|P_{AS}^F - P_{AS}^N|} \qquad (t = 1, 2, \ldots, T).$$

Of particular interest in this respect is $t = 1$ because immediate convergence

TABLE II

NUMBER OF UNITS HELD IN A THEORETICAL EQUILIBRIUM

| | EXPERIMENTS 1, 2, 3, 5 | | | | | |
| --- | --- | --- | --- | --- | --- | --- |
| | Investor Type | | | | | |
| | I | | II | | III | |
| | Period A | Period B | Period A | Period B | Period A | Period B |
| Naive Equilibrium | 0 | 0 | 0 | 9 | 9 | 0 |
| Perfect Foresight Equilibrium | 9 | 0 | 0 | 9 | 0 | 0 |

| | EXPERIMENT 4 | | | |
| --- | --- | --- | --- | --- |
| | Investor Type | | | |
| | I | | II | |
| | Period A | Period B | Period A | Period B |
| Naive Equilibrium | 0 | 0 | 8 | 8 |
| Perfect Foresight Equilibrium | 8 | 0 | 0 | 8 |

would demonstrate that the futures market removes the necessity for any replication at all.

The final set of hypotheses deals with the distribution of certificates. Within these markets each theory makes a rather precise prediction about which individuals will hold certificates. As can be seen the naive expectations model and the perfect foresight model make very precise predictions. They yield two very different hypotheses about certificate holdings.

HYPOTHESIS 9F: Certificate holdings are the same as the holdings predicted by the perfect foresight model (see Table II).

HYPOTHESIS 9N: Certificate holdings are the same as the holdings predicted by the naive expectations model (see Table II).

### 5. EXPERIMENTAL RESULTS

Our analysis of the data is contained in three categories: price convergence, quantity convergence, and individual behavior. In dealing with the data we face some open problems that are being encountered in almost all experimental work where the cost of conducting experiments places a significant constraint on the number of observations. As will be obvious in the figures, the high degree of serial correlation of prices in a given experiment, both within a period and across periods, suggests the simultaneous interaction of the learning process by individuals and a convergence process by the market. Yet, without a theory about these processes, our statistical statements suffer from an inability to use all the data available to us. Furthermore, the statistical tests we report should be regarded more as measures than classical hypothesis tests. Fortunately, the data from these experiments show sufficient regularities so that this should cause no problems.

### A. Price Convergence

Figures 2–6 present the entire time series of transacted prices in the five experiments that were conducted. For every experiment, average price in each period of each year is given at the bottom of the corresponding figure. After repeated trials the period $B$ price is accurately predicted by the simple supply and demand model in all experiments. Period $B$ prices are always within the \$.02 of $P_B$ in dollar terms by the final year. The observation that the observed prices stay consistently \$.01 or \$.02 below the predicted price is consistent with findings by Plott and Smith [13] that participants in these experimental markets impute a slight cost to trading.

Table III summarizes the data from Figures 2–6 and gives price predictions when the simple supply and demand model is modified to take account of transactions costs. Although the observed mean period $B$ prices in the final year of the experiments are all significantly (at the 1 per cent level) less than the

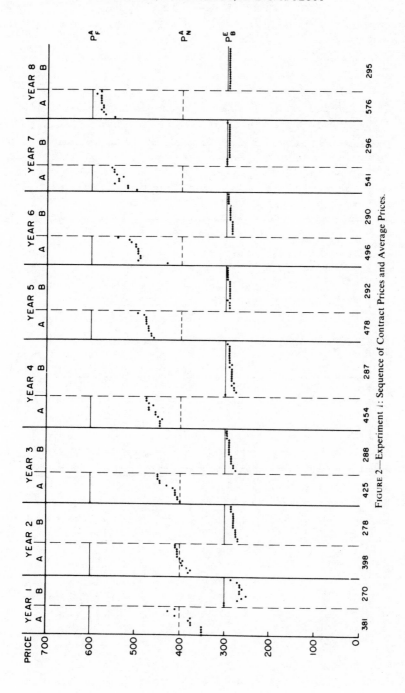

FIGURE 2.—Experiment 1: Sequence of Contract Prices and Average Prices.

ASSET VALUATION                                                    551

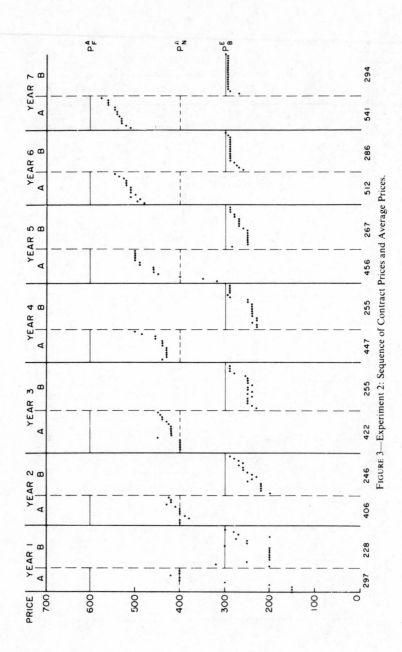

FIGURE 3—Experiment 2: Sequence of Contract Prices and Average Prices.

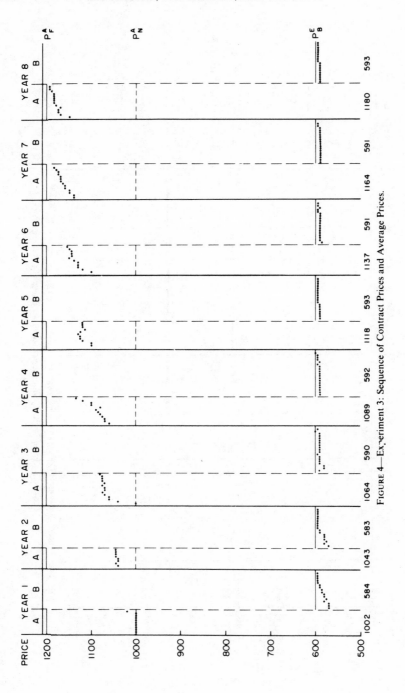

FIGURE 4—Experiment 3: Sequence of Contract Prices and Average Prices.

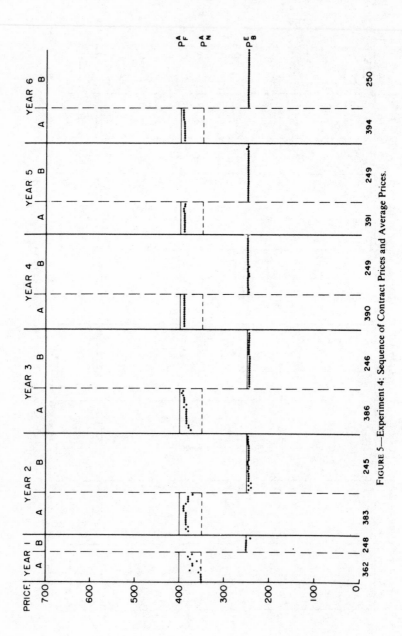

FIGURE 5—Experiment 4: Sequence of Contract Prices and Average Prices.

554

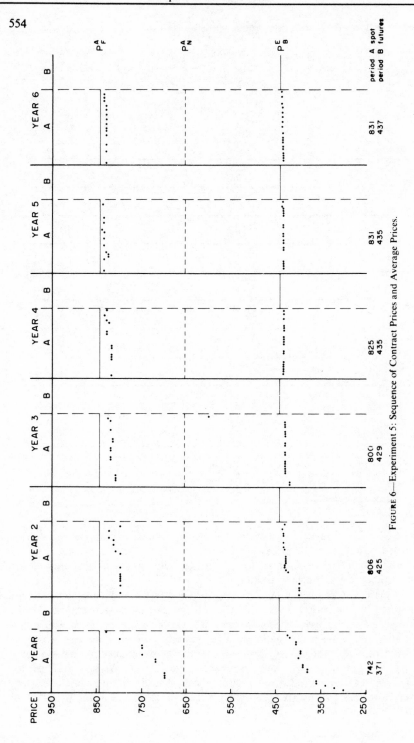

FIGURE 6—Experiment 5: Sequence of Contract Prices and Average Prices.

TABLE III

OBSERVED AVERAGE PRICES AND THEORETICAL PERFECT FORESIGHT PRICE PREDICTIONS
WITH TRANSACTION COSTS

| Experiment Number | Period | Observed Mean Transactions Price in Final Year (Standard Errors are in Parentheses) | Prices (in Francs) Predicted by Hypotheses 1' and 4', Corrected for Transaction Cost, $c$ | | |
|---|---|---|---|---|---|
| | | | $c = \$.01$ | $c = \$.03$ | $c = \$.05$ |
| 1 | A | 576.25[a] (2.76) | 590 | 570 | 550 |
| | B | 295.00[a] (0.0) | 295 | 285 | 275 |
| 2 | A | 541.43[c] (4.73) | 590 | 570 | 550 |
| | B | 293.56[a] (1.43) | 295 | 285 | 275 |
| 3 | A | 1180.36[a] (3.28) | 1180 | 1140 | 1100 |
| | B | 592.50[a] (.61) | 590 | 570 | 550 |
| 4 | A | 393.71[b] (.38) | 398 | 394 | 390 |
| | B | 249.50[a] (.10) | 249 | 247 | 245 |
| 5 | A | 831.07[b] (.57) | 835 | 815 | 795 |
| | B | 437.06[a] (.34) | 437 | 427 | 417 |

[a] At the 10 per cent significance level, one can reject the hypothesis that the observed mean transaction price is less than the predicted price, corrected for a transaction cost of $.01.
[b] At the 10 per cent significance level, one can reject the hypothesis that the observed mean transaction price is less than the predicted price, corrected for a transaction cost of $.03.
[c] At the 10 per cent significance level, one can reject the hypothesis that the observed mean transaction price is less than the predicted price, corrected for a transaction cost of $.05.

predicted prices under an assumption of zero transactions costs, none of these observed mean period *B* prices are significantly less than the predicted prices (even at a significance level as high as 10 per cent) if the participants of the markets impute a $.01 cost to trading.

The perfect foresight equilibrium model (hypotheses 4 and 4') is very strongly supported by the period *A* price data. With one exception (Experiment 2), the average period *A* transacted price in the final year of each experiment was within $.05 at $P_A^F$. Experiment 2 lasted only seven years but the price in year seven was within $.12 of $P_A^F$ and mirrored almost exactly the experience in Experiment 1 which was also about $.12 away from $P_A^F$ in year seven. As was the case for period *B* prices, the period *A* prices also indicate that the imputed cost of trading is very low. In Experiments 1, 3, 4, and 5 the average prices in the period *A* of the final year are not significantly less (at the 1 per cent level) than the predictions of the perfect foresight model if the participants impute a trading cost of $.03 (see Table III).

Hypothesis 3, which states that naive expectations provide a lower bound for prices, is almost a direct implication of Hypothesis 4; it is not particularly surprising that all five experiments support Hypothesis 3 for years beyond year two. Simple hypothesis testing allows us to reject the naive expectations Hypothesis 2 at any significance level. Note that Hypotheses 2 and 4 give mutually inconsistent price predictions for these markets and are sufficiently different that the strong support for Hypothesis 4 implies the rejection of Hypothesis 2.

The "swing-back" Hypothesis 5 that period $B$ convergence precedes period $A$ convergence was supported in all experiments. The relevant inequality was satisfied in every year. This reaffirms the crucial importance of price as a carrier of market information.

The experiments support Hypothesis 6, that convergence in experiments 1–4 will be from below beginning at the naive price. In three out of four experiments average price was at or below $P_A^N$ in year one (Experiments 1, 2, and 3). In two out of four experiments prices were not significantly different from $P_A^N$ (at the 5 per cent level) even during year two (Experiments 1 and 2).

Both Hypotheses 7 and 8 pertain to Experiment 5 alone. Hypothesis 7 (that the first six experiments extend to the case of futures markets) can be accepted on the basis of the above discussion with one important caveat. With a period $B$ futures market (Experiment 5) the period $A$ price in year one was much greater than $P_A^N$. In fact, it was halfway between the naive price and the perfect foresight price. We suggest that this was observed because individuals were able to obtain information about the period $B$ price before making period $A$ transactions. This theory, if ultimately supported, would also explain why Hypothesis 8 was supported. (Hypothesis 8 asserts that period $A$ price will converge more rapidly with a futures market.) The relevant inequality, defined in Hypothesis 8, was satisfied in every case.

Our intuition that the existence of a no-trade equilibrium at naive prices would prevent or impede convergence to the Pareto optimal perfect foresight equilibrium was not supported. In Experiment 4 which was designed to explore this possibility, speculative investment by one investor (who had participated in an earlier experiment) drove the market away from the inefficient price in early years to an efficient, market-clearing (zero excess demand) price by the end of the final year. It appears that this phenomenon permitted the perfect foresight equilibrium to be reached in that experiment.

## B. Quantity Convergence and Efficiency

The predictions about quantity convergence and efficiency of the experimental asset markets were very accurate. Predicted quantities (according to Hypothesis 9F) are 100 per cent accurate after the first year in Experiment 5, the second year

TABLE IV

NUMBER OF UNITS OF ASSET ON "WRONG SIDE OF MARKET"
UNDER PERFECT FORESIGHT HYPOTHESIS

| Experiment Number | Period | Year | | | | | | | |
|---|---|---|---|---|---|---|---|---|---|
| | | 1 | 2 | 3 | 4 | 5 | 6 | 7 | 8 |
| 1[a] | A | 17 | 7 | 3 | 0 | 0 | 0 | 0 | 0 |
| | B | 2 | 2 | 0 | 0 | 0 | 0 | 0 | 0 |
| 2[a] | A | 10 | 3 | 0 | 0 | 0 | 1 | 0 | |
| | B | 5 | 3 | 0 | 0 | 1 | 1 | 0 | |
| 3[a] | A | 16 | 5 | 0 | 0 | 3 | 0 | 0 | 0 |
| | B | 2 | 1 | 0 | 0 | 0 | 0 | 0 | 0 |
| 4[b] | A | 12 | 1 | 0 | 0 | 0 | 0 | | |
| | B | 2 | 0 | 0 | 0 | 0 | 0 | | |
| 5[a] | A | 3 | 0 | 0 | 0 | 0 | 0 | | |
| | B | 5 | 0 | 0 | 0 | 0 | 0 | | |

[a] 18 units in the market.
[b] 24 units in the market.

in Experiment 4, and the third year in Experiment 1. Predicted quantities are 97 per cent accurate after the second year in Experiments 2 and 3. We conclude that Hypothesis 9F cannot be rejected and that Hypothesis 9N can be rejected after the first year. Note that quantity convergence is faster when the period *B* futures market exists in Experiment 5 (especially as compared with Experiment 3 where subjects were also experienced).

Percentage of maximum possible total payout is used as a measure of efficiency in a market year (as opposed to a period) of an experiment. There is only one source of inefficiency in these markets. Inefficiency occurs if and only if a "wrong type" of investor is holding assets at the end of a period. One can easily see the relationship between quantity convergence and efficiency in these experiments. Complete efficiency occurs if and only if quantities are allocated according to Table II. That is, complete efficiency occurs if and only if quantities are allocated according to the rational expectations theory. In each of the experiments, type II investors should be holding all units of the asset in period *B*, and type I investors should be holding all the units at the end of period *A*.

Table IV shows the number of units of the asset which are "on the wrong side of the market." When this number is 0 in periods *A* and *B*, that means that type I investors are the only holders at the end of period *A* and type II investors are the only holders at the end of period *B*. If this is true, *no matter what the price is*, the allocation is efficient. Considering the first year only, of the first four experiments 66 units of 156 were on the wrong side of the market. Then in year three and later in the same experiments only nine out of a possible 804 units are held by investors on the wrong side of the market. Thus, after only three years the quantity predictions by the perfect foresight equilibrium model are almost

TABLE V

PAYOUT AS A PER CENT OF MAXIMUM POSSIBLE EFFICIENCY LEVELS PAYOUT[a]

| Experiment Number | Year | | | | | | | | Per Cent of Maximum Payment under Naive Hypothesis |
|---|---|---|---|---|---|---|---|---|---|
| | 1 | 2 | 3 | 4 | 5 | 6 | 7 | 8 | |
| 1 | 21.19 | 66.67 | 89.05 | 100 | 100 | 100 | 100 | 100 | 33.32 |
| 2 | 50.01 | 99.28 | 100 | 100 | 98.82 | 94.99 | 100 | | 33.32 |
| 3 | 54.74 | 76.19 | 100 | 100 | 89.25 | 100 | 100 | 100 | 59.53 |
| 4 | 60.17 | 98.17 | 100 | 100 | 100 | 100 | | | 60.00 |
| 5 | 77.06 | 100 | 100 | 100 | 100 | 100 | | | 26.58 |

[a] Per cent of maximum total payout was calculated *relative* to original endowments. That is. if all participants in the market make no trades and are just paid on the basis of their original endowments only. then according to our measure. the per cent of maximum total payout is 0.0.

100 per cent correct. In Experiment 5 the model is 100 per cent correct after only one period, thus adding support for the hypothesis that the futures market causes more rapid convergence of the spot market.

The efficiency levels in Table V mirror the quantity predictions. After the second year, efficiency levels remain at near 100 per cent in all experiments. Except for Experiment 5 the efficiency levels attained in the first year approximate those predicted under the naive hypothesis. With a futures market, however, the efficiency level in the first year (77 per cent) was well above that predicted under the naive hypothesis (27 per cent).

Both the quantity and efficiency data provide strong evidence that these markets began at the naive equilibrium but ultimately converged to a rational expectations equilibrium. Only when a futures market existed (Experiment 5) did the market appear to bypass the naive equilibrium and converge immediately to the more efficient perfect foresight equilibrium.

## C. *Individual Behavior*

In simple markets like these one might think that individual behavior is simple or "mechanical" and that the resulting market behavior is therefore "obvious." There are three observations about individual behavior which seemed particularly interesting in this respect and suggest that individual behavior is complicated. Both types of behavior are difficult to explain. One such observed action we will refer to as "overlapping." That is, investors do not always treat transacted price signals as bounds on willingness to pay. Sufficient information exists in the instructions to deduce that each individual has a dividend structure such that each individual's total dividend earnings are linear in the number of certificates held. Such a return structure suggests that in the absence of speculative purchases each transacted price indicates a lower bound on the buyer's willingness to pay. For example, it is hard to understand why subject one would sell subject two an asset for twenty francs if one just sold an asset to two for thirty francs in the previous year and one knows that two has a perfectly flat return structure (but doesn't know two's limit price). From the previous transactions individual one has reason to suspect (especially in period $B$ where there is less opportunity to speculate) that he/she could hold out for thirty. In the experiments one observes trades transacted at $p_1$ and then observes subsequent trades in the same period and in later periods transacted at $p_2$, where $p_2 < p_1$. This frequency of overlapping can be seen in Figures 2–6.

A second observation which seems surprising is the lack of willingness of most individuals to attempt to earn short-term capital gains. Because much of the trading was out of equilibrium and an upward trend in period $A$ prices was fairly well established in the early years, intratemporal arbitrage opportunities abounded. Even in period $B$ the typical pattern of prices within a period started low and increased at the end of the period. Yet such arbitrage rarely occurred. This makes us suspicious of theories of the first type which suggest that equilibria are the result of short-term risky speculation.

A third observation is related to learning. We originally had thought that experience might be an important factor since it seemed likely that inexperienced subjects required several market years to become completely comfortable with trading rules, recording methods, etc. For this reason experienced subjects were used in Experiments 3, 4, and 5. Although convergence with experienced subjects seems to occur somewhat faster than with inexperienced subjects, the same general patterns of convergence to equilibrium are present in the data with both sets of subject pools. Thus, even though experienced subjects were used, the necessity for having done this is not at all evident.

## 6. CONCLUSIONS

Our conclusions are discussed in three sections. The first section deals with the technical models and what has been empirically established (subject, of course, to further replication). The second section concerns itself with the methodological questions alone. The final section deals with conclusions of a more general nature.

It is clear that the rational expectations equilibrium (i.e., the perfect foresight equilibrium) model is an excellent predictor of the behavior in these simple markets. The role of replication is also clear in the markets. In particular, for sequential markets such as those studied here without a futures market, replication is both a necessary and sufficient condition for the applicability of the perfect foresight equilibrium model. Necessity is established because the markets do not converge in the first period. Sufficiency is established by convergence of all markets after replication. Of course, exactly how this result extends to more complicated situations remains to be determined.

With these findings the results of Miller, Plott, and Smith [11] and Plott and

Uhl [14] can be reinterpreted as having provided some experience with the behavior of asset markets. Units in those experiments can be viewed as assets which yield zero dividend returns to the traders[5] and the equilibria can correspondingly be viewed as rational expectations equilibria. Of course the absence of intraperiod trading possibilities (which prevents the intraperiod speculation) and the adjustments on the supply side to aid the equating of market prices over time remove some of the important structural features of asset markets but the application of theory to explain the data is clear.

The convergence pattern in these markets is reminiscent of a dynamic programming algorithm. We have called it the "swingback hypothesis." The last period converges first and the convergence works back from this to earlier periods as the years replicate. Thus, information about prices seems to be the critical variable as the theory suggests. This conclusion is reinforced with the addition of a futures market. It is reasonable to conjecture that the transmission of information about future prices speeds the convergence of the period $A$ spot market.

The observed price convergence has a pattern which supports another theoretical interpretation. The appropriate model may have the markets converging to a temporary (naive) equilibrium *first* and then adjusting to the perfect foresight equilibrium after "sufficient" information has accumulated (Grandmont [5]). Other experimental evidence suggests that a market has converged to an equilibrium when there is "low variance" of transacted prices around the average. This evidence may be used to support a conjecture that Experiments 1 and 2 converged to the naive equilibrium in year 2, and Experiment 3 converged in year 1 (see Figures 2–4).

Several new experimental features were introduced in these experiments. The use of special currency seems to cause no problems. And, the truncation of profits seems to leave behavior unperturbed. For example, a comparison of the behavior of these markets with those reported in Smith [16], which also had rectangular demands and supplies, yields few differences. The lack of a trading commission is thought to prevent "full convergence" (Plott and Smith [13]) but almost all experiments reported here were within \$.03 of predicted perfect foresight equilibrium prices in dollar terms.

There are several general implications which follow from the results above. (a) Any theory which advocates the *general* absence of regularities related to the underlying economic parameters of asset markets is demonstrably wrong. Thus, those who accept such a position must begin to adopt qualifications. (b) Because these markets never converged to the perfect foresight equilibrium during the first period, a *strict* rational expectations theory which does not require replication is inconsistent with the data. Similarly, the efficient market hypothesis can be rejected to the extent that it postulates immediate and instantaneous adjustments. Replication necessarily plays an important role in determining the appli-

---

[5] In these experiments traders had the exclusive right to purchase units in period $A$ for resale in period $B$, but they could not sell units in period $A$ or purchase units in period $B$.

cability of these models, and theories which address the question of how rational expectations are formed should be given serious consideration. (c) The study of futures market institutions can be supplemented by experimental techniques. Danthine [1] and Grossman [7] suggest that futures markets can play an important role in publicizing the private information which exists in an economy. Our initial probe with a single experiment establishes the feasibility of creating a controlled-environment futures market which has some of the properties they suggest will exist. A comparison of the observations from the first four markets with the fifth leads us to conjecture that the existence of a futures market affects the spot market. A futures market may increase the speed with which information is made public through price transactions. We suspect that this increases the speed of convergence to equilibrium, perhaps removes the necessity of replication, and might increase market efficiency. All of these conjectures were supported in the single futures market we studied.

*University of Iowa,*
*Carnegie-Mellon University,*
               *and*
*California Institute of Technology.*

*Manuscript received March, 1980; revision received May, 1981.*

## APPENDIX

### INSTRUCTIONS FOR EXPERIMENTS 1–4

#### GENERAL

This is an experiment in the economics of market decision making. Various research foundations have provided funds for this research. The instructions are simple, and if you follow them carefully and make good decisions, you might earn a considerable amount of money which will be paid to you in cash.

In this experiment we are going to simulate a market in which you will buy and sell certificates in a sequence of market years. Each year consists of two periods, the first of which will be called A, and the second B. Attached to the instructions you will find a sheet, labeled information and record sheet, which helps determine the value to you of any decisions you might make. You are not to reveal this information to anyone. It is your own private information.

The type of currency used in this market is francs. All trading and earnings will be in terms of francs. Each franc is worth ____ dollars to you. Do not reveal this number to anyone. At the end of the experiment your francs will be converted to dollars at this rate, and you will be paid in dollars. Notice that the more francs you earn, the more dollars you earn.

#### SPECIFIC INSTRUCTIONS

Your profits come from two sources—from collecting certificate earnings on all certificates you hold at the end of a period *and* from buying and selling certificates. During each market year you are free to purchase or sell as many certificates as you wish provided you follow the rules below. For each certificate you hold at the end of the period you will be given the number of francs listed on row 19 of your information and record sheet. Notice that this amount may differ from period to period.

Compute your total certificate earnings for a period by multiplying the earnings per certificate by the number of certificates held. That is,

(number of certificates held) × (earnings per certificate) = total certificate earnings.

Suppose for example that you hold 5 certificates at the end of period *A* of year 1. If for that period your earnings are 100 francs per certificate (that is, the number listed on row 19 is 100) then your total certificate earnings in period *A* would be 5 × 100 = 500 francs. This number should be recorded on row 19 at the end of the period.

Sales from your certificate holdings increase your francs on hand by the amount of the sale price. Similarly, purchases reduce your francs on hand by the amount of the purchase price. Thus you can gain *or* lose money on the purchase and resale of certificates. At the end of period *B* of each year all your holdings are automatically sold to the experimenter at a price of 0.

At the beginning of each year you are provided with an initial holding of certificates. This is recorded on row 0 of period *A* in each year's information and record sheet. You may sell these if you wish or you may hold them. If you hold a certificate throughout both periods, then you receive "earnings per certificate" twice—once at the end of period *A*, and again at the end of period *B*. Notice therefore that for each certificate you hold initially you can earn during the year *at least* the *sum* of the two "earnings per certificate" you receive at the end of periods *A* and *B*. You earn this amount if you do not sell that certificate during the entire year.

In addition at the beginning of each year you are provided with an initial amount of francs on hand. This is also recorded on row 0 of period *A* on each year's information and record sheet. You may keep this if you wish or you may use it to purchase certificates.

Thus at the beginning of each year you are endowed with holdings of certificates and francs on hand. You are free to buy and sell certificates as you wish according to the rules below. Your francs on hand at the end of a year are determined by your initial amount of francs on hand, earnings on certificate holdings at the end of each period and by gains and losses from purchases and sales of certificates. All francs on hand at the end of a year in excess of ____ francs are yours to keep. These are your profits for the year.

### TRADING AND RECORDING RULES

(1) All transactions are for one certificate at a time. After each of your sales or purchases you must record the nature of the transaction, a sale (*S*) or purchase (*P*), and the transaction price. The first transaction is recorded on row (1) and succeeding transactions are recorded on subsequent rows.

(2) After each transaction you must calculate and record your new holdings of certificates and your new francs on hand. Your holdings of certificates may never go below zero. Your francs on hand may never go below zero.

(3) At the end of the period record your total certificate earnings on row 19. Compute your end of period totals on row 20 by listing certificate holdings and adding total certificate earnings to your francs on hand.

(4) The totals on row 20 at the end of period *A* should carry forward to row 0 of the next period.

(5) At the end of period *B*, subtract from your francs on hand the amount listed in row 21 and enter this new amount on row 22. This is your profit for the market year and is yours to keep. At the end of each market year, record this number on your profit sheet.

(6) At the end of the experiment add up your total profit on your profit sheet and enter this sum on row 15 of your profit sheet. To convert this number into dollars, multiply by the number on row 16 and record the product on row 17. The experimenter will pay you this amount of money.

### MARKET ORGANIZATION

The market for these certificates is organized as follows. The market will be conducted in a series of years each consisting of two periods. Each period lasts for 7 minutes. Anyone wishing to purchase a certificate is free to raise his or her hand and make a verbal bid to buy one certificate at a specified price, and anyone with certificates to sell is free to accept or not accept the bid. Likewise, anyone

## ASSET VALUATION     563

### PROFIT SHEET

| Row | Market Year | Profit |
|---|---|---|
| 1 | 1 | |
| 2 | 2 | |
| | ⋮ | |
| 14 | 14 | |
| 15 | Total Profit (in Francs) | |
| 16 | Dollars Per Franc | |
| 17 | Total Dollar Profit | |

NAME_____

TRADER NUMBER_____

### INFORMATION AND RECORD SHEET
### YEAR_____

| | Row | PERIOD A | | Certificate Holdings | Francs on Hand | PERIOD B | | Certificate Holdings | Francs on Hand |
|---|---|---|---|---|---|---|---|---|---|
| Beginning of Period Francs on Hand and Certificate Holdings | 0 | | | | | | | | |
| | 1 | S or P | TRANSACTION PRICE | | | S or P | TRANSACTION PRICE | | |
| | 2 | | | | | | | | |
| | | ⋮ | | | | | | | |
| | 18 | | | | | | | | |
| Total Certificate Earnings | 19 | ____ per certificate | | | | ____ per certificate | | | |
| End of Period Totals | 20 | | | | | | | | |
| | 21 | | | | | | | | |
| | 22 | | | | | End of Year Profit | | | |

wishing to sell a certificate is free to raise his or her hand and make a verbal offer to sell one certificate at a specified price. If a bid or offer is accepted, a binding contract has been closed for a single certificate, and the contracting parties will record the transaction on their information and record sheets. Any ties in bids or acceptance will be resolved by random choice. Except for the bids and their acceptance, you are not to speak to any other subject. There are likely to be many bids that are not accepted, but you are free to keep trying. You are free to make as much profit as you can.

### PRACTICE CALCULATIONS

(The substance and much of the wording has been preserved but the format of the practice calculations has been changed to conserve space.)

1. Suppose that at the beginning of period $A$ your initial certificate holding is 1 and your initial francs on hand are 0. Suppose your earnings per certificate are 10 and 15 in periods $A$ and $B$, respectively, and each year you are allowed to keep all francs on hand in excess of 0. If you hold onto your certificate for the entire year, that is, you do not make any transaction in period $A$ or period $B$ certificates, then calculate total certificate earnings in period $A$, end of period francs on hand in period $A$, total certificate earnings in period $B$, end of period francs on hand in period $B$, and profit for the year.

2. Suppose that at the beginning of period $A$ your initial certificate holding is 1 and your initial francs on hand are 100. Your earnings per certificate are 10 in period $A$ and 15 in period $B$. Each year you are allowed to keep all francs on hand in excess of 100. Listed below are seven possible series of trading activities which would be legal for you to do in any given year. In each case you are asked to compute your profit for the year. (i) Make no transactions in period $A$ certificates or period $B$ certificates; (ii) sell one period $A$ certificate for 20, make no transaction in period $B$ certificates; (iii) make no transaction in period $A$ certificates, sell one period $B$ certificate; (iv) purchase one period $A$ certificate for 20, make no transaction in period $B$ certificates; (v) make no transaction in period $A$ certificates, purchase one period $B$ certificate for 20; (vi) sell one period $A$ certificate for 20, purchase one period $B$ certificate for 20; (vii) purchase one period $A$ certificate for 20, sell one period $B$ certificate for 20.

## INSTRUCTIONS FOR EXPERIMENT 5

### GENERAL

This is an experiment in the economics of market decision making. Various research foundations have provided funds for this research. The instructions are simple, and if you follow them carefully and make good decisions, you might earn a considerable amount of money which will be paid to you in cash.

In this experiment we are going to simulate a market in which you will buy and sell certificates in a sequence of market years. Each year consists of two periods, the first of which will be called $A$, and the second $B$. Attached to the instructions you will find a sheet, labeled information and record sheet, which helps determine the value to you of any decisions you might make. You are not to reveal this information to anyone. It is your own private information.

The type of currency used in this market is francs. All trading and earnings will be in terms of francs. Each franc is worth ____ dollars to you. Do not reveal this number to anyone. At the end of the experiment your francs will be converted to dollars at this rate, and you will be paid in dollars. Notice that the more francs you earn, the more dollars you earn.

### SPECIFIC INSTRUCTIONS

Your profits come from two sources—from collecting certificate earnings on all certificates you hold at the end of a period *and* from buying and selling certificates. During each market year you are free to purchase or sell as many certificates as you wish provided you follow the rules below. For each

## ASSET VALUATION                                                565

certificate you hold at the end of the period you will be given the number of francs listed on row 31 of your information and record sheet. Notice that this amount may differ from period to period. Compute your total certificate earnings for a period by multiplying the earnings per certificate by the number of certificates held. That is,

(number of certificates held) × (earnings per certificate) = total certificate earnings.

Suppose for example that you hold 5 certificates at the end of period $A$ of year 1. If for the period your earnings are 100 francs per certificate (that is, the number listed on row 31 is 100) then your total certificate earnings in period $A$ would be $5 \times 100 = 500$ francs. This number should be recorded on row 31 at the end of the period.

Sales from your certificate holdings increase your francs on hand by the amount of the sale price. Similarly, purchases reduce your francs on hand by the amount of the purchase price. Thus you can gain *or* lose money on the purchase and resale of certificates. At the end of period $B$ of each year all your holdings are automatically sold to the experimenter at a price of 0.

At the beginning of each year you are provided with an initial holding of certificates. This is recorded on row 0 of period $A$ in each year's information and record sheet. You may sell these if you wish or you may hold them. If you hold a certificate throughout both periods, then you receive "earnings per certificate" twice—once at the end of period $A$, and again at the end of period $B$. Notice therefore that for each certificate you hold initially you can earn during the year *at least* the *sum* of the two "earnings per certificate" you receive at the end of periods $A$ and $B$. You earn this amount if you do not sell that certificate during the entire year.

All trading for holdings of certificates in period $B$ takes place in period $A$. Therefore, in period $A$, you may make the following two types of trades:

(1) You may purchase (or sell) a certificate to hold throughout *both* periods. These are called period $A$ certificates.

(2) You may purchase (or sell) certificates to hold in only one period. These are called period $B$ certificates since if you purchase it, you hold it only during period $B$. Note that if you sell a period $B$ certificate you hold it only during period $A$ and the trader you sell it to holds it during period $B$.

In addition at the beginning of each year you are provided with an initial amount of francs on hand. This is also recorded on row 0 of period $A$ on each year's information and record sheet. You may keep this if you wish or you may use it to purchase certificates.

Thus at the beginning of each year you are endowed with holdings of certificates and francs on hand. You are free to buy and sell certificates as you wish according to the rules below. Your francs on hand at the end of a year are determined by your initial amount of francs on hand, earnings on certificate holdings at the end of each period and by gains and losses from purchases and sales of certificates. All francs on hand at the end of a year in excess of ____ francs are yours to keep. These are your profits for the year.

#### TRADING AND RECORDING RULES

(1) All transactions are for one certificate at a time. After each of your sales or purchases you must record the nature of the transaction, a sale ($S$) or purchase ($P$), and the transaction price. The first transaction is recorded on row (1) and succeeding transactions are recorded on subsequent rows.

(2) After each transaction for a period $A$ certificate you must calculate and record your new holdings of certificates and your new francs on hand. Your holdings of certificates may never go below zero.

(3) After each transaction for a period $B$ certificate, you must record the net sales of period $B$ certificates in the "Net Sales" column of period $B$. The number in this column must never exceed the number in the "Certificate Holdings" column of period $A$.

(4) At the end of period $B$ your total certificate holdings is equal to your total certificate holdings in period $A$ *minus* your "net sales" of period $B$ certificates.

(5) At the end of the period record your total certificate earnings on row 31 and list your total certificate holdings on row 32.

(6) At the end of period $B$, add your total certificate earnings in both periods to your francs on hand, and enter this amount on row 32. Subtract from your francs on hand the amount listed in row 33 and enter this new amount on row 34. This is your profit for the market year and is yours to keep. At the end of each market year, record this number on your profit sheet.

### R. FORSYTHE, T. R. PALFREY, AND C. R. PLOTT

(7) At the end of the experiment add up your total profit on your profit sheet and enter this sum on row 15 of your profit sheet. To convert this number into dollars, multiply by the number on row 16 and record the product on row 17. The experimenter will pay you this amount of money.

MARKET ORGANIZATION

The market for these certificates is organized as follows. The market will be conducted in a series of years each consisting of two periods. Trading for both periods will be done in period $A$. This period will last ____ minutes. Anyone wishing to purchase a certificate is free to raise his or her hand and make a verbal bid to buy one certificate at a specified price, and anyone with certificates to sell is free to accept or not accept the bid. Likewise, anyone wishing to sell a certificate is free to raise his or her hand and make a verbal offer to sell one certificate at a specified price. When making a bid or offer, you must specify whether you wish to buy or sell a period $A$ or period $B$ certificate. If a bid or offer is accepted, a binding contract has been closed for a single certificate, and the contracting parties will record the transaction on their information and record sheets. Any ties in bids or acceptance will be resolved by random choice. Except for the bids and their acceptance, you are not to speak to any other subject. There are likely to be many bids that are not accepted, but you are free to keep trying. You are free to make as much profit as you can.

The profit sheet for Experiment 5 was the same as that for the other experiments. The information and record sheet for Experiment 5 differed in that the francs-on-hand inventory was carried in a single column on the right-hand side of the form as opposed to the two columns shown on the form above under period $A$ and period $B$.

REFERENCES

[1] DANTHINE, JEAN-PIERRE: "Information, Futures Prices, and Stabilizing Speculation," *Journal of Economic Theory*, 17(1978), 79–98.

[2] EASLEY, DAVID: "The Formation of Expectations in an Uncertain Environment," PhD dissertation, Northwestern University, June, 1979.

[3] FAMA, EUGENE F.: "Efficient Capital Markets: A Review of Theory and Empirical Work," *Journal of Finance*, 25(1970), 383–417.

[4] FRIEDMAN, JAMES W.: "An Experimental Study of Cooperative Duopoly," *Econometrica*, 35(1967), 379–397.

[5] GRANDMONT, JEAN-MICHEL: "Temporary General Equilibrium Theory," *Econometrica*, 45(1977), 535–572.

[6] GROSSMAN, SANFORD: "Further Results on the Informational Efficiency of Competitive Stock Markets," *Journal of Economic Theory*, 18(1978), 81–101.

[7] ———: "The Existence of Futures Markets, Noisy Rational Expectations and Informational Externalities," *Review of Economic Studies*, 44(1977), 431–449.

[8] HARRISON, J. MICHAEL, AND DAVID M. KREPS: "Speculative Investor Behavior with Heterogeneous Expectations," *Quarterly Journal of Economics*, 92(1978), 323–336.

[9] JORDAN, JAMES S.: "Temporary Competitive Equilibrium and the Existence of Self-Fulfilling Expectations," *Journal of Economic Theory*, 12(1976), 455–471.

[10] KEYNES, J. M.: *The General Theory of Employment, Interest and Money*. New York: Harcourt Brace, 1936.

[11] MILLER, R. M., CHARLES R. PLOTT, AND VERNON L. SMITH: "Intertemporal Competitive Equilibrium: An Empirical Study of Speculation," *Quarterly Journal of Economics*, 91(1977), 599–624.

[12] PLOTT, CHARLES R.: "The Application of Laboratory Methods to Public Choice," in *Applications of Social Choice Theory*, edited by Clifford S. Russell. Washington, D.C.: Resources for the Future, 1979.

[13] PLOTT, CHARLES R., AND VERNON L. SMITH: "An Experimental Examinatic . of Two Exchange Institutions," *Review of Economic Studies*, 45(1978), 133–153.

[14] PLOTT, CHARLES R., AND JONATHAN T. UHL: "Competitive Equilibrium with Middlemen: An Empirical Study," *Southern Economic Journal*, 47(1981), 1063–1071.

[15] SMITH, VERNON L.: "Experimental Economics: Induced Value Theory," *American Economic Review*, 66(1976), 274–279.

[16] ———: "Experimental Auction Markets and the Walrasian Hypothesis," *Journal of Political Economy*, 73(1965), 387–393.

[17] TOWNSEND, ROBERT M.: "Market Anticipations, Rational Expectations, and Bayesian Analysis," *International Economic Review*, 19(1978), 481–495.

# Name Index